DATE DUE

			PRINTED IN U.S.A.

SOMETHING ABOUT THE AUTHOR®

Something about
the Author *was named
an "Outstanding
Reference Source"
the highest honor given
by the American
Library Association
Reference and Adult
Services Division.*

R

ISSN 0276-816X

SOMETHING ABOUT THE AUTHOR®

**Facts and Pictures about Authors
and Illustrators of Books for Young People**

EDITED BY
KEVIN S. HILE
DIANE TELGEN
VOLUME 77

 **Gale Research Inc.** • *DETROIT* • *WASHINGTON, D.C.* • *LONDON*

Riverside Community College
Library
4800 Magnolia Avenue
Riverside, California 92506

JUN   '94

Ref
PN
1009
A1C6
v.77

STAFF

Editors: Kevin S. Hile and Diane Telgen

Associate Editor: Marie Ellavich

Senior Editor: James G. Lesniak

Sketchwriters/Copyeditors: Joseph O. Aimone, Joanna Brod, Ira Brodsky, Julie Catalano, Robin Cook, Pamela S. Dear, Elizabeth A. Des Chenes, Stephen Desmond, David Galens, Ronie-Richele Garcia-Johnson, Scott Gillam, Mary Gillis, Jeff Hill, David Johnson, J. Sydney Jones, Denise E. Kasinec, Sharyn Kolberg, Pat Matson Knapp, Thomas F. McMahon, Peg McNichol, Mark F. Mikula, Mary Onorato, Scot Peacock, Wendy Pfeffer, Jani Prescott, Anders J. Ramsay, Vita Richmond, Mary Lois Sanders, Kenneth R. Shepherd, Aarti Stephens, Linda Tidrick, Brandon Trenz, Polly Vedder, and Thomas Wiloch

Research Manager: Victoria B. Cariappa
Research Supervisor: Mary Rose Bonk
Editorial Associates: Reginald A. Carlton, Frank Vincent Castronova, Andrew Guy Malonis, and Norma Sawaya
Editorial Assistants: Laurel Sprague Bowden, Dawn Marie Conzett, Eva Marie Felts, Shirley Gates, Doris Lewandowski, Sharon McGilvray, Dana R. Schleiffers, and Amy B. Wieczorek

Picture Permissions Supervisor: Margaret A. Chamberlain
Permissions Associates: Pamela A. Hayes, Arlene Johnson, and Keith Reed
Permissions Assistants: Susan Brohman and Barbara Wallace

Production Director: Mary Beth Trimper
Production Associate: Mary Kelley
Art Director: Cynthia Baldwin
Desktop Publisher: Sherrell Hobbs
Camera Operator: Willie Mathis

While every effort has been made to ensure the reliability of the information presented in this publication, Gale Research Inc. does not guarantee the accuracy of the data contained herein. Gale accepts no payment for listing; and inclusion of any organization, agency, institution, publication, service, or individual does not imply endorsement of the editors or publisher. Errors brought to the attention of the publisher and verified to the satisfaction of the publisher will be corrected in future editions.

∞™ This book is printed on acid-free paper that meets the minimum requirements of American National Standard for Information Sciences—Permanence Paper for Printed Library Materials, ANSI Z39.48-1984.

This publication is a creative work fully protected by all applicable copyright laws, as well as by misappropriation, trade secret, unfair competition, and other applicable laws. The authors and editors of this work have added value to the underlying factual material herein through one or more of the following: unique and original selection, coordination, expression, arrangement, and classification of the information.

All rights to this publication will be vigorously defended.

Copyright © 1994
Gale Research Inc.
835 Penobscot Building
Detroit, MI 48226-4094

All rights reserved including the right of reproduction in whole or in part in any form.

Library of Congress Catalog Card Number 72-27107

ISBN 0-8103-2287-0 ISSN 0276-816X

Printed in the United States of America

Published simultaneously in the United Kingdom by Gale Research International Limited
(An affiliated company of Gale Research Inc.)

I(T)P™

10 9 8 7 6 5 4 3 2 1

Contents

Authors in Forthcoming Volumes

Below are some of the authors and illustrators that will be featured in upcoming volumes of *SATA*. These include new entries on the swiftly-rising stars of the field, as well as completely revised and updated entries (indicated with *) on some of the most notable and best-loved creators of books for children.

William Vivian Butler: Winner of a Special Edgar Allan Poe award for *The Young Detective's Handbook,* Butler has written popular mysteries and biographies for young people.

Arthur Dorros: Dorros is the author of whimsical stories, including *Pretzel* and *Alligator Shoes,* and bilingual books like *Abuela* that introduce young readers to Spanish vocabulary in an entertaining way.

Karen Gravelle: Award-winning author of *Teenage Fathers: An Inside View,* Gravelle is most noted for her books containing interviews with young adults about serious issues such as cancer and personal loss.

Kevin Hawkes: Author and illustrator of *Then the Troll Heard the Squeak* and *His Royal Buckliness,* Hawkes creates illustrations that have what he calls a ''darker, European look.''

*Patricia Hermes: Hermes' award-winning books, such as *Heads, I Win* and *Mama, Let's Dance,* realistically portray children and teens overcoming trying problems with family and friends.

*Russell Hoban: Author of the modern-day classic, *The Mouse and His Child,* Hoban has created a number of memorable characters, including Frances the badger, Emmet Otter, and Charlie the Tramp.

Liza Ketchum Murrow: A versatile author who has written historical novels, mysteries, and humorous, contemporary tales, Murrow has penned such notable books as *West against the Wind* and *Good-Bye, Sammy.*

*Tom Paisley: Better known by his pen name, T. Ernesto Bethancourt, Paisley worked as an actor and musician before gaining acclaim as a young adult novelist. (Entry contains exclusive interview.)

*Barbara Park: *Operation: Dump the Chump, The Kid in the Red Jacket,* and *Buddies* are just some of the humorous and very popular books by this author. (Entry contains exclusive interview.)

Elizabeth Ring: After gaining experience as a contributor to the magazine *Ranger Rick,* Ring has written a number of successful children's books about the world of nature.

Tricia Springstubb: Springstubb, who has created such memorable characters as Eunice Gottlieb and Lulu, writes light-hearted tales for middle-grade readers.

*Rosemary Sutcliff: The late Sutcliff was widely regarded as one of the finest authors of young adult fiction based on English history and legends, including *The Eagle of the Ninth* and *The Shining Company.*

Janet Wolf: Wolf's picture books are simple and playful works about the daily events in the lives of young children.

*Charlotte S. Zolotow: One of the most respected authors in the field today, Zolotow has written more than sixty acclaimed children's books over the course of her career.

Introduction

Something about the Author (*SATA*) is an ongoing reference series that deals with the lives and works of authors and illustrators of children's books. *SATA* includes not only well-known authors and illustrators whose books are widely read, but also those less prominent people whose works are just coming to be recognized. This series is often the only readily available information source on emerging writers or artists. You'll find *SATA* informative and entertaining whether you are a student, a librarian, an English teacher, a parent, or simply an adult who enjoys children's literature for its own sake.

What's Inside SATA

SATA provides detailed information about authors and illustrators who span the full time range of children's literature, from early figures like John Newbery and L. Frank Baum to contemporary figures like Judy Blume and Richard Peck. Authors in the series represent primarily English-speaking countries, particularly the United States, Canada, and the United Kingdom. Also included, however, are authors from around the world whose works are available in English translation. The writings represented in *SATA* include those created intentionally for children and young adults as well as those written for a general audience and known to interest younger readers. These writings cover the entire spectrum of children's literature, including picture books, humor, folk and fairy tales, animal stories, mystery and adventure, science fiction and fantasy, historical fiction, poetry and nonsense verse, drama, biography, and nonfiction.

Obituaries are also included in *SATA* and are intended not only as death notices but as concise views of people's lives and work. Additionally, each edition features newly revised and updated entries for a selection of *SATA* listees who remain of interest to today's readers and who have been active enough to require extensive revision of their earlier biographies.

Two Convenient Indexes

In response to suggestions from librarians, *SATA* indexes no longer appear in each volume, but are included in alternate (odd-numbered) volumes of the series, beginning with Volume 57.

SATA continues to include two indexes that cumulate with each alternate volume: the Illustrations Index, arranged by the name of the illustrator, gives the number of the volume and page where the illustrator's work appears in the current volume as well as all preceding volumes in the series; the Author Index gives the number of the volume in which a person's Biographical Sketch or Obituary appears in the current volume as well as all preceding volumes in the series.

These indexes also include references to authors and illustrators who appear in Gale's *Yesterday's Authors of Books for Children, Children's Literature Review,* and the *Something about the Author Autobiography Series.*

Easy-to-Use Entry Format

Whether you're already familiar with the *SATA* series or just getting acquainted, you will want to be aware of the kind of information that an entry provides. In every *SATA* entry the editors attempt to give as complete a picture of the person's life and work as possible. A typical entry in *SATA* includes the following clearly labeled information sections:

- *PERSONAL:* date and place of birth and death, parents' names and occupations, name of spouse, date of marriage, and names of children, educational institutions attended, degrees received, religious and political affiliations, hobbies and other interests.

- *ADDRESSES:* complete home, office, and agent addresses.

- *CAREER:* name of employer, position, and dates for each career post; military service.

- *MEMBER:* memberships and offices held in professional and civic organizations.

- *AWARDS, HONORS:* literary and professional awards received.

- *WRITINGS:* title-by-title chronological bibliography of books written and/or illustrated, listed by genre when known; lists of other notable publications, such as plays, screenplays, and periodical contributions.

- *ADAPTATIONS:* a list of films, television programs, plays, and other media presentations that have been adapted from the author's work.

- *WORK IN PROGRESS:* description of projects in progress.

- *SIDELIGHTS:* a biographical portrait of the author's development, either directly from the person—and often written specifically for the *SATA* entry—or gathered from diaries, letters, interviews, or other published sources.

- *FOR MORE INFORMATION SEE:* references for further reading.

- *EXTENSIVE ILLUSTRATIONS:* photographs, movie stills, manuscript samples, book covers, and other interesting visual materials supplement the text.

How a SATA Entry Is Compiled

A *SATA* entry progresses through a series of steps. If the biographee is living, the *SATA* editors try to secure information directly from him or her through a questionnaire. From the information that the biographee supplies, the editors prepare an entry, filling in any essential missing details with research and/or telephone interviews. When necessary, the author or illustrator is sent a copy of the entry to check for accuracy and completeness.

If the biographee is deceased or cannot be reached by questionnaire, the *SATA* editors examine a wide variety of published sources to gather information for an entry. Biographical and bibliographic sources are consulted, as are book reviews, feature articles, published interviews, and material sometimes obtained from the biographee's family, publishers, agent, or other associates. Entries compiled entirely from secondary sources are marked with an asterisk (*).

We Welcome Your Suggestions

We invite you to examine the entire *SATA* series, starting with this volume. Please write and tell us if we can make *SATA* even more helpful to you. Send comments and suggestions to: The Editor, *Something about the Author,* Gale Research Inc., 835 Penobscot Bldg., Detroit, MI 48226-4094.

Acknowledgments

Grateful acknowledgment is made to the following publishers, authors, and artists whose works appear in this volume.

MITSUMASA ANNO. Illustrations by Mitsumasa Anno from his *Anno's Alphabet: An Adventure in Imagination.* Copyright © 1974 by Fukuinkan-Shoten. Reprinted by permission of HarperCollins Publishers, Inc./ Illustrations by Mitsumasa Anno from his *Topsy-Turvies: Pictures to Stretch the Imagination.* Copyright © 1968 and 1970 Fukuinkan-Shoten, Tokyo, publishers of the original Japanese edition: all rights reserved. Reprinted by permission of Mitsumasa Anno./ Photograph courtesy of Mitsumasa Anno.

JENNIFER ARMSTRONG. Jacket of *Steal Away,* by Jennifer Armstrong. Jacket painting copyright © 1992 by Peter Catalanotto. Reprinted by permission of Orchard Books./ Photograph courtesy of Jennifer Armstrong.

MARGARET BARBARLET. Photograph courtesy of Margaret Barbarlet.

JOANNE BARKAN. Photograph courtesy of Joanne Barkan.

BARBARA BERGER. Illustration by Barbara Berger from her *Grandfather Twilight.* Text and illustration copyright © 1984 by Barbara Berger. Reprinted by permission of Philomel Books./ Photograph by Kari Berger, courtesy of Barbara Berger.

JON BOWERMASTER. Photograph by Debra Goldman, courtesy of Jon Bowermaster.

RUTH GEMBICKI BRAGG. Illustration by Ruth Gembicki Bragg from her *The Emperor's Gift.* Copyright © 1986 by Ruth Gembicki Bragg. Reprinted by permission of Ruth Gembicki Bragg./ Photograph courtesy of Ruth Gembicki Bragg.

MARLENE TARG BRILL. Photograph courtesy of Marlene Targ Brill.

HARRY BRUCE. Cover of *Maud: The Life of L. M. Montgomery,* by Harry Bruce. Copyright © 1982 by Harry Bruce. Cover art copyright © 1992 by Steve Assel. Handlettering copyright © 1992 by Ron Zinn. Reprinted by permission of Bantam Books, a division of Bantam Doubleday Dell Publishing Group, Inc./ Photograph courtesy of Harry Bruce.

KATHLEEN BULLOCK. Jacket by Kathleen Bullock from her *A Surprise for Mitzi Mouse.* Copyright © 1989 by Kathleen Bullock. Reprinted by permission of the publisher, Simon & Schuster Books for Young Readers, New York./ Photograph courtesy of Kathleen Bullock.

SYLVIA CASSEDY. Cover of *M. E. and Morton,* by Sylvia Cassedy. Cover art copyright © 1989 by Robert Chronister. Cover copyright © 1989 by Harper & Row, Publishers, Inc. Reprinted by permission of HarperCollins Publishers, Inc./ Cover of *Lucie Babbidge's House,* by Sylvia Cassedy. Copyright © 1989 by Sylvia Cassedy. Reprinted by permission of Avon Books, New York.

SHIRLEY CLIMO. Jacket of *King of the Birds,* by Shirley Climo. Jacket art copyright © 1988 by Ruth Heller. Reprinted by permission of HarperCollins Publishers, Inc./ Cover of *The Egyptian Cinderella,* by Shirley Climo. Cover art copyright © 1989 by Ruth Heller. Reprinted by permission of HarperCollins Publishers, Inc./ Cover of *A Month of Seven Days,* by Shirley Climo. Copyright © 1987 by Shirley Climo. Reprinted by permission of HarperCollins Publishers, Inc./ Photograph courtesy of Shirley Climo.

BARBARA COHEN. Cover of *The Innkeeper's Daughter,* by Barbara Cohen. Cover illustration copyright © 1990 by Ed Marinez. Reprinted by Beech Tree Books, an imprint of William Morrow & Company, Inc./ Cover of *Yussel's Prayer: A Yom Kippur Story,* retold by Barbara Cohen. Illustrations copyright © 1981 by Michael Deraney. Reprinted by permission of Lothrop, Lee & Shepard Books, a division of William Morrow & Company, Inc./ Jacket of *The Long Way Home,* by Barbara Cohen. Jacket illustration copyright © 1990 by Diane de Groat. Reprinted by permission of Lothrop, Lee & Shepard Books, a division of William Morrow & Company, Inc.

PENNY COLMAN. Cover of *Dark Closets and Noises in the Night,* by Penny Colman. Text copyright © 1991 by Penny Colman. Cover design by Tim McKeen. Cover illustration by Pamela T. Keating. Reprinted by permission of Paulist Press./ Photograph by LHB, courtesy of Penny Colman.

BARBARA CORCORAN. Cover of *Which Witch is Which?,* by Barbara Corcoran. Cover illustration copyright © 1992 by Renee Grant. Cover design by Rebecca Tachina. Reprinted by permission of Renee Grant./ Cover of *The Potato Kid,* by Barbara Corcoran. Copyright © 1989 by Barbara Corcoran. Reprinted by permission of Avon Books, New York./ Jacket of *A Dance to Still Music,* by Barbara Corcoran. Atheneum, 1980. Copyright © 1974 by Barbara Corcoran. Illustrations by Charles Robinson. Reprinted by permission of Charles Robinson./ Photograph courtesy of Macmillan Children's Book Group.

BRUCE COVILLE. Cover of *Jeremy Thatcher, Dragon Hatcher,* by Bruce Coville. Text copyright © 1991 by Bruce Coville. Cover illustration by Catherine Huerta. Reprinted by permission of Minstrel and Pocket Books, divisions of Simon & Schuster, Inc./ Cover of *The Ghost in the Third Row,* by Bruce Coville. Copyright © 1987 by Bruce Coville. Cover illustration copyright © 1987 by D. F. Henderson. Reprinted by Bantam Books, a division of Bantam Doubleday Dell Publishing Group, Inc./ Cover of *Jennifer Murdley's*

Toad, by Bruce Coville. Text copyright © 1992 by Bruce Coville. Cover art by Catherine Huerta. Reprinted by permission of Minstrel and Pocket Books, divisions of Simon & Schuster, Inc./ Photograph by Kenneth Tambs, courtesy of Bruce Coville.

LIZ DAMRELL. Illustration from *With the Wind,* by Liz Damrell. Illustrations copyright © 1991 by Stephen Marchesi. Reprinted by permission of Orchard Books.

HELEN K. DAVIE. Illustration by Helen K. Davie from *He Wakes Me,* by Betsy James. Illustrations copyright © 1991 by Helen K. Davie. Reprinted by permission of Orchard Books./ Illustration by Helen Davie from *The Star Maiden* by Barbara J. Esbensen. Copyright © 1988 by Helen K. Davie. Reprinted by permission of Little, Brown and Company.

RUBY DEE. Cover of *Two Ways to Count to Ten,* retold by Ruby Dee. Illustrations copyright © 1988 by Susan Meddaugh. Reprinted by permission of Henry Holt and Company, Inc.

JUDY DELTON. Jacket of *Hired Help for Rabbit,* by Judy Delton. Copyright © 1988 by Macmillan Publishing Company, a division of Macmillan, Inc. Illustrations copyright © 1988 by Lisa McCue. Reprinted by permission of Macmillan Publishing Company, a division of Macmillan Inc./ Jacket of *Angel's Mother's Baby,* by Judy Delton. Houghton Mifflin Company, 1989. Jacket art copyright © 1989 by Margot Apple. Reprinted by permission of Houghton Mifflin Company./ Jacket of *Near Occasion of Sin,* by Judy Delton. Copyright © 1984 by Judy Delton. Original jacket painting by Lucinda Cowell. Reprinted by permission of Lucinda Cowell./ Photograph courtesy of Judy Delton.

GORDON R. DICKSON. Cover of *Lost Dorsai,* by Gordon R. Dickson. Illustrations copyright © 1980 by Fernando Fernandez. Reprinted by permission of Fernando Fernandez.

ANN R. DIXON. Photograph courtesy of Ann R. Dixon.

ANDREJ DUGIN AND OLGA DUGINA. Illustration by Andrej Dugin and Olga Dugina from *Die Drachenfedern* (title of the U.S. edition: *Dragon Feathers*), retold by Arnica Esterl. Copyright © 1993 by Verlag J. F. Schreiber GmbH, Esslingen (Federal Republic of Germany). Reprinted by permission of Verlag J. F. Schreiber GmbH./ Photographs courtesy of Verlag J. F. Schreiber GmbH.

ARNICA ESTERL. Photograph courtesy of Verlag J. F. Schreiber GmbH.

EUGENIE FERNANDEZ. Illustration by Eugenie Fernandez from her *Waves in the Bathtub.* Text and illustrations copyright © 1993 by Eugenie Fernandez. Reprinted by permission of North Winds Press, a division of Scholastic Canada Limited./ Photograph courtesy of Eugenie Fernandez.

MIRKO GABLER. Photograph courtesy of Mirko Gabler.

NANCY GARDEN. Cover of *Monster Hunters, Case 3: Mystery of the Secret Marks,* by Nancy Garden. Copyright © 1989 by Nancy Garden. Cover illustration by Jeffrey Lindberg. Reprinted by permission of Minstrel and Pocket Books, divisions of Simon & Schuster, Inc./ Cover of *Annie on My Mind,* by Nancy Garden. Cover art copyright © 1992 by Elaine Norman. Reprinted by permission of Farrar, Straus and Giroux, Inc./ Photograph by Tim Morse.

LINDA GHAN. Cover of *Muhla, the Fair One,* by Linda Ghan. Text copyright © 1991 by Linda Ghan. Illustrations copyright © 1991 by Elise Benoit. Reprinted by permission of Nuage Editions./ Photograph courtesy of Linda Ghan.

CYNTHIA GRANT. Jacket of *Phoenix Rising; or, How to Survive Your Life,* by Cynthia D. Grant. Copyright © 1989 by Cynthia D. Grant. Jacket illustration copyright © 1989 by Stephen Marchesi. Reprinted by permission of Stephen Marchesi./ Photograph by Rhonda Neuchiller, courtesy of Cynthia D. Grant.

SELI GROVES. Cover of *How on Earth Do We Recycle Paper?,* by Helen Jill Fletcher and Seli Groves. Illustrations copyright © 1992 by Art Seiden and Stearn/Knudsen & Co. Reprinted by permission of The Millbrook Press Inc.

DAN GUTMAN. Photograph courtesy of Dan Gutman.

ELIZABETH HALL. Jacket of *Thunder Rolling in the Mountains,* by Elizabeth Hall and Scott O'Dell. Jacket art copyright © 1992 by Ted Lewin. Reprinted by permission of Houghton Mifflin Company./ Photograph by Allen Raymond, courtesy of Elizabeth Hall.

JUDITH HANN. Photograph courtesy of Judith Hann.

KATE HAYCOCK. Photograph courtesy of Kate Haycock.

MAIRI HEDDERWICK. Illustration by Mairi Hedderwick from her *Katie Morag and the Big Boy Cousins.* Copyright © 1987 by Mairi Hedderwick. Reprinted in the United States by permission of Little, Brown and Company. Reprinted in Canada and the British Commonwealth by permission of The Bodley Head.

JAN HUDSON. Cover of *Sweetgrass,* by Jan Hudson. Copyright © 1984 by Jan Hudson. Reprinted by permission of Scholastic Inc./ Jacket of *Dawn Rider,* by Jan Hudson. Jacket art copyright © 1990 by Jan Spivey Gilchrist. Reprinted by permission of Philomel Books.

DEAN HUGHES. Jacket of *Family Pose,* by Dean Hughes. Atheneum, 1989. Jacket illustration copyright © 1989 by Mary O'Keefe

Young. Reprinted by permission of Mary O'Keefe Young./ Jacket of *Nutty for President,* by Dean Hughes. Atheneum, 1982. Jacket design and illustration copyright © 1981 by Blanche Sims. Reprinted by permission of Blanche Sims./ Jacket of *Honestly, Myron,* by Dean Hughes. Atheneum, 1982. Pictures copyright © 1982 by Martha Weston. Reprinted by permission of Atheneum Publishers, an imprint of Macmillan Publishing Company./ Jacket of *Nutty's Ghost,* by Dean Hughes. Atheneum, 1993. Jacket illustration copyright © 1993 by Jacqueline Garrick. Jacket design by Tania Garcia. Reprinted by permission of Jacqueline Garrick./ Jacket of *Nutty Can't Miss,* by Dean Hughes. Atheneum, 1987. Jacket art copyright © 1987 by Helen Cogancherry. Jacket typography by Mary Ahern. Reprinted by permission of Helen Cogancherry./ Photograph courtesy of Dean Hughes.

BELINDA HURMENCE. Cover of *A Girl Called Boy,* by Belinda Hurmence. Jacket art copyright © 1982 by Steven Assel. Reprinted by permission of Clarion Books, an imprint of Houghton Mifflin Company./ Jacket of *Tancy,* by Belinda Hurmence. Jacket art copyright © 1984 by Charles Lilly. Reprinted by permission of Clarion Books, an imprint of Houghton Mifflin Company./ Cover design of *Before Freedom: 48 Oral Histories of Former North and South Carolina Slaves,* edited by Belinda Hurmence. Copyright © 1990 by Belinda Hurmence. Reprinted by permission of Dutton Signet, a division of Penguin Books USA Inc./ Photograph courtesy of Houghton Mifflin Company.

DAISAKU IKEDA. Jacket of *The Snow Country Prince,* by Daisaku Ikeda. Text copyright © 1990 by Daisaku Ikeda. Jacket art copyright © 1991 by Brian Wildsmith. English version copyright © 1990 by Geraldine McCaughrean. Reprinted in the United States by permission of Alfred A. Knopf, Inc. Reprinted in the British Commonwealth by permission of Oxford University Press./ Photograph courtesy of Daisaku Ikeda.

SHANNON K. JACOBS. Photograph courtesy of Shannon K. Jacobs.

CHARLOTTE FOLTZ JONES. Photograph courtesy of Charlotte Foltz Jones.

JONATHAN D. KAHL. Cover of *Weatherwise: Learning about the Weather,* by Jonathan D. Kahl. Copyright © 1992 Lerner Publications Company. Reprinted by permission of Lerner Publications Company.

TOM KERR. Photograph courtesy of Tom Kerr.

THEODORE O. KNIGHT. Photograph courtesy of Theodore O. Knight.

ELIZABETH LAIRD. Jacket of *The Day Sidney Ran Off,* by Elizabeth Laird. Jacket illustration copyright © 1990 by Colin Reeder. Reprinted in the United States by permission of Tambourine Books, a division of William Morrow & Company, Inc. Reprinted in the British Commonwealth by permission of HarperCollins Publishers Ltd./ Jacket of *Loving Ben,* by Elizabeth Laird. Copyright © 1988 by Elizabeth Laird. Jacket illustration copyright © 1989 by Neil Waldman. Reprinted by permission of Dell Books, a division of Bantam Doubleday Dell Publishing Group, Inc./ Photograph copyright © 1992 by Katie Vandyck, courtesy of Elizabeth Laird.

MARY D. LANKFORD. Photograph courtesy of Mary D. Lankford.

EVAN LEVINE. Photograph courtesy of Evan Levine.

PIJA LINDENBAUM. Photograph courtesy of Pija Lindenbaum.

CLAIRE LLEWELLYN. Cover of *My First Book of Time,* by Claire Llewellyn. Copyright © 1992 Dorling Kindersley Publishing Inc., New York. Reprinted by permission of the publisher.

MEGAN LLOYD. Illustration by Megan Lloyd from *Super Cluck,* by Jane O'Connor and Robert O'Connor. Illustrations copyright © 1991 by Megan Lloyd. Reprinted by permission of HarperCollins Publishers, Inc./ Photograph courtesy of Megan Lloyd.

MELISSA ANN MADENSKI. Photograph courtesy of Melissa Ann Madenski.

ERICA MAGNUS. Illustration by Erica Magnus from her *Around Me.* Copyright © 1992 by Erica Magnus Thomas. Reprinted by permission of Lothrop, Lee & Shepard Books, a division of William Morrow & Company, Inc./ Photograph courtesy of Erica Magnus.

ALAN MARKS. Photograph courtesy of Alan Marks.

JEAN MARZOLLO. Cover of *I'm Tyrannosaurus!: A Book of Dinosaur Rhymes,* by Jean Marzollo. Illustrations copyright © 1993 by Hans Wilhelm, Inc. Reprinted by permission of Scholastic Inc./ Cover of *Uproar on Hollercat Hill,* by Jean Marzollo. Illustrations copyright © 1980 by Stephen Kellogg. Reprinted by permission of Dial Books for Young Readers, a division of Penguin Books USA Inc./ Cover of *I Spy Funhouse: A Book of Picture Riddles,* by Jean Marzollo. Photographs copyright © 1993 by Walter Wick. Reprinted by permission of Scholastic Inc.

COLIN McCARTHY. Photograph courtesy of Colin McCarthy.

GEORGESS McHARGUE. Jacket of *Meet the Vampire,* by Georgess Mchargue. Jacket illustration copyright © 1979 by Tony Ratkus. Reprinted by permission of HarperCollins Publishers, Inc./ Jacket of *The Horseman's Word,* by Georgess McHargue. Copyright © 1981 by Georgess McHargue. Jacket design copyright © 1981 by Giorgetta Bell McRee. Jacket illustration copyright © 1981 by Michael Dudash. Reprinted by permission of Dell Books, a division of Bantam Doubleday Dell Publishing Group, Inc./ Photograph by M. Roberts, courtesy of Georgess McHargue.

BEN MILLSPAUGH. Photograph courtesy of Ben Millspaugh.

PIERR MORGAN. Photograph by Paul Boyer, courtesy of Pierr Morgan.

MARTHA A. MORRISON. Cover photograph of *Judaism: World Religions,* by Martha A. Morrison and Stephen F. Brown. Copyright © 1991 by Martha Morrison and Stephen F. Brown. Cover design reprinted by permission of Brown Publishing Network. Cover photograph reprinted by permission of Giraudon/Art Resource.

JIM MURPHY. Cover of *The Last Dinosaur,* by Jim Murphy. Illustrations copyright © 1988 by Mark Alan Weatherby. Reprinted by permission of Scholastic Inc./ Cover design of *The Boys' War: Confederate and Union Soldiers Talk about the Civil War,* by Jim Murphy. Text copyright © 1990 by Jim Murphy. Jacket design by Ronnie Ann Herman. Reprinted by permission of Houghton Mifflin Company.

SHIRLEY NEITZEL. Photograph courtesy of Shirley Neitzel.

DREW NELSON. Photograph courtesy of Drew Nelson.

SUZANNE NEWTON. Cover of *I Will Call It Georgie's Blues,* by Suzanne Newton. Copyright © 1983 by Suzanne Newton. Cover illustration copyright © Stephen Marchesi. Cover design by Rebecca Laughlin. Reprinted by permission of Puffin Books, a division of Penguin Books USA Inc./ Cover of *Where Are You When I Need You,* by Suzanne Newton. Copyright © 1991 by Suzanne Newton. Cover illustration copyright © 1991 by Ellen Thompson. Reprinted by permission of Viking Penguin, a division of Penguin Books USA Inc./ Cover of *M. V. Sexton Speaking,* by Suzanne Newton. Copyright © 1981 by Suzanne Newton. Puffin cover illustration copyright © 1990 by Robert Barrett. Reprinted by permission of Viking Penguin, a division of Penguin Books USA Inc.

NANCY NIELSEN. Photograph courtesy of Nancy Nielsen.

JANET PACK. Photograph courtesy of Janet Pack.

KIT PEARSON. Cover of *The Daring Game,* by Kit Pearson. Copyright © 1986 by Kathleen Pearson. Cover design by T. M. Craan. Cover illustration by Laura Fernandez. Reprinted by permission of Puffin Books, a division of Penguin Books Canada Limited./ Jacket of *The Sky Is Falling,* by Kit Pearson. Copyright © 1989 by Kathleen Pearson. Jacket design by Monique Oyagi. Jacket illustration by Janet Wilson. Reprinted by permission of Penguin Books Canada Limited./ Photograph by Russell Kelly, courtesy of Kit Pearson.

STELLA PEVSNER. Jacket of *A Smart Kid Like You,* by Stella Pevsner. Copyright © 1975 by Stella Pevsner. Jacket design and frontispiece drawing by Gail Owens. Reprinted by permission of Clarion Books, an imprint of Houghton Mifflin Company./ Cover of *And You Give Me a Pain, Elaine,* by Stella Pevsner. Copyright © 1978 by Stella Pevsner. Cover art copyright © 1989 Maria Jimenez. Reprinted by permission of Archway and Pocket Books, divisions of Simon & Schuster, Inc./ Jacket of *Call Me Heller, That's My Name,* by Stella Pevsner. Copyright © 1973 by Stella Pevsner. Illustrations by Richard Cuffari. Reprinted by permission of Clarion Books, an imprint of Houghton Mifflin Company./ Jacket of *How Could You Do It, Diane?,* by Stella Pevsner. Jacket art copyright © 1989 by Meg Kelleher Aubrey. Reprinted by Clarion Books, an imprint of Houghton Mifflin Company./ Photograph courtesy of Stella Pevsner.

STEPHEN PHILLIP POLLICOFF. Photograph courtesy of Stephen Phillip Pollicoff.

BARBARA G. POLIKOFF. Jacket of *Life's a Funny Proposition, Horatio,* by Barbara Garland Polikoff. Copyright © 1992 by Barbara Garland Polikoff. Jacket illustration copyright © 1992 by Robert Bender. Reprinted by permission of Robert Bender./ Photograph courtesy of Barbara G. Polikoff.

BERNIECE RABE. Cover of *The Balancing Girl,* by Berniece Rabe. Text copyright © 1981 by Berniece Rabe. Illustrations copyright © 1981 by Lillian Hoban. Reprinted by permission of Dutton Children's Books, a division of Penguin Books USA Inc./ Jacket of *The Girl Who Had No Name,* by Berniece Rabe. Copyright © 1977 by Berniece Rabe. Jacket illustration by Muriel Wood. Reprinted by permission of Dutton Signet, a division of Penguin Books USA Inc./ Jacket of *Naomi,* by Berniece Rabe. Copyright © 1975 by Berniece Rabe. Jacket painting by Ned Glattauer. Reprinted by permission of Ned Glattauer./ Photograph courtesy of Berniece Rabe.

ROBIN RAVILIOUS. Illustration by Robin Ravilious from her *The Runaway Chick.* Methuen Children's Books Ltd. Copyright © 1987 by Robin Ravilious. Reprinted in the United States by permission of Macmillan Publishing Company, a division of Macmillan Inc. Reprinted in the British Commonwealth by permission of Robin Ravilious.

FRANK REMKIEWICZ. Jacket by Frank Remkiewicz from his *Greedyanna.* Jacket illustrations copyright © 1992 by Frank Remkiewicz. Reprinted by permission of Lothrop, Lee & Shepard Books, a division of William Morrow & Company, Inc./ Photograph courtesy of Frank Remkiewicz.

JUDITH BENET RICHARDSON. Photograph by Jeanetta Hodges, courtesy of Judith Benet Richardson.

AMINAH ROBINSON. Photograph by Ted Rice, courtesy of Aminah Robinson.

COLBY RODOWSKY. Cover of *Julie's Daughter,* by Colby Rodowsky. Cover art copyright © 1992 by Elaine Norman. Reprinted by permission of Aerial Fiction, a division of Farrar, Straus and Giroux, Inc./ Cover of *Dog Days,* by Colby Rodowsky. Cover illustration copyright © 1993 by Eric Jon Nones. Reprinted by permission of Sunburst Books, a division of Farrar, Straus and Giroux,

Inc./ Cover of *What about Me?,* by Colby Rodowsky. Cover art copyright © 1989 by Diana Deutermann. Reprinted by permission of Farrar, Straus and Giroux, Inc./ Photograph by Sally Foster, courtesy of Colby Rodowsky.

STEPHEN ROOS. Jacket of *You'll Miss Me When I'm Gone,* by Stephen Roos. Copyright © 1988 by Stephen Roos. Jacket illustration copyright © 1988 by Allan Manham. Reprinted by permission of Dell Books, a division of Bantam Doubleday Dell Publishing Group, Inc.

MARIAN SALZMAN. Photograph courtesy of Marian Salzman.

RAGNHILD SCAMELL. Jacket of *Three Bags Full,* by Ragnhild Scamell. Jacket illustration copyright © 1993 by Sally Hobson. Reprinted by permission of Orchard Books.

ROSALYN SCHANZER. Photograph courtesy of Rosalyn Schanzer.

MELANIE SCHELLER. Jacket of *My Grandfather's Hat,* by Melanie Scheller. Jacket illustration copyright © 1991 by Keiko Narahashi. Reprinted by permission of Margaret K. McElderry Books, an imprint of Macmillan Publishing Company.

JOHN SCHINDEL. Photograph courtesy of John Schindel.

ELIZABETH SCHLEICHERT. Photograph courtesy of Elizabeth Schleichert.

CAROL SCHWARTZ. Photograph courtesy of Carol Schwartz.

MARIE-LOUISE SCULL. Photograph courtesy of Marie-Louise Scull.

PEGI DEITZ SHEA. Photograph courtesy of Pegi Deitz Shea.

PATTY SHEEHAN. Cover of *Gwendolyn's Gifts,* by Patty Sheehan. Illustrations copyright © 1988, 1991 by Claudia Bumgarner-Kirby. Reprinted by permission of Pelican Publishing Company./ Photograph courtesy of Patty Sheehan.

ROBERT ALAN SILVERSTEIN. Photograph courtesy of Robert Alan Silverstein.

JEFF SINCLAIR. Photograph courtesy of Jeff Sinclair.

ROBERT KIMMEL SMITH. Cover of *The War with Grandpa,* by Robert Kimmel Smith. Copyright © 1984 by Robert Kimmel Smith. Jacket illustration copyright © 1984 by Richard Lauter. Reprinted by permission of Dell Books, a division of Bantam Doubleday Dell Publishing Group, Inc./ Cover of *Bobby Baseball,* by Robert Kimmel Smith. Copyright © 1989 by Robert K. Smith. Cover illustration copyright © 1989 by Alan Tiegreen. Reprinted by permission of Dell Books, a division of Bantam Doubleday Dell Publishing Group, Inc./ Cover of *Jelly Belly,* by Robert Kimmel Smith. Copyright © 1981 by Robert Kimmel Smith. Jacket illustration copyright © 1981 by Dell Publishing Co., Inc. Illustrations by Bob Jones. Reprinted by permission of Dell Books, a division of Bantam Doubleday Dell Publishing Group, Inc./ Photograph courtesy of Robert Kimmel Smith.

HENRI SORENSEN. Photograph courtesy of Henri Sorensen.

BRADLEY STEFFENS. Photograph courtesy of Bradley Steffens.

IAN STIRLING. Photograph courtesy of Ian Stirling.

GWEN STRAUSS. Photograph courtesy of Gwen Strauss.

R. F. SYMES. Title page photographs from *Rocks & Minerals,* by Dr. R. F. Symes and the staff of the Natural History Museum, London. Copyright © 1988 Dorling Kindersley Limited, London and Editions Gallimard, Paris. Reprinted by permission of Dorling Kindersley Publishing Inc., New York.

SUSAN TERRIS. Jacket of *Stage Brat,* by Susan Terris. Copyright © 1980 by Susan Terris. Jacket design by Susan Gaber. Photograph by Margaretta K. Mitchell, © 1990.

PAT THOMSON. Jacket of *Beware of the Aunts,* by Pat Thomson. Jacket illustration copyright © 1991 by Emma Chichester Clark. Reprinted in the United States by permission of Margaret K. McElderry Books, an imprint of Macmillan Publishing Company. Reprinted in the British Commonwealth by permission of Pan Macmillan Children's Books, a division of Pan Macmillan Ltd., UK.

JAN THORNHILL. Illustration by Jan Thornhill from her *A Tree in a Forest.* Copyright © 1991 by Jan Thornhill. Reprinted by permission of the publisher, Simon & Schuster Books For Young Readers, New York./ Photograph by Ulli Steltzer, courtesy of Jan Thornhill.

COLIN THREADGALL. Illustration by Colin Threadgall from his *Dinosaur Fright.* Text and illustrations copyright © 1992 by Colin Threadgall. Reprinted in the United States by permission of Tambourine Books, a division of William Morrow & Company, Inc. Reprinted in the British Commonwealth by permission of Julia MacRae Books./ Photograph courtesy of Colin Threadgall.

BENETTE TIFFAULT. Photograph courtesy of Benette Tiffault.

INGRID TOMEY. Photograph courtesy of Ingrid Tomey.

ANN TURNER. Cover of *Stars for Sarah,* by Ann Turner. Cover art copyright © 1991 by Mary Teichman. Reprinted by permission of HarperCollins Publishers, Inc./ Cover of *Dakota Dugout,* by Ann Turner. Illustrations copyright © 1985 by Ron Himler. Reprinted by permission of Macmillan Publishing Company, a division of Macmillan Inc.

ROBYN MONTANA TURNER. Photograph by Tara Turner, courtesy of Robyn Montana Turner.

DIZ WALLIS. Photograph courtesy of Diz Wallis.

HELEN WILLIAMS. Photograph courtesy of Helen Williams.

CAROL BEACH YORK. Jacket of *Remember Me When I Am Dead,* by Carol Beach York. Copyright © 1980 by Carol Beach York. Jacket illustration by Lydia Rosier. Reprinted by permission of Dutton Signet, a division of Penguin Books USA Inc./ Jacket of *When Midnight Comes,* by Carol Beach York. Copyright © 1979 by Carol Beach York. Jacket illustration by Lydia Rosier. Reprinted by permission of Dutton Signet, a division of Penguin Books USA Inc./ Jacket of *Once Upon a Dark November,* by Carol Beach York. Copyright © 1989 by Carol Beach York. Jacket art by Alan Olson. Reprinted by permission of Holiday House./ Photograph courtesy of Carol Beach York.

TOSHI YOSHIDA. Jacket by Toshi Yoshida from his *Young Lions.* Jacket artwork copyright © 1982 by Toshi Yoshida. Reprinted in the United States by permission of Philomel Books. Reprinted in the British Commonwealth by permission of the Japan Foreign-Rights Centre./ Photograph courtesy of Toshi Yoshida.

PAULA YOUNKIN. Cover photograph of *Indians of the Arctic and Subarctic,* by Paula Younkin. Copyright © 1992 by Benford Books, Inc. Cover design by Donna Sinisgalli. Cover design reprinted permission of International Book Marketing Ltd. Cover photograph reprinted by permission of Alaska Division of Tourism.

SOMETHING ABOUT THE AUTHOR®

ANNO, Mitsumasa 1926-

■ Personal

Born March 20, 1926, in Tsuwano, Japan; son of Yojiro and Shikano Anno; married Midori Suetsugu, April 1, 1952; children: Masaichiro (son), Seiko (daughter). *Education:* Graduated from Yamaguchi Teacher Training College, 1948.

■ Addresses

Home—3-8-14 Midoricho, Koganei Shi, Tokyo 184, Japan.

■ Career

Artist, educator, essayist, and author and illustrator of children's books. Taught at elementary schools in Tokyo for ten years. *Exhibitions:* Has exhibited in major galleries and museums in Japan, Canada, the United States, and Great Britain.

■ Awards, Honors

"Best Illustrated Books of the Year" citation, *New York Times,* 1970, Spring Book Festival Award, *Chicago Tribune Book World,* 1970, "Brooklyn Art Books for Children" citation, 1973, German Children's and Youth Book Award, 1973, "Notable Book" citation, American Library Association (ALA), and *Horn Book* honor list, all for *Topsy-Turvies: Pictures to Stretch the Imagination;* "Brooklyn Art Books for Children" citation, 1973, for *Upside-Downers: More Pictures to Stretch the Imagi-*

nation; "Fifty Books of the Year" citation, American Institute of Graphic Arts, 1974, Kate Greenaway Medal commendation, 1974, *Boston Globe-Horn Book* award for illustration, 1975, "Best Illustrated Books of the Year" citation, *New York Times,* 1975, Christopher Award, 1976, Children's Book Showcase selection, 1976, "Brooklyn Art Books for Children" citation, 1976, 1977, 1978, and "Notable Book" citation, ALA, all for *Anno's Alphabet: An Adventure in Imagination;* Golden Apple Award, Bratislava International Biennale, 1977; "Outstanding Science Books for Children" citation, New York Academy of Sciences, 1978, and *Horn Book* honor list, both for *Anno's Counting Book;* "Brooklyn Art Books for Children" citation, 1979, "Notable Book" citation, ALA, and *Horn Book* honor list, all for *Anno's Journey;* "Notable Book" citation, ALA, for *The King's Flower;* first prize for graphic excellence, Bologna Children's Book Fair, 1978, for *The Unique World of Mitsumasa Anno: Selected Works (1968-1977);* Parent's Choice Award for illustration in children's books, 1980, for *Anno's Italy;* first prize for graphic excellence, Bologna Children's Book Fair, 1980, for *Nippon no uta;* "Best Illustrated Books of the Year" citation, *New York Times,* 1982, for *Anno's Britain;* prize from Bologna Children's Book Fair, 1982, and "Notable Book" citation, both for *Anno's Counting House;* Hans Christian Andersen Medal, 1985; Jane Addams Children's Book honorary award, 1987, for *All in a Day.*

MITSUMASA ANNO

■ Writings

SELF-ILLUSTRATED; IN ENGLISH TRANSLATION

Topsy-Turvies: Pictures to Stretch the Imagination, Walker/Weatherhill, 1970 (originally published as *Fushigi na e,* Fukuinkan Shoten, 1968).

Upside Downers: More Pictures to Stretch the Imagination, translated by Meredith Weatherby and Suzanne Trumbull, Weatherhill, 1971 (originally published as *Sakasama,* Fukuinkan Shoten, 1969).

Dr. Anno's Magical Midnight Circus, translated by Weatherby, Weatherhill, 1972.

Anno's Alphabet: An Adventure in Imagination, Crowell, 1975 (originally published as *ABC no hon,* Fukuinkan Shoten, 1974).

Anno's Counting Book, Crowell, 1977 (originally published as *Kazoetemiyou,* Kodansha, 1975).

The King's Flower, Collins, 1979 (originally published as *Okina Monono Sukina Osama,* Kodansha, 1976).

Anno's Journey, Collins, 1978 (originally published as *Tabi no Ehon,* Fukuinkan Shoten, 1977).

Anno's Animals, Collins, 1979 (originally published as *Mori no Ehon,* Fukuinkan Shoten, 1977).

Anno's Italy, Bodley Head, 1979, Collins, 1980 (originally published as *Tabi no Ehon II,* Fukuinkan Shoten, 1978).

Anno's Medieval World, Philomel, 1980 (originally published as *Tendo setsu no hon,* Fukuinkan Shoten, 1979).

The Unique World of Mitsumasa Anno: Selected Works (1968-1977), Philomel, 1980 (originally published as *Anno Mitsumasa no Gashu,* Kodansha, 1980).

(With son, Masaichiro Anno) *Anno's Magical ABC: An Anamorphic Alphabet,* Philomel, 1981 (originally published as *Mahotsukai no ABC,* Kuso-kobo, 1980).

(With Masaichiro Anno) *Anno's Counting House,* Philomel, 1982 (originally published as *10-nin no yukai na hikkoshi,* Dowaya, 1981).

Anno's Britain, Philomel, 1982.

(With M. Anno) *Anno's Mysterious Multiplying Jar,* Philomel, 1983.

Anno's USA, Philomel, 1983.

Anno's Flea Market, Philomel, 1984 (originally published as *Nomi no Ichi,* Dowaya, 1983).

(With others) *All in a Day,* Philomel, 1986 (originally published as *Marui Chikyu no Maru Ichinichi,* Dowaya, 1986).

Anno's Peekaboo, Philomel, 1987 (originally published as *Inai Inai Baa no Ehon,* Dowaya, 1987).

Anno's Math Games, Philomel, 1987.

Anno's Sundial, Putnam, 1987.

Anno's Faces, Philomel, 1988 (originally published as *Niko Niko Kabocha,* Dowaya, 1988).

In Shadowland, Orchard, 1988.

Anno's Math Games II, Putnam, 1989.

(Editor) *Anno's Aesop: A Book of Fables by Aesop and Mr. Fox,* Orchard, 1989.

Anno's Masks, Philomel, 1989 (originally published as *Omen no Ehon,* Dowaya, 1989).

Anno's Counting Book Big Book, HarperCollins, 1992.

Anno's Magic Seed, Putnam, 1994.

Also author of *Maze, Dr. Stone-Brain's Computer,* and *The Theory of Set.*

SELF-ILLUSTRATED; UNTRANSLATED WORKS

Nippon no uta (title means "Anno's Song Book"), Kodansha, 1979.

Tsubo no Naka, Dowaya, 1982.

ILLUSTRATOR

Akihiro Nozaki, *Anno's Hat Tricks,* Philomel, 1985 (originally published as *Akai Boshi,* Dowaya, 1984).

Tsuyoshi Mori, *Socrates and the Three Little Pigs,* Philomel, 1986 (originally published as *Sanbiki no Kobuta,* Dowaya, 1985).

(And reteller) Jacob and Wilhelm Grimm, *Anno's Twice-Told Tales: The Fisherman and His Wife and The Four Clever Brothers by The Brothers Grimm and Mr. Fox,* Philomel, 1993.

■ Adaptations

Anno's Journey was adapted as an animated filmstrip, Weston Woods, 1983; *Anno's Math Games,* an interactive CD-Rom, was produced by Putnam New Media, 1994.

Anno fills the pictures of his unusual alphabet book with visual puns and playful surprises. (Illustration by the author from *Anno's Alphabet: An Adventure in Imagination.*)

■ Sidelights

Japanese illustrator and author Mitsumasa Anno is considered one of the most original and accomplished picture-book artists in the field of children's books. Anno is famous for highly detailed, skillful illustrations which display his love of mathematics and science, in addition to his appreciation for foreign cultures and travelling. His drawings, which are often compared to those of Dutch graphic artist M. C. Escher, abound with visual trickery and illusions, and also display a playful sense of humor throughout. Many of Anno's books contain hidden jokes and pranks which are intended to amuse and lead readers into imaginative thinking about numbers, counting, the alphabet, or complex concepts of time and space. Operating on different levels of understanding, Anno's books appeal to both children and adults, while his universal approach has made him a favorite in countries around the world. He has received numerous awards, including the prestigious Hans Christian Andersen Illustrator Medal, awarded every two years for the most outstanding accomplishment in international illustration.

Anno grew up in western Japan in the town of Tsuwano, a small isolated community located in a valley surrounded by mountains. While growing up, Anno had a strong desire to experience places beyond the mountains surrounding his village. "On the other side of the mountains were villages with rice fields, and beyond these rice fields was the ocean, which seemed to be very,

very far away," he stated in an interview with Hisako Aoki for *Horn Book.* "When I reached the ocean for the first time in my life, I tasted it to see if it was really salty. Because my world was cut off from the outside world, first by the mountains and then by the ocean, the desire to go and see what lay on the other side grew stronger." Anno began drawing as a young boy, and was also very interested in mathematics. From a young age onward, as he described in *Fourth Book of Junior Authors,* he "earnestly desired to become an artist."

Anno attended high school in a town far away from Tsuwano, where his studies included art and drawing. "My heart beat when I saw girls in their school uniforms, and drifting clouds in the sky sent me into melancholic moods," Anno wrote in *Fourth Book of Junior Authors.* "I knew something in myself was changing." Anno also became an avid reader, and was influenced by German author Hermann Hesse. Anno described to Aoki his return to Tsuwano after graduation: "I got off the train at the station, feeling happy and proud and a bit shy at the same time, thinking how much I had matured being away from Tsuwano but that the town would accept me as I was.... When I read how Hermann Hesse, as a student, went home to Calw, getting off the train at the end of the town, walking by the river, and crossing the bridge, my heart ached because everything was exactly the same with me." Years later, Anno would have the opportunity to draw sketches of Hesse's Calw, and was startled to discover they were very similar to sketches he'd made of Tsuwano. Anno realized his sketches of the two places represented "the world as seen through my eyes, and they are my own compositions—which other people may see differently. I believe that this is one of the reasons for ... expressing oneself in any form. Through a creative work, people may experience something which they may not have experienced before."

Perspective and Perception

After the Second World War, in which Anno was drafted into the army, he received a degree in 1948 from the Yamaguchi Teacher Training College. Before engaging in an art career, Anno taught elementary school in Tokyo. He commented to Aoki on what he learned from teaching: "As a teacher I tried to present material to pupils so that they could widen their scope of understanding and self-expression. At the same time I learned a lot from them. Children's way of seeing is actually different from that of adults.... For example, children's sense of perspective is different from ours, partly because their faces are smaller and their eyes are closer together. In addition, their experience is more restricted, so they have less to base their judgement on."

Anno's first two picture books reflect his love of playing with visual perception. *Topsy-Turvies: Pictures to Stretch the Imagination,* was published in Japan in 1968, and was followed the next year by *Upside Down-*

ers: More Pictures to Stretch the Imagination. Topsy-Turvies plays visual tricks on perspective and logic, while *Upside Downers* contains illustrations that convey different images depending on the angle or direction from which they are looked at. In presenting such illustrations, Anno hopes to stimulate the powers of young people's imaginations. He wrote in a postscript to *Topsy-Turvies:* "One professor of mathematics claims that in a single picture he has found twelve different 'impossibilities'.... Nothing is impossible to the young, not until we become caught in the problems of living and forget to make-believe. Perhaps these pictures of mine will keep all of us young a little longer, will stretch our imaginations enough to help keep us magically human. I hope so, I believe so—for nothing is impossible."

Anno's more innovative picture books include *Anno's Alphabet: An Adventure in Imagination,* published in 1975. *Anno's Alphabet* features "impossible" woodgrain letters that are framed within decorative borders containing objects beginning with each letter. In 1980, Anno provided the illustrations, while his son, Masaichiro, added the lettering for another alphabet book, *Anno's Magical ABC: An Anamorphic Alphabet.* In *Anno's Magical ABC,* letters and their corresponding objects are viewed through a reflective cylinder provided with the book. *Anno's Mysterious Multiplying Jar,*

In his logic-defying illustrations for *Topsy-Turvies,* Anno challenges readers to stretch their imaginations.

also co-written with his son, demonstrates the mathematical concept of factorials through a series of innovatively connected illustrations that keep increasing in number. *Anno's Medieval World* chronicles the discovery in Western Europe of the fact that the Earth is a round planet which revolves around the sun. Leonard S. Marcus in *The Lion and the Unicorn* noted that *Anno's Mysterious Multiplying Jar* and *Anno's Medieval World* demonstrate Anno's belief that "an interest in science and mathematics is compatible with an interest in art" and that "art and science represent different approaches to the common end of exercising human perception beyond known limits."

Anno's "Journey" Books

In 1977, Anno published his first in a series of acclaimed "journey" books, which recount in pictures Anno's travels through Europe and the United States. *Anno's Journey* arose from travels Anno made in 1963 to Scandinavia, Germany, and England, and was followed by *Anno's Italy, Anno's Britain,* and *Anno's U.S.A. Anno's Journey* is "a wordless book that is a mass of colorful detail, a picture narrative, and a poetic meditation in narrative form," wrote Marcus. "Without a written text as a guide, readers are left to invent stories of their own, which may or may not concern the little man whose journey by boat and on horseback forms the one narrative lifeline or thread running through the book." Throughout the books, Anno hopes to communicate universal messages to his readers. Regarding *Anno's Italy,* he commented in a postscript to the book: "Although it is difficult for me to understand the languages of the western world, still I can understand the hearts of the people. This book [*Anno's Italy*] has no words, yet I feel sure that everyone who looks at it can understand what the people in the pictures are doing, and what they are thinking and feeling."

In addition to his picture books, Anno is also an accomplished painter and graphic artist who has displayed his work in numerous exhibitions throughout galleries and museums in Japan, the United States, Canada, and Great Britain. *The Unique World of Mitsumasa Anno: Selected Works (1968-1977)* offers forty of Anno's best individual works of graphic art which, like his picture books, both challenge the visual and cultural perceptions of their viewers. In a postscript to the book, Anno commented: "Once someone said, upon seeing my pictures, 'You amuse yourself by fooling people; you can't draw without a mischievous spirit.' I really wanted to counter by saying, 'The spirit of noble humanity causes me to do so' . . . . My pictures are like maps, which perhaps only I can understand. Therefore, in following my maps there are some travellers who get lost. There are those who become angry when they discover they have been fooled; but there are also those who enter into the maze of my maps willingly, in an attempt to explore their accuracy for themselves."

■ Works Cited

Anno, Mitsumasa, *Topsy-Turvies: Pictures to Stretch the Imagination,* Walker/Weatherhill, 1970.

Anno, Mitsumasa, entry in *Fourth Book of Junior Authors and Illustrators,* edited by Doris de Montreville and Elizabeth D. Crawford, Wilson, 1978.

Anno, Mitsumasa, *Anno's Italy,* Collins, 1980.

Anno, Mitsumasa, *The Unique World of Mitsumasa Anno: Selected Works (1968-1977),* Philomel Books, 1980.

Aoki, Hisako, "A Conversation with Mitsumasa Anno," *Horn Book,* April, 1983, pp. 137-45.

Marcus, Leonard S., "The Artist's Other Eye: The Picture Books of Mitsumasa Anno," *The Lion and the Unicorn,* Volume 7-8, pp. 24-46.

■ For More Information See

BOOKS

Children's Literature Review, Gale, Volume 2, 1976; Volume 14, 1988.

PERIODICALS

Bookbird, Volume 2, 1984; Volume 4, 1984; October, 1987.

Bulletin of the Center for Children's Books, November, 1983; June, 1984; December, 1984; December, 1987; May, 1988; June, 1988.*

*   *   *

ARMSTRONG, Jennifer 1961-
(Julia Winfield)

■ Personal

Born May 12, 1961, in Waltham, MA; daughter of John (a physicist) and Elizabeth (a master gardener; maiden name, Saunders) Armstrong. *Education:* Smith College, B.A., 1983. *Hobbies and other interests:* Gardening, teaching, music, reading.

■ Addresses

Agent—Susan Cohen, Writers House, 21 West 26th St., New York, NY 10010.

■ Career

Cloverdale Press, New York City, assistant editor, 1983-85; free-lance writer, 1985—; teacher. Girl Scout leader, 1987-89; Smith College recruiter, 1990—; leader of writing workshops. Literacy Volunteers of Saratoga, board president, 1991-93; puppy raiser for Guiding Eyes for the Blind. *Member:* Society of Children's Book Writers and Illustrators, Saratoga County Arts Council.

■ Awards, Honors

Best Book Award, American Library Association (ALA), and Golden Kite Honor Book Award, Society of Children's Book Writers and Illustrators, both 1992, for

JENNIFER ARMSTRONG

Steal Away; Notable Book Citations, ALA, 1992, for *Steal Away* and *Hugh Can Do.*

■ Writings

Steal Away (novel), Orchard Books, 1992.
Hugh Can Do (picture book), illustrated by Kimberly Root, Crown Books for Young Readers, 1992.
Chin Yu Min and the Ginger Cat (picture book), illustrated by Mary GrandPre, Crown Books for Young Readers, 1993.
That Terrible Baby (picture book), illustrated by Susan Meddaugh, Tambourine Books, in press.
Little Salt Lick and the Sun King (picture book), illustrated by Jon Goodell, Crown Books for Young Children, in press.
The Whittler's Tale (picture book), illustrated by Valery Vasiliev, Tambourine Books, in press.

MIDDLE GRADE FICTION; "PETS, INC." SERIES

The Puppy Project, Bantam, 1990.
Too Many Pets, Bantam, 1990.
Hillary to the Rescue, Bantam, 1990.
That Champion Chimp, Bantam, 1990.

YOUNG ADULT FICTION; UNDER PSEUDONYM JULIA WINFIELD

Only Make-Believe (part of "Sweet Dreams" series), Bantam, 1987.
Private Eyes (part of "Sweet Dreams" series), Bantam, 1989.
Partners in Crime (part of "Private Eyes" series), Bantam, 1989.

Tug of Hearts (part of "Private Eyes" series), Bantam, 1989.
On Dangerous (part of "Private Eyes" series), Bantam, 1989.

YOUNG ADULT FICTION; "WILD ROSE INN" SERIES

Bridie of the Wild Rose Inn, Bantam, in press.
Ann of the Wild Rose Inn, Bantam, in press.
Emily of the Wild Rose Inn, Bantam, in press.
Laura of the Wild Rose Inn, Bantam, in press.
Claire of the Wild Rose Inn, Bantam, in press.
Grace of the Wild Rose Inn, Bantam, in press.

■ Work in Progress

Researching nineteenth-century American history.

■ Sidelights

Jennifer Armstrong told *SATA:* "I came to write children's books by accident. When I left college I took the first publishing job I could get, and it turned out to be with the packager of many of the best known juvenile and young adult series on the market. After a year and a half of working on these books, I was convinced that I could do a creditable job of writing them too. And so I began to write for Sweet Valley High. I found that young adult writing came easily to me, and as I worked on the Sweet Valley books, I came up with more and more ideas for books of my own—both for the young adult and the juvenile market. After a number of years working as a full-time writer for the packager, I teamed up with my agent, Susan Cohen of Writers House. With my mass market experience firmly behind me, I was ready to set to work on my own projects.

"The idea for my novel, *Steal Away,* came to me a number of years before I wrote it. At first, it was conceived of as a straightforward adventure story. Having written so many of those books, however, I felt I was ready to tackle something more complex and ambitious. And so, after much thought and nail biting, I settled on the form of the novel as I wrote it—with two narratives interwoven, emphasizing the effect that telling and hearing stories has on us. I intertwined so many threads in *Steal Away* that I was often in danger of getting hopelessly confused. But those issues—race relations, feminism, friendship, and loyalty, and the importance of telling stories—were and still are important to me."

Race Relations Explored in *Steal Away*

Armstrong's desire to write about what is important to her is evident in her historical novel *Steal Away.* Written for youngsters in grades five to eight, the story begins in the year 1896 when Mary, a thirteen-year-old, travels with her grandmother to visit Gran's sick friend, Bethlehem. Gran (Susannah) and Bethlehem soon relate the story of how they became fast friends when they, like Mary, were thirteen-years-old. *Steal Away* is a story of courage, friendship, and interracial understanding. The title is derived from a spiritual which was used in those days as a signal to slaves that the time had come for them to run for freedom.

In the story, both of Susannah's parents die in an accident in 1855, and she is sent to live with an uncle who keeps slaves on a plantation in Virginia. Susannah believes that slavery is wrong, and so, when she is given Bethlehem as her own personal slave, Susannah befriends her. The basic difference between her uncle's beliefs and what Susannah believes forms the nucleus for difficulties and is the catalyst for relationships among the characters around which the plot revolves. Emotions in the story run high as Bethlehem deals with her hatred of slavery, resentment of her white "friend," and her need to leave Susannah and go her own way. Young Susannah must resolve her own feelings about the black race just as her granddaughter, Mary, must do when Susannah, or Gran, tells her the story years later. Ann Welton in *School Library Journal* commented that "the issues explored in this book run deep . . . . This will go a long way toward explicating the damage done by slavery."

Partners in Crime was also written for children in grades six to nine. Part of the "Private Eyes" series, this book has a likeable, modern heroine who is not afraid to voice

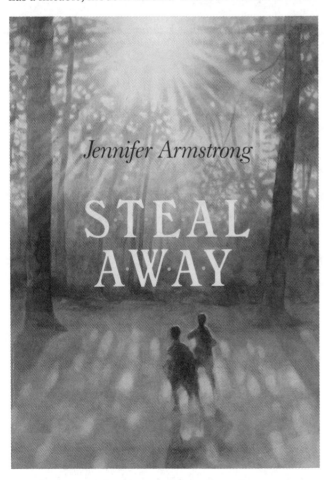

In Armstrong's award-winning tale, two girls bond together to escape the culture of slavery in the American South in 1855. (Cover illustration by Peter Catalanotto.)

her opinions and act on her beliefs. A *Publishers Weekly* reviewer stated that *Partners in Crime* "blends romance with a fairly uncomplicated mystery, providing light entertainment." Another Armstrong book in the "Private Eyes" series, *Tug of Hearts*, "is a cut above most series books and will appeal to a lot of young adult readers," according to Jeanette Larson in *School Library Journal*. The heroine is different from those in many young romance books in that she is not afraid to risk losing her boyfriend.

For readers in grades three to six, Armstrong has written her "Pets, Inc." series. *The Puppy Project*, the first book in the series, features two sisters who love animals, have a menagerie of their own, and yet desperately want a puppy that was born to a neighbor's dog. The second book in the series, *Too Many Pets*, details the escapades of four girls who try to set up a pet care business. *That Champion Chimp*, the fourth book in the "Pets, Inc." series, also revolves around love and respect for animals and the responsibilities of having a pet. "Armstrong's plot is tightly focused and filled with well-integrated facts," assessed a *Booklist* contributor.

The versatile Armstrong has also written several picture books, including *Chin Yu Min and the Ginger Cat* and *Hugh Can Do*. The latter book, with its cumulative theme and rhythmic text, is similar to poetry and is fun to read aloud, as many reviewers noted. Moreover, as is typical of many folktales, the story offers "a valuable lesson presented in a book to be valued," found a contributor to *Publishers Weekly*. Kate McClelland in *School Library Journal* decided that *Hugh Can Do* is "an especially nice balance of dramatic tension, droll humor, and positive philosophy."

About the topic of books in general, Armstrong told *SATA:* "More and more these days I see people—grown-up people—trying to control what kids can see and do and read. I know teachers and librarians who scorn the mass market books which I wrote and still write, and insist on giving kids exclusively 'good' books. But adults have access to a variety of fiction, and I think all kinds of fiction should be available to kids so that they can make their own decisions about what they enjoy."

■ Works Cited

Review of *Hugh Can Do, Publishers Weekly*, June 29, 1992, p. 62.

Larson, Jeanette, review of *Tug of Hearts, School Library Journal*, June, 1989, p. 125.

McClelland, Kate, review of *Hugh Can Do, School Library Journal*, October, 1992, p. 78.

Review of *Partners in Crime, Publishers Weekly*, March 24, 1989, p. 73.

Review of *That Champion Chimp, Booklist*, October 1, 1990, p. 344.

Welton, Ann, review of *Steal Away, School Library Journal*, February, 1992, p. 85.

■ For More Information See

PERIODICALS

Bulletin of the Center for Children's Books, March, 1992,
    p. 173.
Kirkus Reviews, July 15, 1992, p. 917.
Publishers Weekly, July 13, 1990, p. 55.
School Library Journal, July, 1990, p. 74.
Voice of Youth Advocates, August, 1992, p. 165.

*   *   *

AUER, Martin 1951-

■ Personal

Born January 14, 1951, in Vienna, Austria; son of Georg
(a journalist) and Gertrude (a homemaker; maiden
name, Sokopp) Auer; married Sylvia, 1973 (divorced
1975); children: Nadja Auer. *Education:* Two years at
Vienna University.

■ Addresses

Rotenmuhlgasse, 44/30 A-1120 Wien, Austria.

■ Career

Actor and musician with the Theater in Borseplatz and
Theater in Kunstlerhaus, Vienna, Austria, 1971-77.
Also was a member of the music group, Dreschflegel.
Involved in marketing, public relations, and journalism,
beginning in 1979. Has worked as an entertainer,
musician, and filmmaker, though primarily as a poet
and magician, 1984—.

■ Awards, Honors

German Youth Book Prize honor list, 1989, and Chil-
dren's Book Prize, by the Ministers of Culture in
Nordrheinwestfalen, 1990, both for *Now, Now, Markus;*
Austrian Prize of the Children's Jury—poetry, 1993.

■ Writings

IN ENGLISH TRANSLATION

Now, Now, Markus, illustrated by Simone Klages,
    Greenwillow Books, 1989 (originally published as
    Bimbo und sein Vogel, Beltz & Gelberg, 1988).
The Blue Boy, illustrated by Klages, Macmillan, 1992
    (originally published as *Der blaue Junge,* Beltz &
    Gelberg, 1991).

UNTRANSLATED WORKS

(With Reinhart Honold and Rudi Tinsobin) *Der Dresch-
    flegel* (songs; title means "The Flail"), Liederbuch,
    Eigenverlag, 1977.
Was niemand wissen kann (poetry and stories; title
    means "What No One Can Ever Know"), Beltz &
    Gelberg, 1986.
Der Sommer des Zauberers (stories; title means "The
    Summer of the Magician"), Beltz & Gelberg, 1988.

(With Klaus Trabitsch) *Zum Mars und zurueck* (songs;
    title means "To Mars and Back"), Coppenrath-
    Verlag, 1988.
Von Pechvogeln und Unglucksraben (stories; title means
    "Hard Luck and Misery"), Beltz & Gelberg, 1989.
Und wir flogen tausend Jahre (title means "So We Flew
    a Thousand Years"), illustrated by Klages, Beltz &
    Gelberg, 1990.
In der wirklichen Welt (title means "In the Real
    World"), Beltz & Gelberg, 1990.
(With Christina Zurbrugg) *A Butten voll Kinder, an
    rotzigen Mann* (song book and recording; title
    means "A Basket Full of Children and an Unkempt
    Man"), IDI-Ton, 1990.
Die Jagd nach dem Zauberstab (title means "The Hunt
    for the Magic Wand"), Beltz & Gelberg, 1991.
Der wunderbare Zauberer von Oz (based on the tales of
    L. Frank Baum), Beltz & Gelberg, 1992.
Die seltsamen Leute vom Planeten Hortus (title means
    "The Strange People from Planet Hortus"), Diester-
    weg, 1992.
Tri-Tra-Trallala ("Punch and Judy" plays), Otto Maier
    Verlag, 1992.

PLAYS

Schlumperwald, Piatnik & Sohne, 1987.

Also author of *Wenn 55 Jahre Vergehen,* 1991, and
Sonnenuntergang, 1992, both performed at Cafe de
Chinitas.

OTHER

Contributor of prose to the following anthologies: *Der
Eingang ins Paradies,* Suhrkamp Taschenbucher, 1988;
Die Erde ist mein Haus, Beltz & Gelberg, 1988; *Die
Arche Noah,* Suhrkamp Taschenbucher, 1989; *Die Sir-
ene,* Suhrkamp Taschenbucher, 1990; and *Daumesdick,*
Beltz & Gelberg, 1990. Contributor of poetry to the
following anthologies: *Uberall und neben dir,* Beltz &
Gelbert, 1986; *Schmah ohne,* Jugend & Volk, 1987;
Danke, man lebt, Osterreichischer Bundesverlag, 1987;
and *Die Wundertute,* Philipp Reclam Junior, 1989.

■ Adaptations

A Butten voll Kinder, an rotzigen Mann was adapted as a
live performance by Gruppe Regenpfeifer, 1986; *Zum
Mars und zurueck* was recorded by the Krachorchester,
MC Coppenrath-Verlag, 1988, and adapted as a revue
for children, with the Krachorchester, 1989.

■ Work in Progress

A biography of nineteenth-century French entomologist
Jean Henri Fabre.

■ Sidelights

Martin Auer went from his two-year studies of German
history to a career as a performer, starting in 1971 with
Austria's Borseplatz Theatre, then with the Kunstlerhaus. Auer joined the music group Dreschflegel and held
"many jobs," he told *SATA.* He's worked in marketing,

public relations and journalism since 1979. "From there," he said, "it was not too far a jump to magician." Actually, since 1984, he has made a living as an entertainer, actor, musician, and above all, a storyteller.

One of Auer's many books, *Bimbo und sein Vogel* (literally, "Bimbo and His Bird") was renamed *Now, Now, Markus* and printed in the U.S. in 1989. It's a lyrical story about a red-haired boy whose parents don't pay too much attention to him unless he pretends to drop dead. One day, Markus does this to get a bird. His parents don't know he'll bring home a large, beautiful swan! Markus runs away with the clever swan and the two have many adventures, including a run-in with a giant, before returning home.

The story of Markus and his swan benefitted from Auer's poetic gift—the book appeared on the 1989 German Youth Book Prize honor list and was also selected by the Ministers of Culture of Nordrheinwestfalen in 1990 for the Children's Book Prize. *Now, Now, Markus* was eventually printed in the United States, Canada, Japan, France, Holland, Sweden, Finland, and Norway.

Auer uses a similar whimsical, rhyming approach to the big world in his other writings, but tempers it with thoughts about some big questions, as with *The Blue Boy*. This book, published in 1992, features the adventures of a boy whose parents have been killed in a war. The blue boy (he's from the Blue Planet) avoids everyone who tries to befriend him. It isn't until he flies away from the Blue Planet that he learns the reason for war and why it must be avoided.

Several of Auer's books which have not been published in the United States talk about other planets: *Zum Mars und zurueck,* which means "To Mars and Back," is a songbook for children; *Die seltsamen Leute vom Planeten Hortus,* or "The Strange People from Planet Hortus," is a storybook. He also has written about a 1,000-year flight and a chase after a magic wand, and compiled short stories about magicians.

■ For More Information See

PERIODICALS

Booklist, September 15, 1992, p. 148.
Horn Book, March, 1990, p. 232.
Kirkus Reviews, August 15, 1989, p. 1241.
New York Times Book Review, April 15, 1990, p. 23.
Publishers Weekly, August 11, 1989, p. 458; August 3, 1992, p. 72.
Quill and Quire, September, 1990, p. 22.
School Library Journal, January, 1990, p. 74.

B

BARBALET, Margaret 1949-

■ Personal

Born December 19, 1949, in Adelaide, Australia; daughter of John Evans (a general practitioner doctor) and Anne Caroline (maiden name, Beckwith) Hardy; married Jack Barbalet, May 12, 1970 (divorced January 10, 1989); children: Tom, Felix, David. *Education:* Adelaide University, M.A., 1973. *Religion:* Anglican.

■ Addresses

c/o Penguin Books, P.O. Box 257 Ringwood, VIC 3134 Australia.

■ Career

Adelaide Children's Hospital, Adelaide, historian, 1973-74; Adelaide City Council, research officer, 1973-75; Commonwealth Schools Commission, research consultant, 1984-88; Department of Foreign Affairs and Trade, 1990—, desk officer, Middle East and North Africa section, 1992—. *Member:* Australian Society of Authors.

■ Awards, Honors

Vogel Award shortlist, for *Steel Beach,* 1983; Children's Book of the Year Award shortlist, for *The Wolf,* 1992.

■ Writings

Far from a Low Gutter Girl: The Forgotten World of State Wards (non-fiction), Oxford University Press, 1983.
Blood in the Rain (novel), Penguin, 1986.
Steel Beach (novel), Penguin, 1988.
Lady, Baby, Gypsy, Queen (novel), Penguin, 1992.

FOR CHILDREN

The Wolf, illustrated by Jane Tanner, Macmillan, 1991.

MARGARET BARBALET

■ Work in Progress

The Sea of Sand, a children's book.

■ Sidelights

A working historian and author of a historical and social study on state wards in Australia in the late 19th and early 20th centuries, Margaret Barbalet has also written several novels (including *Blood in the Rain, Steel Beach,* and *Lady, Baby, Gypsy, Queen*) and a book for children. This last work, *The Wolf,* a somewhat unusual picture-book, has received much attention from critics for its rich symbolism. As Don Pemberton writes in *Magpies,* "Margaret Barbalet's story ... is a psychological thriller with something of the resonance of a folk tale.... Her wolf comes out of an old fable and threatens a contemporary home."

The Wolf begins when Tal, the eldest of three children living in the Australian countryside with their mother, awakens to the screams of his younger brother. A wolf has begun to howl outside the family's home. This wolf, which is never pictured in the book's illustrations, howls every night and attempts to find a way into the house, which has been boarded up and tightly locked against it. "The howling went on and on. He knew it was the wolf coming closer. It was worse than he could have imagined. It was worse than his nightmares." As time passes, the children, especially Tal, and their mother try to cope with the wolf and the way it changes their lives. Writes Carolyn Noah in *School Library Journal*, "the lesson is clear: confront fears and they dissolve." Pemberton similarly reports that Barbalet began to develop the story one day when she was driving and the words "Let it in" came to mind. "They *are* the heart of the matter," writes Pemberton. "Let the wolf in."

Although most critics acknowledge the symbolic depth of *The Wolf*, some express concern that the tale might prove too frightening or ambiguous for young children. A reviewer in the *Bulletin of the Center for Children's Books* writes, "Unlike the wolves and witches of folklore, the threat in Barbalet's story is never made concrete and knowable, and therefore tameable. Readers won't be fooled by the happy ending." Still others, like a reviewer for *Publishers Weekly,* advise parents of younger children: "While older readers may grasp the deeper lesson about mastering one's own terrors, some children may find the tale confusing and even alarming."

Despite these arguments, Noah, citing Barbalet's "finely honed prose" and illustrator Jane Tanner's "dark, realistic illustrations," describes *The Wolf* as "a treasure to be read again and again." Pemberton also praises how "Margaret Barbalet and Jane Tanner have succeeded vibrantly in dramatising the need to 'take responsibility,' as Jane phrased it, 'for your own inner darkness.' ... This fine book will appeal to people from 9 to 90."

■ Works Cited

Barbalet, Margaret, *The Wolf,* Macmillan, 1991.
Noah, Carolyn, review of *The Wolf, School Library Journal,* April, 1992, p. 112.
Pemberton, Don, review of *The Wolf, Magpies,* November, 1991.
Review of *The Wolf, Bulletin of the Center for Children's Books,* April, 1992, pp. 198-199.
Review of *The Wolf, Publishers Weekly,* April 13, 1992.

*   *   *

BARKAN, Joanne
(J. B. Wright)

■ Personal

Born in Chicago, IL; married Jon R. Friedman (a painter/sculptor). *Education:* Goucher College, B.A.; University of Wisconsin, M.A.; Johns Hopkins Univer-

JOANNE BARKAN

sity, further graduate study. *Politics:* Leftist/democratic socialist. *Hobbies and other interests:* Art, dance, movies, politics, European travel.

■ Addresses

Home and office—711 West End Ave., New York, NY 10025.

■ Career

Editor, Croft-NEI Publications, 1976-78; national news editor, *Seven Days Magazine,* 1978; book editor and staff writer for "The Muppets," Jim Henson Productions, 1985-87; editor and project coordinator, Brooke-House Publishing, 1988-92; executive editor, *Dissent* magazine; freelance writer and editor. *Member:* Democratic Socialists of America, National Writers Union, Phi Beta Kappa.

■ Awards, Honors

Parents Choice Reference Book Honor and National Association of Science Teachers/Children's Book Council Joint award for a science trade book, for *Creatures That Glow;* Children's Choices selection, for *Ann Marie's Blanket.*

■ Writings

Baby Piggy and the Thunderstorm, Muppet Press, 1987.
The Christmas Toy, Scholastic, Inc., 1987.
Kermit's Mixed-up Message, illustrated by Lauren Attinello, Scholastic, Inc., 1987.
Baby Gonzo's Unfinished Dream, illustrated by Tom Cooke, Muppet Press, 1988.
Baby Kermit's Old Blanket, illustrated by Tom Brannon, Muppet Press, 1988.

Boober's Colorful Soup, illustrated by John Nez, Longmeadow Press, 1988.

Doozers Big and Little, illustrated by Nez, Longmeadow Press, 1988.

My Cooking Pot, illustrated by Jody Wheeler, Warner Books, 1989.

My Cooking Spoon, illustrated by Wheeler, Warner Books, 1989.

My Frying Pan, illustrated by Wheeler, Warner Books, 1989.

My Measuring Cup, illustrated by Wheeler, Warner Books, 1989.

My Rolling Pin, illustrated by Wheeler, Warner Books, 1989.

My Spatula, illustrated by Wheeler, Warner Books, 1989.

What's So Funny, illustrated by Normand Chartier, Houghton, 1989.

The Girl Who Couldn't Remember, Simon & Schuster, 1989.

The Secret of the Sunken Treasure, Simon & Schuster, 1989.

My Pruning Shears, illustrated by Wheeler, Warner Books, 1990.

My Rake, illustrated by Wheeler, Warner Books, 1990.

My Trowel, illustrated by Wheeler, Warner Books, 1990.

My Watering Can, illustrated by Wheeler, Little, Brown, 1990.

Whiskerville Bake Shop, illustrated by Karen L. Schmidt, Grosset & Dunlap, 1990.

Whiskerville Firehouse, illustrated by Schmidt, Grosset & Dunlap, 1990.

Whiskerville Post Office, illustrated by Schmidt, Grosset & Dunlap, 1990.

Whiskerville School, illustrated by Schmidt, Grosset & Dunlap, 1990.

Anna Marie's Blanket, illustrated by Deborah Mase, Barron's, 1990.

Glow in the Dark Spooky House, illustrated by Rose Mary Berlin, Western Publishing, 1990.

My Birthday Adventure with TeddyO (a computer-personalized picture book), illustrated by Wheeler, Franco American Products, 1991.

A Very Scary Haunted House, illustrated by Wheeler, Scholastic, Inc., 1991.

A Very Scary Jack O'Lantern, illustrated by Wheeler, Scholastic, Inc., 1991.

Easter Egg Fun, illustrated by Betsy Franco-Feeney, Warner Books, 1991.

Easter Surprise, illustrated by Franco-Feeney, Warner Books, 1991.

Where Do I Put My Toys?, illustrated by Laura Rader, Scholastic, Inc., 1991.

Where Do I Put My Clothes?, illustrated by Rader, Scholastic, Inc., 1991.

Where Do I Put My Books?, illustrated by Rader, Scholastic, Inc., 1991.

Where Do I Put My Food?, illustrated by Rader, Scholastic, Inc., 1991.

Whiskerville Train Station, illustrated by Schmidt, Grosset & Dunlap, 1991.

Whiskerville Theater, illustrated by Schmidt, Grosset & Dunlap, 1991.

Whiskerville Grocery, illustrated by Schmidt, Grosset & Dunlap, 1991.

Whiskerville Toy Shop, illustrated by Schmidt, Grosset & Dunlap, 1991.

(Under pseudonym J. B. Wright) *Dinosaurs,* illustrated by Gene Biggs, Western Publishing, 1991.

Boxcar, illustrated by Richard Walz, Macmillan, 1992.

Caboose, illustrated by Walz, Macmillan, 1992.

Locomotive, illustrated by Walz, Macmillan, 1992.

Passenger Car, illustrated by Walz, Macmillan, 1992.

A Very Merry Santa Claus Story, illustrated by Cristina Ong, Scholastic, Inc., 1992.

A Very Merry Snowman Story, illustrated by Ong, Scholastic, Inc., 1992.

A Very Scary Ghost Story, illustrated by Wheeler, Scholastic, Inc., 1992.

A Very Scary Witch Story, illustrated by Wheeler, Scholastic, Inc., 1992.

That Fat Hat, illustrated by Maggie Swanson, Scholastic, Inc., 1992.

Animal Car, illustrated by Ong, Macmillan, 1993.

Circus Locomotive, illustrated by Ong, Macmillan, 1993.

Clown Caboose, illustrated by Ong, Macmillan, 1993.

Performers' Car, illustrated by Ong, Macmillan, 1993.

The Magic Carpet's Secret, illustrated by Brooks Campbell and Kenny Thompkins, Walt Disney, 1993.

Elves for a Day, Walt Disney, 1993.

Numbers Add Up at Home, illustrated by Peggy Tagel, Book Club of America, 1993.

The Ballet Mystery, Simon & Schuster, 1994.

Home, Creepy Home, Steck-Vaughn, 1994.

The Krystal Princess and the Grand Contest, Scholastic, Inc., 1994.

CHILDREN'S NONFICTION

Abraham Lincoln: A Biography, illustrated by Lyle Miller, Silver Press, 1990.

Air, Air, All Around, illustrated by Heidi Petach, Silver Press, 1990.

Fire, Fire, Burning Bright, illustrated by Petach, Silver Press, 1990.

Rocks, Rocks, Big and Small, illustrated by Petach, Silver Press, 1990.

Water, Water, Everywhere, illustrated by Petach, Silver Press, 1990.

Creatures That Glow, Doubleday, 1991.

ADULT NONFICTION

Visions of Emancipation: The Italian Workers' Movement since 1945, Greenwood Press, 1984.

OTHER

"The Apple Tree behind the House," in *Kick Up Your Heels,* Scott, Foresman, 1981; "SFX! The Secrets Behind Special Effects in the Movies," in *ROBOFORCE Magazine*; "Molly's Great Swim," in *On Stage,* Riverside Publishing, 1986; "People Who Help People," in *Blue Ribbon,* Riverside Publishing, 1986; "Pobi's New Pen Pal," in *On Stage,* Riverside Publishing, 1986. Contributor, sometimes under undisclosed pseudonyms, of original stories for reading textbooks for Scott, Foresman, and Riverside Publishing, and author of social studies textbooks for Holt, Rinehart and Winston, and Ginn and Co. Contributor of articles on politics and economics to *Attenzione, Progressive, Commonweal, Monthly Review, Dissent, In These Times* and other publications in the United States, and to *Renewal* (Britain), *Tiden* (Sweden), and *Il Manifesto,* a daily newspaper in Italy.

■ Sidelights

Joanne Barkan is a prolific author of both fiction and nonfiction children's books. Her award-winning *Creatures That Glow* is a science book for young readers that explains bioluminescence. The book features color photographs that glow in the dark and a text that was praised for its clear, straightforward presentation of a complicated but fascinating topic.

Barkan is also the author of *Abraham Lincoln and Presidents' Day,* a biography for first readers that reviewers noted reads like fiction. Other nonfiction titles for this age group include *Air, Air, All Around* and *Water, Water, Everywhere,* featuring riddles and simple experiments as a way to introduce youngsters to science topics.

Barkan's fiction titles include board books such as *Locomotive, Boxcar, Passenger Car,* and *Caboose.* This series features information about trains that is geared for the youngest of children. The books, which are shaped like the train car they depict, may be joined together end-to-end like a train. Another board book series, this one from Grosset and Dunlap, including such titles as *Whiskerville Bake Shop, Whiskerville Firehouse, Whiskerville Post Office,* and *Whiskerville School,* introduces the youngest children to the workings of various public institutions. The reviewer for *Publishers Weekly* commented: "This hospitable town is worth a stop on any young traveler's itinerary."

The list of Barkan's picture books includes two Halloween tales, *A Very Scary Witch Story* and *A Very Scary Ghost Story,* both of which feature glow-in-the-dark illustrations and friendly supernatural beings in search of fun. *Anna Marie's Blanket* is a more realistic story concerning a young girl whose excitement about starting school is tempered by the realization that she will have to leave her beloved blanket at home.

■ Works Cited

Review of *Whiskerville Bake Shop, Whiskerville Firehouse, Whiskerville Post Office,* and *Whiskerville School, Publishers Weekly,* April 27, 1990, p. 59.

■ For More Information See

PERIODICALS

Booklist, November 1, 1991, p. 511.
Publishers Weekly, March 30, 1990, p. 60; April 13, 1992, pp. 85-86; September 7, 1992, p. 59.
School Library Journal, July, 1990, p. 67; March, 1991, p. 181; January, 1992, pp. 118, 123.

BERGER, Barbara (Helen) 1945-

■ Personal

Born March 1, 1945, at Edwards Air Force Base in CA; daughter of Knute E. (a physician, medical artist, and research pathologist) and Margaret (a nurse, medical editor, executive research secretary, and poet; maiden name, Haseltine) Berger. *Education:* Attended University of Washington, 1963-66, 1967-68, Yale University, 1966, and Temple University's Tyler School of Art in Rome, Italy, 1966-67; University of Washington, B.F.A., 1968. *Politics:* "Non-political." *Religion:* "Christianity and Buddhism."

■ Career

Freelance artist, author and book illustrator. *Exhibitions:* Berger had regular gallery shows in Seattle, 1971; various children's book art shows throughout the United States. *Member:* Society of Children's Book Writers, Authors Guild, International Society of Folk Harpers and Craftsmen.

■ Awards, Honors

Parents' Choice Foundation Award, 1984, Washington State Governor's Writer's Award, 1985, and *Horn Book* Graphic Gallery Selection, 1986, all for *Grandfather Twilight;* Golden Kite Award for picture illustration, Society of Children's Book Writers, 1985, for *The Donkey's Dream;* Washington State Governor's Writer's Award, 1991, for *Gwinna;* art from *The Donkey's Dream* and *When the Sun Rose* was selected for inclusion in the United States exhibit at the Biennale of Illustrations, Bratislava, Czechoslovakia, in 1987.

BARBARA BERGER

■ Writings

SELF-ILLUSTRATED

Animalia, Celestial Arts, 1982.
Grandfather Twilight, Philomel, 1984.
The Donkey's Dream, Philomel, 1985.
When the Sun Rose, Philomel, 1986.
Gwinna, Philomel, 1990.
The Jewel Heart, Philomel, 1994.

OTHER

(Illustrator) Jane Yolen, *Brothers of the Wind,* Philomel, 1981.

■ Work in Progress

The Unicorn Ship and "many other original story ideas in various stages of development."

■ Sidelights

Barbara Berger is a highly praised children's book author whose detailed paintings accentuate stories filled with magical elements. A professional artist before turning to children's books, Berger often gets new story ideas from paintings she has done or wishes to do.

In her first project as author and illustrator, *Animalia,* Berger collected and retold thirteen stories that celebrate a harmonious relationship between humans and animals. While Cheryl Lynn Gage, reviewing this work for *School Library Journal,* felt that the prose might be too "grandiose" and "didactic" for most children, she added: "The paintings accompanying each tale are highly detailed works of art in their own right and reflect the warmth and wisdom of the tales." *Animalia* received the following accolade from *Publishers Weekly:* "Berger's creation is impossible to overpraise as an inducement to contemplation on the wonders of nature."

With her first wholly original effort, *Grandfather Twilight,* Berger garnered praise for both her prose and the accompanying pictures. The story mystically renders the rising of the moon each twilight as the gift of a pearl from a kindly old man to the sky each night. Janice Prindle, reviewing *Grandfather Twilight* in the *New York Times Book Review,* remarked: "Berger's words in this illustrated bedtime story have been selected with such devotion that they stand, like a hymn, on their own.... Her full-color paintings tell the story just as beautifully, and in greater, more original detail." While some critics felt the story lacked plot or action, *People* magazine commented: "This is a bedtime story for dreams to be made of." In a review in *Horn Book,* Robert D. Hale enthused: "*Grandfather Twilight* is a book that enriches our heritage of mythology and legends—one to call upon frequently—'whenever the world falls apart.'"

Christian Story Told Anew

The Donkey's Dream, Berger's next publication, tells the story of the birth of Jesus from the point of view of the donkey who bears Mary to Bethlehem. Berger incorpo-

Berger's self-illustrated *Grandfather Twilight* depicts the magic of moonrise as an old man presenting a pearl to the sky each night.

rates Christian symbols into both the illustrations and the story as the donkey imagines he is carrying a city, a ship, a fountain, and then a rose upon his back—all symbols of Christian religious import. Jane Langton commented in the *New York Times Book Review:* "The artist-author has brought a reverent simplicity to one of the oldest stories in the world." Again, Berger's illustrations were singled out for praise. *Publishers Weekly* remarked: "The paintings are glorious, reverent versions of the Nativity in which colors intensify the impact of visions and reality."

Like *Grandfather Twilight, When the Sun Rose* is a fantasy story illuminated by colorful, unusual paintings. In this work, a rose-covered girl arrives with the rising of the sun in a carriage pulled by a golden lion to play with the story's narrator. The two girls play with their dolls, have tea, and paint rainbows before the friend departs with the setting of the sun and a promise to return. *Publishers Weekly* commented: "Berger's skillful blending of the metaphysical and a child's inner life make this an inspired work of art."

Berger's *Gwinna* is the fairy tale story of a child with wings who is placed in the home of human parents until she is old enough to fulfill her dream of traveling to a faraway mountain, where she carves herself a harp to play. The review in *Publishers Weekly* summarized: "No brief recap of *Gwinna*'s plot can do justice to all its subtleties or to its profound imagery. Berger tells her long tale in simple, direct prose that illuminates its allegorical aspects with impressive clarity while keeping the action and adventure flowing smoothly.... With the publication of this story, Berger takes her place with the best talents in the field, past and present."

"One time in the summer," Berger reminisced to *SATA*, "we kids were sleeping out in a friend's backyard. After the popcorn was gone and all our giggling was done, I lay awake in my sleeping bag, looking up at the stars. I was thinking about infinity, wondering, trying to imagine the space around the stars really and truly having no end. It was hard. Suddenly for one tiny moment, I did understand. It was less than a second. I couldn't hold the moment and make it last, but it did happen. I still remember the great feeling of mystery, something so wondrous and vast that even if you could hold it, you might break into pieces unless your heart and mind were big enough. I want all my books and paintings to have a touch of that feeling, a small breath of the big, beautiful mystery."

"My sister and I both loved to draw, from the first time we could hold a crayon," Berger continued. "Every year before Christmas, Dad would take us to his office in 'secret.' He gave us paints and brushes, and we made paintings for Mom for Christmas. He framed them, and she hung them up on the kitchen walls until there was no more room.

"One year, instead of a painting for Christmas, I wanted to make her a book. I wrote my own poems in pencil, and made pictures for each one. She loved it, but still the book wasn't all I hoped it would be. I thought, 'When I grow up, I'm going to learn how to do this. I'm going to make my own books, with words and pictures together.'

Stories from Paintings

"After college I kept on painting. Sometimes a painting seemed to have a story in it somewhere, even if I didn't quite know what it was. Or the painting might be one moment in a bigger story. Every couple of years, I had a show in a gallery. When I hung the paintings on the walls, they seemed to be all connected. Something invisible held them together. It might be a story you would 'read' by going from one painting to another, around the gallery. But the story had no words, only the title of each painting, and it might be a different story to every person.

"Finally I began to do my own books. *Grandfather Twilight* came from a painting I had done of an old man made of sky. In his hand he held a pearl, or the moon, and his beard turned into clouds. I asked, 'What is the story? Where did he come from and where is he going?' I daydreamed about it, went for long walks in the woods with my dog, imagined and sketched, and wrote it all down, and that is how it grew into a book. *When the Sun Rose* grew the same way, from a different painting of a big yellow rose coming in through an open door. This was the best way for me to start writing stories because I think in pictures. I love words too, but an image comes to my mind first, almost always.

"My Dad used to say that colors can sing. It is true, yet for me it isn't easy. The paintings in my books take a long time. First I do piles and piles of drawings. I work all the pictures out in a dummy. When everything feels right at last, then I start with the paint. It's always like coming home again to mix the colors on my big white china plates. Each book has its own 'flavor' and as I paint, the colors often surprise me.

"New ideas can come any time, you never know when. I jot them down and put them in folders so I can find them later. An idea might come with a word or two, like 'Unicorn Ship.' Then I wonder what the story is. I love to play with the ideas. So I keep the folders in the toy box my Dad painted for me when I was a baby, with blue inside and 'Barbara's Toys' on the lid. Now it's my idea box. There are more ideas in it than I can ever make into finished books. But I hope to do at least ten more, and there's plenty more room in the box."

■ Works Cited

Review of *Animalia, Publishers Weekly,* December 24, 1982, p. 64.
Review of *Animalia, School Library Journal,* April, 1983, p. 109.
Review of *The Donkey's Dream, Publishers Weekly,* September 13, 1985, p. 132.
Review of *Grandfather Twilight, People,* December 17, 1984.
Review of *Gwinna, Publishers Weekly,* August 10, 1990, p. 445.
Hale, Robert D., "Musings," *Horn Book,* March, 1985, pp. 215, 218-19.
Langton, Jane, review of *The Donkey's Dream, New York Times Book Review,* December 15, 1985, p. 24.
Prindle, Janice, review of *Grandfather Twilight, New York Times Book Review,* February 24, 1985, p. 30.
Review of *When the Sun Rose, Publishers Weekly,* September 26, 1986, p. 79.

■ For More Information See

PERIODICALS

Bulletin of the Center for Children's Books, September, 1985.
Kirkus Reviews, August 15, 1986, p. 1287.

*   *   *

BOWERMASTER, Jon 1954-

■ Personal

Born June 29, 1954, in Normal, IL; son of Ralph E. (a school administrator) and Barbara (a teacher; maiden name, Cryer) Bowermaster; married Debra Goldman (a photographer), September 4, 1982. *Education:* Drake University, B.A., 1976; American University, M.A., 1977.

JON BOWERMASTER

■ Addresses

Home—Box 730, Stone Ridge, NY 12484. *Agent*—(literary) Stuart Krichevsky, Sterling Lord Literistic, One Madison Avenue, New York, NY 10010.

■ Career

Rockford Newspaper Co., Rockford, IL, reporter, 1974-75; *Des Moines Register,* Des Moines, IA, reporter, 1975-76; *Planet,* Des Moines, editor, 1977-82; Busby Productions, Des Moines, film producer, 1982-84; *Record,* New York City, managing editor, 1985, contributing editor, *Outside, American Photo;* freelance writer, 1985—.

■ Writings

Governor: An Oral Biography of Robert D. Ray, Iowa
    State University Press, 1987.
Saving the Earth, Knopf, 1991.
Crossing Antartica, Knopf, 1992.
*The Adventures and Misadventures of Peter Beard in
    Africa,* Little, Brown/Bulfinch, 1993.

Contributor of articles to periodicals, including *New York Times, National Geographic, Rolling Stone,* and *Playboy.*

■ Work in Progress

Paradise Lose: East Africa in the Nineties and *North to South: Travels in the New Chile.*

■ Sidelights

"It has taken several years for me to come up with a response to the inevitable 'What do you do?' question," Jon Bowermaster told *SATA.* "I've finally come up with a reply that will have to do, even though it prompts even more queries: I am a writer who travels."

* * *

BRAGG, Ruth Gembicki 1943-

■ Personal

Born June 22, 1943, in Marietta, GA; daughter of Stanley (an inventor) and Florence Elizabeth (a teacher; maiden name, Johnson) Gembicki; married Alan Bragg (a principal engineer), February 5, 1966; children: Hannah, Andrew. *Education:* Attended University of Illinois at Urbana-Champaign, 1961-63; School of the Art Institute of Chicago, B.F.A., 1966; attended American Students' and Artists' Center (Paris), 1974-76; attended Harvard Graduate School of Design. *Politics:* Democratic. *Religion:* Unitarian-Universalist. *Hobbies and other interests:* Camping, beach-going, theater, reading, "sitting and talking and laughing with friends."

■ Addresses

Home—51 Hancock St., Bedford, MA 01730.

■ Career

Writer and illustrator. Villagio Dei Franciulli (orphanage), Polcinego, Italy, art instructor, 1966-70; Maison des Jeunes et de la Culture, Chaville, France, ceramics instructor, 1974-77; Bedford Adult Education Program, Bedford, MA, drawing and painting instructor, 1978; Middlesex Community College, Bedford, book design instructor, 1979; artist in residence through the Groton Center for Arts, Groton, MA, 1983-87 and 1992—. Appeared in sculpting demonstration films produced at the School of the Art Institute of Chicago, 1965; leader of workshops on literacy and bookmaking; two paintings commissioned for "God Images," a Unitarian-Universalist religious education program, 1986. Bedford Art Council, member, 1981—, chair, 1981-82 and 1984-87; member of Democratic Town Committee, beginning in 1987; member of Housing Authority, beginning in 1988. *Exhibitions:* Frequent exhibitor at various shows and galleries in the U.S. and Europe, 1977—, including Cambridge, Bedford, Boston, Framingham, Lowell, West Concord, Arlington, South Hamilton, Wellfleet, Concord, Plymouth, and Cohasset, MA,

RUTH GEMBICKI BRAGG

Appalachia, Bethesda, MD, Little Rock, AK, Rolling Green, OH, Lacey, WA, Rhode Island School of Design, Bologna, Italy, Japan, and Chaville, France; one-artist shows in Carlisle, Boston, Billerica, Concord, Worcester, and First Parish, Lynn, MA; *FISH, The Emperor's Gift,* and *The Generals* were all entered into the Archives of Modern Christian Art. *Member:* Habitat for Humanity, Amnesty International, War Resistors' League.

■ Writings

SELF-ILLUSTRATED

Mrs. Muggle's Sparkle, Picture Book Studio, 1990.
The Birthday Bears, Picture Book Studio, 1991.
Alphabet out Loud, Picture Book Studio, 1991.
Colors of the Day, Picture Book Studio, 1992.

Also author and illustrator of *The Emperor's Gift,* 1986, *The Generals,* 1986, and *FISH,* 1987.

ILLUSTRATOR

Mary Ellen Kiddle and Brenda Wegmann, *Perspectivas: Temas de hoy y de siempre,* Holt, 1974, 5th edition, Harcourt, 1993.
Loring Knecht, Suzanne Toan Knecht, and Jean Tromme, *Echos de Notre Monde,* Holt, 1975.
Brenda Wegmann, *Ocho Mundos: Themes for Vocabulary Building and Cultural Awareness,* Holt, 1978, 4th edition, Harcourt, 1990.

Also illustrator with Sue Baldauf of *Every-day Magic,* 1992. Illustrator of other textbooks, booklets, and filmstrips.

■ Work in Progress

The Miser's Three Wishes, an operatic libretto for two voices, with composer Ilya Levinson; illustrating *Daniel Jazz,* Vachel Lindsay's retelling of the story of Daniel; *The Uncertain Angel,* a picture book based on the nativity story of St. Luke, to be illustrated by Madeleine Lord; *Long Tall Deep Wide,* a picture book about directions; a series of short stories for older readers; a booklet on the prevention of child abuse, with Sue Baldauf and Katherine Del Rossi.

■ Sidelights

Ruth Gembicki Bragg told *SATA:* "Writing and illustrating depend more on the observation of the details of reality than on extraordinary bursts of imagination. Imagination is the salt, not the main ingredient of such work. From teachers, studies, travels, my husband, our two children, and friends, I have been introduced to a wide variety of realities, and the process continues. But it was begun when I was a child, when my parents read to me, played music, told stories, when my grandmother talked to me in smatterings of German, when my grandfather counted fingers and toes in Swedish. Books and magazines were everywhere in my parents' home, and these were our museums; the stained-glass-windowed church was our theater. When I asked, I was told that yes, the Bible was true, but no, God wasn't likely to speak through any burning bushes these days, and no, they didn't know why. Questions are parts of truth too. As early and as easily as that, I was taught to doubt the permanence of the status quo.

"Given paper, pencils, crayons, and years and years of time empty of schedules and expectations, I scribbled curls of waxy color until I learned to modify random motion into gestures that would result in lines with definite destinations, like a tottering baby grown to a child sent on an errand. I could think of a tree and put marks on a paper and someone else seeing the marks would know that it was a tree. Like that, I was an artist. The work of becoming a writer was going on at the same time. When my parents read to me, they pointed to the markings on pages, and eventually I came to know that the things that my parents traced when they read were not random markings, but lines sent on errands; they were the words that my parents would say when they saw those straight lines and curls, and if someone else traced the same lines, they would say the same words. I had learned to read. From there it was a simple step to learn to make the same letter marks, put the letters into patterns that were words, and then to juggle words into different patterns. I was a writer.

"Before I was an illustrator, I was a painter. Before I was an author, I wrote letters to my friends and stories for my children and journals for my husband and myself. A great leap of faith is necessary in order for a painter to become an illustrator and for a journal writer to become an author. However, it is not the painter or the journal writer who takes a deep breath and crosses fingers and says prayers and appropriate lucky words, but the publisher—most notably in my case, Robert Saunders of Picture Book Studio and Andrew Clements. If a tree falls in the forest, does it make a sound? Maybe yes, maybe no. And what of the manuscript that slides through the transom, across a desk, and no one reads it? Does it become a book? Definitely not! Andrew read *Mrs. Muggle's Sparkle,* and that started everything rolling. I will be a long time in his debt for having the simple courtesy of reading something by someone no one had ever heard of and seeing it could be done. Renee Davis, once of Holt Rinehart and Winston, performed the same service: 'yes, we'll take a chance.'

"When I am working on the text of a book, the words engulf the page. When I am illustrating, the pictures swallow up the words. A balance must be struck. I've been asked whether accepting suggestions from editors or art directors compromises my work. As the original meaning of 'compromise' is 'mutual promise of excellence,' then listening to suggestions is a compromise. But I can always refuse suggestions. An editor at one publishing house thought that 'yo-yo' was too difficult a word, so I packed up my papers and went elsewhere.

"If writing is sending words on an errand, what sort of errands do I set for mine? I believe that it is the responsibility of an artist to make common experiences uncommon, thereby bringing these into the realm of contemplation, and where appropriate, into the realms of celebration and action. Or, as I've said to classes of schoolchildren: 'to change the world.'

Story Sparks First Children's Book

"Parents, friends, and associates are not always at the ready to tell a person that he or she is a proud miracle worthy of celebration. But a book can do this. *Mrs. Muggle's Sparkle* is based partly on a story my grandfather told about a bird in a nest in a tree in a forest (all modified with the words 'teeny tiny') which concludes with the line, 'and then the teeny tiny bird opened its teeny tiny beak and said, "*CHIRP!*"' The second inspiration for the book was a true story about a doctor who advised the parents of hearing-impaired children to shout endearments to their babies on the theory that people with partial hearing learn not to listen because command and reprimands are most commonly shouted, while 'sweet nothings' are normally whispered. In *Mrs. Muggle's Sparkle,* 'I love you' is murmured, cried, yelled, shouted 'as loud as you can' for a grand total of seven 'I love you's,' which I hope will cancel out some of the less attractive words directed at children (and elders). Another message of the book is that a person should determinedly seek what is important, even if the seeking means some silliness.

"I have been told that St. Augustine invented silent reading. Before that, everyone who could read did it out loud. Silent reading is fine, but sometimes it seems that children are required to be quiet while the babble of machines goes on and on. Hushed too often, children stop asking the questions that fuel society's changes, or else they resort to obscenity and violence to get atten-

tion. That sounds pretty solemn an errand for *Alphabet out Loud,* where children shout, caterwaul, and howl through the alphabet *E*ating *F*udge, making *V*alentines and *W*ishes, and finish by having a snoring contest: *ZZZZZZ.* But that is the book's message. I want the reader and the 'listener' to be equally vocal. The only way the story—and our lives—make sense is to participate.

"Likewise, with *The Birthday Bears* comes an invitation to actively share in the celebration of memory and imagination: what do *you* see? what do *you* remember? what do *you* think will happen next? The combination of science and poetry that is *Colors of the Day* may seem to have a different goal than the others, just as science and poetry may seem to have little in common. However, science and poetry have the same basis: direct observation, participation in life. I want children to refuse to accept cliches for answers. When I was writing *Colors of the Day,* I don't know how many obviously silly, inaccurate reasons I heard for why the sky is blue, before I asked an astronomer, Alan MacRobert, and a physicist who does work for NASA, David Knecht. The truth of the world is startlingly wonderful, available to anyone who has time to stop and look. And when they know this, just by stopping, just by looking, just by asking, the children will change the world.

A carved box inlaid with fierce tigers contains a precious gift of friendship in Bragg's self-illustrated version of the traditional tale *The Emperor's Gift.*

"To someone who is considering a career in book-making, I recommend Vachel Lindsay's advice: 'Do not stuff them with children's songs,/The neat and the pretty sugary words,/The cheap, the tawdry, the tinkling tunes./Give them knives and forks, as well as spoons.' Then, because librarians are the people who sort the 'cutlery,' I would suggest that a writer- or illustrator-to-be spend some time at a library. Make an appointment to talk with the librarians about which books they and the children like and why, not to copy what's there, but to see what company your work will keep. Look for three books that you like above all others, and three you dislike. (Some of my favorite writer/illustrators are Brian Wildsmith, Maurice Sendak, Eric Carle, Lisbeth Zwerger, and Nancy Ekholm Burkert.) Count the pages, count the words: a picture book is more a haiku than a novel. Also, because the words will be read out loud, a writer has to consider the sounds and rhythms words make as much as the meanings they convey. As for illustrations, these have to be absolutely yours. Beware of pseudo-Snoopys, faux Babars, and animals with eyelashes. Look at books by painters who incorporate words into their paintings and drawings: Henri Matisse's *Jazz*, Saul Steinberg's *Labyrinth*, Ben Shahn's *The Love and Joy of Letters*, Sister Mary Corita's *Headlines and Footnotes*, among others.

"My work day begins about 9:30. If I'm starting the text of a story, I write using a pen and typing paper, then rewrite on a personal computer that has an ink jet printer with variable type that helps me visualize type space requirements when sketching illustrations. For serious rewrite problems, I go back to pen and ink. Maybe the process of manually forming the letters helps because writing becomes drawing, or maybe because when I scratch out a pen-and-ink line and then change my mind, I can recover it. When I'm happy with the text, I begin the illustrations by making page divisions. The illustrations may require changes in the text (one of the benefits of being both a writer and an illustrator), and the text changes may affect the drawings. When both balance to my satisfaction, I contact publishers. To finish the sixteen drawings that illustrate text, end papers, title page and covers takes at least four or six months; a book from beginning to end takes about two years. My working day ends around 5:00 or 6:00. After 6:00, the light is bad and the colors are not true. If I work on drawings after 6:00, the way various people hold their forks at dinner remind me of the illustrations in progress; if I work on writing after that time, my mind will saunter off in the midst of a sentence to contemplate whether the right word is 'shriek' or maybe 'bellow'—to the detriment of polite conversation."

■ For More Information See

PERIODICALS

Bulletin of the Center for Children's Books, May, 1991, p. 211.
Newsweek, December 3, 1990, p. 66.
School Library Journal, April, 1992, p. 103.
Wilson Library Bulletin, September, 1991, p. 107.

BRILL, Marlene Targ 1945-

■ Personal

Born September 27, 1945, in Chicago, IL; daughter of Irving Targ (a pharmacist) and Genevieve Worshill Targ (a homemaker); married Richard Brill (a consultant in marketing and public relations), February 4, 1973; children: Alison Targ Brill. *Education:* University of Illinois, B.S., 1967; Roosevelt University, M.A., 1973; Loyola University, Administrative Certificate, 1978.

■ Addresses

Office—Marlene Targ Brill Communications, 314 Lawndale, Wilmette, IL 60091; or c/o Children's Press, 5440 North Cumberland Ave., Chicago, IL 60656.

■ Career

Worked as a curriculum specialist, media coordinator and special education classroom teacher, 1967-80; Marlene Targ Brill (MTB) Communications, Wilmette, IL, children's book author, speaker about writing, and writer/editor for businesses and textbook publishers, 1980—. Consultant and advocate for special education. Children's Memorial Hospital, member of Health Edu-

MARLENE TARG BRILL

cation Committee, 1990-92; DePaul University Nursing School, community representative to education committee, 1993—. *Member:* Society of Children's Book Writers and Illustrators, Independent Writers of Chicago, Children's Reading Round Table.

■ Awards, Honors

Chicago Women in Publishing merit award, 1988, for *Hide-and-Seek Safety;* listed in *Outstanding Young Women of America,* 1982-83.

■ Writings

JUVENILE

(With Kathi Checker) *Unique Listening/Mainstreaming Stories,* Instructional Dynamics, 1980.
John Adams, Children's Press, 1986.
I Can Be A Lawyer, Children's Press, 1987.
Libya, Children's Press, 1987.
James Buchanan, Children's Press, 1988.
Hide-and-Seek Safety, World Book, 1988.
Rainy Days and Rainbows, World Book, 1989.
Algeria, Children's Press, 1990.
Why Do We Have To?, World Book, 1990.
Mongolia, Children's Press, 1992.
Daniel in the Lion's Den, Publications International, 1992.
David and Goliath, Publications International, 1992.
Jonah and the Whale, Publications International, 1992.
Joseph's Coat of Many Colors, Publications International, 1992.
Noah's Ark, Publications International, 1992.
Allen Jay and the Underground Railroad, Carolrhoda Books, 1993.
(With Harry Targ) *Guatemala,* Children's Press, 1993.
(With Targ) *Guyana,* Children's Press, in press.
Trail of Tears, Millbrook Press, in press.

OTHER

Project Aware (slide-tape production), Illinois Association for Retarded Citizens, 1980.
Washington D.C. Travel Guide, World Book, 1982.
Infertility and You, Budlong Press, 1984.
Parenting a Child with Down Syndrome, Barron's Educational Series, 1993.

Contributor of two chapters to *The President's World,* World Book, 1982; author of "The Important You" column for *Career World,* 1981.

■ Work in Progress

Honduras, Children's Press, 1995; *Amazing Kids; Kids for Change;* two biographies.

■ Sidelights

Marlene Targ Brill loved books from a very young age. "My parents read constantly, and I remember being jealous of my older brother, who had a smaller bedroom but one full of books and records," she recalled to *SATA.* She especially remembers the excitement of

receiving a box of books each year from her uncle, an editor in New York. Each box contained surprises that encouraged her reading and expanded her intellectual horizons. If a topic intrigued her she spent hours investigating it. Biographies were of particular interest and became, and still are, an obsession. Over the years her habit of researching topics of intense interest, and her love of biographies, resulted in nonfiction books about people and places.

As a child she had an active imagination. She would sit in the window of the family's apartment and watch people passing on the street below, making up stories about where they were going and what they were doing. In school, essay questions on tests helped sustain grades, as words flowed with ease. "Still, I never thought of becoming an author," Marlene said. Instead, she studied special education, devoting thirteen years to teaching students with disabilities and training teachers. During these years she published her first stories. "As a special education teacher in the days before there were so many exciting textbooks, I developed my own classroom materials," she told *SATA.* "I determined to do better than what was already published."

Working with a psychologist friend, Kathi Checker, Marlene wrote the first set of four special education fiction stories published as *Unique Listening/Mainstreaming Stories.* The stories drew on Marlene's classroom experiences, Kathi's psychology skills, and family experiences. Although Kathi Checker died before the project was completed, Marlene continued, and the series was published on cassette tapes. Still, it took years before Marlene thought of herself as a full-time author.

Her first venture into full-time freelance writing was in editorial work and writing textbooks. "However, I kept being drawn back to writing books for children," she commented. Now Marlene writes books for readers of all ages, toddlers to adults. "I like variety," she noted. "Just recently I completed a historical fiction story for primary-grade kids and a guidebook for parents of children who have Down syndrome."

Marlene finds all kinds of writing challenging and involving, with the research being just as enjoyable as the writing. "I feel like an explorer, delving into old newspapers, tracking down historical documents and locating famous and not-so-famous people to interview," she told *SATA.* The challenge is in condensing all of the materials she finds. "To me research is an endless treasure hunt with many pots of gold."

Marlene especially enjoys writing for young children, finding this a great challenge. "With fewer, simpler words, every word counts," she stated. *Allen Jay and the Underground Railroad,* written for first- to fourth-graders, is the true story of a boy who helped someone escape danger. The story includes several complicated subjects: the Underground Railroad, slavery and the Quaker religion. The challenge was to tell the story in words the beginning and young reader could understand.

In all of her projects Marlene cares about her subjects and puts time and energy into the research needed to tell the stories. A current project, *Amazing Kids,* is a collection of biographies and essays about children who are brave and talented. "I investigated many resources about each person and information about the time and place in which they lived," she told *SATA.* "I wanted to be true to my subjects. Their lives became very important to me."

Now, when speaking to groups of children, Marlene encourages them to read about subjects that interest them. She encourages them to explore their emotions and expand their talents through writing. "Whatever their future, I hope they find a career that brings them as many rewards as writing does for me."

* * *

BRUCE, (William) Harry 1934-

■ Personal

Born July 8, 1934, in Toronto, Ontario, Canada; son of Charles Tory and Agnes (maiden name, King) Bruce; married Penny Meadows, September 10, 1955; children: Alexander, Annabel, Max. *Education:* Mount Allison University, B.A., 1955; London School of Economics, 1956-57; Massey College, University of Toronto, 1969-70; University of King's College, Halifax, D.C.L., 1985; University St. Francis Xavier, Antigonish, Nova Scotia,

HARRY BRUCE

LL.D., 1991. *Hobbies and other interests:* Sailing, walking, fly-fishing.

■ Addresses

Home—General Delivery, St. Andrews, New Brunswick, Canada EOG2XO. *Office*—Atlantic Salmon Federation, P.O. Box 429, St. Andrews, New Brunswick, Canada EOG2XO. *Agent*—Bella Pomer, 22 Shallmar Blvd., PH2, Toronto, Ontario, Canada MSN 2Z8.

■ Career

Ottawa Journal, reporter, 1955-59; *Globe and Mail,* reporter, 1959-61; *Maclean's,* assistant editor, 1961-64; *Saturday Night,* managing editor, 1964-65; *Canadian Magazine,* managing editor, 1965-66; *Star Weekly,* associate editor and featured columnist, 1967-68; *Toronto Daily Star,* columnist, 1968-69; *Maclean's,* columnist and reports and reviews editor, 1970-71; Nova Scotia Light and Power Co. Ltd, executive editor, 1971; *Atlantic Insight,* editor, 1979-80, executive editor, 1981; *Atlantic Salmon Journal,* editor, 1991—. Freelance writer, 1973-79. Gazette East Coast Editorial Ltd., Canadian Broadcasting Corporation, Halifax, TV talk-show host, 1972. Founding board member, Writers' Federation of Nova Scotia.

■ Awards, Honors

Nellie for best radio drama, Association of Canadian Television and Radio Artists, 1977, for *Word from an Ambassador of Dreams;* first winner of the Evelyn Richardson Memorial Literary Award for best nonfiction book by a Nova Scotian, 1978, for *Lifeline;* Brascan Award for Culture, National Magazine Awards, 1981; top prize for magazine writing, Atlantic Journalism Awards, 1983, 1984, 1986, 1993; Toronto-Dominion Bank Award for Humour, National Magazine Awards, 1983; First National Business Book Award runner-up, 1886, for *The Man and the Empire: Frank Sobey;* City of Dartmouth Book Award winner, and Booksellers' Choice Award, Atlantic Provinces Booksellers' Association, both for *Down Home: Notes of a Maritime Son,* both 1989.

■ Writings

NONFICTION FOR ADULTS

A Basket of Apples: Recollections of Historic Nova Scotia, photographs by Chic Harris, Oxford, 1982.
The Gulf of St. Lawrence, photographs by Wayne Barrett and Anne MacKay, Oxford, 1984.
Each Moment as It Flies, Methuen, 1984.
Movin' East: The Further Writings of Harry Bruce, Methuen, 1985.
Down Home: Notes of a Maritime Son, Key Porter, 1988.

NONFICTION FOR YOUNG ADULTS

Maud: The Life of L. M. Montgomery, Bantam, 1992.

Also author of *The Short Happy Walks of Max Mac-Pherson,* 1968; *Nova Scotia,* 1975; *Lifeline,* 1977; *R. A.: The Story of R. A. Jodrey, Entrepreneur,* 1979; and *The Man and the Empire: Frank Sobey,* 1985. Contributor of essays, reviews and articles to commentaries, anthologies, and periodicals.

■ Work in Progress

Mr. Lawyer: Frank Covert, QC., a biography and *The Beginner's Encyclopedia of Fly-Fishing.*

■ Sidelights

Although he once worked as a television interviewer, Harry Bruce's career has been devoted almost exclusively to writing. He has skillfully performed as a reporter, feature writer, and editor for several Canadian newspapers and magazines, and has won many awards and honors for these efforts. While his collections of essays are very popular, he has also received praise for a biography for young adults, *Maud: The Life of L. M. Montgomery.* By 1992, Bruce had become one of the better-known writers of nonfiction in Canada.

Popular Adult Nonfiction

Bruce has successfully written text to accompany photographs for two books. *Books in Canada*'s Gary Michael Dault wrote of Bruce's skills in *A Basket of Apples: Recollections of Historic Nova Scotia,* "Together [with photographer Chic Harris] they have made an attractive little book that has genuine warmth and charm. Not a mean accomplishment." *The Gulf of St. Lawrence* received praise also. Applauding Bruce's wry humor, *Quill and Quire*'s George Meyers remarked that "Bruce's witty introduction and commentary enhance one's understanding of Anne MacKay and Wayne Barrett's photographs." "Bruce's captions are at once chatty and factual. A lot of history—on both the human and the national scale—has happened in the St. Lawrence, and he does his best to convey it," commented John Oughton in *Books in Canada.*

Each Moment As It Flies, a collection of the best essays Bruce wrote for national and regional magazines, has also received favorable reviews. The subjects of the pieces include the Christmas blues, jogging, profiles, travelogues on Crete and Barbados, and sailing on the East Coast of Canada. Noting that readers will be reminded of similar experiences, *Books in Canada* contributor Sherie Posesorski found that by "digging deep, Bruce has chronologically arranged the essays to flow from childhood memories to his own children's experiences, skillfully recreating his youth." Rob Davidson, writing in *Quill and Quire,* commended Bruce's work in *Each Moment as It Flies:* "Harry Bruce knows how to turn a fleeting impression into an essay and an essay into a lasting memory."

Movin' East: The Further Writings of Harry Bruce provides Bruce's fans with another collection of essays and tales. Steven Slipp in his review for *Quill and Quire*

lauded the collection for its warmth pointing out that Bruce's "familiar voice is freshwater clear, and his taste for life is as sharp and true as the salt in his adopted Atlantic surf." *Books in Canada* contributor Nanci White remarked, "As a compendium of Canadian political, sporting, and cultural activities over the last two decades, *Movin' East* is a rare and pleasant combination of side-wrenching laughter and thoughts too deep for tears."

First Young Adult Book Praised

Maud: The Life of L. M. Montgomery, Bruce's first book for young adults, has brought him additional acclaim. This biography reveals the life of Lucy Maud Montgomery, the author of the beloved book, *Anne of Green Gables,* and the "Avonlea" series. Bruce demonstrates that Maud's life was similar to that of Anne: like her fictional creation, Maud was left without parents, determined to write despite the disapproval of guardians, and attended college at a time when few women did so. While highlighting her bold characteristics, Bruce also relates the idea that Maud was a very caring woman who was devoted to her family and friends.

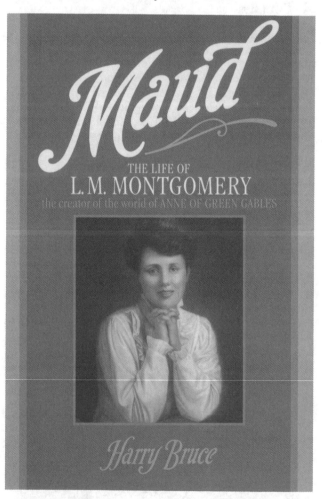

A noted fiction writer for adults, Bruce has also penned a nonfiction work on the author of the classic children's book *Anne of Green Gables.* (Cover illustration by Steve Assel.)

In general critics applauded Bruce's skill in making Maud, the creator of a vivid heroine, come alive herself. According to a contributor to the *Kirkus Reviews,* "quotes from her [Montgomery's] works capture her lively spirit, while social context conveys the magnitude of obstacles she overcame." "With a tender and sympathetic eye, Bruce reveals the quiet heroism" of Maud, asserted a reviewer in *Publishers Weekly.*

Bruce's biography of Montgomery may be enjoyed by adults as well as young adults. "Since *Maud* has appeared," Harry Bruce wrote to *SATA,* "I have found that while teenagers are taking to it as my publisher had hoped, many adults also find it fascinating, and say it does not read like a book meant exclusively for children. Maybe this means that, if the prose style is sufficiently simple and straightforward and the story being told happens to be interesting—as the real life of Maud Montgomery was—then the same book can appeal to people aged anywhere from 12 to 82, or more. I like to think so anyway."

■ Works Cited

Dault, Gary Michael, review of *A Basket of Apples: Recollections of Historic Nova Scotia, Books in Canada,* November, 1982, pp. 15, 17.

Davidson, Rob, review of *Each Moment as It Flies, Quill & Quire,* October, 1984.

Review of *Maud: The Life of L. M. Montgomery, Kirkus Reviews,* August 1, 1992, p. 986.

Review of *Maud: The Life of L. M. Montgomery, Publishers Weekly,* July 27, 1992, p. 64.

Meyers, George, review of *The Gulf of St. Lawrence, Quill & Quire,* December, 1984.

Oughton, John, review of *The Gulf of St. Lawrence, Books in Canada,* November, 1984, p.14.

Posesorski, Sherie, review of *Each Moment as It Flies, Books in Canada,* January-February, 1985, p. 22.

Slipp, Steven, review of *Movin' East: The Further Writings of Harry Bruce, Quill & Quire,* February, 1986.

White, Nanci, review of *Movin' East: The Further Writings of Harry Bruce, Books in Canada,* November, 1985, p. 24.

■ For More Information See

PERIODICALS

Quill & Quire, February, 1989.
School Library Journal, August 1992, p. 181.

—*Sketch by Ronie-Richele Garcia-Johnson*

*   *   *

BULLOCK, Kathleen (Mary) 1946-

■ Personal

Born April 28, 1946, in San Francisco, CA; daughter of John T. (a traffic manager) and Mary G. (a secretary; maiden name, McAllister) Donohue; married Walter H.

KATHLEEN BULLOCK

Bullock (a landscaper), December 22, 1967 (deceased); children: Patrick, Amy, Mary. *Education:* Attended College of San Mateo and Canada College (CA). *Politics:* Independent. *Religion:* Christian.

■ Addresses

Home and office—795 Tolman Creek, Ashland, OR 97520.

■ Career

Freelance commercial and fine artist, 1980—. *Member:* Children's Writers and Illustrators Workshop, Paperback Writer Writing Workshop.

■ Awards, Honors

American Book Award for Educational Material, 1988, for *Shakin' Loose with Mother Goose.*

■ Writings

SELF-ILLUSTRATED

The Little Gardener's Cook Book, BestSellers, 1986.
It Chanced to Rain, Simon & Schuster, 1989.
A Surprise for Mitzi Mouse, Simon & Schuster, 1989.
A Friend for Mitzi Mouse, Simon & Schuster, 1990.
The Rabbits Are Coming!, Simon & Schuster, 1991.
She'll Be Comin' 'Round the Mountain, Simon & Schuster, 1993.

ILLUSTRATOR

Shakin' Loose with Mother Goose (four-book series), Kids Matter Inc., 1986.
Marjorie Frank, *Complete Writing Lessons for the Middle Grades,* Incentive Publishers, 1987.

Frank, *Complete Writing Lessons for the Primary Grades,* Incentive Publishers, 1987.

Imogene Forte, Frank, and Joy MacKenzie, *The Kid's Stuff Book of Reading and Language Arts,* Incentive Publishers, 1987.

MacKenzie, *The Bible Read-to-Me "ABC",* David C. Cook Publications, 1988.

MacKenzie, *The Bible Read-to-Me "123",* David C. Cook Publications, 1988.

Frank, *The Kid's Stuff Book of Math for the Primary Grades,* Incentive Publishers, 1988.

Frank, *The Kid's Stuff Book of Math for the Middle Grades,* Incentive Publishers, 1988.

Frank, *202 Science Investigations,* Incentive Publishers, 1990.

Donald Peet and Marcia Stille, *Latin for Americans, Workbook I,* Macmillan, 1990.

Peet and Stille, *Latin for Americans, Workbook II,* Macmillan, 1990.

Cherrie Farnette, Forte, and Barbara Los, *Special Kid's Stuff High-Interest, Low-Vocabulary Reading and Language Skills,* Incentive Publishers, 1990.

Maria Pertik and Sandra Senter, *Stress Management and Me,* Incentive Publications, 1990.

The Twelve Days of Christmas, Allan Publishers, 1991.

Also illustrator of *Benziger Family Life Program Series (K-8),* Benziger Publishing.

■ Work in Progress

"I plan to write an adventure story for older children, and a series of chapter books for beginning readers."

■ Sidelights

"Though I was born in San Francisco," Kathleen Bullock told *SATA,* "I spent most of my childhood in the South Peninsula suburb of Redwood City where our burgeoning family settled. I was to be the oldest of ten children.

"We grew into a noisy bunch of Irish comedians, cut-ups and jokesters; a legend in our neighborhood. Someone was always 'on', singing, dancing, storytelling, or doing whatever it took to capture attention. It's not surprising that I developed into a storyteller. Everyday life provided not only hours of entertainment, but the raw material for most of my future children's books.

"My earliest dreams were artistic. When I was two, I decorated the walls of my bedroom closet with crayon. In kindergarten, at the age of five, I created a painting that set the course of my life. It was a brilliant depiction of ghosts floating over a haunted house and a field of leering pumpkins. Nothing I've accomplished since has been as satisfying.

"Putting words and pictures together, a favorite pastime, led to the creation of homemade comic books. I sent a sample to Walt Disney, hoping for a job as the world's youngest cartoonist. I never did hear from Mr. Disney.

Being part of a large family gave Bullock the inspiration for the character of Mitzi Mouse, who has some trouble adjusting to a growing household in this story. (Cover illustration by the author.)

"My first truly original illustrated, hand-lettered picture book was done as a project in freshman art class. My teacher, the great Jackie White, trained and encouraged me to open my inner eye. When I saw characters from my own imagination come to life on the page, I was forever hooked.

"I enjoy my work (though it is hard work). Every time I sit at my drawing table I fall into a world that is limited only by the bounds of my imagination and the level of my ability. I learn from each project, and try to put that newfound knowledge into the next book.

"Sometimes people ask how they, too, might become published. The ingredients for success include some talent, and some experience, mixed with generous portions of luck, motivation and perseverance.

"Children often want to know which book is my favorite. I usually prefer the book I'm working on at the moment. I do have a special place in my heart for the story of the little mouse named Mitzi who has to adjust every time the size of her family changes. Understandably, many of my ideas for Mitzi come from my own childhood experiences, and the unique perspective one develops growing up in a large family."

■ For More Information See

PERIODICALS

Children's Book Review Service, June, 1989, p. 117;
    March, 1990, p. 86.
Horn Book, July, 1989, p. 48; July, 1990, p. 51; fall,
    1991, p. 223.

Kirkus Reviews, May 1, 1989, p. 686; December, 1989,
    p. 77; April, 1991, p. 88; June 15, 1991, p. 796.
Parents, May, 1992, p. 130.
Publishers Weekly, May 24, 1991, p. 56.
School Library Journal, August, 1989, p. 116.

C

CASSEDY, Sylvia 1930-1989

■ Personal

Born January 29, 1930, in Brooklyn, NY; died of cancer, April 6, 1989, in Manhasset, NY; daughter of Jacob (a pharmacist) and Minnie (Singer) Levine; married Leslie Verwiebe, June 19, 1949 (died September 3, 1950); married Edward S. Cassedy Jr. (a professor), March 28, 1952; children: Ellen (Mrs. Jeffrey Blum), Steven, Amy, Susannah. *Education:* Brooklyn College, B.A., 1950; attended Johns Hopkins University writing seminar, 1959-60.

■ Career

Queens College of the City University of New York, Saturday Enrichment Program, Flushing, NY, teacher of creative writing to children, 1973-74; Great Neck Public Library, Great Neck, NY, teacher of creative writing to children, 1975-79; Manhasset Public Schools Parent-Teacher Association, Saturday Enrichment Program, Long Island, NY, teacher of creative writing to children, 1977-84. Instructor in teaching creative writing to children for Nassau County Board of Cooperative Education, Nassau County, NY, 1978-79.

■ Awards, Honors

Notable Books for Children citations, American Library Association, 1983, for *Behind the Attic Wall*, and 1987, for *M.E. and Morton;* Children's Choice book, 1983, for *Behind the Attic Wall.*

■ Writings

FOR CHILDREN

Little Chameleon, illustrated by Rainey Bennet, World, 1966.
Pierino and the Bell, illustrated by Evaline Ness, Doubleday, 1966.
(Editor and translator with Kunihiro Suetake) *Birds, Frogs, and Moonlight* (verse), illustrated by Vo-Dinh, Doubleday, 1967.

SYLVIA CASSEDY

Marzipan Day on Bridget Lane, illustrated by Margot Tomes, Doubleday, 1967.
(Editor and translator with Parvathi Thampi) *Moon-Uncle, Moon-Uncle: Rhymes from India,* illustrated by Susanne Suba, Doubleday, 1972.
In Your Own Words: A Beginner's Guide to Writing, Doubleday, 1979, revised edition, 1990.
Behind the Attic Wall, Crowell, 1983.
M.E. and Morton, Crowell, 1987.
Roomrimes (verse), illustrated by Michele Chessare, Crowell, 1987.
Lucie Babbidge's House, HarperCollins, 1989.
Best Cat Suit of All, Dial, 1991.

(Editor and translator with Kunihiro Suetake) *Red Dragonfly on My Shoulder: Haiku,* HarperCollins, 1992.

Zoomrimes: Poems about Things That Go (verse), HarperCollins, 1993.

■ Sidelights

Sylvia Cassedy, who died in 1989 at the age of 59, left behind an impressive body of work in several genres. This encompassed books of verse such as *Roomrimes,* an alphabetical tour of places which includes rhymed, unrhymed, and haiku poetry, and nonfiction such as *In Your Own Words: A Beginner's Guide to Writing,* a manual in which she uses an informal, direct style to provide information on the writing of prose and poetry. However, she is best remembered as writer of fiction for middle graders, having produced such highly praised volumes as *Behind the Attic Wall, M.E. and Morton,* and the posthumously published *Lucie Babbidge's House.* Sylvia Cassedy's fiction centers on the healing role of fantasy and daydream in children's daily life.

Critics have celebrated Cassedy's work for exploring the inner world of children in a detailed, understanding, and insightful manner. Cassedy's protagonists are young girls who are outsiders—withdrawn, unpopular, or fearful—who learn to appreciate themselves through their own imaginations as well as their own sensitive inner natures. Cassedy portrays this development by showing the contrast between the harsh reality of the daily lives of the girls at home or in school and the positive nature of their fantasy lives. "Against the warmth and color and infinite possibilities of the inner worlds of her characters, Sylvia Cassedy sets their painful realities," noted Christine McDonnell *Horn Book.* Maggie, of *Behind the Attic Wall,* is orphaned and slighted; Mary Ella, the "M.E." of *M.E. and Morton,* is isolated and lonely; and Lucie, in *Lucie Babbidge's House,* is ridiculed by others in her boarding school/orphanage, even as she attempts to cope with her scattered memories of her parents' death. "This backdrop of pain is so intense and unrelenting that, were it not for the reprieve of the inner worlds, neither characters nor readers could endure it," writes McDonnell.

A painful childhood is something to which Sylvia Cassedy was no stranger. She candidly recounted in an autobiographical sketch in *Sixth Book of Junior Authors:* "On the whole, I was not an unpopular kid. I had some good friends. I got invited to birthday parties. When I was eleven a boy asked me to dance. But I felt unpopular. My good friends had better friends of their own, or seemed to. My place card at those birthday parties was somehow always at the end of the table, farthest from the hostess. The boy who asked me to dance was the shortest boy in the class; I was the shortest girl. He picked me for my size."

Citing her intense experiences growing-up as the motivation behind her writing, she continued: "I spent much of my time suffering. I collected hurts .... And remembered. Not only then, but now. Except that now I don't

suffer over them; I write about them. All those troubled 11- and 12-year old girls in my novels are, in their way, recreations not of my actual childhood but how I perceived it at the time and remember those perceptions now .... I remembered all that suffering, in what can only be described as loving detail."

Turning to the Novel

Behind the Attic Wall, Cassedy's first novel, deals explicitly with the issue of a young girl's suffering and alienation. A reviewer commented in *Junior Bookshelf:* "The central character of Sylvia Cassedy's ghost story *Behind the Attic Wall* is most powerfully drawn, a twelve year old orphan girl who has been thrown out of one institution after another as unmanageable." After being sent to live with her two old great-aunts, Maggie, hearing voices, discovers two dolls living secret lives within the attic. Through her imaginary interactions with these dolls Maggie learns to love and care. Sylvia Cassedy herself, in a letter to her editor, Marilyn Kriney, wrote: "Throughout the book I have emphasized the main character's need not only to be cherished, but to cherish in return—to fix, to heal, to look after— and insofar as the story has a theme at all, it can be characterized as the power of such cherishing to alter the life of a troubled human being." Zena Sutherland,

In this book by Cassedy, M.E. gains a new appreciation for her self and her "dumb" older brother through the imaginative energy of her friend Polly.

calling the book a "memorable story" in the *Bulletin of the Center for Children's Books,* concluded that "the conversion of Maggie from a suspicious cynic to a concerned participant is made credible."

In her next novel, *M.E. and Morton,* Cassedy again centers on the healing power of fantasy: lonely Mary Ella (M.E.) is taught by her newfound friend, Polly, how to change her negative self-image through daydream and play. In the process Mary Ella comes to love and appreciate her awkward older brother, Morton, whom she had previously despised. A *Publishers Weekly* reviewer praised not only Cassedy's sensitivity to children's alienation but also the artful flow of her pen: "Cassedy's story unfolds deliberately, interspersed with stories about Mary Ella's own creativity, which reveal her growing ability to cherish Morton.... The strokes are broad and textured, and unutterably intense." Marcia Hupp similarly observed in *School Library Journal* that *M.E. and Morton* is "a beautifully crafted novel, one to be lingered over and shared."

It is *Lucie Babbidge's House,* published posthumously, that stands as Sylvia Cassedy's most eloquent meditation on the healing power of children's imaginative play. Of the book, Mary M. Burns in *Horn Book* argued that as readers we first see Lucie as "the unkempt, withdrawn Goosey-Loosey, tormented by her classmates at Norwood Hall—a school about as appealing as a Dickensian orphanage—and dismissed by her teacher as uncooperative and stupid. However, when she enters her house after school, she is the beloved, admired daughter of a closely knit—if somewhat eccentric—family." It is only as the novel progresses that the reader discovers that Lucie's house is a secret doll house, hidden in the school's basement, and that Lucie's loving family exists only in her imagination.

However, healing and maturity come to Lucie as they did to Maggie and, for that matter, Mary Ella. "In Lucie, Cassedy has created another unforgettable, vivid character," wrote Ellen Fader in *School Library Journal,* and Lucie's story will prove a "highly satisfying novel for readers who delight in complex characterization, and the inventive use of language and plotting."

Sylvia Cassedy's fiction grapples with the alienation that can often encompass childhood, how this alienation is mitigated through fantasy, and, ultimately, how fantasy itself provides the knowledge to deal successfully with many real-life problems. "Without ever resorting to superficial psychologizing, Cassedy always showed a deep understanding of the imaginative obsessions behind children's most ordinary games," Roger Sutton observed in *Bulletin of the Center for Children's Books.* As McDonnell, lamenting Cassedy's recent death, concluded in *Horn Book:* "A writer of great skill, originality, insight, and compassion, Sylvia Cassedy believed in the healing power of creativity and love. Sadly, we can only wonder what other stories she would have shared with us had her life not been shortened by cancer. Wonder, and be thankful for the daring books she left us."

Lucie Babbidge is taunted by her peers and scolded by her teacher but finds comfort and healing in a world of fantasy in Cassedy's last work.

■ Works Cited

Burns, Mary M., review of *Lucie Babbidge's House, Horn Book,* November-December, 1989, pp. 768-769.

Cassedy, Sylvia, entry in *Sixth Book of Junior Authors and Illustrators,* Wilson, 1989, pp. 49-50.

Review of *Behind the Attic Wall, Junior Bookshelf,* October, 1984.

Fader, Ellen, review of *Lucie Babbidge's House, School Library Journal,* September, 1989, p. 272.

Hupp, Marcia, review of *M.E. and Morton, School Library Journal,* June-July, 1987, p. 93.

McDonnell, Christine, "Sylvia Cassedy: Valuing the Child's Inner Life," *Horn Book,* January-February, 1991, p. 101-105.

Review of *M.E. and Morton, Publishers Weekly,* July 10, 1987, p. 70.

Sutherland, Zena, review of *Behind the Attic Wall, Bulletin of the Center for Children's Books,* November, 1983, p. 45.

Sutton, Roger, review of *Lucie Babbidge's House, Bulletin of the Center for Children's Books,* September, 1989, p. 5.

■ For More Information See

BOOKS

Children's Literature Review, Volume 26, Gale, 1992.

PERIODICALS

Bulletin of the Center for Children's Books, December, 1979, p. 68; February, 1988, p. 112.
Christian Science Monitor, May 2, 1973, p. B4.
Horn Book, February, 1984; March-April, 1988.
New York Times Book Review, November 6, 1966, p. 60; November 5, 1967, p. 61; November 20, 1983, pp. 39-40.
School Library Journal, November, 1979, pp. 85-86; October, 1987, p. 120; February, 1991.
Times Literary Supplement, May 4, 1984, p. 506.
Voice of Youth Advocates, June, 1987, p. 76.
Washington Post Book World, November 5, 1972.*

* * *

CHASE, Alice
See McHARGUE, Georgess

* * *

CLIMO, Shirley 1928-

■ Personal

Born November 25, 1928, in Cleveland, OH; daughter of Morton J. (a paving contractor) and Aldarilla (a writer; maiden name, Shipley) Beistle; married George F. Climo (a corporate historian), June 17, 1950; children: Robert, Susan, Lisa. *Education:* Attended DePauw University, 1946-49. *Politics:* "Variable." *Religion:* Protestant.

■ Addresses

Home—24821 Prospect Ave., Los Altos, CA 94022.
Agent—Kendra Marcus, *Bookstop,* 67 Meadow View Rd., Orinda, CA 94563.

■ Career

WGAR-Radio, Cleveland, OH, scriptwriter for weekly juvenile series. "Fairytale Theatre," 1949-53; freelance writer, 1976—. President, Los Altos Morning Forum, 1971-73. *Member:* California Writers, Society of Children's Book Writers.

■ Writings

(Reteller) *Piskies, Spriggans, and Other Magical Beings: Tales from the Droll-Teller* (juvenile), illustrated by Joyce Audy dos Santos, Crowell, 1981.
The Cobweb Christmas (picture book), illustrated by Joe Lasker, Crowell, 1982.
(Contributor) Sylvia K. Burack, *Writing and Selling Fillers, Light Verse, and Short Humor,* Writer, Inc., 1982.

SHIRLEY CLIMO

Gopher, Tanker, and the Admiral (juvenile), illustrated by Eileen McKeating, Crowell, 1984.
Someone Saw a Spider (juvenile) illustrated by Dirk Zimmer, Harper, 1985.
A Month of Seven Days (juvenile historical novel), Crowell, 1987.
King of the Birds (picture book), illustrated by Ruth Heller, Harper, 1988.
The Egyptian Cinderella (picture book), illustrated by Ruth Heller, Crowell, 1989.
T. J.'s Ghost (juvenile), Crowell, 1989.
City! New York (juvenile history), illustrated with photographs by George Ancona, Macmillan, 1990.
City! San Francisco (juvenile history), illustrated with photographs by George Ancona, Macmillan, 1990.
City! Washington, D. C. (juvenile history), illustrated with photographs by George Ancona, Macmillan, 1991.
The Match between the Winds (picture book), illustrated by Roni Shepherd, Macmillan, 1991.
The Korean Cinderella (picture book), illustrated by Ruth Heller, HarperCollins, 1993.
Stolen Thunder (picture book), illustrated by Alexander Koshkin, Clarion, 1994.
Atalanta's Race (picture book), illustrated by Alexander Koshkin, Clarion, in press.
The Irish Cinderlad, HarperCollins, in press.

King of the Birds
by Shirley Climo
illustrated by Ruth Heller

Many of Climo's retellings of traditional tales are "why" stories; this book tells why the wren was named king of all the birds. (Cover illustration by Ruth Heller.)

Contributor to magazines, including *Family Weekly, The Writer, Cricket, Ranger Rick,* and *Seventeen,* and to newspapers.

■ Work in Progress

The Princess Treasury for HarperCollins, publication expected in 1996.

■ Sidelights

"To be a children's book writer always seemed the most wonderful aspiration in the world to me—and the most natural," Shirley Climo told *SATA.* "My earliest memory is of being rocked in a creaky wicker carriage while my mother, a children's author, recited her stories. Long before I could read, I'd begun telling my own tales to myself and to anyone else willing to listen."

"I grew up, raised three children, a half dozen dogs, a clutch of cats, a horse, and a straggle of chickens. Each new addition provided additional story-telling material, and many two-legged and four-legged household members have found their way into print. Most important, I have found that writing books for youngsters is, indeed, quite wonderful."

The Start of a Writing Career

"From 1976 until 1980," Climo continues, "I fulfilled a typical writer-reentry apprenticeship doing a series of newspaper articles and selling a number of travel and humor pieces to adult magazines. I learned a great deal, but all along my target was not bigger but smaller. I kept my eye on other people's kids. A trip to Cornwall and a stay in a four-hundred-year-old cottage provided the necessary information and inspiration for my first juvenile book, a collection of Cornish folklore called *Piskies, Spriggans, and Other Magical Beings.*

"My second book, *The Cobweb Christmas,* is also a folktale, from Germany. Writing it turned a fear of spiders into a fascination, and now I'm thoroughly enmeshed in spider lore and legend and have ... completed a collection of spidery tales called *Someone Saw a Spider.* My book, *Gopher, Tanker and the Admiral* is strictly a contemporary humor/adventure story for youngsters and the *A Month of Seven Days* is a historical novel for pre-teens that borders on being a ghost story. With the picture book version of *Betty Stoggs and the Small People* (one of the Cornish tales) and *King of the Birds,* I'm back in the realm of folklore."

A Troll Book
$2.95 U.S.
$3.95 CAN.

Can Zoe outsmart the Yankees?

A MONTH OF SEVEN DAYS

Shirley Climo

A girl living in the South during the Civil War tries to scare away the Northern soldiers who have occupied her home in this novel by Climo.

Climo's works are often inspired by traditional folktales and legends. In her first children's story book, *Piskies, Spriggans, and Other Magical Beings: Tales from the Droll-Teller,* Climo retells nine Cornish folktales filled with magical creatures, surrounding the stories with informative introductions and humorous codas that explain the dialect used and the superstitions presented. In a review in the *New York Times Book Review,* Selma G. Lanes commented on Climo's "lean, no-nonsense prose, which will give her credibility with today's possibly skeptical children." *Publishers Weekly* called the collection "a folklore aficionado's paradise."

For her next project, Climo recalls a 300-year-old German legend that explains the tradition of hanging tinsel on Christmas trees. *The Cobweb Christmas* tells the story of Cristkindel, who takes pity on the cold spiders which have been ejected from a newly-cleaned house on Christmas eve by bringing them inside with him. The spiders cover the Christmas tree in cobwebs which Cristkindel turns to silver and gold. *The Bulletin of the Center for Children's Books* called *The Cobweb Christmas* a "pleasant but rather sedate modern example of a 'why' story."

King of the Birds is another picture book in the "why" genre of children's books. In this work, Climo retells the ancient legend that places the homely wren as king of the birds due to his clever use of the eagle to fly higher and longer than any other bird in the animal kingdom. *Publishers Weekly* remarked, "Climo has created a lively, elegant version of an ancient legend." Richard Peck, reviewing *King of the Birds* in *Los Angeles Times Book Review* concluded that the combination of Climo's text and illustrator Ruth Heller's pictures is nearly ideal: "When the birds take wing across a double-page spread, the soul soars." With *The Match between the Winds,* Climo produced another picture book based on legend, praised for its evocative setting and the charm of the author's rendering.

In *The Egyptian Cinderella,* Climo blends ancient Egyptian folklore and fact in the picture book story of a young Greek slave girl who marries an Egyptian Pharoah with the help of a pair of magic slippers. While some reviewers found an element of racism in the tale's depiction of the fair-haired protagonist's triumph over the darker servant girls, most found the story an exotic take to the traditional, and much-loved, Cinderella tale. Martha Rosen, reviewing this work for *School Library Journal,* called *The Egyptian Cinderella* "a stunning combination of fluent prose and exquisitely wrought illustrations. Climo has woven this ancient tale . . . with clarity and eloquence."

In *Someone Saw a Spider: Spider Facts and Folktales,* Climo collects and retells legends and facts about these insects, and includes a bibliography of further sources for the enterprising young reader. Although some reviewers commented that the book's main asset is as a source for storytelling, *Kirkus Reviews* remarked: "Climo's collection is fact-filled and fun . . . . She is to be praised for her sparkling retellings."

Mysteries for Young Readers

Climo's first title for young readers, *Gopher, Tanker, and the Admiral,* was also well received by reviewers. This story pairs a young boy nicknamed Gopher and the cranky retired admiral who is his neighbor. Together, the unlikely duo solve the mystery behind the rash of burglaries on their block. *School Library Journal* praised the humorous elements in Climo's short novel, and *Bulletin of the Center for Children's Books* remarked: "There's appeal in the bridging of a generation gap."

T. J.'s Ghost is Climo's second mystery for middle readers. Set on the California coast, this story tells of a young girl who expects a dull time when she stays with her aunt and uncle while her parents vacation in Hawaii. Instead she meets a ghost and helps him find the ring that keeps him returning to the material world. Critics praised the evocative setting of Climo's novel more than the plot of the work itself, but Margaret Mary Ptacek, reviewing *T. J.'s Ghost* in *Voice of Youth Advocates* concluded: "This isn't a great adventure but a pleasant tale."

A Month of Seven Days is a historical novel for middle readers set during the American Civil War. The novel's heroine, twelve-year-old Zoe, and her mother, are terrified when their home is commandeered by Yankee troops just when Zoe's father is expected home on leave from the Confederate army. Zoe attempts to protect her father by scaring away the superstitious Yankee captain, and in the process learns that even the enemy is human. The review in *Publishers Weekly* was mixed, stating that Zoe's emerging confidence in herself, her teasing of the Northern soldiers, and her perception that her enemies are not monsters but human beings "are just a few of the tantalizing issues that are brought to light but never satisfactorily resolved." *Kirkus Reviews,* however, remarked: "Zoe is believable; her anger and bewilderment are well portrayed, as is the experience of being part of an occupied country."

In a departure from her earlier works for the young, Climo has published three travel guides for young tourists, illustrated with photographs by George Ancona. Comprising *City! New York, City! San Francisco,* and *City! Washington, D. C.,* this series has been commended for its entertainment value as well as for its suggestions for activities and sights to see in each of the cities featured. Elizabeth S. Watson, reviewing the volume on San Francisco in *Horn Book,* comments that Climo has "produce[d] a superbly clear picture of the city."

In an article on writing children's books that Climo contributed to *The Writer* magazine, she noted: "Some view the world of children's literature as a land of gloom and doom. Libraries across the country have cut their book-buying budgets, and many publishers have cut their production accordingly." "But I'm not necessarily discouraged," Climo concludes. "When I talk to fifth- and six-grade students about writing, most of them want to write for adults, even before they've grown up themselves. When I speak to adult groups, most of them want to write for children. I encourage all of them. For while fewer picture books get into print now than a decade or so ago, today's books are better than ever. Editors are still willing to stop, look, and listen to a good picture book."

■ Works Cited

Climo, Shirley, "Creating a Picture Book," *The Writer,* July, 1983, pp. 18-20, 44.

Review of *The Cobweb Christmas, Bulletin of the Center for Children's Books,* October, 1982, p. 23.

Review of *Gopher, Tanker, and the Admiral, Bulletin of the Center for Children's Books,* September, 1984.

Review of *Gopher, Tanker, and the Admiral, School Library Journal,* May, 1984, p. 101.

Review of *King of the Birds, Publishers Weekly,* January 15, 1988, p. 94.

Lanes, Selma G., review of *Piskies, Spriggans, and Other Magical Beings: Tales from the Droll-Teller, New York Times Book Review,* July 5, 1981.

Review of *A Month of Seven Days, Kirkus Reviews,* November 15, 1987, p. 1625.

Review of *A Month of Seven Days, Publishers Weekly,* December 11, 1987, p. 66.

Peck, Richard, review of *King of the Birds, Los Angeles Times Book Review,* March 27, 1988.

Review of *Piskies, Spriggans, and Other Magical Beings: Tales from the Droll-Teller, Publishers Weekly,* March 20, 1981.

Ptacek, Margaret Mary, review of *T. J.'s Ghost, Voice of Youth Advocates,* August, 1989, p. 156.

Rosen, Martha, review of *The Egyptian Cinderella, School Library Journal,* October, 1989.

Review of *Someone Saw a Spider: Spider Facts and Folktales, Kirkus Reviews,* November 15, 1985, p. 1266.

Watson, Elizabeth S., review of *City! San Francisco, Horn Book,* May-June, 1990, p. 346.

■ For More Information See

BOOKS

Contemporary Authors New Revision Series, Volume 24, Gale, 1988, pp. 123-24.
Something about the Author, Volume 39, Gale, 1985, pp. 46-48.

PERIODICALS

Bulletin of the Center for Children's Books, March, 1986; October, 1987; February, 1988.
Horn Book, January-February, 1991, p. 94.
Kirkus Reviews, March 15, 1989, pp. 460-61.
New York Times Book Review, November 12, 1989, p. 50.

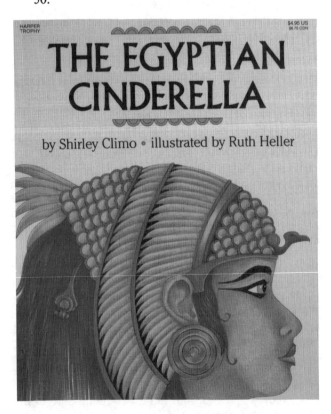

HARPER TROPHY

$4.95 US
$6.75 CDN

THE EGYPTIAN CINDERELLA

by Shirley Climo ● illustrated by Ruth Heller

Climo combined history and myth to create this tale of a Greek slave girl who becomes the wife of an Egyptian pharoah. (Cover illustration by Ruth Heller.)

Publishers Weekly, August 6, 1982, p. 70; September 29, 1989, p. 67; May 10, 1991, p. 256.

School Library Journal, February, 1981; December, 1985, p. 87; December, 1987, p. 84; August, 1988, p. 79; November, 1989, p. 105; March, 1991; December, 1991.

—Sketch by Mary Gillis

*   *   *

COHEN, Barbara 1932-1992

■ Personal

Born March 15, 1932, in Ashbury Park, NJ; died of cancer, November 22, 1992, in Bridgewater, NJ; daughter of Leo Kauder and Florence (an innkeeper; maiden name, Marshall) Kauder Nash; married Eugene Cohen (an innkeeper), September 14, 1954; children: Leah, Sara, Rebecca. *Education:* Barnard College, B.A., 1954; Rutgers University, M.A., 1957. *Religion:* Jewish.

■ Addresses

Home—540 Foothill Rd., Somerville, NJ 08876.

■ Career

Educator and author. Public high school teacher of English in Tenafly, NJ, 1955-1957, Somerville, NJ, 1958-60, and Hillsborough, NJ, beginning 1970. *Member:* Authors Guild, Authors League of America, League of Women Voters, Society of Children's Book Writers,

BARBARA COHEN

This story of an isolated teenager is partly based on Cohen's own experiences growing up. (Cover illustration by Ed Martinez.)

Association of Jewish Libraries, Hadassah, Phi Beta Kappa.

■ Awards, Honors

American Library Association Best Books for Young Adults citations, 1980, for *Unicorns in the Rain,* and 1982, for *Seven Daughters and Seven Sons;* National Jewish Book Awards for *King of the Seventh Grade* and *Yussel's Prayer;* Kenneth Smilen Present Tense award for *King of the Seventh Grade;* Association of Jewish Libraries Best Picture Book Award for *Yussel's Prayer;* American Library Association Notable Children's Books citations for *Thank You Jackie Robinson, I Am Joseph,* and *Seven Daughters and Seven Sons;* Sydney Taylor Award for lifetime work.

■ Writings

The Carp in the Bathtub, illustrated by Joan Halpern, Lothrop, 1972.
Thank You Jackie Robinson, Lothrop, 1974.
Where's Florrie?, Lothrop, 1976.
Bitter Herbs and Honey, Lothrop, 1976.

The Binding of Isaac, illustrated by Charles Mikolaycak, Lothrop, 1978.

My Name Is Rosie, Lothrop, 1978.

The Innkeeper's Daughter, Lothrop, 1979.

I Am Joseph, illustrated by Mikolaycak, Lothrop, 1980.

Unicorns in the Rain, Atheneum, 1980.

Fat Jack, Atheneum, 1980.

Lovely Vassilisa, Atheneum, 1980.

Queen for a Day, Lothrop, 1981.

Yussel's Prayer, Lothrop, 1981.

The Demon Who Would Not Die, illustrated by Antoly Ivanov, Atheneum, 1982.

Seven Daughters and Seven Sons, Atheneum, 1982.

Gooseberries to Oranges, illustrated by Beverly Brodsky, Lothrop, 1982.

King of the Seventh Grade, Lothrop, 1982.

Lovers' Games, Atheneum, 1983.

Molly's Pilgrim, illustrated by Michael Deraney, Lothrop, 1983.

Here Comes the Purim Players!, illustrated by Brodsky, Lothrop, 1984.

Roses, Lothrop, 1984.

The Secret Grove, illustrated by Deraney, Union of American Hebrew Congregations, 1985.

Coasting, Lothrop, 1985.

When Sally's mother develops breast cancer, the whole family must learn to communicate their feelings and fears in Cohen's young adult novel. (Cover illustration by Diane de Groat.)

Four Canterbury Tales, illustrated by Tina Schart Hyman, Lothrop, 1987.

The Christmas Revolution, Lothrop, 1987.

First Fast, Union of American Hebrew Congregations, 1987.

Headless Roommate, Bantam, 1987.

The Donkey's Story, Lothrop, 1988.

The Orphan Game, Lothrop, 1988.

(With Louise Taylor) *Dogs and Their Women,* Little, 1989.

People Like Us, Bantam, 1989.

Tell Us Your Secret, Bantam, 1989.

The Long Way Home, Lothrop, 1990.

Two Hundred Thirteen Valentines, Holt, 1991.

(With Taylor) *Cats and Their Women,* Little, 1992.

(With Taylor) *Horses and Their Women,* Little, in press.

Also author of *Make a Wish Molly.*

■ Adaptations

A film version of *Molly's Pilgrim* was written and directed by Jeff Brown, 1985.

■ Sidelights

Prolific author Barbara Cohen often voiced the opinion that all works of the imagination—even those fraught with fantasy—have deep biographical/autobiographical elements. Referring to her own work, she commented in an essay for *Something about the Author Autobiography Series (SAAS)*: "I understand that everything I write grows out of my own experience. It has nowhere else to come from. Sometimes I still write about talking purple pods and thundering herds of elephants. Now, however, I understand that they too are in some way connected to what has happened to me, and always were. But I also understand that in transmuting an experience into fiction, I am going beyond the experience. I write not so much to reflect what has occurred as to shape it, to give it meaning, to control it."

Cohen was interested in books at an early age. She recounted in *SAAS:* "I loved reading right from the beginning, and wanted ... to make things like those books I loved so much." When the author was eight, her father purchased the Somerville Inn where Cohen spent many of her formative years. "We were Jewish in a town where anti-Semitism was still close to the surface. My mother worked at a time when most other mothers didn't. And she worked not in a school or an office, but selling liquor and renting rooms to strangers. All these things served to make me feel isolated from other kids my age and forced me to depend on my brother, sister and books," Cohen noted in her essay.

Cohen wrote constantly all the way through high school and college. In 1954, she graduated as an English major and married Gene Cohen. Ironically—given her youthful passion for literature—Cohen wrote almost nothing for the next twenty years. She explained that she was "too busy being Gene's wife, Leah, Sara, and Becky's mother, and a high-school teacher to have time or energy left over for much writing."

All of this changed very dramatically when, in the early seventies, Cohen was struck by newfound inspiration and wrote *The Carp in the Bathtub,* which revolves around the tension that arises when two children fall in love with a live fish they find stored in their bathtub. When they discover that their mother plans to turn the carp into a Jewish dish called "gefilte fish" for Passover dinner, the children vow to save the their new friend. *The Carp in the Bathtub* was an instant success. Of the book, Cohen remarked in *SAAS:* "A universal idea cast in a particular ethnic mold, it is a story to which children (and grown-ups) of every background can relate. At the same time it provides insight into Jewish customs and ceremonies."

Her experience as a Jew was something that Cohen felt very deeply. "As a Jew who was alive, even though very young, during the years of the Holocaust, I of course [was] scarred for life by that event. I have not been scarred in anything like the way survivors or their children have been, but I do feel that in some sense any Jew over forty is a survivor," she remarked. This sensibility can be traced in much of Cohen's work. For example, of writing *King of the Seventh Grade*—a story about a once wayward boy choosing to become a Jew and celebrate his bar mitzvah—the author related that she was "able to do it because the central issues of the book, Jewish identity and survival, have always been of great concern to me."

It was in *Bitter Herbs* that Cohen dealt most directly with the alienation she felt growing up in the 1930s and 1940s. The book chronicles a year in the life of a Jewish girl, Rebecca, who lives in a small New Jersey town circa 1915. Cohen emphasized in *SAAS:* "Although *Bitter Herbs* takes place sixteen years before I was born, once again the feelings it reflects are my own. The simultaneous constriction and comfort of small-town life, the pain caused by a community's subtle anti-Semitism, the excitement and guilt attendant upon a romance with a boy who isn't Jewish—these are all part of my own high school experience."

Additional influences in Cohen's writings were numerous and complex. In books like *Lover's Games, Roses,* and *Fat Jack,* she drew her inspiration from earlier readings. Alternatively, *The Christmas Revolution, The Orphan Game,* and *Coasting* were inspired by the comings and goings of her three children. It was Cohen's own childhood experience as an outsider, however, that truly marked her work, a fact exemplified by books like *Where's Florrie?, Seven Daughters and Seven Sons, People Like Us,* and *My Name is Rosie,* which all feature a young heroine somehow set apart from her peers by circumstance.

The Innkeeper's Daughter was perhaps the most directly autobiographical of Cohen's books. The story revolves around the trauma experienced by sixteen-year-old Rachel Gold, who arrives at a classmate's party in a

The true meaning of the holiday of Yom Kippur is hightlighted in this picture book. (Cover illustration by Michael J. Deraney.)

black dress only to discover everyone else is wearing a sweater and skirt. This incident serves as a metaphor for the loneliness that often encompasses adolescence. Of the book, Cohen candidly admitted: "I went to that party in that dress when I was sixteen, and the misery of that never-to-be-forgotten occasion was finally exorcised in writing about it. Teenagers often mention that chapter to me. It strikes them as the truth."

During the years Cohen was writing novels, she was also producing picture storybooks such as *The Binding of Isaac,* and *Lovely Vassilisa.* With regard to these works, Cohen noted: "Why do I as a picture book writer select one story to retell out of the thousands and thousands of stories which are available? Because that story in some way reflects my concerns, my needs, my feelings. In that story I find particular delight. I want to play with it. I want to do things with it which will make other people connect with it as I do, and love it too."

Cohen wove a very graphic literary tapestry from the many threads, forces and events that shaped her life. She once commented: "I think I'm a writer because I spent much of my childhood listening to my relatives tell stories about each other. I don't write the stories they told, but I absorbed atmosphere and the tale-telling habit from them. All my writing is in some way inspired by my experience, but is only now and then a direct recounting of that experience." For Cohen, artistic creation came at the somewhat mystical meeting point of fantasy and reality, an idea she expressed in her essay.

"I can tell you which parts of a book came out of my own experience and which from my imagination," she wrote. "But I can only tell you that once the book is finished. Though I write and rewrite, when a book is done, I have the sense that it was written by a stranger. The process remains mysterious."

■ Works Cited

Cohen, Barbara, essay in *Something about the Author Autobiography Series,* Volume 7, Gale, 1982.

■ For More Information See

PERIODICALS

Booklist, December 1, 1979; April 1, 1980.
Chicago Tribune Book World, May 3, 1981.
New York Times Book Review, June 15, 1980.
Washington Post Book World, June 8, 1980; August 10, 1980.

OBITUARIES:

BOOKS

The Writers Directory: 1992-1994, St. James Press, 1992.

PERIODICALS

Los Angeles Times, December 5, 1992, p. A26.
New York Times, December 1, 1992, p. B13.
School Library Journal, January, 1993, p. 18.*

—*Sketch by Stephen Desmond*

*   *   *

COLMAN, Penny (Morgan) 1944-

■ Personal

Born September 2, 1944, in Denver, CO; daughter of Norman Charles Morgan (a psychiatrist) and Maritza (an artist; maiden name, Leskovar) Morgan; married Robert Archer Colman, separated January 1992; children: Jonathan, David, and Stephen. *Education:* University of Michigan, A.B. (with distinction), 1966; Johns Hopkins University, M.A.T., 1967; University of Oklahoma, postgraduate work, 1977; New York University, book publishing program certificate, 1980. *Hobbies and other interests:* "Exploring cemeteries to find graves of historic people I write about; adventure sports; going to every type of bookstore, especially used books; driving on long trips; jogging and bicycling; doing puzzles and playing Scrabble; thinking and talking about ideas."

■ Addresses

Home and office—146 Cambridge Ave., Englewood, NJ 07631.

■ Career

Free-lance writer and editor, 1975—; seminar leader and speaker, 1975-; United Presbyterian Church, New York City, program developer, 1977-81; Granger Galleries, New York City, founder and president, 1981-85; Center for Food Action, Englewood, NJ, executive director, 1986-87. Appointed to New Jersey Commission on Hunger, 1986, and New Jersey State Women Infant Children Advisory Council, 1987. Has appeared on radio and television programs. *Member:* Authors Guild, American Society of Journalists and Authors, Society of Children's Book Writers and Illustrators.

■ Awards, Honors

Silver Award, Lidman Prize Competition, 1990, for "Stamps!"; Paul A. Witty Short Story Award nomination, International Reading Association, 1990, for "But Not Ms. Anderson!"

■ Writings

JUVENILE NONFICTION

Breaking the Chains: The Crusade of Dorothea Lynde Dix, Betterway Publications/Shoe Tree Press, 1992.
Spies! Women and the Civil War, Betterway Publications/Shoe Tree Press, 1992.
Fannie Lou Hamer and the Fight for the Vote, Millbrook Press, 1993.
A Woman Unafraid: The Achievements of Frances Perkins, Atheneum, 1993.
101 Ways to Do Better in School, Troll Associates, 1994.
Madame C.J. Walker: Building a Business Empire, Millbrook Press, 1994.
Mother Jones and the Children's Crusade, Millbrook Press, 1994.
Toilets, Bathtubs, Sinks and Sewers: The History of the Bathroom, Atheneum, 1994.

Also contributor to *Sports Illustrated for Kids, Cricket,* and *U.S. Kids.*

PENNY COLMAN

JUVENILE FICTION

I Never Do Anything Bad, Paulist Press, 1988.
Dark Closets and Noises in the Night, Paulist Press, 1991.

ADULT NONFICTION

(Editor) *Spiritual Disciplines for Everyday Living,* Character Research Press, 1982.
Grand Canyon Magic, PMC Books, 1987.
This is Bergen County Where People Make a Difference, League of Women Voters, 1989.
(With Stella Chess and Alexander Thomas) *Fifty Years Together: Researchers, Psychiatrists, Professors, and Parents,* self-published, 1993.
Equal Rights Amendment: A Curriculum Guide, National Education Association, 1993.

Also contributing editor, *The American Way,* Viking Press, 1976. Consulting editor, *The Cheyenne Way,* National Endowment for the Humanities, 1978. Contributor to *Teens: A Fresh Look,* John Muir Publications, 1991.

OTHER

Also author of *Dare to Seek* (one-act play), Granger Publications, 1976. Author and editor of human resource manuals, including *Knowing Me and You,* Granger Publications, 1976; and *Use and Power of Language,* National Council of Churches, 1981. Editor of newsletters, including *ACCESS* and *Sharing.* Author of script for videotape, *Education is the Key,* Broad Street Productions, 1988.

■ Work in Progress

Mary McLeod Bethune, Millbrook Press; *Hospital Transport Ships in the Civil War,* Simon & Schuster; *Rosey the Riveter: Women Fighting the War from Home in World War II,* Crown; *Women in Society USA,* Times Books International; *Strikes!,* Millbrook Press; *In Search of Women,* "a photoessay book about the many landmarks to women in America—monuments, plaques, historical sites, museums, etc."

■ Sidelights

In between her many projects, author Penny Colman told *SATA:* "I grew up in a noisy family. Very noisy. My three brothers and I were close in age, and we were always into something—backyard baseball games; canoeing, swimming, and fishing in the creek that ran behind our house; and fighting with each other about this and that. There was also always music. We had a family orchestra—my Dad played the piano, my Mom and brother Vin played the cello, my brother Kip and I played the violin, and my brother Jon played the clarinet. We kids weren't very good, but we played anyhow. For several years, my parents also owned a farm with a huge barn and a swimming hole. We had three horses, six sheep, a goat who jumped on the hood of moving cars, and a flock of exotic-looking chickens that my Dad and I ordered from a catalog. When all the noise and activity got to be too much, I would go for

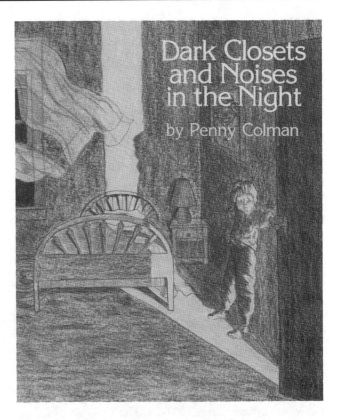

Susan and Alex learn not to be afraid of nighttime sights and sounds in this humorous story by Colman. (Cover illustration by Pamela T. Keating.)

long bike rides. I loved to ride with 'no hands' on the handle bar, and I got to be so good that I could read a book and ride my bike at the same time!

"When I was seventeen years old, my parents had another child—my sister Cam. With a new baby in the house, things got even noisier!

"After I grew up, I had three children who were *really* close in age. Jonathan was one year old when his identical twin brothers David and Stephen were born! They were noisy, too! And always into something—backyard basketball and breakdancing. They sang all the time and even performed at a nightclub in New York City. One summer when Jonathan was twelve and David and Stephen were eleven, we drove across the United States in a red van called the 'Road Radish.' All the activities and adventures and noises of my life have given me lots to write about."

■ For More Information See

PERIODICALS

National Observer, July 4, 1977.
Record, July 8, 1992.
Woman's Newspaper, July, 1987.

CORCORAN, Barbara 1911-
(Paige Dixon, Gail Hamilton)

■ Personal

Born April 12, 1911, in Hamilton, MA; daughter of John Gilbert (a physician) and Anna (Tuck) Corcoran. *Education:* Wellesley College, B.A., 1933; University of Montana, M.A., 1955; post-graduate study at University of Denver, 1965-66. *Politics:* Democrat. *Religion:* Episcopalian.

■ Addresses

Home—P.O. Box 4394, Missoula, MT 59806.

■ Career

Worked at a variety of jobs in New York City and Hamilton, MA, 1933-49, including writing for the Works Progress Administration, working as a theater manager, and working as a playwright and free-lance writer; Celebrity Service, Hollywood, CA, researcher, 1945-53; University of Kentucky, Covington, instructor in English, 1956-57; Columbia Broadcasting System, Hollywood, researcher, 1957-59; Marlboro School, Los Angeles, CA, teacher of English, 1959-60; University of Colorado, Boulder, instructor in English, 1960-65; Palomar College, San Marcos, CA, instructor in English, 1965-69; author of books for children and young adults, 1969—. Instructor in expressive writing, Austin Community College, 1983; instructor in writing for children, Women's Center, University of Montana, Missoula, 1984—. *Wartime service:* Worked as a Navy inspector at a proximity-fuse factory in Ipswich, MA, and for the Army Signal Corps in Arlington, VA, 1940-45. *Member:* Authors League of America, PEN.

BARBARA CORCORAN

■ Awards, Honors

Samuel French Award for original play, 1955; Children's book of the year citation, Child Study Association, 1970, for *The Long Journey;* William Allen White Children's Book Award, 1972, for *Sasha, My Friend;* Pacific Northwest Book Sellers' Award, 1975; two outstanding science trade book for children citations, National Science Teachers Association, 1977, for *Summer of the White Goat,* and for *The Loner;* Merriam Award, 1991, for distinguished contributions to Montana literature. *A Star to the North, A Trick of Light, Child of the Morning, I Am the Universe, You Put up with Me, I'll Put up with You,* and *The Hideaway* were Junior Literary Guild selections.

■ Writings

YOUNG ADULT NOVELS

Sam, illustrated by Barbara McGee, Atheneum, 1967.
(With Jeanne Dixon and Bradford Angier) *The Ghost of Spirit River,* Atheneum, 1968.
A Row of Tigers, illustrated by Richard L. Shell, Atheneum, 1969.
Sasha, My Friend, illustrated by Allan Eitzen, Atheneum, 1969 (English edition published as *My Wolf, My Friend,* Scholastic).
The Long Journey, illustrated by Charles Robinson, Atheneum, 1970.
(With Angier) *A Star to the North,* Thomas Nelson, 1970.
The Lifestyle of Robie Tuckerman, Thomas Nelson, 1971.
This Is a Recording, illustrated by Richard Cuffari, Atheneum, 1971.
A Trick of Light, illustrated by Linda Dabcovich, Atheneum, 1972.
Don't Slam the Door When You Go, Atheneum, 1972.
All the Summer Voices (historical), illustrated by Robinson, Atheneum, 1973.
The Winds of Time, illustrated by Gail Owens, Atheneum, 1973.
A Dance to Still Music, illustrated by Robinson, Atheneum, 1974.
Meet Me at Tamarlane's Tomb (mystery), illustrated by Robinson, Atheneum, 1975.
The Clown, Atheneum, 1975, published as *I Wish You Love,* Scholastic Book Services, 1977.
Axe-Time, Sword-Time (historical), Atheneum, 1976.
The Faraway Island, Atheneum, 1977.
Make No Sound, Atheneum, 1977.
(With Angier) *Ask For Love and They Give You Rice Pudding,* Houghton, 1977.
Hey, That's My Soul You're Stomping On, Atheneum, 1978.
Me and You and a Dog Named Blue, Atheneum, 1979.
Rising Damp, Atheneum, 1980.
The Person in the Potting Shed (mystery), Atheneum, 1980.
Making It, Little, Brown, 1980.
You're Allegro Dead (mystery), Atheneum, 1981.
Child of the Morning, Atheneum, 1982.
A Watery Grave (mystery), Atheneum, 1982.

Strike!, Atheneum, 1983.
Which Witch Is Which? (mystery), Atheneum, 1985.
August, Die She Must (mystery), Atheneum, 1984.
The Woman in Your Life, Atheneum, 1984.
Mystery on Ice (mystery), Atheneum, 1985.
The Shadowed Path (Moonstone Mystery Romance), Archway, 1985.
Face the Music, Atheneum, 1985.
A Horse Named Sky, Atheneum, 1986.
When Darkness Falls (Moonstone Mystery Romance), Archway, 1986.
I Am the Universe, Atheneum, 1986 (also published as *Who Am I Anyway?,* Field Enterprises).
You Put up with Me, I'll Put up with You, Atheneum, 1987.
The Hideaway, Atheneum, 1987.
The Sky Is Falling, Atheneum, 1988.
The Private World War of Lillian G. Adams, Atheneum, 1989.
The Potato Kid, Atheneum, 1990.
Stay Tuned, Atheneum, 1991.
Family Secrets, Atheneum, 1992.
Wolf at the Door, Atheneum, 1993.

HISTORICAL ROMANCE NOVELS

Abigail, Ballantine, 1981.
Abbie in Love (continuation of *Abigail*), Ballantine, 1981.
A Husband for Gail (conclusion to *Abigail*), Ballantine, 1981.
Beloved Enemy, Ballantine, 1981.
Call of the Heart, Ballantine, 1981.
Love Is Not Enough, Ballantine, 1981.
Song for Two Voices, Ballantine, 1981.
By the Silvery Moon, Ballantine, 1982.

UNDER PSEUDONYM PAIGE DIXON; JUVENILE NOVELS

Lion on the Mountain, illustrated by J.H. Breslow, Atheneum, 1972.
Silver Wolf (wildlife), illustrated by Ann Brewster, Atheneum, 1973.
The Young Grizzly (wildlife), illustrated by Grambs Miller, Atheneum, 1973.
Promises to Keep, Atheneum, 1974.
May I Cross Your Golden River?, Atheneum, 1975, published as *A Time to Love, A Time to Mourn,* Scholastic Book Services, 1982.
The Search for Charlie, Atheneum, 1976.
Cabin in the Sky (historical), Atheneum, 1976.
Pimm's Cup for Everybody, Atheneum, 1976.
Summer of the White Goat (wildlife), Atheneum, 1977.
The Loner: A Story of the Wolverine, illustrated by Miller, Atheneum, 1978.
Skipper (sequel to *May I Cross Your Golden River?*), Atheneum, 1979.
Walk My Way, Atheneum, 1980.

UNDER PSEUDONYM GAIL HAMILTON; JUVENILE NOVELS

Titania's Lodestone, Atheneum, 1975.
A Candle to the Devil (mystery), illustrated by Joanne Scribner, Atheneum, 1975.
Love Comes to Eunice K. O'Herlihy, Atheneum, 1977.

OTHER

From the Drawn Sword (play), first produced in Boston, 1940.
Yankee Pine (play), first produced at Bard College, NY, 1940.
The Mustang and Other Stories (short stories), Scholastic Book Services, 1978.

Contributor of Radio scripts to "Dr. Christian" program; contributor of short stories and other pieces to *Glamour, Charm, Woman's Day, Redbook, American Girl,* and *Good Housekeeping.*

■ Work in Progress

The View from Here, a novel about a boy who loses an eye in a fireworks accident.

■ Sidelights

Barbara Corcoran, who has also written as Paige Dixon and Gail Hamilton, characteristically produces fiction that investigates the physical and emotional problems of young men and women. Some of her protagonists suffer deafness, learning disabilities, or terminal illness. Others must endure chronic shyness, minority status, eccen-

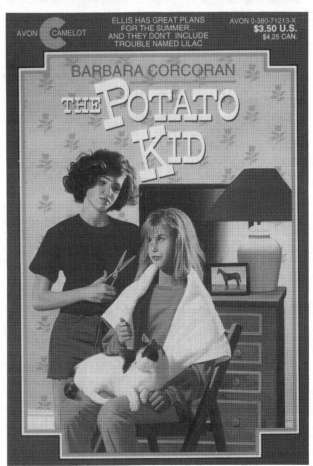

Ellis's plans for a "perfect" summer are jeopardized by the arrival of a troublesome ten-year-old that she must watch over.

tric parents, or family break-up. In the end, Corcoran's protagonists transcend their problems and attain self-confidence and wisdom. Since her first book in 1967, she has written over seventy novels and has been consistently acclaimed by reviewers of children's and young adult books.

Corcoran was born in Hamilton, Massachusetts, on April 12, 1911, to Anna Tuck and John Gilbert Corcoran, a physician. She was an only child, which may have prompted her to make up characters and stories out of a need to occupy herself. She had been writing since childhood and recalled later, as Mary Lou White quoted in *Dictionary of Literary Biography,* that she used to start stories on her father's prescription pads. Corcoran stated: "My parents were encouraging although I think my dad thought that I'd probably starve to death." Noting, also, her love for reading, she divulged in *Contemporary Authors Autobiography Series* (*CAAS*): "I was an avid reader, everything from *Bobbsey Twins on a Houseboat* to *David Copperfield*. I startled my father when I was thirteen by asking for Darwin's *Origin of the Species* for Christmas. I still have it."

In 1933 Barbara Corcoran graduated from Wellesley College with a B.A. degree. She began writing plays and thought she had found her niche in writing. She recalled in *CAAS:* "Two of my father's patients were writers, George Brewer, who wrote *Dark Victory,* and Judith Kelly, author of *Marriage is a Private Affair* and other novels. They had me to lunch and gave me encouragement. Mrs. George Patton called me with kind words, as did Mrs. C.C. Williams, daughter of the elder Henry Cabot Lodge. But on the whole, my fellow-townsmen thought I was wasting my time, throwing away that expensive college education. They felt sorry for my father." As it turned out Corcoran did, in fact, have a few plays produced in Boston and college theaters, but success was limited. "Although friends told me I reminded them of Lillian Hellman (I think they meant the way I wore my hair), I wasn't having the Hellman effect on Broadway producers," Corcoran said, according to White. "In time, sanity prevailed and I turned to other kinds of writing, always with the feeling that I'd lost something."

Over the following decades, Corcoran's fiction came to span many genres: children's books, young adult realism, mystery, romance, historical romance, wildlife. However, her enduring fascination with young people coming of age through a series of difficult adventures is something which surfaces regardless of the genre in which she is working. Corcoran's interest in transcending adversity can be partially traced to situations she herself confronted in her life. Her parents' divorce, for example, created tremendous anxiety for the young Corcoran. She recounted in *CAAS:* "Thirteen was a traumatic year. My parents separated. I was an only child, and my foundation was the three of us. Now there were two of us. My mother and I moved out of the house that I had thought of as the only conceivable place to live. My father, who had his office there, stayed alone with a housekeeper, and we moved to a house in North

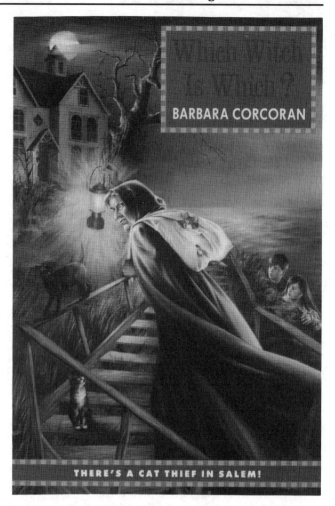

In this mystery for young readers, an amateur detective uncovers the reason for the theft of a number of cats in the town of Salem. (Cover illustration by Renee Grant.)

Beverly. We stayed five years, and to this day I shudder when I pass it." Years later, Corcoran retains an ambivalence to parent figures in many of her works. *Ask for Love and They Give You Rice Pudding* is typical in this regard. In this novel, Robbie, a rich, friendless seventeen-year-old, deals with the fact of his parents' weakness and their absence from his life.

In 1933 Corcoran had occasion to visit a friend in Chapel Hill, North Carolina, and was exposed to the dire poverty experienced by many people in the area. She later recounted in *CAAS:* "I spent a few months with my college friend Cappy Lambeth.... She had a job distributing flour and corn meal for President Roosevelt's CWA, and we spent many hours bouncing across roadless fields and down country roads visiting the poor. I had never seen that kind of poverty, and I was appalled." She went on to describe their living conditions: "A heavy smell of pork fat saturated the air. Women worked in the fields wearing bonnets, like the ones my great grandmother wore. They were old, many of these women, and so frail one wondered how they survived. A young woman whose husband was on the chain-gang was angry at having to accept government

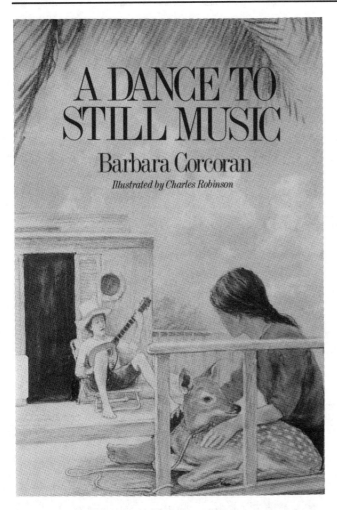

A DANCE TO STILL MUSIC

Barbara Corcoran

Illustrated by Charles Robinson

Margaret runs away from her new home in Key West in order to return to her beloved Maine, but she ends up finding something even better—a new friend. (Cover illustration by Charles Robinson.)

handouts. Cappy's Mother said, 'They ask for bread and you give them a stone.' My consciousness was being raised." These memories and images form the backdrop to several of Corcoran's novels. *The Long Journey,* for example, revolves around a young girl's search to get help for her grandfather, who is going blind. On the way, she meets unusual characters and learns about the amenities of modern life that were unknown to her prior to her trip.

Corcoran's understanding of everyday heroism in the face of hardship was broadened during wartime. She was a Navy inspector, working on a mass-production line, at the Sylvania factory in Ipswich. She recalled in *CAAS:* "It was a new world for me. I had got to know women who had been working on the line all their lives. They were tough, funny, wary women, to whom I had to prove that I was okay in spite of being a college graduate. I made some good friends. Rosalie Gosbee, an Essex girl who knew my Corcoran relatives, became one of the best friends I would ever have. Mary Conley, a fellow-inspector, also was to be a lifelong friend." Corcoran eventually used these navy experiences as a basis for the book *Axe-time, Sword-time,* a story about a

girl with a learning disability who comes to establish her independence by getting a job in a factory.

Of the incredible amount of literature Barbara Corcoran has produced, one book, *A Dance to Still Music,* remains emblematic of her basic theme: the capacity of a young protagonist to overcome adversity. Margret is the newly-deaf heroine of the story. Having recently recovered from a severe illness, Margret "is trying in a bitter way to accept her handicap but not to overcome it," explained Jean Fritz in the *New York Times Book Review.* She runs away from her unfeeling mother in Key West, intending to return to her home in Maine. "En route," commented White, "she has the good fortune to be cared for by a wonderful woman on a houseboat." She brings Margret aboard and gradually coaxes her to come to terms with her disability. *A Dance to Still Music* includes topics that are characteristic of Corcoran's fiction. "The themes of alienation and self-discovery appear with frequency in contemporary fiction," explained Charity Chang in *Children's Literature,* and in *A Dance to Still Music* "these themes are paramount and handled by Barbara Corcoran with finesse."

A Dance to Still Music had its genesis in the author's own experience; when she was in sixth grade, Corcoran had surgery on her mastoids, the air-filled bones behind the ears, which left her temporarily without hearing. As she explained in *CAAS:* "I used my memory of mastoid days to recreate what it feels like to suddenly be deaf. It was a subject I had thought a lot about, not only because of my own experience but because my cousin Ralph's mother was deaf, and I had had a friend in the 1930s who was also deaf. It seemed to me that the deaf got a lot less sympathy than, for instance, the blind. People got tired of repeating, of having to raise their voices, of being misunderstood, and they were often impatient, or, worse, behaved as if the deaf person were not there. *A Dance to Still Music* remains my favorite of my own books."

Other novels by Corcoran range from historicals to mysteries to wildlife tales to stories of contemporary young adult life. *The Person in the Potting Shed,* for instance, tells of a brother and sister who discover a body while on an unwanted summer trip to New Orleans; Margaret Mary Ptacek praises the novel in *Voice of Youth Advocates* as "containing suspense without being melodramatic." *Child of the Morning* recounts Susan's discovery that she has epilepsy, and Corcoran "manages to allow the reader to empathize with the fears and hopes, the despairs and triumphs of Susan's life," according to *Voice of Youth Advocates* contributor Jan Van Wiemokly. And *You Put up with Me, I'll Put up with You* deals with Kelly's efforts to adjust to a new town and new friends. "Humor, mystery, and a sympathetic but realistic analysis of a young girl's feelings, fears, and self-discoveries are combined in this creative and highly readable story," notes Judy Butler in *School Library Journal.*

Barbara Corcoran continues to write furiously and remains tremendously up-beat about her future. At age eighty-two, she told *SATA,* "I am blind in one eye and have a cataract in the other. However, I just finished a new book." She still enjoys writing for children; "there are many reasons why . . . , but one is that children seem to me more individual than adults," the author said in a publicity statement. "Everybody of every age is a unique individual, but children are still finding out who they are and discovering their own ways of living the life that lies ahead of them. They don't worry much about being like other people. People always ask me where I get my ideas. That's where I get them: from every one of you. Each one of you is a story waiting to be written. I'm glad I found you."

■ Works Cited

Butler, Judy, review of *You Put up with Me, I'll Put up with You, School Library Journal,* March, 1987, p. 169.

Chang, Charity, entry in *Children's Literature: Annual of the Modern Language Association Seminar on Children's Literature and the Children's Literature Association,* edited by Francelia Butler, Volume 4, Temple University Press, 1975.

Corcoran, Barbara, entry in *Contemporary Authors Autobiography Series,* Volume 2, Gale, 1985.

Corcoran, Barbara, publicity statement from Atheneum Publishers, 1989.

Fritz, Jean, review of *A Dance to Still Music, New York Times Book Review,* November 17, 1974, p. 8.

Ptacek, Margaret Mary, review of *The Person in the Potting Shed, Voice of Youth Advocates,* April, 1981, p. 32.

Van Wiemokly, Jan, review of *Child of the Morning, Voice of Youth Advocates,* August, 1982, p. 29.

White, Mary Lou, "Barbara Corcoran," *Dictionary of Literary Biography,* Volume 52: *American Writers for Children since 1960: Fiction,* Gale, 1986.

■ For More Information See

BOOKS

Contemporary Literary Criticism, Volume 17, Gale, 1981.

PERIODICALS

Bulletin of the Center for Children's Books, March, 1987, p. 123.

Christian Science Monitor, November 2, 1967.

Horn Book, August, 1969; October, 1969; October, 1970; February, 1971; December, 1971; June, 1978.

In Review: Canadian Books for Children, summer, 1971.

Journal of Reading, February, 1976; March, 1976.

New York Times Book Review, October 3, 1971; November 3, 1974; January 4, 1976.

School Library Journal, February, 1992, p. 85.

Voice of Youth Advocates, April, 1987, p. 30; June, 1992, p. 92.

BRUCE COVILLE

COVILLE, Bruce 1950-

■ Personal

Born May 16, 1950, in Syracuse, NY; son of Arthur J. (a sales engineer) and Jean (an executive secretary; maiden name, Chase) Coville; married Katherine Dietz (an illustrator), October 11, 1969; children: Orion Sean, Cara Joy. *Education:* Attended Duke University and State University of New York at Binghamton; State University of New York at Oswego, B.A., 1974. *Politics:* "Eclectic." *Religion:* Unitarian.

■ Addresses

Agent—Curtis Brown Ltd., 10 Astor Pl., New York, NY 10003.

■ Career

Author and playwright. Wetzel Road Elementary, Liverpool, NY, teacher, 1974-81. Co-host and co-producer of *Upstage,* a cable program promoting local theater, 1983. Has also worked as a camp counselor, grave digger, and toy maker. *Member:* Society of Children's Book Writers and Illustrators.

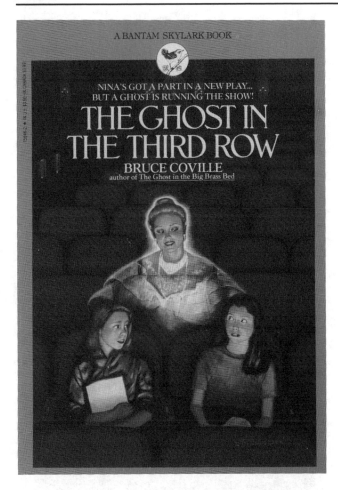

A BANTAM SKYLARK BOOK

NINA'S GOT A PART IN A NEW PLAY...
BUT A GHOST IS RUNNING THE SHOW!

THE GHOST IN
THE THIRD ROW

BRUCE COVILLE
author of The Ghost in the Big Brass Bed

When a school play is beset with strange and destructive incidents, many people blame the ghost of a woman who was killed on the stage years earlier—but Nina and Chris find another answer.

■ Writings

JUVENILE FICTION

The Foolish Giant, illustrated by wife, Katherine Coville, Lippincott, 1978.
Sarah's Unicorn, illustrated by K. Coville, Lippincott, 1979.
The Monster's Ring, Knopf, 1982.
Spirits and Spells, Dell, 1983.
The Eyes of the Tarot, Bantam, 1983.
Sarah and the Dragon, illustrated by Beth Peck, Harper, 1984.
Waiting Spirits, Bantam, 1984.
Amulet of Doom, Dell, 1985.
The Brave Little Toaster Storybook, Doubleday, 1987.
The Ghost in the Third Row, Bantam, 1987.
Murder in Orbit, Scholastic, 1987.
How I Survived My Summer Vacation, Pocket Books, 1988.
The Ghost Wore Grey, Bantam, 1988.
Prehistoric People, Doubleday, 1990.
The Dinosaur That Followed Me Home, illustrated by John Pierard, Pocket Books, 1990.
Ghost in the Big Brass Bed, Bantam, 1991.

Jeremy Thatcher, Dragon Catcher, illustrated by Gary A. Lippincott, Harcourt, 1991.
My Teacher Fried My Brains, Pocket Books, 1991.
My Teacher Glows in the Dark, Pocket Books, 1991.
My Teacher Flunked the Planet, Pocket Books, 1992.
Goblins in the Castle, Pocket Books, 1992.
Jennifer Murdley's Toad, illustrated by Lippincott, Harcourt, 1992.
Space Brat, illustrated by K. Coville, Pocket Books, 1992.
Space Brat Two: Blork's Evil Twin, illustrated by K. Coville, Pocket Books, 1993.
Aliens Ate My Homework, illustrated by K. Coville, Pocket Books, 1993.

JUVENILES; "A.I. GANG" SERIES

Operation Sherlock, NAL Books, 1986.
Robot Trouble, NAL Books, 1986.
Forever Begins Tomorrow, NAL Books, 1986.

OTHER

(Author of book and lyrics) *The Dragon Slayers,* music by Angela Peterson, first produced at Syracuse Musical Theater, 1981.
(Author of book and lyrics) *Out of the Blue,* music by Peterson, first produced at Syracuse Musical Theater, 1982.
(Author of book and lyrics with Barbara Russell) *It's Midnight: Do You Know Where Your Toys Are?,* music by Peterson, first produced at Syracuse Musical Theater, 1983.
(With others) *Seniority Travel Directory,* Schueler Communications, 1986.
(With others) *The Sophisticated Leisure Travel Directory,* Schueler Communications, 1986.
(Editor) *The Unicorn Treasury,* Doubleday, 1987.
The Dark Abyss, Bantam, 1989.
(Editor) *Unicorn Treasury: Stories, Poems and Unicorn Lore,* Doubleday, 1991.
(Editor) *Herds of Thunder: Manes of Gold* (collection of stories and poems), Doubleday, 1991.
(Reteller) William Shakespeare, *The Tempest,* illustrated by Ruth Sanderson, Bantam, 1993.

Contributor to anthologies, including *Dragons and Dreams,* 1986, and *Read On! Two,* Books 4 and 6, 1987. Contributor to *Harper's Bookletter, Sesame Street Parent's Newsletter, Cricket,* and *Wilson Library Bulletin.* Associate editor, *Syracuse Business* and *Syracuse Magazine,* both 1982-83; editor and columnist, *Seniority,* 1983-84.

■ Adaptations

The Ghost Wore Gray is available on cassette from Recorded Books, 1993.

■ Sidelights

Bruce Coville is well known as a writer of juvenile fiction and the author of children's best sellers such as *Jeremy Thatcher, Dragon Hatcher.* His novels draw heavily on mythic creatures, such as unicorns and dragons, and science fiction traditions, such as aliens and space stations, often with a humorous twist. He has also contributed to and edited volumes of short stories, and completed several musical plays for younger audiences.

As he once told *SATA,* Coville cherishes memories of his childhood, noting that his early surroundings nurtured his vivid imagination: "I was raised in Phoenix, a small town in central New York. Actually, I lived well outside the town, around the corner from my grandparents' dairy farm, which was the site of my happiest childhood times. I still have fond memories of the huge barns with their mows and lofts, mysterious relics, and jostling cattle. It was a wonderful place for a child to grow up. In addition to the farm there was a swamp behind the house, and a rambling wood beyond that, both of which were conducive to all kinds of imaginative games." It was during this period that Coville began to develop the heightened sensibility usually possessed by writers of fantasy.

Coville's father, not bookish himself, was instrumental in exposing the young Bruce to the delightful world of literature. Coville recounted in *SATA:* "Despite this wonderful setting, much of what went on at that time went on in my head, when I was reading, or thinking and dreaming about what I had read. I was an absolute bookaholic. My father had something to do with this." Coville went on to explain: "He was a traveling salesman, a gruff but loving man, who never displayed an overwhelming interest in books. But if anyone was to ask me what was the best thing he ever did for me I could reply without hesitation that he read me *Tom Swift in the City of Gold.* Why he happened to read this to me I was never quite certain. But it changed my life. One night after supper he took me into the living room, had me sit in his lap, and opened a thick, ugly brown book (this was the *original* Tom Swift) and proceeded to open a whole new world for me. I was enthralled, listened raptly, waited anxiously for the next night and the next, resented an intrusion, and reread the book several times later on my own. It was the only book I can ever remember him reading to me, but it changed my life. I was hooked on books."

Coville may have loved books, but like many other authors, the realization that he wanted to be a writer came very abruptly. He told *SATA:* "I think it was sixth grade when I first realized that writing was something that I could do, and wanted to do very much. As it happened, I had spent most of that year making life miserable for my teacher by steadfastly failing to respond to the many creative devices she had to stimulate us to write. Then one day she simply (finally!) just let us write—told us that we had a certain amount of time to produce a short story of substance. Freed from writing topics imposed from without, I cut loose, and over several days found that I loved what I was doing. This may not be the first time that I knew I wanted to write, but it's the time that I remember." In addition to writing, Coville himself went on to be a teacher. He held a full-time position at Wetzel Road

Elementary School, in Liverpool, New York for seven years starting in 1974.

However, writing was always to be Coville's first love. He was introduced to the possibilities of writing for children by the woman who would later become his mother-in-law. He explained in *SATA* that she "gave me a copy of *Winnie the Pooh* to read, and I suddenly knew that what I really wanted to write was children's books—to give to other children the joy that I got from books when I was young. This is the key to what I write now. I try with greater or lesser success, to make my stories the kinds of things that I would have enjoyed myself when I was young; to write the books I wanted to read, but never found. My writing works best when I remember the bookish child who adored reading and gear the work toward him. It falters when I forget him."

As he developed into an experienced writer, Coville worked in different genres. He created musical plays such as *The Dragon Slayers,* first produced at Syracuse Musical Theater in 1982. He contributed to anthologies of fantasy stories, such as *Dragons and Dreams.* But it was in the area of juvenile fiction, beginning with the publication of *The Foolish Giant* in 1978, that Coville made a significant mark. That first tale, for younger

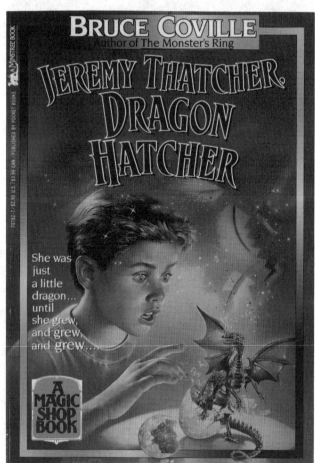

In this best-selling book by Coville, Jeremy's adventures begin in Mr. Elive's Magic Shop, where he buys a very unusual egg. (Cover illustration by Catherine Huerta.)

readers, tells of a mild, clumsy giant who has difficulty being accepted by the ordinary people of his village until he saves them from an evil wizard. In the years since that first book, Coville has published over twenty other tales for children, culminating in the appearance of several of his works on children's best seller lists.

Many of Coville's books are jam-packed with the trappings of traditional mythic imagery: supernatural spirits, tarot cards, unicorns, prehistoric monsters, futuristic creatures at the outer edge of the universe. He discussed this in *SATA:* "Myth is very important to me. My picture books have firm roots in basic mythic patterns. Hopefully, the patterns do not intrude, but provide a structure and depth that enhances my work." Coville often combines imaginary creatures with present-day people to create a tale of mystery or adventure. In *The Ghost in the Third Row,* for instance, Nina discovers an actual ghost haunting the theater where she is acting in a murder drama. Nina returns with her friend Chris in *The Ghost Wore Gray,* where the two try to discover the story behind the spirit of a Confederate soldier who appears in a New York hotel. "Despite the fantasy element of a ghost, this is a

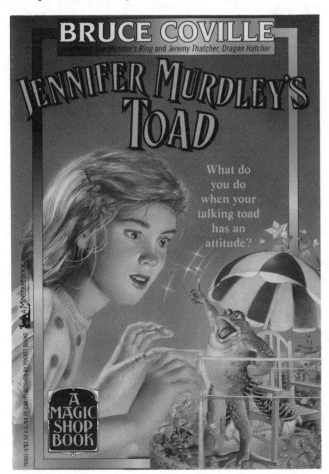

Elive's Magic Shop is revisited in this story about Jennifer Murdley, who learns about her own inner strength when she tries to help the toad she buys from the strange store. (Cover illustration by Catherine Huerta.)

mystery," notes *School Library Journal* contributor Carolyn Caywood, who adds that the tale "evokes real feeling."

Some of Coville's most popular books have been those that involve Mr. Elive's Magic Shop. In the first, *Jeremy Thatcher, Dragon Hatcher,* young Jeremy escapes his tormenter Mary Lou only to find himself in a strange shop where he buys an unusual egg. When the egg hatches a baby dragon—that no one else but Mary Lou can see—Jeremy finds himself in the midst of adventure. "The book is filled with scenes that will bring laughter and near tears to readers," Kenneth E. Kowen notes in *School Library Journal,* while Kathleen Redmond writes in *Voice of Youth Advocates* that the story is a good combination of real and fantasy worlds and "is right on target." Coville returns to the magic shop in *Jennifer Murdley's Toad,* where Jennifer purchases a lonely toad hatched from a witch's mouth. In aiding her pet, Bufo, who seeks his lost love and is chased by the witch, Jennifer herself is turned into a toad and learns to appreciate her inner strengths. Margaret C. Howell of *School Library Journal* praises Coville's theme as "particularly well handled," and adds that "the story moves well, with realistic characterizations."

Coville believes that a knowledge of mythic patterns and imagery can facilitate children's growth and social understanding. He argued in *SATA:* "This 'making sense' is a process that generally takes a lifetime and yet, sadly, it is all too often never even begun. To utilize myth as a guide in this quest one must be familiar with its patterns and structures, a familiarity that is best gained from reading or hearing myth and its reconstructions from earliest childhood on." Coville feels that the literature he himself writes plays a part in exposing young people to the mythological realm. "I do not expect," he explained in *SATA,* "a child to read my picture books and suddenly discover the secret of the universe. I do hope that something from my works will tuck itself away in the child's mind, ready to present itself as a piece of a puzzle on some future day when he or she is busy constructing a view of the world that will provide at least a modicum of hope and dignity."

Of this necessity to educate young people through literature, he explained in *SATA:* "This may seem like a long-term goal and a minimal result for the work involved, but I am, after all, a teacher. This has always been our lot. We deal with a child for a year, pour our hearts and souls into his development, and then send him on his way with the scant hope that somehow, someday, some little of what we have tried to do may present itself to him when it is needed." Coville concluded, qualifying his theory with a practical turn of phrase: "But this is idle speculation. The first and foremost job in writing is to tell a whacking good story. You just have to hope it might mean something before you're done."

■ Works Cited

Caywood, Carolyn, review of *The Ghost Wore Gray,* *School Library Journal,* September, 1988, p. 183.
Howell, Margaret C., review of *Jennifer Murdley's Toad,* *School Library Journal,* September, 1992, p. 250.
Kowen, Kenneth E., review of *Jeremy Thatcher, Dragon Hatcher, School Library Journal,* May, 1991, p. 91.
Redmond, Kathleen, review of *Jeremy Thatcher, Dragon Hatcher, Voice of Youth Advocates,* June, 1991, p. 106.

■ For More Information See

PERIODICALS

Bulletin of the Center for Children's Books, February, 1991, p. 133; July, 1992, p. 292.
Locus, November, 1991, p. 53; April, 1992, p. 45; July, 1992, p. 48.
School Library Journal, December, 1984, p. 100; February, 1988, p. 72; December, 1989, p. 98; September, 1990, p. 239; January, 1992, p. 108.
Times Educational Supplement, November 20, 1987, p. 30.
Voice of Youth Advocates, October, 1989, p. 221.*

D

DAMRELL, Liz 1956-

■ Personal

Born November 30, 1956, in Tulsa, OK; daughter of Jack Tucker and Thelma Lee (maiden name, Back) Teed; married Charles S. Damrell, 1980; children: Devin, Matthew. *Education:* Received B.A. from Lafayette College.

■ Addresses

Home—656 Kingston Road, Lexington, KY 40505. *Office*—Lexington-Fayette Urban County Government, Rm. 104, 200 East Main Street, Lexington, KY 40507.

■ Career

Lexington-Fayette Urban County Government, Lexington, KY, council clerk. Central Kentucky Riding for the Handicapped, volunteer and member of board of directors.

■ Awards, Honors

American Booksellers Pick of the List, 1991, for *With the Wind.*

■ Writings

With the Wind (picture book), illustrated by Stephen Marchesi, Orchard Books, 1991.

■ For More Information See

PERIODICALS

Atlanta Journal, April 3, 1991, section D, p. 2.
Children's Book Review Service, spring, 1991, p. 134.
Kirkus Reviews, February 15, 1991, p. 254.
School Library Journal, June, 1991, p. 74.

The freedom a handicapped boy feels while riding on horseback is captured in Damrell's *With the Wind,* illustrated by Stephen Marchesi.

DAVIE, Helen K(ay) 1952-

■ Personal

Born July 2, 1952, in Los Angeles, CA; daughter of Andrew Nelder (an industrial engineer) and Dorothy Drews Davie; married David W. Rickman, December 2, 1978 (divorced, 1989); married Frank A. Cawley (a college bookstore manager), December 30, 1989. *Education:* Attended De Anza Community College, 1970-72; California State University, Long Beach, B.A., 1975. *Politics:* "Liberal, Feminist, Green." *Hobbies and other interests:* Natural history, gardening, "entertaining 3 cats," traveling.

■ Career

Worked part-time creating business cards and logos; illustrator of greeting cards for Windemere Press; illustrator for textbooks until 1988; illustrator of children's books. Midpeninsula Regional Open Space District, docent; Castlemont School, San Jose, CA, tutor. *Member:* Society of Children's Book Writers and Illustrators, Center for Children's Environmental Literature (CCEL), Sierra Club, Audubon Society, Orion, Humane Society, California Academy of Sciences, Smithsonian, World Wildlife Federation, Greenpeace, Childfree, NOW.

■ Awards, Honors

Minnesota Book Award, children's book, 1988, for *The Star Maiden: An Ojibway Tale; The Star Maiden* was named to the International Reading Association Teacher's Choice List, 1989.

■ Illustrator

Caroline Arnold, *What We Do When Someone Dies,* F. Watts, 1987.
Sing with Me Christmas Carols (collection of well-known carols with an audiocassette), Random House, 1987.
Barbara Juster Esbensen (adapter), *The Star Maiden: An Ojibway Tale,* Little, Brown, 1988.
Esbensen (adapter), *Ladder to the Sky: How the Gift of Healing Came to the Ojibway Nation,* Little, Brown, 1989.
Betsy James, *He Wakes Me,* Orchard Books, 1991.
Esbensen, *The Great Buffalo Race: How the Buffalo Got Its Hump* (poems), Little, Brown, 1993.
Kathy Zoehfeld, *A Shell Is Someone's Home,* Harper-Collins, 1994.

■ Work in Progress

Illustrations for *Echoes for the Eye,* by Barbara Juster Esbensen, for HarperCollins, publication expected, summer, 1995; a self-illustrated work, tentatively titled *Was That You?,* dealing with natural history.

■ Sidelights

"When I begin to illustrate a book, I do extensive research: collecting information from libraries and museums, making photocopies and notes, and taking photographs," Helen K. Davie told *SATA.* "Some books I've worked on have required as much as six months of preparation before I even drew the first sketch. Usually I'm surrounded by so much reference material I can't find a clear space on my desk to work!"

Davie's commitment to research and accuracy has won her the respect of both critics and readers of children's books. The illustrations she produced for Barbara Juster Esbensen's adaptations of Native American legends have received much attention and praise for their careful rendering of Ojibway traditions. In the first of these books, *The Star Maiden: An Ojibway Tale,* a star appears as a woman in a young man's dreams. She tells him that she is tired of wandering the skies and asks if he can help her join his tribe. He agrees to help, and the star comes to earth in various guises, on one occasion appearing as a rose. None of her various incarnations are successful in gaining her inclusion in the tribe. Finally, she sees herself reflected in a lake and, along with her sister stars, chooses to become a water-lily, where she will always be close to the canoe people, as the Ojibway call themselves.

Sally M. Hunter, a reviewer for *Five Owls,* credited Davie with "incredibly stylized and exquisite pictures and borders. The stylization of floral and geometric border designs appear to be copies of authentic Ojibw[ay] beadwork and Great Lakes tribal ribbon work.... Each illustration is bursting with details of Indian life." Davie's illustrations elicited similar praise from Ethel R. Twichell, a *Horn Book* reviewer who acknowledged that "the book carefully and beautifully re-creates the details of clothing from moccasin to feathered headdress."

The second collaboration between Esbensen and Davie resulted in another Ojibway retelling, *Ladder to the Sky: How the Gift of Healing Came to the Ojibway Nation.* In this tale, a distraught grandmother attempts to follow her grandson to the land of the dead. The journey, which no mortal can make unaccompanied by a spirit-

Davie conducted extensive research into Native American traditions in order to create the illustrations for Barbara J. Esbensen's *The Star Maiden: An Ojibway Tale.*

Davie's pictures capture the affectionate bond between a cat and his adoring owner in *He Wakes Me.* (Text by Betsy James.)

messenger, results in the grandmother's death and the introduction of disease among the Ojibway with the return of her body. In an act of compassion, the Great Spirit teaches the Ojibway to use medicinal plants to heal themselves. "In lucid, dramatic watercolors, imaginatively bordered with stylized motifs based on plant life, Davie extends this gracefully retold story," commented a writer for *Kirkus Reviews.*

After working on *Ladder to the Sky,* Davie illustrated Betsy James's children's book *He Wakes Me,* in which a young girl follows a cat through his daily routine. In addition to commenting on the variety of the illustrations, Jane Saliers in the *School Library Journal* noted that the drawings "perfectly picture the cat as he runs, plays and is cuddled."

Commenting on her profession, Davie said: "I believe an illustrator has an obligation to be accurate, even if, for example, a young reader doesn't know the differences in the clothing worn by various tribes. But beyond accuracy, a good illustration must be engaging. It should do more than merely depict a scene from the story. It should also bring another level of richness and meaning to the author's words."

■ Works Cited

Hunter, Sally, review of *The Star Maiden, Five Owls,* July/August, 1988, p. 88.
Review of *Ladder to the Sky, Kirkus Reviews,* October 1, 1989.

Saliers, Jane, review of *He Wakes Me, School Library Journal,* August, 1991.
Twichell, Ethel R., review of *The Star Maiden, Horn Book,* July/August, 1988.

■ For More Information See

PERIODICALS

Booklist, April 1, 1988.
Kirkus Reviews, May 15, 1988; July 1, 1991.
Publishers Weekly, October 27, 1989.

*   *   *

DEE, Ruby 1923(?)-

■ Personal

Born Ruby Ann Wallace, October 27, 1923 (some sources say 1924), in Cleveland, OH; daughter of Marshall Edward (a railroad porter and waiter) and Emma (a teacher; maiden name, Benson) Wallace; professionally known as Ruby Dee; married Ossie Davis (an actor, writer, director, and producer of stage and motion picture productions), December 9, 1948; children: Nora, Guy, Hasna Muhammad. *Education:* Hunter College (now of the City University of New York), B.A., 1945; attended Actors Workshop in the 1950s, Fairfield University, Iona College, and Virginia State University; studied acting with Paul Mann, Lloyd Richards, and Morris Carnovsky.

■ Addresses

Office—P.O. Box 1318 New Rochelle, NY, 10802.

■ Career

Actor and writer. American Negro Theatre, apprentice, 1941-44; actor in Broadway plays, including *South Pacific* 1943, *Jeb,* 1946, *A Raisin in the Sun,* 1959, *Purlie Victorious,* 1961, and *Boesman and Lena,* 1970. Actor in motion pictures, including *No Way Out,* 1950, *The Jackie Robinson Story,* 1950, *Edge of the City,* 1957, *St. Louis Blues,* 1958, *A Raisin in the Sun,* 1961, *Gone Are the Days* (also released as *Purlie Victorious* and *The Man from C.O.T.T.O.N.*), 1963, *Do the Right Thing,* 1989, and *Jungle Fever,* 1991. Actor in television productions, including *Black Monday,* 1961, *Roots: The Next Generation,* 1979, *The Atlanta Child Murders,* 1985, and an *American Playhouse* broadcast of "Zora is My Name," 1990. Co-host of radio program *Ossie Davis and Ruby Dee Story Hour,* 1974-78, and of the television series *With Ossie and Ruby,* Public Broadcasting System (PBS), 1981. Performer on recordings for Caedmon, Folkways Records, and Newbery Award Records. *Member:* Screen Actors Guild, Actors' Equity Association, American Federation of Television and Radio Artists, National Association for the Advancement of Colored People, Negro American Labor Council, Southern Christian Leadership Conference, Students for Non-Violence (member of coordinating committee).

Two Ways
to Count to Ten

A Liberian Folktale | Retold by Ruby Dee
Illustrated by Susan Meddaugh

Best known for her acting career, Dee has also penned some books for children, including this retelling of a Liberian folktale. (Cover illustration by Susan Meddaugh.)

■ Awards, Honors

Emmy Award nomination for outstanding single performance by an actress in a leading role, Academy of Television Arts and Sciences, 1964, for *Express Stop from Lenox Avenue;* (with husband Ossie Davis) Frederick Douglass Award from the New York Urban League, 1970; Obie Award, 1971, for *Boesman and Lena;* Martin Luther King, Jr., Award from Operation PUSH, 1972; Drama Desk Award, 1973, for *The Wedding Band;* (with Ossie Davis) Actors' Equity Association Paul Robeson Citation, 1975, for outstanding creative contributions in the performing arts and in society at large; Award for Cable Excellence (ACE), 1983, for role as Mary Tyrone in *Long Day's Journey into Night;* inducted into Theater Hall of Fame, 1988, and NAACP Image Award Hall of Fame, 1989; Literary Guild Award, 1989, for *Two Ways to Count to Ten;* Literary Guild Award, 1989, for *Two Ways to Count to Ten;* Emmy Award, Academy of Television Arts and Sciences, for *Decoration Day;* honorary doctorates from Fairfield University, Iona College, and Virginia State University.

■ Writings

FOR ADULTS

(With Jules Dassin and Julian Mayfield) *Up Tight* (screenplay; adapted from Liam O'Flaherty's novel *The Informer*), Paramount, 1968.

(And director) *Take It from the Top* (musical play), first produced Off-Broadway at New Federal Theatre, January 19, 1979, revised version presented as *Twin Bit Gardens,* 1979.
My One Good Nerve: Rhythms, Rhymes, Reasons (stories, poems, and essays), Third World Press, 1987.
Zora is My Name (television play), broadcast on *American Playhouse,* PBS, 1990.

FOR CHILDREN

(Editor) *Glowchild, and Other Poems,* Third Press, 1972.
Two Ways to Count to Ten, Holt, 1988.
Tower to Heaven, Holt, 1991.

OTHER

Columnist for *New York Amsterdam News.* Associate editor for *Freedomways.*

■ Sidelights

One of America's premiere African American performers, Ruby Dee has illuminated stages on Broadway as well as popular films ranging from *Edge of the City* to Spike Lee's *Do The Right Thing* and *Jungle Fever.* Dee's talents, however, are not limited to acting; with her husband, Ossie Davis, Dee has produced a number of specials and series for various television and radio broadcasts. She is also the editor and author of books, including the well-received children's publications *Glowchild, and Other Poems, Two Ways to Count to Ten,* and *Tower to Heaven.*

Dee began her career while she was studying at Hunter College in the early 1940s. Describing herself to *SATA* as a "product of Harlem and The American Negro Theater," Dee studied acting with Paul Mann, Lloyd Richards, and Morris Carnovsky. Along with Sidney Poitier and Harry Belafonte, Dee starred in the productions of the American Negro Theater. She also contributed her talents to radio plays and acted in the Broadway production of *South Pacific.* When she found a role in Robert Ardrey's *Jeb,* she met the production's principal actor, Ossie Davis, whom she later married. Dee continued her stage work while starring in television and film roles such as *Edge of the City,* a film in which Dee portrayed the wife of a young African American working on New York's docks, and *A Raisin in the Sun,* where she duplicated the role of Lorraine that she had originally presented in the Broadway play. Dee then portrayed Lutiebelle Gussie Mae Jenkins in her husband Ossie Davis's satirical play, *Purlie Victorious.*

Dee told *SATA* that her role in *Purlie Victorious* was one of her favorites, and she has also enjoyed her Obie award-winning performance as Lena in Athol Fugard's play *Boesman and Lena.* Another favorite for Dee is her role as Julia in Alice Childress's *Wedding Band,* a role that netted her a Drama Desk Award, and she also noted her experiences working on numerous films and television productions, including Sidney Poitier's film *Buck and the Preacher,* Alex Haley's *Roots: The Next Generation,* Lorraine Hansberry's *To Be Young, Gifted and*

Black, and James Baldwin's *Go Tell It On the Mountain.* Dee further expressed her appreciation of two projects where she exercised her writing skills, *Up Tight* and *Take It From the Top.*

Success With Words

Up Tight was Dee's 1968 debut as a writer, and the film was praised by critic Vincent Canby of the *New York Times* as "such an intense and furious movie that it's impossible not to take it seriously." Later, Dee wrote and directed a stage musical, *Take It from the Top,* which was produced Off-Broadway at the New Federal Theatre in 1979. Dee then turned to books as an outlet for her writing talents and released a compilation of short stories, humorous writings, and poetry entitled *My One Good Nerve.*

Dee's next book project was to collect and compile poetry written by and for young people. The result was *Glowchild, and Other Poems,* her first book addressed to children. Grouped into sections such as "Thoughts and Questions About 'Me'" and "City Happenings," *Glowchild* earned positive notices for the passionate writings contained in the book. Georgess McHargue of the *New York Times Book Review* wrote that "there is enough anger here to melt down the World Trade Center." A reviewer in *Publishers Weekly* was also impressed by the selection of poems in *Glowchild,* commenting that "all are eminently worth reading."

Dee's next work for children, *Two Ways to Count to Ten,* was an adaption of a Liberian folk tale. In the story, King Leopard challenges his daughter's potential suitors to throw a spear high enough so that he can count to ten before it falls. The antelope cleverly counts by twos and thus meets the King's challenge. In the opinion of a reviewer in *Publishers Weekly* "readers and listeners of all ages will find this an irresistibly satisfying tale." *Two Ways to Count to Ten* won Dee the 1989 Literary Guild Award.

Tower to Heaven, Dee's next work, is also an adaptation of an African tale. In this book, the blows of an old woman named Yaa forces the sky god, Onyankopon, to flee higher in the sky. Missing his company, Yaa and others build a tower to heaven. The tower, however, cannot be completed for lack of one more mortar, which the builders try to obtain by taking pieces from the bottom of the tower. A reviewer for *Kirkus Reviews* considered the work to be an "appealing presentation of a wise, witty tale," while a *Publishers Weekly* reviewer noted the book's "sly humor enlivened by boldly defined and vividly colored primitive art." Denia Lewis Hester, writing for the *School Library Journal,* was also enthusiastic, stating that "good, solid telling makes this an easy choice for reading aloud."

In summing up her varied pursuits, Dee explained to *SATA* that she is a "word worker." Discussing her projects for stage, television, and movies, Dee noted that "as an actor I want to explore life rhythms and the sounds in the silences." This dedication to sound and expression also extends to her work in other fields, including writing. "I love language and authors and music," Dee notes, "and how it can all interconnect."

■ Works Cited

Canby, Vincent, review of *Up Tight, New York Times,* December 19, 1968.
Review of *Glowchild, Publishers Weekly,* November 27, 1972, p. 40.
Hester, Denia Lewis, review of *Tower to Heaven, School Library Journal,* July, 1992, p. 67.
McHargue, Georgess, review of *Glowchild, New York Times Book Review,* November 5, 1972.
Review of *Tower to Heaven, Kirkus Reviews,* June 1, 1991, p. 728.
Review of *Tower to Heaven, Publishers Weekly,* May 17, 1991, p. 63.
Review of *Two Ways to Count to Ten, Publishers Weekly,* June 10, 1988, p. 80.

■ For More Information See

PERIODICALS

Bulletin of the Center for Children's Books, April, 1973, p. 122; July, 1988, p. 226.
School Library Journal, June-July, 1988, p. 96.
Children's Book Review Service, August, 1991, p. 163.

—*Sketch by Ronie-Richele Garcia-Johnson*

*   *   *

DELTON, Judy 1931-

■ Personal

Born May 6, 1931, in St. Paul, MN; daughter of Alfred Frank (a plant engineer) and Alice (Walsdorf) Jaschke; married Jeff J. Delton (a school psychologist), June 14, 1958; children: Julie, Jina, Jennifer, Jamie. *Education:* Attended School of Association Arts, 1950, and College of St. Catherine, 1954-57.

■ Addresses

Home—St. Paul, MN.

■ Career

Elementary school teacher in parochial schools of St. Paul, MN, 1957-64; free-lance writer. Teacher of writing in colleges, 1974-89.

■ Awards, Honors

Two Good Friends was named an American Library Association Notable Book, 1975; *Two Good Friends, Three Friends Find Spring, Brimhall Turns to Magic* were named Junior Literary Guild selections.

JUDY DELTON

■ Writings

JUVENILE

Two Good Friends, Crown, 1974.
Rabbit Finds a Way, Crown, 1975.
Two Is Company, Crown, 1976.
Three Friends Find Spring, Crown, 1977.
Penny Wise, Fun Foolish, Crown, 1977.
My Mom Hates Me in January, Albert Whitman, 1977.
It Happened on Thursday, Albert Whitman, 1978.
Brimhall Comes to Stay, Lothrop, 1978.
Brimhall Turns to Magic, Lothrop, 1979.
On a Picnic, Doubleday, 1979.
The New Girl at School, Dutton, 1979.
Rabbit's New Rug, Parents Magazine Press, 1979.
The Best Mom in the World, Albert Whitman, 1979.
Kitty in the Middle, Houghton, 1979.
Kitty in the Summer, Houghton, 1980.
Lee Henry's Best Friend, Albert Whitman, 1980.
My Mother Lost Her Job Today, Albert Whitman, 1980.
Groundhog's Day at the Doctor, Parents Magazine Press, 1981.
I Never Win, Carolrhoda, 1981.
Blue Ribbon Friends, Houghton, 1982.
A Walk on a Snowy Night, Harper, 1982.
I'm Telling You Now, Arthur Ray, Dutton, 1982.
The Goose Who Wrote a Book, Carolrhoda, 1982.
Only Jody, Houghton, 1982.
A Pet for Bear and Duck, Albert Whitman, 1982.
Backyard Angel, Houghton, 1983.
Brimhall Turns Detective, Carolrhoda, 1983.
Near Occasion of Sin (young adult), Harcourt, 1984.
Kitty in High School, Houghton, 1984.
Angel in Charge, Houghton, 1985.
Bear and Duck on the Run, Houghton, 1985.
A Birthday Bike, Houghton, 1985.
I'll Never Love Anything Ever Again, Albert Whitman, 1985.

Rabbit Goes to Night School, Albert Whitman, 1986.
Angel's Mother's Boyfriend, Houghton, 1986.
Xmas Gift for Brimhall, Houghton, 1986.
An Elephant in the Garden, Houghton, 1986.
The Mystery of the Haunted Cabin, Houghton, 1986.
(With Dorothy Tucker) *My Grandma's in a Nursing Home*, Houghton, 1986.
Angel's Mother's Wedding, Houghton, 1987.
Kitty from the Start, Houghton, 1987.
No Time for Christmas, Carolrhoda, 1988.
Hired Help for Rabbit, Macmillan, 1988.
Angel's Mother's Baby, Houghton, 1989.
My Mom Made Me Go to Camp, Doubleday, 1990.
Sonny's Secret, Dell, 1991.
The Perfect Christmas Gift, Macmillan, 1992.
My Mom Made Me Go to School, Bantam, 1992.
My Mom Made Me Take Piano Lessons, Doubleday, 1993.

"PEE WEE SCOUT" SERIES; ILLUSTRATED BY ALAN TIEGREEN

Cookies and Crutches, Dell, 1988.
Camp Ghost-Away, Dell, 1988.
Lucky Dog Days, Dell, 1988.
Blue Skies, French Fries, Dell, 1988.
Grumpy Pumpkins, Dell, 1988.
Peanut-Butter Pilgrims, Dell, 1988.
A Pee Wee Christmas, Dell, 1988.
That Mushy Stuff, Dell, 1989.
Spring Sprouts, Dell, 1989.
The Pooped Troop, Dell, 1989.
The Pee Wee Jubilee, Dell, 1989.
Bad, Bad Bunnies, Dell, 1990.
Rosy Noses, Freezing Toes, Dell, 1990.
Sonny's Secret, Dell, 1990.
Sky Babies, Dell, 1990.
Trash Bash, Dell, 1990.
Pee Wees on Parade, Dell, 1992.
Lights, Action, Land-Ho!, Dell, 1992.
Piles of Pets, Dell, 1993.
Fishey Wishes, Dell, 1993.
Pee Wees on Skis, Dell, 1993.

"THE CONDO KIDS" SERIES; ILLUSTRATED BY TIEGREEN

Hello Huckleberry Heights, Dell, 1990.
Summer Showdown, Dell, 1990.
The Artificial Grandma, Dell, 1990.
Huckleberry Hash, Dell, 1990.
Scary Scary Huckleberry, Dell, 1990.
Merry Merry Huckleberry, Dell, 1990.

OTHER

The Twenty-Nine Most Common Writing Mistakes (adult), Writers Digest, 1985.

Contributor of over two hundred essays, articles, poems, and short stories to popular magazines, including *Wall Street Journal, Saturday Review, Humpty Dumpty, Instructor,* and *Highlights for Children.*

■ Work in Progress

More titles in the "Pee Wee Scouts" for Dell; a middle-grade series about a mother who wins the lottery, for Hyperion/Disney.

■ Sidelights

Judy Delton, who began writing when she was thirty-nine, once explained to *SATA* how she embarked on writing fiction: "Suddenly I had reached middle age and I sat down and took stock of the situation. I asked myself what I'd done with my life besides raise four children, bake cakes for the PTA, and donate blood. I began to put my thoughts on paper, and a city newspaper published a very poor verse of mine. The check for six dollars looked like six hundred at the time and I was inspired to plunge ahead, oblivious to pitfalls, competition, rejection, and depression."

Delton continued: "Without a writing class or a textbook on the subject, I unknowingly was saved from the hazards of structure and confinement, however many editors shuddered at my abuse of the English language. I was admonished that one must 'know the rules before breaking them' and phone calls from editors said, 'Your spelling is atrocious, your grammar poor, and the way you change tense in the middle of the paragraph makes me extremely nervous.' Their reluctant words, however, said 'I'll buy.'"

Indeed, success has proved abundant for Delton. Of her early fortunes as a writer, she commented in *SATA:* "Through trial and error, kind help of editors, and mainly *experience,* I sold, in two and a half years, 115 of my essays, articles, verse, short stories, children's stories, and newspaper features. *Two Good Friends* was my first hardcover book."

In her books Judy Delton draws heavily on her childhood experiences. Growing up in a very strict Catholic environment, she was regularly subject to a sense of overwhelming fear and guilt: "I remember my terror at the thought of hell and my scrupulousness over sin," she revealed in an article she wrote for *Something about the Author Autobiography Series* (*SAAS*). "I once found a small rosary case...and kept it, and suffered untold anguish worrying if keeping it was a mortal sin or venial sin. Sister had told us it was a mortal sin to steal something over five dollars. How was I to find out the cost or value of the case? My nightmares grew so great at the thought of hell's fire that I put it back under the bush in the alley where I'd found it, despite my great desire to own it."

Delton continued in *SAAS* that even after she returned the case "I lived in terror of committing mortal sin and going to hell. Around every corner lurked temptation. More than any friend or classmate, I probed into the makings of sin and deeply analyzed my actions. I could find sin in any act. In second grade we made our first confession and, although for a while I was relieved by the act of forgiveness, the sacrament's intricacies in-

Angel feels that getting a new father and a new house is hard enough, but the thought that her mother will have a new baby worries the young girl in this book by Delton. (Cover illustration by Margot Apple.)

volved me even more deeply in analysis. Those who say childhood is an innocent time of joy are wrong. I think it is a period filled with a distorted universe where experiences and judgement lack perspective, and everywhere danger waits to swallow you up. I fretted over 'B' movies, disobedience to my parents, death, war—to name just a few."

This episode, along with others from her childhood, is chronicled in Delton's "Kitty" series of books, which she described in *SAAS* as being about "growing up Catholic in St. Paul during the forties." The first book, *Kitty in the Middle,* relates young Kitty's escapades with friends in the fourth grade at Catholic school. "Lively and funny, their exploits will evoke chuckles," Mary I. Purucker notes in *School Library Journal,* and adds that the even non-Catholic readers will "appreciate the fun." *Kitty in the Summer* follows Kitty's visit to her aunt's house in a small farming town, and is based on the author's own childhood visits to her Aunt Katie's. A *Bulletin of the Center for Children's Books* critic praises the "appealing" story for "so faithfully creat[ing] a believable ten-year-old in a flavorful community." Later books take Kitty to high school and return to third grade to show her adjustment to a new school.

Hired Help for Rabbit

story by Judy Delton & pictures by Lisa McCue

In this picture book by Delton, Rabbit decides he needs some help around the house, but his "helpers" only cause him more trouble. (Cover illustration by Lisa McCue.)

Delton's Catholic upbringing is also reflected in her first novel for young adults, 1984's *Near Occasion of Sin.* The novel tells of the growing up and coming of age of Tess, a young girl whose narrow focus on the meaning of sin and the rules of religion leads her into a hasty marriage. Although her new husband is unstable and abusive, Tess is determined to make her marriage work; it is only after she becomes pregnant that she resolves to leave her husband and start a new life. Ethel R. Twichell of *Horn Book* observes that "Tess's protected, devoutly Catholic girlhood recalls the author's stories about Kitty," although *Near Occasion of Sin* is a much darker story. Nevertheless, the critic continues, "the unhappiness of the story is alleviated by the occasional touches of humor, a well-realized family, and an authentic recreation of the 1940's." Pat Harrington of *School Library Journal,* while stating that a girl of that time may be "incomprehensible to teens coming of age today," notes that "Tess is a memorable character, and her dialogue is often bitter, ... witty and insightful." And Susan B. Madden describes the book in the *Voice of Youth Advocates* as a "stark and powerful novel which will probably prove controversial."

Much of Judy Delton's work reflects, either directly or indirectly, the emotional questioning and general condition of childhood. Her "Angel" books reflect common situations many children face today, showing Angel dealing with her mother's new boyfriend, subsequent marriage, and pregnancy. Other books show children confronting problems such as having to give up a pet (*I'll Never Love Anything Ever Again*), being reluctant to leave home (*My Mom Made Me Go to Camp* and *My Mom Made Me Go to School*), and dealing with a infirm grandparent (*My Grandma's in a Nursing Home*). Del-

ton has also written a mystery for younger readers, *The Mystery of the Haunted Cabin,* a cheerful story which takes place during a summer vacation.

"I have heard that all a person needs is to live the first five years of life and he or she will have enough material and experience to write about for the rest of his or her life," Delton wrote in *SAAS.* She added: "Someone said that the things you learn in childhood are engraved in stone, and the things you learn as an adult are written on ice. It is not just 'memories' but values and motivation and personality that are developed then." These recollections of what it is like to be a child help Delton create her realistic portraits of everyday children.

Delton continues to work at a feverish pace, lecturing when not in front of her typewriter. Her "Pee Wee Scouts" series is approaching thirty books, and has sold over 7.5 million copies. Although her books are very popular, she admitted in *Publishing Research Quarterly* that "I find I write to entertain myself. I write because I like an audience. Because I can't talk all the time. Because it's easier than acting. Because I can't tap dance like Shirley Temple.... I find this reversal of writing for myself serendipitous. Because only when I write for

Tess's determination to avoid sin fulfills her Catholic beliefs, but also leads her into a troubled marriage. (Cover illustration by Lucinda Cowell.)

myself can I write for others. It's like making people happy. You can't go out and 'make' people happy. You have to be happy for yourself and then hope that it affects others."

■ Works Cited

Delton, Judy, essay in *Something about the Author Autobiography Series,* Volume 9, Gale, 1990, pp. 127-140.

Delton, Judy, "Writing for Today's Child," *Publishing Research Quarterly,* fall, 1991.

Harrington, Pat, review of *Near Occasion of Sin, School Library Journal,* October, 1984, p. 165.

Review of *Kitty in the Summer, Bulletin of the Center for Children's Books,* January, 1981, p. 90.

Madden, Susan B., review of *Near Occasion of Sin, Voice of Youth Advocates,* April, 1985, p. 48.

Purucker, Mary I., review of *Kitty in the Middle, School Library Journal,* May, 1979, p. 60.

Something about the Author, Volume 14, Gale, 1978.

Twichell, Ethel R., review of *Near Occasion of Sin, Horn Book,* November/December, 1984, p. 762.

■ For More Information See

PERIODICALS

Bulletin of the Center for Children's Books, January, 1980, p. 92; December, 1982, p. 2; December, 1984, p. 64.

Horn Book, October, 1980, p. 519.

New York Times Book Review, November 14, 1976, p. 25; February 13, 1983, p. 30; September 9, 1984, p. 43; February 17, 1985, p. 25.

St. Paul Dispatch, April 2, 1977.

St. Paul Pioneer Press, May 31, 1981.

School Library Journal, March, 1981, p. 130; November, 1983, p. 75; February, 1991, p. 68; April, 1992, p. 90.

*   *   *

DICKSON, Gordon R(upert) 1923-

■ Personal

Born November 1, 1923, in Edmonton, Alberta, Canada; came to the United States in 1936; naturalized citizen; son of Gordon Fraser (a mining engineer) and Maude Leola (a teacher; maiden name, Ford) Dickson. *Education:* University of Minnesota, B.A., 1948, graduate study, 1948-50.

■ Addresses

Office—P.O. Box 11569, St. Paul, MN, 55111. *Agent*—Kirby McCauley, Box 20447, 1539 First Ave., New York, NY 10028.

■ Career

Writer. Instructor in writers' workshops, including the Intensive Institute on the Teaching of Science Fiction,

University of Kansas. *Military service:* U.S. Army, 1943-1946. *Member:* Authors Guild, Mystery Writers of America, World S.F., Authors League of America, Science Fiction Writers of America (founding member; president, 1969-71), Science Fiction Research Association, Minnesota Science Fiction Society.

■ Awards, Honors

Hugo Award, 1965, for short story "Soldier, Ask Not"; Nebula Award, Science Fiction Writers of America, 1966, for short story "Call Him Lord"; E.E. Smith Memorial Award for Imaginative Fiction, 1975; August Derleth Award, British Fantasy Society, 1976, for *The Dragon and the George;* Jupiter Award, Instructors of Science Fiction in Higher Education, 1978, for *Time Storm;* Hugo Award nominations, 1978, for *Time Storm,* and 1979, for *The Far Call;* Hugo Awards, 1981, for the novellas *Lost Dorsai* and *The Cloak and the Staff.*

■ Writings

FOR YOUNG ADULTS

Secret under the Sea, Holt, 1960.

Secret under Antarctica, Holt, 1963.

Secret under the Caribbean, Holt, 1964.

Space Winners, Holt, 1965.

Alien Art, Dutton, 1973.

(With Ben Bova) *Gremlins, Go Home!,* St. Martin's, 1974.

(With Poul Anderson) *Star Prince Charlie,* Putnam, 1975.

FOR ADULTS; NOVELS

Alien from Arcturus (bound with *The Atom Curtain,* by Nick Boddie Williams), Ace Books, 1956, revised edition published as *Arcturus Landing,* 1979.

Mankind on the Run (bound with *The Crossroads of Time,* by Andre Norton), Ace Books, 1956, published as *On the Run,* 1979.

Naked to the Stars, Pyramid Press, 1961.

Delusion World [and] *Spacial Delivery,* Ace Books, 1961.

The Alien Way, Bantam, 1965.

Mission to Universe, Berkley Publishing, 1966.

(With Keith Laumer) *Planet Run,* Doubleday, 1967.

The Space Swimmers, Berkley Publishing, 1967.

Wolfling, Dell, 1969.

Spacepaw, Putnam, 1969.

None but Man, Doubleday, 1969.

Hour of the Horde, Putnam, 1970.

Sleepwalker's World, Lippincott, 1971.

The Pritcher Mass, Doubleday, 1972.

The Outposter, Lippincott, 1972.

The R-Master, Lippincott, 1973, revised edition published as *The Last Master,* Tor, 1984.

(With Harry Harrison) *The Lifeship,* Harper, 1976, published in England as *Lifeboat,* Futura, 1978.

Timestorm, St. Martin's, 1977, published as *Time Storm,* Baen, 1992.

The Far Call, Dial, 1978.

Pro, Ace Books, 1978.

Home from the Shore, Sundridge, 1978.
Masters of Everon, Ace Books, 1980.
(With Roland Green) *Jamie the Red,* Ace, 1984.
The Forever Man, Ace, 1987.
Way of the Pilgrim, Ace, 1987.
The Earth Lords, Ace, 1989.
Wolf and Iron, St. Martin's Press, 1990.
Naked to the Stars [and] *The Alien Way,* Tor, 1991.
Blood and War, Baen, 1993.

NOVELS IN THE CHILDE CYCLE

Time to Teleport [and] *The Genetic General,* Ace Books, 1960, *The Genetetic General* was expanded and published as *Dorsai!* (also see below), DAW Books, 1976.
Necromancer (also see below), Doubleday, 1962, published as *No Room for Man,* Macfadden, 1963, reprinted under original title, DAW Books, 1978.
Soldier, Ask Not, Dell, 1967.
The Tactics of Mistake (also see below), Doubleday, 1971.
Three to Dorsai! (contains *Necromancer, Dorsai!,* and *Tactics of Mistake*), Science Fiction Book Club, 1975.
The Final Encyclopedia, Ace, 1985.
The Chantry Guild, Ace, 1988.
Young Bleys, Tor, 1991.

NOVELS IN THE SIR DRAGON SERIES

The Dragon and the George, Doubleday, 1976.
The Dragon Knight, St. Martin's Press, 1990.
The Dragon on the Border, Berkley/Ace, 1992.
The Dragon at War, Berkley/Ace, 1992.

COLLECTIONS OF SHORT SCIENCE FICTION

(With Poul Anderson) *Earthman's Burden,* Gnome Press, 1957.
Danger—Human, Doubleday, 1970, published as *The Book of Gordon R. Dickson,* DAW Books, 1973.
Mutants: A Science Fiction Adventure, Macmillan, 1970.
(With others) *Five Fates,* Doubleday, 1970.
(With Anderson and Robert Silverberg) *The Day the Sun Stood Still: Three Original Novellas of Science Fiction* (contains "A Chapter of Revelation," by Anderson, "Thomas the Proclaimer," by Silverberg, and "Things Which Are Caesar's," by Dickson), Thomas Nelson, 1972.
The Star Road, Doubleday, 1973.
Ancient, My Enemy, Doubleday, 1974.
Gordon R. Dickson's SF Best, Dell, 1977.
The Spirit of Dorsai (contains "Brothers" and "Amanda Morgan"), Ace Books, 1979.
In Iron Years, Doubleday, 1980.
Lost Dorsai (includes novellas *Lost Dorsai* and *Warrior*), Ace Books, 1980.
Love Not Human, Ace, 1981.
The Man from Earth, Tor, 1983.
Dickson!, New England Science Fiction Association, 1984.
Beyond the Dar Al-Harb (contains "Beyond the Dar Al-Harb," "On Messenger Mountain," and "Things Which Are Caesar's"), Tor, 1985.
Forward!, Baen, 1985.

Invaders!, Baen, 1985.
(With Anderson) *Hoka!,* Tor, 1985.
Steel Brother, Tor, 1985.
The Man the Worlds Rejected, Tor, 1986.
The Dorsai Companion, Ace, 1986.
The Last Dream (includes "St. Dragon and the George"), Baen, 1986.
Survival!, Baen, 1987.
In the Bone: The Best Science Fiction of Gordon R. Dickson, Ace, 1987.
Ends (includes "Call Him Lord"), Baen, 1988.
The Stranger, Tor, 1987.
Guided Tour, Tor, 1988.
Beginnings (includes "Soldier, Ask Not"), Baen, 1988.
Space Dogfights, Ace, 1992.
Mindspan, Baen, 1993.

EDITOR

1975 Annual World's Best Science Fiction, DAW Books, 1975.
Combat SF, Doubleday, 1975.
Futurelove, Bobbs-Merrill, 1977.
Nebula Award Winners Twelve, Harper, 1979.
(With others) *Robot Warriors,* Ace, 1991.
The Harriers, Baen, 1991.

Also author of *Secrets of the Deep* (includes *Secret under the Sea, Secret under Antarctica,* and *Secret under the Caribbean*) and editor of *Devils and Demons* and *Witches, Warlocks and Werewolves* (anthologies). Author of over 150 published short stories. Author of radio plays. Contributor of introductions and essays to anthologies and periodicals.

■ Work in Progress

Bleys and *The Antagonist,* both novels in the *Childe Cycle,* and several more "Sir Dragon" books.

■ Sidelights

Although Gordon R. Dickson was just four years old when he learned to read, he already knew that he wanted to become a writer, reports Robert L. Jones in the *Dictionary of Literary Biography.* The son of a mining engineer from Sydney, Australia, and an American teacher, Dickson began writing his first stories as a child living in the mining camps of Alberta, Canada, in the 1920s and '30s. After the death of his father in 1936, Dickson, his younger brother Craig, and their mother moved to Minneapolis. Dickson studied at the University of Minnesota from 1939 to 1943, when he entered the U.S. Army. Although asthma prevented him from serving overseas during World War II, he was decorated for his service on the West Coast. After the war, Dickson returned to the university (where his instructors included noted American writers Sinclair Lewis, Allan Tate, and Robert Penn Warren) and earned a B.A. in Creative Writing in 1948. Two years in graduate school convinced him that he was a writer, not an academic; he has been a full-time writer ever since. Dickson made his publishing debut with *Alien from Arcturus* in 1956 and went on to become one of the best-known and most prolific contemporary writers of science fiction. One of the rare science fiction authors to make a living solely by his writing, Dickson has by his own count published over forty-nine novels and 150 short stories, and his books have sold over 20 million copies. He also has become a sought-after personality at science-fiction gatherings around the world. By 1992, he had spoken as a guest of honor at over two hundred meetings of science fiction readers and writers and had appeared at over four hundred and fifty conventions and other gatherings.

Dickson has published several novels specifically for young adults, including *Space Winners,* about a group of young people stranded on an alien world, and *Alien Art,* which imagines the struggles of environmentalists on a planet of the future. Moreover, although most of his work is, as Raymond H. Thompson comments in *Canadian Children's Literature,* "obviously written for adults," much of Dickson's "adult fiction" has proven very popular with younger readers. Set in richly imagined worlds of the future or the past, Dickson's stories are "studded with those marvelous scientific 'discoveries' ... which allow the hero to perform feats impossible at present," Thompson points out. Many of these "discoveries" involve highly developed paranormal skills like mental telepathy and teleportation across time and space. In addition, Thompson continues, at their core most of Dickson's novels are about growing up. The typical Dickson hero is a young man setting out in his career who proves himself in the face of his older colleagues' skepticism and assumptions of their own superiority. The hero triumphs because he possesses youthful qualities of flexibility, optimism, and willingness to take risks, and because he has matured by learning to care about others and to take responsibility for his own actions.

The *Childe Cycle*

Dickson's major work is the ongoing *Childe Cycle,* which on completion, Dickson told *SATA,* "will consist of sixteen novels—three historical, three contemporary, and ten set in the future." The first book in the cycle, *Dorsai!,* appeared in 1960, and six others had been published as of 1992: *Necromancer; Soldier, Ask Not; The Tactics of Mistake; The Final Encyclopedia; The Chantry Guild;* and *Young Bleys.* Dickson has also published several Cycle-related short stories and novellas, collected in *Lost Dorsai, Spirit of Dorsai,* and *The Dorsai Companion,* which in addition to four short stories includes descriptions of the various worlds of the Cycle, sketches of major characters, a Cycle chronology, and lineage charts. The completed *Childe Cycle,* Dickson told *SATA,* "will connect to form a single 'novel of thematic argument,'" although the individual titles also "stand easily on their own, complete novels in themselves." While some readers refer to the novels of the *Childe Cycle* as the "Dorsai" novels, Dickson told *SATA* that this label is not "strictly accurate." Nonetheless, fans of the Cycle books have created an organization based on the Dorsai and hold an annual Dorsai convention.

Part of Dickson's larger *Childe Cycle* series, this collection of "Dorsai" science fiction stories won a prestigious Hugo award. (Cover illustration by Fernando Fernandez.)

While establishing Dickson as a serious writer of science fiction, the Cycle books also gave him a reputation as a war author, which, Jones insists, he is not. "The Dorsai are indeed warriors of formidable abilities, but they are only a part of the total picture," Jones writes, pointing out that Dickson's books, especially those of the *Childe Cycle,* reflect a complex and fairly consistent philosophical outlook. In the Cycle, Dickson explained to Clifford McMurray of the *Science Fiction Review,* "I'm making the argument that a type of characteral, moral—spiritual, if you like—evolution began with the Renaissance, is presently continuing unnoticed, and will culminate five hundred years from now in what I call the Responsible Man." In Dickson's vision of the future, three successful lines, which he calls Splinter Cultures, have evolved from humankind: the warrior (the Dorsai), the philosopher (the Exotics of the planets Mara and Kultis), and the faith-holder (the Friendlies of the planets Harmony and Association). Dickson added: "My assumption is that the Splinter Cultures have only one character-facet, instead of being full spectrum in character like you and me and the people of old Earth. Concentrated in this way, they are nonviable. If all the rest of the human race was killed off and they were left alone they would eventually die off, too, because they don't have the full spectrum of humanity in them—yet." Consistent themes in Dickson's work include the conflict between individualism and social conformity, as well as the problems that arise when different cultures meet and the need for mutual understanding and flexibility to resolve those problems.

Medieval Adventures, Fantastic Futures

The same philosophical ideas permeate Dickson's numerous novels outside the Cycle, many of which are more readable and faster paced than the somewhat ponderous Cycle volumes. Several of his most popular books make up the "Sir Dragon" series, which began with *The Dragon and the George* and includes *The Dragon Knight, The Dragon on the Border,* and *The Dragon at War.* In *The Dragon and the George,* a young twentieth-century mathematician, Jim Eckert, and his wife, Angie, are whisked into a parallel universe that is much like fourteenth-century England, except that this world includes real-life wizards and magical beasts. Angie is transported accidentally, and when Jim tries to follow her he materializes on the other side in the form of a dragon. In this and the subsequent books of the series, Jim learns how to change back and forth between his human and dragon bodies and slowly grows in stature as a magician. While his powers quickly gain him respect among the people he meets, Jim also must struggle with the burden of responsibility, for as a magician from another world he has become a target of the evil powers that exist in his new-found home.

Time Storm, which Jones describes as "the most conceptually complete of Dickson's novels," is set in the future, rather than the past. In this novel a young man, Marc Despard, is assisted by a leopard, a young woman, and an alien in calming a "time storm" that threatens permanently to disrupt the space-time continuum and to destroy the universe. Another of Dickson's best-known works is *The Far Call,* which is set at the end of the twentieth-century and concerns international attempts to launch the first manned spaceflight to Mars. *Wolf and Iron* also takes place in the late twentieth century. Civilization has collapsed, and young Jeebee Walthar joins forces with a wolf he has rescued from captivity as he makes his way west across dangerous territory towards his brother's ranch in Montana. In *The Forever Man,* an ace starship fighter pilot, Jim Wander, becomes a single entity with his spaceship. Accompanied by the disembodied mind of a scientist, Mary Gallegher, he investigates an enemy alien culture. *Hour of the Horde* features a crippled painter, Miles Vander, who becomes the only man who can save the earth from the invading forces of the "Silver Horde."

Dickson has also written several books in collaboration with other science fiction writers. *Lifeship,* co-authored with Harry Harrison, takes place in a future society which has become highly stratified and is dominated by a fascistic elite. When members of the society's various classes, as well as some aliens, find themselves adrift in a space-going lifeboat, their survival hinges on their ability to learn to get along. Dickson joined forces with Poul Anderson, a former classmate at the University of Minnesota, in writing the collections *Earthman's Burden* and *Hoka!,* which contain stories about small, bear-like creatures called Hokas who behave remarkably like humans.

"One of the Old Guard"

Some reviewers find Dickson's work somewhat old-fashioned. "Dickson is one of the old guard, and his stories are earnest, carefully plotted, and unabashedly pro-space exploration," remarks Kenneth Von Gunden in *Fantasy Review.* "Dickson's work harks back to an earlier decade: there are no cyberpunks here; many of the [science fiction] trappings, ... seem outdated; women are practically invisible," remarks a reviewer of *Young Bleys* in *Publishers Weekly.* Thompson reports that "Dickson's heroines have earned the criticism of feminist critics for their subservience and for the unquestioning loyalty they finally adopt." An exception to these reviewers' comments about female characters is Amanda Morgan, the title character of a novella published in *The Spirit of Dorsai.* Writing in *Booklist,* reviewer Roland Green calls Morgan "one of the ... best female characters in [science fiction] or fantasy during the last decade." Dickson is widely recognized as a master of his craft. "To read the first page of a Dickson book is to know that you will read them all," states Don Sakers in *Wilson Library Bulletin,* while Thompson suggests that young readers "can find no better introduction to the field of science fiction."

■ Works Cited

Green, Roland, Review of *Spirit of Dorsai, Booklist,* February 1, 1980, p. 760.

Jones, Robert L., "Gordon R. Dickson," *Dictionary of Literary Biography,* Volume 8: *Twentieth-Century American Science Fiction Writers,* Gale, 1981, pp. 141-147.

McMurray, Clifford, "An Interview with Gordon R. Dickson," *Science Fiction Review,* July, 1978, pp. 6-12.

Sakers, Don, "S.F. Universe," *Wilson Library Bulletin,* June, 1989, p. 108.

Thompson, Raymond H., "Gordon R. Dickson: Science Fiction for Young Canadians," *Canadian Children's Literature,* Number 15/16, 1980, pp. 38-46.

Von Gunden, Kenneth, review of *In the Bone: The Best Science Fiction of Gordon R. Dickson, Fantasy Review,* June, 1987, p. 35.

Review of *Young Bleys, Publishers Weekly,* March 1, 1991, p. 61.

■ For More Information See

PERIODICALS

Algol, spring, 1978, pp. 33-38.

Analog, August, 1984, pp. 169-170; October, 1984, pp. 147-148; May, 1987, pp. 179-180; May, 1989, pp. 180-181; May, 1991, pp. 181-182; September, 1991, pp. 164-165.

Booklist, February 15, 1992, p. 1065; November 1, 1992, p. 51.

Bulletin of the Center for Children's Books, October, 1973.

Bulletin of the Science Fiction Writers of America, fall, 1979.

Destinies, February-March, 1980.

Extrapolation, number 18, 1976, pp. 8-9; fall, 1979.

Fantasy Review, August, 1985, pp. 16, 18; December, 1985, p. 17; July/August, 1986, p. 24; October, 1986, p. 23.

Kirkus Reviews, August 15, 1984, p. 779.

Los Angeles Times Book Review, July 29, 1990, p. 6.

New York Times Book Review, August 2, 1987.

Publishers Weekly, September 7, 1984.

Times Literary Supplement, May 25, 1967.

Voice of Youth Advocates, April, 1986, p. 39; December, 1986, p. 236; August/September, 1987, p. 129; June, 1989, p. 116; June, 1991, p. 107; August, 1991, p. 164; June, 1992, p. 108.*

*   *   *

DIXON, Ann R. 1954-

■ Personal

Born February 26, 1954, in Richland, WA; daughter of David S. (an engineer) and Barbara (a homemaker; maiden name Cook) Dixon; married Walter R. Pudwill (a carpenter), May 30, 1982; children: Linnea C. Pudwill, Noranna N. Dixon. *Education:* University of Washington, B.A. (magna cum laude), 1976. *Religion:* Christian. *Hobbies and other interests:* Storytelling, gardening, skiing, nonmotorized outdoor recreation.

■ Addresses

Home—P.O. Box 1009, Willow, AK 99688.

■ Career

Free-lance writer, Willow, AK, 1982—; librarian, Matanuska-Susitna Borough, Willow, AK, 1987—. Reforestation contractor, Hoedads, Inc., Eugene, OR, 1977-81; vice president and member, Willow Library Board, 1981-87. *Member:* Society of Children's Book Writers and Illustrators, Alaska Library Association, Phi Beta Kappa.

■ Writings

How Raven Brought Light to People, Macmillan, 1992.

■ Work in Progress

The Sleeping Lady, for Alaska Northwest, 1995; various children's stories.

ANN DIXON

■ Sidelights

Author and librarian Ann R. Dixon told *SATA:* "Stories, nature, and children are the threads that have anchored my life.

"As a child I was hooked on the combination of fresh air and books by riding my bicycle several miles to the local one-room library. Reading and writing stories were my favorite subjects in school.

"I spent much of my college time working in or otherwise hanging around libraries. It was there that I discovered storytelling and the oral tradition and rediscovered children's books. In the big city I also learned that proximity to clean air and water, mountains, trees, birds, dirt, rocks, etc. was essential to my soul.

"I began learning about other cultures, first by learning languages, then by traveling. Finally, I became more aware of and interested in the various cultures within my own land. I was/am fascinated with the ways people express their beliefs and imaginations through story.

"These days, the seemingly divergent threads of my life seem to be braiding into a single strand. I spend most of my days either writing stories or working at a library, where I also tell and read stories to young children. My own children provide plenty of opportunity for story in all senses. And as I learn more about the stories, both oral and written, of other cultures—especially the many within my own country—I have great hope for the power of story to build bridges of understanding. I hope to be part of that process."

*   *   *

DIXON, Paige
See CORCORAN, Barbara

DUGIN, Andrej 1955-

■ Personal

First name also transliterated as Andrey; born November 3, 1955, in Moscow, U.S.S.R. (now Russia); son of Viatcheslav Dugin (an actor) and Ninel Ternovskaya (an actress) Dugina; married Olga Kotikova (an artist), June 30, 1984. *Education:* Attended Krasnopresnenskaya Art School, 1968-72; studied under Rostislav N. Barto, 1970-72; Surikov Art Institute, 1972-79. *Politics:* "Prefer Democracy to Dictatorship." *Religion:* Protestant.

■ Addresses

Office—c/o Heike Brillmann-Ede, J. F. Schreiber Verlag GmbH, Postfach 285, 7300 Esslingen, Germany.

■ Career

Krasnopresnenskaya Art School, teacher, 1978-79, and 1980-84; collaborated with various Soviet magazines, including *Pioneer, Krokodil, Sputnik,* and *Literaturnaya Gazeta;* illustrator, 1989—. *Exhibitions:* Works on exhibition in Moscow in 1984. *Military service:* Served in the Soviet army, 1979-80.

ANDREJ DUGIN

Dugin and his wife, Olga Dugina, co-created the elaborate and fantastical illustrations in the book *Dragon Feathers.*

■ Illustrator

G. Ansimov, *The Producer of a Musical Theatre,* VTO, 1980.

M. Lermontov, *The Lyric Poetry,* Detskaya Literatura, 1984.

M. Morozov, *The Shakespeare's Theatre,* VTO, 1984.

R. Saito, *The Fiery Horse,* Detskaya Literatura, 1985.

F. Schiller, *The Goblet,* Detskaya Literatura, 1986.

A. Kazantsev, *The Flamed Island,* Detskaya Literatura, 1987.

Michael Bulgakov as a Dramatist and the Artistic Life of His Time, compiled by A. Ninov, VTO, 1988.

(With wife, Olga Dugina) *The Fine Round Cake,* adapted by Arnica Esterl (based on the Joseph Jacobs story "Johnny-cake"), translated by Pauline Hejl, Four Winds Press, 1991 (originally published as *Das Maerchen vom schoenen runden Kuchen*).

(With Olga Dugina) *Dragon Feathers,* Thomasson-Grant, 1993.

Chief artist for *The Bird Catcher* (animation), directed by E. Prorokova, 1984-85.

■ Sidelights

Andrej Dugin told *SATA:* "I have seriously occupied myself with drawing since I was twelve years old, because my mother wanted her son to be engaged in something else besides hanging around with other teenagers on the streets. She thought that, in this way, I would make my right way in life. I began to attend a night art school for children where most of the pupils had been studying a long time. They were, of course, more skillful in drawing than I was, and I had to work hard to achieve the same quality. I liked to draw and drew a lot. Little by little it became the need and then the life.

"Now I am working as an illustrator. It seems to me that I can do something interesting in this field. I think that it is possible to say something unusual about common things and, conversely, to show the usual of the miracle. For me a plot serves as a ground for creating my own parallel visual stories. Without destroying a plot I try to show that it has many meanings.

"I think that only few work as slowly, persistently, and carefully as I do. I hope very much that I shall succeed in keeping these qualities in the future. I think they will help me (as they are now) to achieve positive results."

■ For More Information See

PERIODICALS

Publishers Weekly, November 1, 1993, pp. 79-80.

* * *

DUGINA, Olga 1964-

■ Personal

Born September 5, 1964, in Moscow, U.S.S.R. (now Russia); daughter of Valentin Kotikov (a journalist) and Elena Silina Kotikova (a textile-designer); married Andrej Dugin (an artist), June 30, 1984. *Education:* Attended Krasnopresnenskaya Art School, 1978-81; Moscow Art College, 1984-88. *Politics:* "I am indifferent to politics." *Religion:* "I do not belong to any confession." *Hobbies and other interests:* Taking photographs, cooking, watching good movies and performances, listening to music (classical, songs of Russian bards, rock).

■ Addresses

Office—c/o Heike Brillmann-Ede, J. F. Schreiber Verlag GmbH, Postfach 285, 7300 Esslingen, Germany.

■ Career

Krasnopresnenskaya Art School, Moscow, secretary, 1981-82; Gossnab, Moscow, architectural artist, 1982-83; Kuntsevo Cinema, Moscow, designer, 1985; *Energija* magazine, Moscow, designer, 1988-90; illustrator, 1989—.

■ Illustrator

M. Sholokhov, *The Fate of a Man* (stories), Raduga, 1990.

OLGA DUGINA

V. Yan, *Chingiz-Han,* Raduga, 1990.
Y. Rajnis, *The Lake* (poetry), Raduga, 1990.
(With husband, Andrej Dugin) *The Fine Round Cake,* adapted by Arnica Esterl (based on the Joseph Jacobs story "Johnny-cake"), translated by Pauline Hejl, Four Winds Press, 1991 (originally published as *Das Maerchen vom schoenen runden Kuchen*).
(With A. Dugin) *Dragon Feathers,* J. F. Schreiber, 1993, Thomasson-Grant, 1993.

Also illustrator of book covers, including *The Road Accident,* by Y. Nagibin, Raduga, 1989, and *Nothing in Particular,* by V. Tokareva, Raduga, 1991.

■ Sidelights

Olga Dugina told *SATA:* "I began to draw when I was a little girl, before I could read and write. My parents were not artists. But really I can say that they were my first teachers. In our house lots of things were made by hand. My father gathered some pieces of wood, metal, and stones and turned them into sculptures, pictures, decorations. Each of them was the only one of its kind. My mother's embroideries were unique and worthy of museum exhibition. It was easier for me to manage with a pencil and a brush than with a needle. But I must say that my parents (especially my mother) taught me how to be patient, persevering, and attentive to the smallest details in the work. These qualities are very useful for me now in illustrating.

"Studying at the elementary school I was friends with a girl whose mother was an illustrator. I used to call on them often. There were so many interesting things—particular colors, special instruments, and the pictures for fairy-tale that attracted me most of all. I was told about making books, which interested me very much. Of course for a small girl it was difficult to understand those magic words—a frontispiece, a flyleaf, a fillister—but I liked them anyway. And afterwards I was shown a printed book and there were the pictures in it which I had seen lying incomplete on the desk a while ago. It seemed like magic, a miracle. My friend and I organized our own publishing house where we were artists and editors, writers and proofreaders. Of course the only readers of our manuscript books and magazines were our parents.

"Then I entered the children's art school. There I met Andrej Dugin, who later became my husband. In this art school he worked as a teacher. Until now I remain his pupil and I am proud of this. Working together with him I understood that illustration could be not a simple picture identified with the text. It gives a chance to open and show an artist's own perception of the world."

■ For More Information See

PERIODICALS

Publishers Weekly, November 1, 1993, pp. 79-80.

E

ARNICA ESTERL

ESTERL, Arnica 1933-

■ Personal

Born July 2, 1933, in The Hague, Holland; daughter of L. F. C. Mees (a doctor) and A. Weissenberg (a nurse); married Dietrich Esterl (a teacher); children: Iris, Andrea, Beate, Lukas. *Education:* Studied German philology, philosophy, and the Frisian language in Amsterdam, Netherlands, and Tuebingen, Germany.

■ Addresses

Home—Lange Morgen 10 B, DW 70619 Stuttgart, Germany.

■ Career

Storyteller, 1975—. *Member:* Europaische Maerchengesellschaft e.V. (European Fairy Tale Association), Stuttgarter Maerchenkreis e.V. (regional group of the European Fairy Tale Association, based in Stuttgart; founder).

■ Writings

(Edited with Wilhelm Solms) *Tiere und Tiergestaltige im Maerchen: Im Auftrag der europaischen Maerchengesellschaft herausgegeben* (papers from a conference organized by the Europaische Maerchengesellschaft, 1988), Erich Roth, 1991.

(Adapter) *The Fine Round Cake* (based on the Joseph Jacobs story "Johnny-cake"), translated by Pauline Hejl, illustrated by Andrej Dugin and Olga Dugina, Four Winds Press, 1991 (originally published as *Das Maerchen vom schoenen runden Kuchen*).

*   *   *

EVSLIN, Bernard 1922-1993

OBITUARY NOTICE—See index for *SATA* sketch: Born April 9, 1922, in Philadelphia, PA; died of cardiac arrest, June 4, 1993, in Kauai, HI. Film producer, playwright, mythologist, and writer. While a producer of documentaries filmed in the United States, Europe, and Asia, Evslin also wrote stage plays and screenplays for a wider audience. His comedy *Geranium Hat* won acclaim on Broadway in 1959. The same year, his *Face of the Land* was named best television film in a poll by *Variety*. Evslin used his experience as a screenwriter to inform his 1964 novel *Merchants of Venus*. In the mid-1960s, Evslin began writing books concerning mythology and history, including *The Greek Gods, Heroes and*

Monsters of Greek Myth, and *The Trojan War.* His background in mythology helped him write such works for children as *The Green Hero, Adventures of Ulysses, Jason and the Argonauts,* and *Hercules,* which received the Washington Irving Children's Book Choice Award in 1986.

OBITUARIES AND OTHER SOURCES:

BOOKS

Authors of Books for Young People, 3rd edition, Scarecrow, 1990, pp. 216-217.

PERIODICALS

New York Times, June 26, 1993, p. 27.

F

FERNANDES, Eugenie 1943-

■ Personal

Born September 25, 1943, in Huntington, NY; daughter of Creig Flessel (an illustrator for D.C. Comics) and Marie Flessel (a homemaker; maiden name, Marino); married Henry Fernandes (an illustrator), October 1, 1966; children: Kim, Matthew. *Education:* Attended School of Visual Arts, New York City, 1963-65. *Politics:* "Human."

■ Addresses

Office—c/o Annick Press, 15 Patricia Ave., Willowdale, Ontario M2M 1H9, Canada.

■ Career

Freelance illustrator and author, 1966—.

■ Writings

SELF-ILLUSTRATED

Wickedishrag, C. R. Gibson, 1968.
Jenny's Surprise Summer, Western Publishing, 1981.
The Little Boy Who Cried Himself to Sea, Kids Can Press, 1982.
A Difficult Day, Kids Can Press, 1983 (black and white), 1987 (color).
(Co-written and illustrated with husband, Henry Fernandes) *Ordinary Amos and the Amazing Fish,* Western Publishing, 1986.
The Very Best Picnic, Western Publishing, 1988.
Jolly Book Box: Early Learning for Toddlers (contains "ABC and You," "Alone-Together," "Picnic Colors," "Dreaming Numbers," and "Busy Week"), Ladybird Books, 1990.
(Illustrated with daughter, Kim Fernandes) *Just You and Me,* 1993.
Waves in the Bathtub, Scholastic Canada, 1993.
The Tree that Grew to the Moon, Scholastic Canada, 1994.

EUGENIE FERNANDES

Also writer, designer, and producer of animated television-spots for the *Sesame Street* Children's Television Workshop.

ILLUSTRATOR

Lucille Hammond, *Dog Goes to Nursery School,* Western Publishing, 1982.
Ronne Peltzman, *My Book of the Seasons,* Western Publishing, 1982.
Ronne Peltzman, *Ned's Number Book,* Western Publishing, 1982.

Lucille Hammond, *When Dog Was Little,* Western Publishing, 1983.

Linda Hayward, *I Had a Bad Dream,* Western Publishing, 1985.

Kathleen N. Daly, *Little Sister,* Western Publishing, 1986.

Anne Baird, *Ride Away!,* Simon & Schuster, 1987.

Anne Baird, *Belly Buttons,* Simon & Schuster, 1987.

Lucille Hammond, *When Dog Grows Up,* Western Publishing, 1987.

Eve Merriam, *Daddies at Work,* Simon & Schuster, 1989.

Eve Merriam, *Mommies at Work,* Simon & Schuster, 1989.

Marianne Borgardt, *Going to the Dentist* (case-bound pop-up), Simon & Schuster, 1991.

Stacie Strong, *Going to the Doctor* (case-bound pop-up), Simon & Schuster, 1991.

Jean Lewis, *Glow in the Dark—Under the Sea,* Western Publishing, 1991.

Suzan Reid, *Grandpa Dan's Toboggan Ride,* Scholastic Canada, 1992.

Lily Barnes, *Lace Them Up,* Hyperion, 1992.

Patricia Quinlan, *Brush Them Bright,* Hyperion, 1992.

Lucille Hammond, *Little Kitten Dress-Up,* Ladybird Books, 1992.

Larry Dane Brimner, *The Leaving of Elliot Fry,* Boyds Mills Press, 1993.

Ginny Clapper, *My Mommy Comes Back* (book and tape), Western Publishing, 1993.

Judy Rothman, *Today I Took My Diapers Off* (book and tape), Western Publishing, 1993.

David Suzuki, *Nature in the Home,* Stoddart, 1993.

Also illustrator for United Nations Children's Fund, 1987 and 1988, and for *One Light, One Sun,* published as part of "Raffi Songs to Read," Crown, 1988; illustrator for *One Light, One Sun* album cover.

ILLUSTRATOR; BOARD BOOK SERIES; PUBLISHED BY LADYBIRD BOOKS, EXCEPT WHERE NOTED

My Bath Time Book, 1987.
My Bedtime Book, 1987.
My Going Out Book, 1987.
My Playtime Book, 1987.
My Busy Day Book, 1988.
My Rainy Day Book, 1988.
My Sunny Day Book, 1988.
My Birthday Book, 1988.
Jan Colbert, *Good Morning,* HarperCollins, 1993.
Jan Colbert, *Good Night,* HarperCollins, 1993.

ILLUSTRATOR; BOOKS WRITTEN BY RICHARD THOMPSON AND PUBLISHED BY ANNICK PRESS

Sky Full of Babies, 1987.
Foo, 1988.
I Have to See This!, 1988.
Gurgle, Bubble, Splash, 1989.
Effie's Bath, 1990.
Jesse on the Night Train, 1990.
Maggee and the Lake Minder, 1991.
Tell Me One Good Thing: Bedtime Stories, 1992.
Don't be Scared, Eleven, 1993.

■ Work in Progress

Six new books.

■ Sidelights

Eugenie Fernandes is a freelance illustrator and author of several children's books. Among her recent works is *Just You and Me,* which is her first professional collaboration with her daughter Kim Fernandes, who has published children's books of her own. *Just You and Me* tells of how young Heather and her mother wish to spend some time alone but must bring Heather's infant sibling with them on a walk after the baby refuses to fall asleep. No matter where they go—out to sea, up into the clouds, even to the moon—the baby remains awake. The baby finally falls asleep only after the other characters give up pursuing the task. *Quill and Quire* contributor Janet McNaughton found the work a "winning effort," stating that "children five and under will appreciate the combination of the mundane and the wildly improbable in *Just You and Me.*"

Fernandes told *SATA:* "We moved to a lake in Ontario, Canada, in 1984. Before that my studio was always the corner of a bedroom, protected only by a strip of tape on the floor that said 'please knock.' Our two children were quite good about that invisible door. They often sat next to me creating pictures and stories of their own, just as I had done when I was a child sitting beside by father, Creig Flessel. He was one of the early comic book artists in the 1930s with D.C. Comics.

"I spent much of my growing-up-time in my father's studio. The rest of the time you could find me swimming with mermaids and romping with pirates, climbing trees, taking care of baby birds, and enjoying the picnic lunches that my mother often brought to the beach. *Tell Me One Good Thing, Gurgle, Bubble, Splash,* and *Jenny's Surprise Summer* are filled with images of that childhood.

"*Waves in the Bathtub* is a story that has been with me since I was small enough to feel that the tub was huge. It brewed quietly over the years as I watched my own children play for hours in the tub with toy dolphins and boats and whales. And the song—I don't quite know where that came from. I just found myself singing it. The trick was putting it down on paper.

"The story for *A Difficult Day* was built around an angry moment that I shared with my son when he was five. He went to his room and slammed the door. 'You can't come in. Don't you try to come in,' he said. 'I don't like you any more. I don't like anybody!' Then there was a pause. By now I was listening *very* carefully and writing very quickly—because I knew that he was giving me some important feelings. Then came his best line, 'Why don't you love me better!' I can feel the emotion in this story, both as the child and as the mother.

"So . . . here I am in a nutshell, perhaps a coconut shell. I've always been grateful that my work could be done at

Kady frolicks with colorful fish, playful dolphins, friendly polar bears, and other ocean creatures in Fernandes's self-illustrated *Waves in the Bathtub*.

home where I could be with the kids, snug as a bug on snowy days, splashing into the lake on hot summer afternoons, and doing something that I love—writing and illustrating children's books. Kids often ask me which is my favorite book. I have a few favorites—*A Difficult Day, Ordinary Amos, Waves in the Bathtub,* and *Just You and Me.*"

■ Works Cited

McNaughton, Janet, review of *Just You and Me, Quill and Quire,* August, 1993.

G

GABLER, Mirko 1951-

■ Personal

Born March 20, 1951, in Teplice, Czechoslovakia; son of Vladimir (a building engineer) and Vlasta (a secretary) Gabler; married Ann Gourlay (a writer) May, 1973; children: Alec, Luke. *Education:* Attended School for Industrial Arts, Prague, 1965-68; School for Applied Arts, Zagreb, Yugoslavia (now Croatia), graduated, 1973.

■ Addresses

Office—Read Road, Box 100-B, Red Hook, NY 12571.

■ Career

Zagreb [Yugoslavia] Film, animator, 1973; self-employed as furniture and exhibit designer, 1973-82; designer, Gallery Association of New York State, 1982-84; Bard College, Annandale-on-Hudson, NY, exhibitions designer, 1984-87; self-employed in furniture and exhibition design, 1987—; writer and illustrator of children's books, 1989—. Coach of youth soccer team. *Member:* Society of Children's Book Writers and Illustrators.

■ Writings

AUTHOR AND ILLUSTRATOR

The Alphabet Soup, Holt, 1992.
Brakus Krakus ..., Holt, 1993.
Tall, Wide and Sharpeye, Holt, in press.

■ Work in Progress

Golem and Other Legends of Prague, "a travel guide to Prague and its magical places" for children.

■ Sidelights

Mirko Gabler told *SATA:* "Someone once said that we Czechs are late bloomers. Now, I don't know whether

MIRKO GABLER

my writing career is already blooming or still sprouting. But whatever it is doing, it has done it late—at the age of thirty-nine, after years of designing and building exhibits, furniture, and other hard-edged things. Curiously, the urge to write books came to me a few months after the long-awaited revolution in my old country, Czechoslovakia, in 1989. Suddenly, the years of my childhood there seemed much closer to me, and I said to myself: 'Why don't I write a little book about growing up in Czechoslovakia, with lots of pictures?' And so I did, made a dummy of it, and went off to look for a publisher. While my collections of rejections grew, I wrote many other stories, and a year and a half later I found a publisher for two of them: one set in Czechoslovakia, the other a full-blooded American tale.

"Today, thanks to the wild turn of history, I'm writing and drawing for children, getting published, reading my books to kids, signing books, and having a great time (as, ironically, Czechoslovakia is breaking in two).

"In my work, I draw on Czech folklore quite a bit. I like the mix of things supernatural and ordinary, the hair-raising drama and plain silliness found in Czech story-telling. I admire the directness and eloquence of folk-tales in general, especially American and English tales. Having always suffered from a short attention span, I have no patience with humorless and longwinded sagas. As a father of two boys, I can appreciate the holding power of a good yarn, with plenty of action to keep even the jumpiest third graders on the edge of their seats. I find great satisfaction in reading my stories in schools, especially when a supposedly hyperactive bunch sits mesmerized and biting their nails, following every turn as our hero struggles against all odds. I then feel what my grandmother must have felt, when in the evenings, with the lights out and only the stove door open for illumination, she told us her wild tales.

"Once I have written a story, I find that reading it aloud to a group of kids is the true test. It helps me sharpen the plot and also fine-tune the sound of the lines for smoother delivery. I think that reading aloud is the best way to teach effective use of language.

"Once the story is polished up, then come the pictures. It surprises me sometimes to see that the best pictures I draw remind me of something I saw as a child. I like to keep my pictures breezy. The pictures run ahead of the text. Every picture is something of a mystery that only can be understood upon reading the whole page—like a film with delayed sound.

"To be honest I have very few ground rules when it comes to my work. Each story is a different experience. Each has its own birthing pains and joys. And as long as it stays that way, I'll enjoy doing it."

*　　*　　*

GARDEN, Nancy 1938-

■ Personal

Born May 15, 1938, in Boston, MA. *Education:* Columbia University, B.F.A. from School of Dramatic Arts, 1961, M.A. from Teacher's College, 1962. *Hobbies and other interests:* Gardening, weaving, hiking, running, cross-country skiing, traveling.

■ Addresses

Home—Carlisle, MA, and West Tremont, ME.

NANCY GARDEN

■ Career

Scholastic Magazines, New York City, began as assistant editor, became associate editor, 1966-70; Houghton Mifflin Co., Boston, MA, editor, 1971-76; writing teacher, freelance writer, and book reviewer, 1976—. Has also worked in theater as an actress and lighting designer, taught at various levels, and done freelance editorial work for various publishers. Gives talks at schools and libraries to children on writing and speaks at writer's conferences for adults. *Member:* Society of Children's Book Writers and Illustrators, PEN American Center.

■ Awards, Honors

Annie on My Mind was selected as a 1982 *Booklist* Reviewer's Choice, and was on the 1982 American Library Association (ALA) Best Books list and the 1970-83 ALA Best of the Best list; *Fours Crossing* was on the 1983-84 William Allen White Award Master List.

■ Writings

FICTION

What Happened in Marston, illustrated by Richard Cuffari, Four Winds, 1971.
The Loners, Viking, 1972.
Maria's Mountain, illustrated by Barbara Brascove, Houghton, 1981.
Annie on My Mind, Farrar, Straus, 1982.
(Adaptor) *Favorite Tales from Grimm,* illustrated by Mercer Mayer, Four Winds, 1982.

Prisoner of Vampires, illustrated by Michele Chessare, Farrar, Straus, 1984.

Peace, O River, Farrar, Straus, 1986.

Lark in the Morning, Farrar, Straus, 1991.

My Sister, the Vampire, Knopf, 1992.

"FOURS CROSSING" SEQUENCE

Fours Crossing, Farrar, Straus, 1981.

Watersmeet, Farrar, Straus, 1983.

The Door Between, Farrar, Straus, 1987.

"MONSTER HUNTERS" SERIES

Mystery of the Night Raiders, Farrar, Straus, 1987.

Mystery of the Midnight Menace, Farrar, Straus, 1988.

Mystery of the Secret Marks, Farrar, Straus, 1989.

Mystery of the Kidnapped Kidnapper, Minstrel, 1994.

Mystery of the Watchful Witches, Minstrel, 1994.

NONFICTION

Berlin: City Split in Two, Putnam, 1971.

Vampires, Lippincott, 1973.

Werewolves, Lippincott, 1973.

Witches, Lippincott, 1975.

Devils and Demons, Lippincott, 1976.

Fun with Forecasting Weather, Houghton, 1977.

The Kids' Code and Cipher Book, Linnet, 1981.

■ Adaptations

What Happened in Marston was adapted for television and broadcast by American Broadcasting Company (ABC) as an "ABC Afterschool Special" under the title *The Color of Friendship; Annie on My Mind* was adapted for television and first broadcast by the British Broadcasting Corporation (BBC) in 1992.

■ Work in Progress

The Joining, a fourth volume in the "Fours Crossing" sequence.

■ Sidelights

Boston-born Nancy Garden is the author of fiction and nonfiction books for children and young adults. Her books address many difficult topics, including race issues, homosexuality, teen drug use, teen suicide, and runaways. She has also written horror fiction. Garden is sensitive to young people's point of view in a complicated and very real world. She described her thinking in her essay in *Something about the Author Autobiography Series* (*SAAS*): "I see a child walking to or from school and that triggers memories of my own childhood and questions about the child I see: What is his or her life like? Who is she/he? What is he going to do when he gets home? Is a dog waiting for her—a little brother—an ailing grandmother—piles of homework—farm chores—a beating—a special surprise?"

As a young child, Garden had a love for books and stories. Many writers influenced her, from childhood into adulthood. She recalls Rudyard Kipling's *Jungle Book* with great fondness, along with Anna Sewell's *Black Beauty,* and A. A. Milne's *Pooh* books. She sometimes ended up in trouble, misunderstood by a teacher, for being "lost in a story." Her favorite teachers, in contrast, read aloud, told stories and encouraged her imagination. She recalls listening avidly to a radio program on which children's books were read aloud; the same program once awarded her honorable mention in a book report competition. Garden also enjoyed more conventional radio programs such as *Sky King, Gene Autry,* and *Land of the Lost.* As a young adult she enjoyed and was influenced by the works of authors Ernest Hemingway, John Dos Passos, and Thomas Wolfe.

But stories were not just something that came from outside her home and family. Her father told tales about his youthful pranks, and made up stories about "Mr. Talkie"—an inept man whose clothes had to point out to their owner that he'd put them on wrong—and about the "Flounderie," a fish who talked a diner out of eating him. She also remembers her parents reading aloud to her. The sense of close and loving support she associates with her father's storytelling is borne out in a story she recounted in *SAAS:* "Dad used to tell me that a girl could do anything a boy could do, but that in order to get recognition, she had to do it twice as well. I could do anything I wanted, he'd say, if I worked hard enough at it. Those were unusually understanding and encouraging words for a man to say to his daughter in those days—in any day, perhaps!"

Garden's mother, whom the author describes as "my confidante, my rock," told stories too. Her tales were bits of household folklore, such as the mysterious noise made by a mouse trapped in a soup bowl, or the games she and her siblings played on their chicken farm. And Garden would sometimes participate as well, helping make up stories with her mother about people they saw in stores or on the streets. Her Uncle Dan, a Unitarian minister, delighted in puns and would read Kipling aloud to her and her cousins. Her Tante Anna, known as "Tanna" for ease of pronunciation, not only also read aloud to her, but required her to provide recitals of plot summaries from the movies she went to.

Other features of Garden's childhood made the impulse to live in the imagination even stronger. An only child, she was somewhat isolated, and although she made a few very close friends, they were often lost because of the frequent moves her family had to make. And illnesses—from colds and measles to scarlet fever—frequently kept her at home. At one point she even created an imaginary twin for herself. This desire to create new characters turned into a serious interest in drama and writing by the time Garden was in high school. There she was exposed to the works of Eugene O'Neill, Sean O'Casey, and other playwrights. In *SAAS* she described her feeling for acting then as "akin to what I imagine a religious vocation is like for a girl of the same age." This commitment led her to the Bachelor of Fine Arts program in the School of Dramatic Arts at Columbia University and to summer stock and off-Broadway theater. Realizing the economic realities of

Garden's "Monster Hunters" series of mystery stories feature Brian Larabee and Numbles Crane—two young sleuths who take on a number of spooky cases. (Cover illustration by Jeffrey Lindberg.)

theatrical life, she got an M.A. from Columbia Teachers College and supplemented her income with part-time teaching and office work while continuing to write. One of these jobs brought her the friendship of budding author and illustrator Barbara Seuling, with whom she collaborated in a novice try at a children's book.

The taste of writing was apparently sweet. She tried, living on her savings and the generosity of her parents, a year of freelance writing. "It was a glorious way to live," she related in *SAAS.* "I'd get up in the morning, have breakfast, go to my desk, and work." Eventually she sold her first story, to the children's magazine *Jack and Jill.* This was glorious, too, as were a couple of poetry sales, but it was not a living. She went to work for a man who called himself a literary agent (but who actually ran an editorial service), where she edited, evaluated, and even ghostwrote work by would-be writers. She later found work with Scholastic Magazines on several of their children's publications. After several years there, she returned to New England with her partner Sandra Scotti and began writing for Houghton Mifflin's text division in Boston.

By then Garden had published her first two books. "I wrote my first published book, *Berlin: City Split in Two,*

at least partly because my mother's side of the family was German (although not from Berlin)," the author once told *SATA.* Later nonfiction included the four volumes *Vampires, Werewolves, Witches,* and *Devils and Demons,* edited by her good friend Barbara Seuling, who was by then also in publishing. Garden's first novel, *What Happened in Marston,* was published around the same time as *Berlin.* Inspired by the race riots of the 1960s, when many black neighborhoods were destroyed by angry mobs, the novel looks at similarly frightening events through the eyes of a young white boy whose black best friend lives in one of the affected neighborhoods. *Marston* was later dramatized as an "ABC Afterschool Special," under the title *The Color of Friendship. The Loners,* published in 1972, "came out of interviews I did for *Junior Scholastic* magazine with teenagers who had troubles with drugs," the author related.

Garden turned to fantasy in 1981 with *Fours Crossing,* the first of a sequence of novels set in a modern-day New Hampshire town. Thirteen-year-old Melissa, whose mother has died, has just arrived in Fours Crossing to stay with her grandmother while her father travels. She soon befriends Jed, another near-orphan. It soon becomes clear that something mysterious is preventing spring from coming to the town. The two friends gradually realize that a sinister hermit is the culprit; Melissa and Jed determine to foil his plans. In "a genuinely exciting episode," according to *Horn Book* contributor Paul Heins, the two children are captured and imprisoned by the hermit. How they escape and save spring for the town is a story "likely to satisfy" most readers, as Patricia Dooley writes in *School Library Journal.*

Garden has written three more books in the "Fours Crossing" sequence. In 1983's *Watersmeet,* Jed and Melissa meet a mysterious visitor, testify at the hermit's trial, and realize that the hermit still wants to destroy the town. In *The Door Between,* published in 1987, Melissa learns more about the old hermit's bitterness and the role she must play in thwarting his evil intentions. In a forthcoming final volume entitled *The Joining,* Melissa puts the hermit to rest at last, saving the town. These sequels, like the first book, are steeped in Celtic mythology and pagan lore; Virginia Golodetz remarks in a *School Library Journal* review of *The Door Between* that "a mood of suspense and powerful magic pervades the story until almost the very end."

While she has penned fantasies such as the "Fours Crossing" books and mysteries such as her "Monster Hunters" series, Garden is also known for realistic young adult novels like *The Loners, Peace, O River,* and *Lark in the Morning.* Perhaps her best known—and most controversial—is *Annie on My Mind,* a pioneering story of two teenage girls who fall in love and come to terms with their homosexuality. Told from hindsight, while the two girls are attending college on different coasts, *Annie on My Mind* details the meeting of Annie and Liza at a New York museum and their growing love for each other. When their relationship is discovered by

NANCY GARDEN

Annie
on
My Mind

aerial fiction

Garden provides a realistic look at two girls coming to terms with their homosexuality in her young adult novel *Annie on My Mind.* **(Cover illustration by Elaine Norman.)**

school officials, it precipitates a crisis for Liza. The conclusion of the book, in which the two girls reaffirm their feelings for each other, provides a happy ending rare in books of this type for young adults. *Annie on My Mind* was dramatized by the BBC in England and first broadcast in 1992.

Many critics have recognized Garden's pioneering efforts in their positive assessments of the book. "I think the body of adolescent literature has waited for this book a long time, and it is superior to all its predecessors," Mary K. Chelton asserts in *Voice of Youth Advocates.* She adds that "the writing is clear, consistent, at times lyrical, but best of all gut-level believable." A *Bulletin for the Center of Children's Books* reviewer explains that the story is "candid, dignified, perceptive, and touching," with "strong characters" providing its focus. "By allowing readers to see Annie and Liza first as detailed, vivid characters," Roger D. Sutton observes in *School Library Journal,* Garden "gives the relationship a solid resonance that until now has been absent

from this genre." Terming *Annie on My Mind* a "significant" work, Sutton concludes that Garden raises her story above the typical teen "problem" novel "to become instead a compelling story of two real and intriguing young women."

Garden once commented that whatever the topic, "I write for young people because I like them, and because I think they are important. Children's books can be mind-stretchers and imagination-ticklers and builders of good taste in a way that adult books cannot, because young people usually come to books with more open minds. It's exciting to be able to contribute to that in a small way." When Garden offers advice to young writers, her enthusiasm is likewise evident. She urges them to work diligently at something she considers supremely satisfying, the very best kind of fun. And like a kid at the playground who wants to play just a little more, no matter how late it gets, she always wants to write another book. As she concludes in *SAAS:* "I keep feeling there's a book just out of reach, no matter how many I write."

■ Works Cited

Review of *Annie on My Mind, Bulletin of the Center for Children's Books,* December, 1982, p. 66.

Chelton, Mary K., review of *Annie on My Mind, Voice of Youth Advocates,* August, 1982, p. 30.

Dooley, Patricia, review of *Fours Crossing, School Library Journal,* May, 1981, p. 72.

Garden, Nancy, essay in *Something about the Author Autobiography Series,* Volume 8, Gale, 1989.

Golodetz, Virginia, review of *The Door Between, School Library Journal,* December, 1987, pp. 99-100.

Heins, Paul, review of *Fours Crossing, Horn Book,* August, 1981, p. 431.

Sutton, Roger D., review of *Annie on My Mind, School Library Journal,* August, 1982, p. 125.

■ For More Information See

PERIODICALS

Bulletin of the Center for Children's Books, May, 1981, p. 170; November, 1983, p. 48; October, 1987, p. 27.

Horn Book, December, 1983, p. 580.

School Library Journal, September, 1983, p. 134; November, 1987, p. 104.

Voice of Youth Advocates, February, 1984, p. 338.

—*Sketch by Joseph O. Aimone*

*   *   *

GHAN, Linda (R.) 1947-

■ Personal

Born January 9, 1947, in Winnipeg, Manitoba, Canada; daughter of Sydney (an owner of a general store and trailer park) and Esther (a public school teacher and piano teacher; maiden name, Hoffer) Ghan. *Education:* University of Saskatchewan, Saskatoon, B.A. (literature and fine arts), 1968, B.A. (literature; with honors), 1969; University of Saskatchewan, Regina, M.A., 1971; Concordia University, Montreal, Quebec, TESL (Teaching of English as a Second Language) Certificate, 1978; doctoral study at University of Montreal, 1990—. *Religion:* Jewish. *Hobbies and other interests:* Swimming, scuba diving, cross-country skiing, cycling, yoga, theatre, film, traveling.

■ Addresses

Home—5368 Hutchison, Montreal, Quebec, Canada H2V 4B3. *Office*—Concordia University, 1455 de Raisonneuve Blvd. W., Montreal, Quebec, Canada H3G 1M8.

■ Career

University of Regina, Regina, Saskatchewan, instructor in English, 1969-70; Ocho Rios Secondary School, Ocho Rios, St. Ann, Jamaica, instructor, 1971-72; St. Joseph's Teachers College, Kingston, Jamaica, instructor, 1973-76; Concordia University, Montreal, Quebec, instructor in TESL department, 1976-79, instructor in creative writing, 1979-93. *Daily News,* Kingston, feature writer, 1975-76; CINQ-FM Radio, Montreal, producer and host of "Art and Eggs" (weekly arts program), 1979-82.

LINDA GHAN

Playwrights' Workshop, Montreal, member of board, 1983-87; Black Theatre Workshop, Montreal, member of board, 1987-93.

■ Awards, Honors

Second prize winner, Chatelaine Fiction Contest, 1979, for "The Conversion"; honourable mention, Flare Humour Contest, 1980, for "A Touch of Nordic Madness"; prize winner, Quebec Multi-Cultural Theatre Festival, 1982, for *Coldsnap;* Canada Council Explorations grant, 1983, for *A Gift of Sky;* Concordia Advancement of Scholarly Activity (CASA) grant, Concordia University, 1988; Canadian Children's Book Centre Choice Award, 1991, for *Muhla the Fair One.*

■ Writings

FOR CHILDREN

Muhla the Fair One, Nuage Press, 1991.

Also author of "Anancy" (script), for JTV in Kingston, Jamaica, 1974-75; author of "Where's Zelda?," published in *Robin Run,* Gage Publishing, Ltd., 1980; and *Beauty and the Beast* (play), produced in Montreal schools, 1985.

FOR ADULTS

Coldsnap (play), produced in Edmonton, Alberta, at Rice Theatre, 1980, later in Montreal, Quebec, at Centaur Theatre, 1985.
Toros' Daughter (play), produced in Montreal, by Playwrights' Workshop, 1985.
O'Hara, A Coming of Age (play), produced by Canadian Broadcasting Company (CBC) Radio, 1986.
A Gift of Sky (novel), Prairie Books, 1988.
Waiting for David in Saudi Arabia (play), produced in Montreal, by Generic Theatre, 1993.

Also author of "The Conversion," published in *Between Two Worlds,* 1983. Contributor to periodicals, including *Flare* and *Commonwealth.*

■ Work in Progress

Colours of the Moon (a novel); various short stories.

■ Sidelights

Linda Ghan has been telling stories and writing for most of her life. "I grew up in Hoffer, a hamlet in the midwest (southern Saskatchewan), just seven miles north of the American border," she told *SATA.* "My father had the general store which sold everything from blue jeans to watermelon to chicken feed. Growing up with the silence and space was important to me: I believe it is the reason I write." By the time she was ten, she was writing for the children's page of *Western Producer* under the pen name Jenny Wren. In the seventh grade, Ghan and two other students started a newspaper, and in high school, she wrote and edited another school paper as well as the school yearbook.

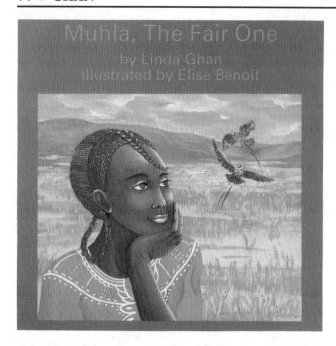

Based on a West African folktale, *Muhla, the Fair One* was first written by Ghan as a play that would teach black Canadian students about their heritage. (Cover illustration by Elise Benoit.)

During her college years, the content of Ghan's writing changed. She explained: "When I went to university, I wrote 'political stuff'—articles about the racism in Saskatoon, for instance. In Saskatoon, a city in northern Saskatchewan, there were some students—not many, but some—from Africa, India, etc., who found it difficult to rent apartments because of their skin color. After that, I spent a summer living on an Indian Reserve, and because I am dark and in the summer look like an Indian, I had the experience of being treated like one—ignored or mistreated."

When Ghan went to Jamaica to teach, she began to write again. One of her stories, "Where's Zelda," about "a little girl from Saskatchewan who suddenly finds herself in Jamaica talking to Mule, Frog, and Doctor Bird," was published in a fourth-grade reader that is still being used in schools in Canada. Since then, Ghan has been writing for both adults and children. She continued: "I've written radio drama, and adult and children's theatre; I've had one novel published, and most recently, another children's story published—*Muhla the Fair One.*

Ghan described this story for *SATA:* "*Muhla the Fair One* was first written as a children's play that was performed in Montreal Schools by Black Theatre Workshop. It is an adaptation of a West African folktale. The cast was young black actors, and a large percentage of the students in the schools were West Indian immigrants. There is very little writing in Canada that speaks to them and tells them how beautiful they are.

"I learned a lot from the research for *A Gift of Sky, Muhla the Fair One,* and *Colours of the Moon.* I love learning, and it is one of the aspects of writing—the research—that I particularly enjoy. However, I am also working on some stories which do not require research, and it is a lot of fun, too. I feel like I'm on holiday!"

In 1993, Ghan was working on her Ph.D. at the University of Montreal, Quebec, and continuing work on *Colours of the Moon.* She told *SATA:* "I live in a city now—Montreal. I believe, though, that my heart is with the geography of the prairie, with the wide skies and the space."

*   *   *

GOULD, Jean R(osalind) 1909(?)-1993

OBITUARY NOTICE—See index for *SATA* sketch: Born May 25, 1909 (some sources say 1919), in Greenville, OH; died of cancer of the jaw, February 8, 1993, in Perrysburg, OH. Editor and writer. Gould received her undergraduate degree from the University of Toledo and went on to write literary biographies for young readers on such notables as novelist Herman Melville and black poet Paul Laurence Dunbar. After traveling to New York City in the early 1950s, she worked as an editor and writer at the Amalgamated Clothing Workers Union. In the 1960s she began a string of biographies for adults, including *The Story of F. D. R.'s Conquest of Polio,* which concerns President Franklin Delano Roosevelt, *Winslow Homer: A Portrait, Robert Frost: The Aim Was Song,* and *The Poet and Her Book: A Biography of Edna St. Vincent Millay.* She was nominated for a National Book Award in 1975 for *Amy: The World of Amy Lowell and the Imagist Movement.*

OBITUARIES AND OTHER SOURCES:

BOOKS

The Writers Directory: 1990-1992, St. James Press, 1990.

PERIODICALS

New York Times, February 12, 1993, p. B7.
School Library Journal, April, 1993, p. 24

*   *   *

GRANT, Cynthia D. 1950-

■ Personal

Born November 23, 1950, in Brockton, MA; daughter of Robert C. and Jacqueline (Ford) Grant; married Daniel Heatley (marriage ended); married Erik Neel, 1988; children: (first marriage) Morgan; (second marriage) Forest. *Education:* Attended high school in Palo Alto, CA.

■ Addresses

Home—Box 95, Cloverdale, CA, 95425.

CYNTHIA D. GRANT

■ Career

Writer, 1974—.

■ Awards, Honors

Annual book award from Woodward Park School, 1981, for *Joshua Fortune;* Best Book of the Year award, Michigan Library Association's Young Adult Caucus, 1990, PEN/Norma Klein award, 1991, and Author Day Award, Detroit Public Library, 1992, all for *Phoenix Rising.*

■ Writings

JUVENILE

Joshua Fortune, Atheneum, 1980.
Summer Home, Atheneum, 1981.

YOUNG ADULT

Big Time, Atheneum, 1982.
Hard Love, Atheneum, 1983.
Kumquat May, I'll Always Love You, Atheneum, 1986.
Phoenix Rising; or, How to Survive Your Life, Atheneum, 1989.
Keep Laughing, Atheneum, 1991.
Shadow Man, Atheneum, 1992.
Uncle Vampire, Atheneum, 1993.

■ Work in Progress

Another young-adult novel, *Mary Wolf.*

■ Sidelights

Cynthia D. Grant told *SATA:* "As a child, I was in love with the magic of words, their power to create worlds on paper. Childhood is a vivid time of intensely felt emotions and experiences. Now I write what I feel strongly about.

"One reason I write for teenagers is those years remain so vivid in my mind. Junior high and high school were difficult times. The kids were so mean to each other! If you stuck out in any way, by being especially smart, or handicapped, or saddled with a hideous home permanent, you were picked on until you bled to death of a thousand tiny cuts. Kids who were picked on took it out on smaller kids. Hurt people hurt people—and themselves. Is this a system?

"In my writing I try to reach out to readers and let them know that they are not alone; that, unique as each of us is, we all feel lonely and scared and confused sometimes. And to say, in the words of an anonymous author: Be kind; everyone you meet is fighting a hard battle."

One of the hallmarks of Grant's work is her use of non-stereotypical characters. In the *School Library Journal,* Steve Matthews writes about the people in *Joshua Fortune* as "a cast of well-drawn and often bizarre characters." Some of them are depicted as offspring of the Haight-Ashbury flower children of the late 1960s. Josh, the main character, is adjusting to life in a new town, a new man in his mother's life, and his two new friends who are considered odd characters. The *Bulletin of the Center for Children's Books* says that, "in fact, everybody in the story is an odd character."

One of the colorful characters in *Summer Home* is Baby Boris Schmaltzman, a lazy, obnoxious, oversized fifteen-year-old bully, who is "built like a Frigidaire." Another is a social outcast and owner of a "Junkarama" who is the best friend of the main character, Max. Still another is the elderly female author with gleaming eyes who wrote a dime-store detective novel that has gone out of print. This novel and its author become Max's inspiration, helping him to overcome his fear of water, open communications with his adolescent sister, and deal with Baby Boris.

Gabriel McCloud, a well-liked eighteen-year-old who is an alcoholic high-school drop-out and member of a dysfunctional family, is the main character in Grant's book *Shadow Man.* Gabe is killed before the book begins, when he drives his pickup truck into a tree. As the plot develops, interior monologues by the survivors, in addition to excerpts from Gabe's high-school journal, show readers a bright student, the victim of an abusive background, who might have overcome the consequences of his past had he been given the chance. Gary Young in *Booklist* says that Gabe's suicide transforms the lives of those he leaves behind and "moves the mood from sadness to strength."

Grant features unusual characters in her other books as well. Missy is a nine-year-old dreaming of show business in *Big Time,* urged on by an ambitious, pushy stage mother. Seventeen-year-old Stephen, in *Hard Love,* thinks he is in love with an older woman and has as a best friend a troubled, complex young man named Paulie. Paulie is portrayed as losing touch with reality and headed for self-destruction. In *Kumquat May, I'll Always Love You* Livvy, a high-school senior, lives alone in a big isolated house for two years by cleverly covering up her mother's absence. Seventeen-year-old Jesse, torn by tragedy, filled with grief, and haunted by nightmares, finds some help in the diary of her sister, Helen, a teenager who died from cancer, in *Phoenix Rising; or, How To Survive Your Life.*

Even though Grant's books often deal with serious issues, she uses humor to make a point. In *Keep Laughing* Shep, whose comedian father left home when the boy was only a toddler, has seen more of his dad on TV than he has in real life; he jokes that he had long thought his father was only six inches tall. Carol Shama in *Voice of Youth Advocates* reports that "*Keep Laughing* is not a funny book." Over the course of the story Shep learns that his father is more interested in his own life and gratification than in him. Shep covers the hurt and anger he feels by his use of bitter humor. Debra S. Gold reports in the *School Library Journal,* "With its well-mixed balance of humor and serious contemplation, this title handles contemporary issues in a fresh, candid voice."

In *Kumquat May, I'll Always Love You* humor and pathos are well mixed as Livvy, often lonesome living in a house all alone, misses her mother and does some very funny things to make people believe her mother still lives there. One of the schemes Livvy employs is buying her mother's Harlequin romances and favorite lipsticks. The *Bulletin of the Center For Children's Books* says, "The plot is preposterous but rendered totally entertaining by a humorous sense of itself: a witty style ... and plenty of quirky caricatures to lift the underlying sadness of Livvy's loss of family."

Grant told *SATA* that "in *Phoenix Rising,* Helen says, 'I'd like to be able to make readers laugh and cry; to reach across the page and say, Hey, we're alive! I want to show the courage of fathers and mothers who bring forth babies who brave the maze of childhood; learning to crawl, standing up, oops, falling, starting over, getting up, going on, finding love, losing hope, enduring pain and disappointment; believing that happiness is just around the corner, if we don't give up, if we keep moving forward. There is so much I want to say.' She speaks for me."

■ Works Cited

Gold, Debra S., review of *Keep Laughing, School Library Journal,* September, 1991, pp. 278, 281.

Review of *Joshua Fortune, Bulletin of the Center for Children's Books,* January, 1981, p. 93.
Review of *Kumquat May, I'll Always Love You, Bulletin of the Center for Children's Books,* September, 1986, p. 7.
Matthews, Steve, review of *Joshua Fortune, School Library Journal,* November, 1980, pp. 85-86.
Shama, Carol, review of *Keep Laughing, Voice of Youth Advocates,* February, 1992, pp. 370-71.
Young, Gary, review of *Shadow Man, Booklist,* November 1, 1992, p. 504.

■ For More Information See

PERIODICALS

Bulletin of the Center for Children's Books, April, 1982, p. 148; December, 1983, p. 67; February, 1989, p. 147.
Children's Book Review Service, July, 1982, p. 127; January, 1984, p. 52.
Kirkus Reviews, November 1, 1991, p. 1402; November 1, 1992, p. 1375.
Kliatt, winter, 1985, p. 10.

In this young adult novel by Grant, the grief of losing her sister Helen to cancer causes nightmares and other troubles in teen-age Jessie, who eventually finds solace in Helen's diary. (Cover illustration by Stephen Marchesi.)

Publishers Weekly, June 27, 1986, p. 95; February 10, 1989, p. 73; October 11, 1991, p. 64; November 1, 1991, p. 1402.

School Library Journal, September, 1981, p. 125; April, 1982, p. 82; October, 1983, p. 168; May, 1986, pp. 103-4; February, 1989, p. 100; October, 1992, p. 140.

Voice of Youth Advocates, April, 1982, p. 34; August/October, 1986, pp. 142, 144; June, 1989, p. 101.

*   *   *

GREAVES, Nick 1955-

■ Personal

Born July 10, 1955, in Huddersfield, England; son of Roland Meynell (an antiques dealer) and Gwendoline (Ritchie) Greaves; married Janet Phillipa Slack (marriage ended); married Stephanie Anne Weedon (a manager at an employment agency), July 20, 1990; children: (first marriage) Douglas. *Education:* Attended University of Aston, 1974-76. *Politics:* Conservative. *Religion:* Atheist.

■ Addresses

Home—9 Caithness Rd., Hillside, Bulawayo, Zimbabwe. *Office*—L&L Mining & Industrial Suppliers, 136A Moyo St., Bulawayo, Zimbabwe.

■ Career

Anglo American Corp., Botswana, field geologist, 1976-80; Retreatments Group, East Transvaal, Zimbabwe, contracts manager, 1980-83; O. Connoly & Co., Bulawayo, Zimbabwe, sales manager, 1983-88; L&L Mining & Industrial Suppliers, Bulawayo, administrative manager, 1988—. *Member:* Wildlife Society of Zimbabwe (coordinator of Hwange Game Count, 1987-89), Zimbabwe Falconers Club (treasurer, 1982—).

■ Writings

When Hippo Was Hairy and Other Tales from Africa, illustrated by Rod Clement, Lutterworth, 1988.
When Lion Could Fly and More Tales from Africa, illustrated by Clement, Barron's, 1993.

■ Adaptations

When Hippo Was Hairy was recorded on audio cassette by The Nature Company of California.

■ Work in Progress

Stories from the Great Turtle Island; Hwange: Retreat of the Elephants; wildlife folklore of Australia/New Zealand, Asia, and Europe.

■ Sidelights

Nick Greaves wrote *When Hippo Was Hairy* when he noted the lack of children's stories relating to African wildlife and nature. "Unfortunately, the Africa of old is fast disappearing," Greaves told *SATA.* "Most black youngsters either are urbanized or grow up in communities devoid of wildlife and, in some cases, of vegetation. It is my hope that these books will encourage African youngsters to want to see the animals of their traditional stories and ensure the animals' existence into a sometimes bleak looking future. If any kid, black or white, has been encouraged to take an active role in conservation academically or practically as a result of reading my books, I will feel I have contributed something useful to the future of Africa's, and maybe the world's, wildlife."

■ For More Information See

PERIODICALS

Junior Bookshelf, December, 1988, p. 290.
School Library Journal, February, 1989, p. 94.

*   *   *

GREENLEE, Sharon 1935-

■ Personal

Born January 12, 1935, in Des Moines, IA; daughter of Gordon and Lillian (maiden name, Reynolds) Bittle; married second husband, Richard Greenlee (a school administrator), August, 1973; children: (first marriage) David, Kimberly, Julie Ann, Kathleen. *Education:* Attended Simpson College, 1953-54; Drake University, B.S., 1966, M.S., 1973; postgraduate work at University of Nebraska at Kearney, 1982. *Religion:* "Baptized and raised a Lutheran. Now member of Episcopal Church." *Hobbies and other interests:* Cross-country skiing, mountain hiking, nature photography, and reading.

■ Addresses

Home and office—P.O. Box 104, Centennial, WY 82055.

■ Career

University of Wyoming, Laramie, WY, instructor, 1985—. Freelance consultant, conducts workshops to develop self-esteem, communication and thinking skills, and creativity, 1983—; private counselor, 1984—. Taught elementary school for several years. *Member:* Zonta International, PEO (continuing education chair), Phi Delta Kappa, Delta Kappa Gamma (vice-president), Alpha Delta Kappa.

■ Writings

When Someone Dies, Peachtree, 1992.

Also author of *Images of Me: A Guide for Those Who Work with Pre-School Age Children,* self-published.

■ Work in Progress

Self-Esteem, Communication and High-level Thinking Skills, for Allyn and Bacon; and *Ways to Help Yourself and Others, When Someone Dies*. Researching children and grief and adults with unresolved childhood grief.

■ Sidelights

Sharon Greenlee told *SATA:* "It's amazing that my first publication should be a book of comfort about death, as I avoided everything surrounding the subject, including the grieving process, after the death of my mother when I was eleven.

"It wasn't until the sudden and tragic deaths of my son and step-son that I began the long and lonely pilgrimage into my own past regarding grief and loss. It took me half a lifetime of burying feelings and emotions before I could finally come to grips with my own sorrow and the feelings I had at the time of my mother's death. The journey was slow and painful and had it not been for my son's three-year-old daughter, Anna, and her grief over the loss of her daddy, I might never have made the first step."

"Anna's grief was heartbreaking to witness. She was quiet and withdrawn, and whenever David's name was mentioned, she would experience and speak of painful stomach aches. This reminded me of my own childhood attempts to bury my sorrow, mainly because I didn't have anyone who knew how to encourage me to express it. I asked Anna to tell me everything she remembered about her daddy and recorded her story word for word in an attempt to help her give voice to the feelings and emotions that were held hostage in her young mind.

"*When Someone Dies* expresses the feelings and emotions of the child who was finally heard, and the wisdom of the adult that emerged as the result of the experience."

*   *   *

GRIEGO, Tony A. 1955-

■ Personal

Born July 10, 1955 in Seattle, WA; son of Leonard (a teacher) and Manuelita Griego (a homemaker); married Colleen C. (a homemaker), March 22, 1985; children: Nancy Lynn. *Education:* Attended Long Beach State University; San Diego State University, B.F.A. *Religion:* Catholic. *Hobbies and other interests:* Reading, movies, World War II history.

■ Addresses

Home—4906 West 57th Terrace, Roeland Park, KS 66205. *Office*—Hallmark Cards, 2501 McGee, Kansas City, MO 64141.

■ Career

Artist, Hallmark Card Co., Kansas City, MO, 1982-84, 1990—; freelance illustrator.

■ Illustrator

C. W. Hunter, *Green Gourd: A North Carolina Folktale*, Putnam Publishing Group, 1992.

■ Sidelights

"I started drawing when I was a little kid," Tony Griego told *SATA*. "My uncle gave me a cartoon book with a pad, a pencil and a kneaded eraser. I drew a caricature of Bob Hope and was astonished at how well it came out." Griego was greatly influenced by the humor and sarcasm he found in the comics he read as a child, including *Marvel* comics, *Spiderman* and *The Hulk*—and especially *Peanuts*. "I cut them out of the paper and saved them in a notebook," he said.

Griego loves his job illustrating greeting cards for Hallmark. "My drawing has always been whimsical and humorous," he stated. "I tried to draw in a realistic way once and it made me nervous. Humor is my bread and butter.

"Finding the time to do *The Green Gourd* was difficult. I would like to do more children's books. I want to illustrate a book that I would consider good enough to buy and add to my collection of favorite books."*

*   *   *

GROVES, Seli

■ Personal

Born in Brooklyn, New York; daughter of Philip (a writer) and Florence (a musician; maiden name, Seligman) Steinberg; married Freddy Groves (died September 9, 1991); children: Linda Carol Groth (stepdaughter). *Education:* Hunter College, A.B. *Politics:* Liberal.

■ Addresses

Agent—Dorothy Stearn, 500 E. 77th, New York, NY, 10021.

■ Career

Developed prototype for first soap magazine later called *Daytime TV;* worked as a contributing editor for *Soap Opera Digest*, media editor for *Youngperson*, London editor for *16*, and editor for *VIBES, Movie Mirror*, and *America's Music;* editor for *Health Beat*, Williams Publishing, London, England; creator and editor of *Soap Beat, Weekday TV, Fun Fair*, and *Young Hollywood;* King Features Weekly Service, columnist on entertainment, television, medical and nutrition news, working women, seniors, and veterans; columnist for *Young Miss;* WGCH, Greenwich, CT, producer and

HELEN JILL FLETCHER AND SELI GROVES

This book by Groves provides readers with a number of fun ways to recycle and reuse paper products—instead of putting them in landfills.

host of *Seli on the Telly.* Curator of "Summer of Soaps—60 Years of Soap Operas," Chicago Museum of Broadcast Communications, 1991. Lecturer. Contributor to the creation of "Stage II," a trivia game for Hasbro. *Member:* Council of Writers Organizations (former vice president); American Medical Writers Association, American Society of Journalists and Authors, Mystery Writers of America, Society of Children's Book Writers, American Society of Journalists and Authors (former vice president), Press Women of New York (former president), Newswomen of New York, New York Academy of Sciences, Hollywood Women's Press Club (former secretary).

■ Writings

NON-FICTION FOR YOUNG ADULTS

(With Joanna Randolph Rott) *How in the World Do We Recycle Glass?,* Millbrook Press, 1992.
(With Helen Jill Fletcher) *How in the World Do We Recycle Paper?,* Millbrook Press, 1992.

NON-FICTION FOR ADULTS

(With the editors of the Associated Press and Robert Waldron) *Soaps: A Pictorial History of America's Daytime Dramas,* Contemporary Books, 1983.
(With Dian Dincin Buchman) *The Writer's Digest Guide to Manuscript Formats,* Writer's Digest Books, 1987.

Also coauthor of *50 Blinks that Changed the World.* Ghost writer of publications, including *Socialism and Women,* 1974. Contributor to *Careers in Art;* contributor of entries on international law, maritime law, the British legal system, and political science to *Encyclopedia Britannica.* Contributor to *Celebrity Plus* magazine.

■ Work in Progress

A mystery novel; a book written with a New York-based fitness trainer; a biography written with a widow of a Metropolitan Opera singer.

■ Sidelights

Seli Groves began writing at an early age. She told *SATA:* "My first 'sold' piece to a publication for young people was during my elementary school years when I contributed a poem to *Calling All Girls,* the predecessor to *Young Miss* which, itself, is the predecessor of *YM.* The poem came out of an afternoon with my father at Coney Island, where we lived for a year before he died. It was a cold autumn day, and we looked at the sea gulls riding the gray-white waves. I recall saying that if I could have 'miracle eyes' (I remember using that term) then I could see Europe from where we were standing. He told me that even with 'miracle eyes,' I'd have to keep moving closer to Europe because of the way the earth curves at the farthest end of our sight line. I wrote the poem that night—or at least, it was within several days of that wonderful afternoon. I don't recall it entirely, but it started with 'As I stand on familiar sands / Trying to look out to foreign lands / I know that I'll never see too far, / Unless I leave where I am and go to where they are.' My dad died the following spring, but he lived long enough to see my poem in print.

"Over the years, I've done a great many things: I studied drama at the Dramatic Workshop—and did a few workshop productions; I worked in advertising; I was a patent law researcher; I was active in social causes including civil rights and anti-Vietnam war protests. When my late husband and I lived in Santa Monica, we were part of a group that organized a boycott of companies that provided various war materials, including napalm. While we lived in London for two years, I joined a group protesting the Royal Society to Prevent Cruelty to Animals because of evidence that animals were being sold to labs by the society and otherwise abused. Often, when I'd be asked why I was an activist for this or that cause, I'd give the usual reasons such as my belief in justice and the rightness of cause, etc. But part of me reflected back on that time with my dad and the fact that it's not enough just to be an observer: to get somewhere, you have to move.

"As for my interest in writing for children, that, too, comes out of my relationship with both my parents. Regardless of whatever other gift they might have given me at any time, they always included a book. My mother got me my own library card when I was six. I read all the children's books at the Brooklyn Public Library in Williamsburgh, Brooklyn, and my parents signed to be responsible for any books I would take out from the adult collection. Although I could still continue to borrow books from that library for a while, I remember how sad I felt when there were no more children's books on the shelf for me. I wouldn't want any other child to ever have to feel the same."

* * *

GUTMAN, Dan 1955-

■ Personal

Born October 19, 1955, in New York, NY; son of Sidney J. Gutman (in advertising) and Adeline Berlin (a homemaker; maiden name, Wernick); married Nina Wallace (an illustrator), September 25, 1983; children: Sam. *Education:* Rutgers University, B.A., 1977, conducted graduate work at Rutgers University's Institute for Cognitive Studies. *Hobbies and other interests:* Travel, history, technology, sports, pop culture, movies.

■ Addresses

Home and office—224 Euclid Ave., Haddonfield, NJ 08033. *Agent*—Liza P. Voges, Kirchoff/Wohlberg Inc., 866 United Nations Plaza, Suite 525, New York, NY 10017.

■ Career

Video Review Publications, coeditor of *Electronic Fun* (magazine), 1982-83; Carnegie Publications, founder and editor in chief of *Computer Games* (magazine), 1983-84; freelance writer, 1984—. *Member:* National Writer's Union, Society for American Baseball Research.

■ Writings

FOR CHILDREN

Baseball's Biggest Bloopers: The Games That Got Away, Viking Children's Books, 1993.
Baseball's Greatest Games, Viking Children's Books, 1994.
Baseball's Greatest World Series, Viking Children's Books, 1994.

FOR ADULTS

The Greatest Games, Compute Books, 1984.
I Didn't Know You Could Do THAT with a Computer!, Compute Books, 1986.
(With Douglas Herrmann) *Super Memory,* Rodale, 1990.
It Ain't Cheatin' If You Don't Get Caught, Penguin, 1990.
Baseball Babylon, Penguin, 1992.
Banana Bats and Ding Dong Balls: A Century of Baseball Invention, Macmillan, 1994.

Dan Gutman with wife Nina and son Sam.

Also author of the syndicated newspaper column "I Didn't Know You Could Do THAT With a Computer!," 1983-92, and a monthly column in *Success.* Contributor to periodicals, including *Esquire, Discover,* and *Science Digest.*

■ Work in Progress

They Came from Centerfield, a children's book, for Scholastic, publication expected in 1995; collaborating with a group of third graders on a baseball book.

■ Sidelights

Dan Gutman told *SATA:* "As a kid, I was a skinny, nerdy right fielder for the Galante Giants, a little league team sponsored by the Galante Funeral Home in Newark, New Jersey. I was terrible, but I loved baseball. It's a real thrill to be making a living writing about the game today.

"What really turns me on is to dig into old newspapers to research classic ballgames, and then re-create them so the readers feel like they're sitting in the stands watching.

"I know that boys are often reluctant to read (I sure was). My hope is that they'll pick up my books because they like baseball and then look up hours later to realize they've been *reading* the whole time. That would give me a lot of satisfaction.

"In addition to my writing career, I give talks in schools in which I use baseball to get kids interested in reading and writing."

H

HALL, Elizabeth 1929-

■ Personal

Born September 17, 1929, in Bakersfield, CA; daughter of Edward Earl (an accountant) and Ethel Mae (maiden name, Butner) Hall; married Fred Roy Mason (a teacher), 1946 (divorced, 1966); married Scott O'Dell (a writer), 1967 (died October 15, 1989); children: (first marriage) Susan Elizabeth, David Frederic. *Education:* Bakersfield College, A.A., 1947; Fresno State College (now California State University, Fresno), A.B. (with highest honors), 1962, post graduate studies, 1963-65. *Politics:* Democrat. *Religion:* Episcopalian. *Hobbies and other interests:* Snorkeling, traveling, reading, "playing with my dog Nylak, a Siberian husky."

■ Addresses

Home and office—Make Peace Hill, Box 4, Waccabuc, NY 10597. *Agent*—Dorothy Markinko, McIntosh & Otis, 310 Madison, New York, NY, 10017.

■ Career

Shafter Branch Library, Shafter, CA, librarian, 1958-66; University of California, Irvine, librarian, 1966-67; *Psychology Today,* Del Mar, CA, associate editor, 1967-68, assistant managing editor, 1968-72, managing editor, 1972-75, managing editor in New York City, 1975-76; Harcourt, Brace, Jovanovich, Inc., New York City, editor of *Human Nature,* 1976-79, vice-president of Human Nature Corporation, 1976—; writer and behavioral science journalist, 1979—. Consultant in human sciences for Giunti Gruppo Editoriale, Florence, Italy, 1984-91. Appeared in the 1972 CRM Films production, *A Conversation With B. F. Skinner,* and planned, edited, and appeared in series of nine films produced by BNA Films, including *The Manager as Entrepreneur, The Innovative Organization, Social Needs as Business Opportunities,* and *Coping with Technological Change. Member:* International Dickens Fellowship, Authors Guild, Authors League of America, Society for Research

Elizabeth Hall with her late husband, Scott O'Dell

in Child Development, Gerontological Society of America, Textbook Author's Association.

■ Awards, Honors

National Merit Award honorable mention, American Psychological Foundation, 1974, for *Why We Do What We Do,* and 1976, for *From Pigeons to People;* ALA Notable Book for young adults, American Library Association, for *Possible Impossibilities: A Look at Parapsychology;* notable children's trade book in the field of social studies, National Council for Social Studies, for *Thunder Rolling in the Mountains.*

■ Writings

Voltaire's Micromegas, Golden Gate Press, 1967.
Phoebe Snow, Houghton Mifflin, 1968.
Stand Up, Lucy!, Houghton Mifflin, 1971.

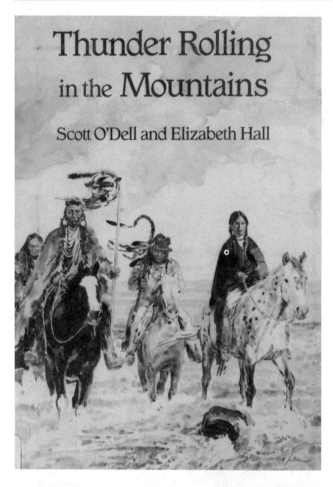

Thunder Rolling in the Mountains

Scott O'Dell and Elizabeth Hall

The fate of the Nez Perce tribe, who lose their fight to remain on their native land, is recounted through the eyes of the chief's daughter, Sound of Running Feet, in this historical novel by Hall. (Cover illustration by Ted Lewin.)

Why We Do What We Do: A Look at Psychology, Houghton Mifflin, 1973.

From Pigeons to People: A Look at Behavior Shaping, Houghton Mifflin, 1975.

(Editor) *Developmental Psychology Today,* 2nd edition, CRM Books, 1975, 3rd edition (with Robert E. Schell), 1979, 4th edition, 1983, 5th edition, (with Lois Hoffman and Scott Paris), McGraw-Hill, 1988, 6th edition, (with Hoffman and Paris), 1994.

Possible Impossibilities: A Look at Parapsychology, Houghton Mifflin, 1977.

(With Michael Lamb and Marion Perlmutter) *Child Psychology Today,* Random House, 1982, 2nd edition, 1986.

(Co-author) *Psychology Today: An Introduction,* 5th edition, Random House, 1983, 6th edition, 1986, 7th edition, (with Richard Bootzin, Gordon Bower, and Jennifer Crocker), 1991.

(With Ray Rosen) *Sexuality,* Random House, 1984.

(With Perlmutter) *Adult Development and Aging,* Wiley, 1985, 2nd edition, 1990.

(Editor) *Principles of Psychology Today,* Random House, 1987.

(With John Kotre) *Seasons of Life,* Little, Brown, 1990.

(With husband Scott O'Dell) *Thunder Rolling in Mountains,* Houghton Mifflin, 1992.

Contributor to *Everywoman's Emotional Well-being,* edited by Carol Tavris, Doubleday, 1986. Also contributor to numerous periodicals including *Psychology Today* and *America Illustrated.*

■ Work in Progress

Venus Among the Fishes, a novel for children begun in collaboration with her late husband Scott O'Dell.

■ Sidelights

"Since infancy, I have moved within a world of books," Elizabeth Hall told *SATA.* "Both my grandparents were librarians, and since we were a three generation family, I was exposed to print at a tender age. Each evening I sat on a grandparent's lap during the ritual reading of the evening paper, and by the age of 18 months, I had learned my letters from the headlines. This was during the Great Depression, and so it is no wonder that the first word I learned to spell was CAPONE, the last name of the notorious gangster whose exploits filled the news.

"Once I had unlocked the gates of print, I read incessantly, This happened before I was old enough to go to school and created a problem for my elementary school teachers, who kept shoving me through the grades, a semester at a time. As a result, I started college a few weeks before my sixteenth birthday.

"When I met Scott O'Dell, I was librarian in a small agricultural town in central California, Scott was convinced that I should write, and my first two books were on topics he suggested. His writings inspired my own, and I embarked on a 23-year apprenticeship with a master writer, which consisted of sharing his research, talking continually about works in progress, and typing (later entering on a computer) his handwritten manuscripts.

"And so, of all the books I have written, *Thunder Rolling in the Mountains* has given me the most pleasure. Together Scott and I followed the trail taken in 1877 by Chief Joseph's band of Nez Perce on their flight from the U.S. Army. We drove from Oregon to Bear Paws, Montana, stopping at the site of each battle, reading the accounts collected from the Nez Perce and from U.S. soldiers. After Scott's death, when I picked up the uncompleted manuscript, the story seemed to write itself.

"Our posthumous collaboration continues. At present, I am working on an unusual story that Scott began some months before his death, but put aside to return to the Chief Joseph story. This tale, narrated by a dolphin, was inspired by my swim with dolphins at Hawk's Cay, Florida. Scott was entranced by the dolphins and interrupted his work to begin spinning their story. My own research for the book has given me the opportunity to study marine biology, snorkel to my heart's content, and swim many times with the dolphins in an unstructured setting."

*   *   *

HAMILTON, Gail
See CORCORAN, Barbara

*   *   *

HANN, Judith 1942-

■ Personal

Born September 8, 1942, in Derby, England; daughter of Ralph and Connie Hann; married John Exelly (a journalist), October 17, 1964; children: Jake, Daniel. *Education:* Durham University, B.Sc., 1964. *Hobbies and other interests:* Walking, gardening, food, travel.

■ Addresses

Home—Kensington House, Richmond Way, London W14 0AX, England.

■ Career

Writer. Journalist for Westminster Press, beginning in mid-1960s; free-lance journalist; British Broadcasting Corporation (BBC), London, England, presenter of *Tomorrow's World*, 1974-94.

JUDITH HANN

■ Awards, Honors

Two-time recipient of the Glaxo Science Writers Award.

■ Writings

But What about the Children?: A Working Parents' Guide to Child Care, Bodley Head, 1976.
The Family Scientist, Macdonald & Jane's, 1980.
The Perfect Baby?, Weidenfield & Nicolson, 1982.
The Food of Love, Partridge Press, 1987.
How Science Works: One Hundred Ways Parents and Kids Can Share the Secrets of Science, Reader's Digest Association, 1991.

Also author of *Judith Hann's Total Health Plan*, 1984, revised edition, 1986.

■ Sidelights

Judith Hann began her writing career as a journalist, and in five years as science columnist with Westminster Press, she established a reputation for presenting sometimes confusing scientific theories and issues in a clear, easily understood manner. After receiving monetary awards for her journalism, Hann was free to pursue other book-length writing projects. She described her first book, 1976's *But What about the Children?: A Working Parents' Guide to Child Care*, to *SATA* as "a working parent's guide to child care that incorporates the results of sociological and psychological research." Her second book, *The Perfect Baby?*, explores the issues of obstetrics and genetic engineering, and pays particular attention to "future developments in the Biological Revolution," according to the author.

Hann's first book for children, *The Family Scientist*, is a collection of scientific facts accompanied by simple experiments easily done at home. In a review of *The Family Scientist*, John Coleman of the *New Statesman* wrote: "Profusely illustrated, this elegant compendium embraces plants and animals, body and mind, heat and cold, the sky, physics, chemistry, food and cooking, light, sound, water and the atmosphere, proposing along the way masses of plausible projects and experiments." Hann's follow-up book was a similar work, titled *How Science Works: One Hundred Ways Parents and Kids Can Share the Secrets of Science*, which became a bestseller after its 1991 publication. In a *Booklist* review, Barbara Jacobs noted that "enough projects are designed to satisfy inquisitive minds of all ages." *School Library Journal* contributor Sylvia V. Meisner commended the book as well, praising the "lively, understandable text," and finding the work "a cut above most how-to science books."

Hann continues to write about science and serves as host of the British Broadcasting Corporation (BBC) television program *Tomorrow's World*, a survey of technological advances. Her other works include *Judith Hann's Total Health Plan*, which followed an eight-part television series by BBC on healthy food called *The*

Taste of Health. Her book on healthy gourmet food is titled *The Food of Love.*

■ Works Cited

Coleman, John, "Home Truths," *New Statesman,* November 9, 1979, p. 732.

Jacobs, Barbara, review of *How Science Works, Booklist,* July, 1991, p. 2017.

Meisner, Sylvia V., review of *How Science Works, School Library Journal,* July, 1991, p. 80.

■ For More Information See

PERIODICALS

Junior BookShelf, April, 1980, p. 83.
Kirkus Reviews, May 15, 1991, p. 671.
Voice of Youth Advocates, December, 1991, p. 336.

* * *

HAYCOCK, Kate 1962-

■ Personal

Born December 28, 1962, in Banbury, England; daughter of Philip John Haycock (a teacher) and Anne Haycock (a company director; maiden name, Mellish). *Education:* University of Sussex, B.A., 1985. *Politics:* Liberal Democrat. *Religion:* None.

■ Addresses

Home—64 Beaks Hill Rd., Kings Norton, Birmingham B38 8BY, England.

■ Career

Aston Technology, Birmingham, England, management trainee, 1986-87; Acton College, London, England, lecturer in computing and business, 1987-89; Gamester Kenyon, London, public relations account executive, 1989-90.

■ Writings

Fitness, Wayland (Sussex, England), 1990.
(Edited by Rebecca Stefoff) *Plays,* Wayland, 1990, Garrett Educational Corporation, 1991.
Pasta, Carolrhoda, 1991.
Skiing, Macmillan Child Group, 1991.
Gymnastics, Macmillan Child Group, 1991.
Science Fiction Films, Macmillan Child Group, 1992.

■ Work in Progress

Homelessness, forthcoming from Wayland; research on the history of skiing and the social journalist Henry Mayhew.

KATE HAYCOCK

■ Sidelights

Kate Haycock told *SATA:* "I came to writing quite by accident, as a friend of mine who edits children's books suggested I try writing one. *Pasta* ensued, and I enjoyed the research aspect and the discipline of presenting my research in an interesting way for young readers.

"As I often find writing a bit lonely, I am moving into the area of television research. I am working three days a week at a television documentary production company and hope to see some of my research projects come to fruition.

"My career has been very 'bitty'—I have ventured on several careers and have learned and gained from each so far. There is a common thread throughout and, in any case, I consider life to be a career."

* * *

HEDDERWICK, Mairi 1939-

■ Personal

Born May 2, 1939, in Gourock, Renfrewshire, Scotland; daughter of Douglas Lindsay (an architect) and Margaret (Gallacher) Crawford; married Ronnie Hedderwick, June 24, 1962 (divorced); children: Mark, Tamara. *Education:* Edinburgh College of Art, Diploma of Art, 1962; Jordanhill College of Education, Glasgow, art teaching certificate, 1963; primary teaching certificate, 1981.

MAIRI HEDDERWICK

■ Addresses

Home—Crossapol, Isle of Coll, Argyll PA78 6TB, Scotland. *Agent*—Pat White, Rogers, Coleridge & White, 20 Powis Mews, London W11 1JN, England.

■ Career

Traveling art teacher in Mid Argyll, Scotland, 1962-64; crofter and mother, Isle of Coll, Scotland, 1964-69; Malin Workshop (art stationery, prints), Isle of Coll and Fort William, Scotland, artist, designer, and owner with husband, 1969-80; community cooperatives advisor in Highlands and Islands (based in Inverness), Scotland, 1986-89. Freelance writer, illustrator, and public speaker, 1980—.

■ Awards, Honors

Souvenirs of Scotland Award, Scottish Design Centre, 1971 and 1974; Smarties Award finalist, for *Katie Morag and the Tiresome Ted*, 1986; Earthworm Award (with others), Friends of the Earth, 1993, for *Venus Peter Saves the Whale*.

■ Writings

SELF-ILLUSTRATED; FOR CHILDREN

Katie Morag Delivers the Mail, Bodley Head, 1984, Little, Brown, 1988.
Katie Morag and the Two Grandmothers, Little, Brown, 1985.
Katie Morag and the Tiresome Ted, Little, Brown, 1986.

Katie Morag and the Big Boy Cousins, Little, Brown, 1987.
P. D. Peebles' Summer or Winter Book, Little, Brown, 1989 (published in England as *Peedie Peebles' Summer or Winter Book*, Bodley Head, 1989).
Katie Morag and the New Pier, Bodley Head, 1993.
Peedie Peebles' Colour Book, Bodley Head, 1994.

SELF-ILLUSTRATED; FOR ADULTS

Mairi Hedderwick's Views of Scotland, Famedram (Scotland), 1981.
An Eye on the Hebrides: An Illustrated Journey, Canongate, 1989.
Highland Journey: A Sketching Tour of Scotland Retracing the Footsteps of Victorian Artist John T. Reid, Canongate, 1992.

ILLUSTRATOR

Rumer Godden, *The Old Woman Who Lived in a Vinegar Bottle*, Viking, 1972.
Jane Duncan, *Herself and Janet Reachfar*, Macmillan (London), 1975.
Duncan, *Brave Janet Reachfar*, Houghton, 1975.
Duncan, *Janet Reachfar and the Kelpie*, Houghton, 1976.
E. R. Taylor, *The Gifts of the Tarns*, Collins, 1977.
Duncan, *Janet Reachfar and Chickabird*, Houghton, 1978.
(With others) Enid Fairhead, editor, *The Book of Bedtime Stories*, Collins, 1979.
Alexander Maclean, *The Haggis*, State Mutual Book & Periodical Service, 1987.
Jamie Fleeman's Country Cookbook, State Mutual Book & Periodical Service, 1987.
Alan Keegan, *Scotch in Miniature*, revised edition, State Mutual Book & Periodical Service, 1987.
Christopher Rush, *Venus Peter Saves the Whale*, Canongate, 1992.
Joan Lingard, *Hands off Our School*, Hamish Hamilton, 1992.

Also illustrator of *A Cat Called Rover; A Dog Called Smith*, by Wendy Body, 1981; *Hamish and the Wee Witch*, 1986, *Hamish and the Fairy Bairn*, 1989, *A Kist of Whistles* and *Meet Maggie McMuddle*, both 1990, all by Moira Miller; *Our Best Stories*, edited by Anne Wood and Ann Pilling, 1986; and *The Spell Singers and Other Stories*, edited by Beverley Mathias, 1990.

■ Sidelights

Mairi Hedderwick's perceptive depictions of Scottish island life have found a wide audience in Great Britain, the United States, and Scandinavia. Hedderwick has illustrated works by other children's writers, but she is best known for her own picture books. Most of these feature Katie Morag, a youngster growing up on an island in the Hebrides. The author told *Horn Book* magazine: "When I started creating the Katie Morag books, there were very few books about, and for, Scottish children by Scottish authors. This may sound a trifle chauvinistic, but it is pleasing to see that the major publishers are more aware of the demand.... I have been very lucky; I had little restriction put on my expression of my culture."

Hedderwick was born and raised in Scotland, the granddaughter of a missionary to Africa. Both her grandfather and her father painted, so her own artistic ambitions were encouraged at home and at school. Hedderwick told *Horn Book* that, although her economic circumstances were comfortable during childhood, she felt emotionally deprived. "I had a mother who did not show much affection," she said. "I do not have any memories of being held or cuddled by her .... I was an only child. My father was often ill with 'nerves,' as it used to be called. He died when I was thirteen. That may be why I became a children's writer and illustrator—perhaps I am still trying to find that lost childhood."

As a youngster Hedderwick discovered a book in which the children went to an island in the Hebrides. The description of that region's beauty filled her with a longing she never quite forgot. "I wanted with all my heart to go to that island and sail on that sea," she told *Horn Book.*

Hedderwick attended Edinburgh College of Art from 1957 until 1961 and then earned a teaching certificate from Jordanhill College of Education. She served as a traveling art teacher in several Scottish towns and married in 1962. For slightly more than a year she and her husband worked together on a dairy farm, then they moved to the Hebridean Isle of Coll. There they lived "in splendid isolation" in an old farmhouse at the end of a beach. Hedderwick found they could support themselves by manufacturing postcards of Coll and neighboring islands.

"We started with a hand duplicator because there was no electricity on the island, and we made island map postcards of the West Coast," the author told *Horn Book.* "We churned out sixty-five thousand postcards in one season .... We expanded the range of stationery

Causing mischief with her older cousins is fun, but Katie and the boys feel better when they make up for their shenanigans by helping Granny with some chores. (Illustration by the author from *Katie Morag and the Big Boy Cousins.*)

products and prints from my sketching tours on other islands and the mainland of Scotland. Our two small children had plenty of scrap paper to be creative with!"

When their two children became old enough to attend secondary school, Hedderwick and her husband reluctantly left Coll for the mainland city of Inverness. By that time Hedderwick had begun to illustrate children's books by other authors, including *The Old Woman Who Lived in a Vinegar Bottle* by Rumer Godden and several "Janet Reachfar" books by Jane Duncan. In the mid-1980s Hedderwick began to write and illustrate her own books, featuring island-dwelling Katie Morag and her family.

The "Katie Morag" books have been praised for their strong sense of place, their non-sexist role models, and their sensitive exploration of everyday life in Scotland. "Hedderwick makes her fictitious Scottish island an elegant, yet thoroughly plausible setting," write Donnarae MacCann and Olga Richard in the *Wilson Library Bulletin*. "Whether she is depicting boats, bridges, animals, villagers, or Grannie's tractor, there is a delicacy and a down-to-earth grasp of details in each composition. Nothing appears alien in this environment because the artist is consistent in building simple, jewel-like areas with her varied techniques."

"I'd like to think that all my work is more than pretty pictures," Hedderwick told *Horn Book*. "My children's books all have, at base, a moral message. That must be the missionary grandfather emerging from me. I would never lose the message of a story by hiding it behind a really gorgeous picture. For young children art appreciation is way down the line—the story and the characters are paramount." At the same time, the author notes, illustrations are crucial to the formation of young imaginations. "Illustrations in books are often the first place a small child sees and learns about what is beyond its own experience," she concluded. "That is a big responsibility!"

In 1990 Hedderwick returned to rent the old farmhouse at the end of the beach on her beloved Isle of Coll. In 1993 she bought back the house from the people the Hedderwicks had sold it to in 1973.

■ Works Cited

Hedderwick, Mairi, "The Artist at Work: A Sense of Place," *Horn Book*, March-April, 1990, pp. 171-77.
MacCann, Donnarae, and Olga Richard, "Picture Books for Children," *Wilson Library Bulletin*, October, 1988, pp. 76-77.

■ For More Information See

BOOKS

Kingman, Lee, and others, compilers, *Illustrators of Children's Books: 1967-1976*, Horn Book, 1978.
Twentieth-Century Children's Writers, 3rd edition, St. James Press, 1989.

PERIODICALS

Children's Literature in Education, Volume 22, number 1, 1991.

* * *

HICYILMAZ, Gay 1947-

■ Personal

Born May 5, 1947, in Surrey, England; daughter of Harry (an engineer) and Dorothy (a teacher; maiden name, Hart) Campling; married Muzaffer Hicyilmaz (a banker), 1970; children: Timur, Kubilay, Hulagu, Mewgu. *Education:* University of Sussex, B.A., 1969.

■ Addresses

Home—c/o Fenton, 18 Durrington Ave, Wimbledon, London SW20 8NT, England. *Agent*—Rosemary Bromley, Juvenalia, Avington, Winchester, Hampshire SO21 1DB, England.

■ Career

British Council teacher in Ankara, Turkey, in the 1970s; writer. *Member:* Society of Authors.

■ Awards, Honors

Silver Pen Award, Holland, 1992.

■ Writings

Against the Storm (children's novel), Viking, 1990.
The Frozen Waterfall, Faber, 1993.

■ Work in Progress

Walking a Circle of Dust.

■ For More Information See

PERIODICALS

Junior Bookshelf, August, 1993, p. 152.
Times (London), March 10, 1990.

* * *

HILDER, Rowland 1905-1993

OBITUARY NOTICE—See index for *SATA* sketch: Born June 28, 1905, in Great Neck, Long Island, NY; died in 1993. Publisher, educator, and illustrator. Hilder, who moved to England with his family when he was ten years old, taught at Goldsmith's College School of Art in London during the 1920s and 1930s and at the Blackheath School of Art in the 1980s. He founded the Heron Press in 1945 and, in 1960, became a director at Rezle Publications. Before 1940, Hilder illustrated children's books, including *The Adventures of a Trafalgar Lad, Moby Dick,* and *Treasure Island.* His own writings include *Horse Play, Starting with Watercolor,* and *Expressing Land, Sea, and Sky in Watercolor* (also known as *Painting Landscapes in Watercolour*).

OBITUARIES AND OTHER SOURCES:

BOOKS

Spalding, Frances, *Twentieth Century Painters and Sculptors,* Volume 6, Antique Collectors' Club, 1990.
Who's Who, 145th edition, St. Martin's, 1993.

PERIODICALS

Junior Bookshelf, June, 1993, pp. 87-88.

*   *   *

HOLLAND, Lynda (H.) 1959-

■ Personal

Born May 30, 1959, in Barrie, Ontario, Canada. *Education:* University of Akron, B.S., 1987, M.S., 1989. *Religion:* Fellowship Baptist.

■ Addresses

Home—7600 Waterton Drive, Richmond, British Columbia V7A-464, Canada.

■ Career

Private tutor in Richmond, British Columbia, Canada.

■ Writings

The Snicker-Snees, Winston-Derek, 1992.

■ Work in Progress

The Gloppy Green Goop, and a young adult novel.

*   *   *

HORTON, Madelyn (Stacey) 1962-

■ Personal

Born May 29, 1962, in Escanaba, MI; daughter of Daniel (a right-of-way agent) and Marilyn (an artist; maiden name, Harkins) Stacey; married Christopher Horton (a writer), May 30, 1987; children: Nicholas. *Education:* St. Norbert College, B.A., 1984; University of Louisville, M.A., 1986; doctoral study at University of Washington, 1988—. *Hobbies and other interests:* Reading, film, hiking, skiing, and travel.

■ Addresses

Home and office—7053 13th Ave. NW, Seattle, WA 98117.

■ Career

University of Louisville, Louisville, KY, writing instructor, 1984-87; children's book writer.

■ Writings

The Lockerbie Airline Crash, Lucent Books, 1991.

■ Work in Progress

Dissertation on the fiction of Canadian women writers; *The Importance of Mother Jones,* to be published by Lucent Books, 1994.

■ Sidelights

Madelyn Stacey Horton told *SATA:* "The best I knew growing up was reading. I read everything—stories and novels, encyclopedias and dictionaries, even the backs of cereal boxes, if they were lying around. And I read everywhere—in a gnarly crook of the crab apple tree, in my mother's broom closet (with a flashlight!), and, naturally, in my bed, every single night. Now I have a child of my own, and reading all my early favorites to him is a singular joy. I'm saving up all his three-year-old escapades and adventures and charming comments, and plan to turn them into stories someday."

*   *   *

HUDSON, Jan 1954-1990

■ Personal

Born April 27, 1954, in Calgary, Alberta, Canada; died April, 1990; daughter of Laurie (a school librarian and professor) and Marie (a teacher; maiden name, Haugen) Wiedrick; married in 1977; children: (stepdaughter) Cindy. *Education:* University of Calgary, B.A., 1978; University of Alberta, LL.B., 1983. *Religion:* Society of Friends (Quaker).

■ Career

Legal editor and writer. Legal researcher, administrative assistant, and editor for attorney general of British Columbia. *Member:* Writers Union of Canada (British Columbia/Yukon representative to national council, 1986-87), Canadian Bar Association, Free-Lance Editors Association, Canadian Society of Composers, Authors, Illustrators, and Performers.

■ Awards, Honors

Children's Literature Prize, Canada Council, and Best Children's Book of the Year, Canadian Association of Children's Librarians, both 1984, and Notable Book and Best Book for Young Adults citations, American Library Association, 1989, all for *Sweetgrass.*

point

Scholastic 0-590-43486-1 / $2.95

Can a fifteen-year-old girl save her people?

SWEETGRASS

Jan Hudson

A fifteen-year-old Blackfoot girl proves to her father that she is old enough to marry by nursing her family through a disastrous smallpox epidemic in this novel, which Hudson based on actual Native American history.

■ Writings

Sweetgrass (juvenile novel), Tree Frog Press, 1984, Philomel Books, 1989.
Dawn Rider (juvenile novel), Philomel Books, 1990.

■ Sidelights

"My area of interest is social anthropology—the little things that make up most people's lives," explained the late Jan Hudson in a 1989 *Publishers Weekly* interview with Bella Stander. In Hudson's two novels, *Sweetgrass* and *Dawn Rider,* the Canadian writer, who died in 1990, employed this love of daily details to re-create bygone worlds of the Blackfoot Indians of northern Montana and south central Alberta. But these are more than just stories with historical settings. They are timeless tales with a universal theme: young girls overcoming adversity to find their true place in the world.

Hudson herself had a fair amount of adversity to overcome in the publishing of the first of these books,

Sweetgrass. The first draft was finished in 1979, but for the next several years the manuscript made the rounds of dozens of American publishers without finding a home. Like her female heroines, Hudson persevered. "I was going to keep rewriting it and keep resubmitting it until someone took it," she told Stander.

Finally, after several rewrites the book was picked as a finalist from Alberta Province in the first Writing for Young People contest. The prize: publication. Hudson's trials were not over, however, for the publisher involved in the contest ultimately backed off its pledge. It was not until late 1984 that a small regional Canadian house, Tree Frog Press, published *Sweetgrass.* Within the year it won both the Canadian Library Association Book of the Year for Children, as well as the Canada Council Children's Literature Prize. Since then, the book has been published in eight languages.

Hudson, who was born in Calgary, Alberta in 1954, loved words even as a child, writing stories and reading everything that came her way. At the age of ten, she read the *Rubaiyat* of Omar Khayyam. Hudson's mother recalls asking her if she understood it and the young Jan replied, "It's the music that I liked." In 1977 Hudson married a Native American and adopted his daughter, Cindy Lynn. This young girl, to whom *Sweetgrass* was dedicated, was the inspiration for the book. Reading histories of the Blackfoot people to familiarize herself with her daughter's heritage, Hudson came across accounts of a smallpox epidemic among the Blackfoot Indians which destroyed half the tribe in the harsh winter of 1937. At the time, Hudson was a law student at the University of Alberta, and the reports of the suffering of the Blackfoot people so moved her that she wanted to incorporate the historical records into a story of one young girl's bravery.

Sweetgrass, a fifteen-year-old Indian girl, is out picking strawberries the summer of 1837 when the story opens. With her is her friend Pretty-Girl, whose name explains it all. She is only thirteen, yet already her parents have given her away in marriage. Sweetgrass dreams of the handsome young warrior Eagle-Sun, hoping that he will be able to capture enough horses to pay her father, Shabby Bull, her bride-price. But her father is not keen on losing his favorite daughter, insisting that she is not yet a woman nor strong enough to marry. At the annual Sun Dance, Sweetgrass hopes her father will announce her marriage. Instead he decrees that she must prepare twenty-eight buffalo hides, alone, before spring. Only then will he consider her a woman and arrange her marriage. Meanwhile, Eagle-Sun, who is from a different family group, steals shy looks at Sweetgrass and dispatches his brother to talk to her father. At the end of the summer when the two families break camp to depart for their separate winter homes, the young lovers must part.

Life among the Blackfoot is an endless cycle of food gathering in preparation for the long, cold months of winter. Sweetgrass and other young girls gather berries, butcher and prepare the buffalo which the braves kill, and prepare pemmican, all activities that Hudson recreates with accuracy and skill. As Sarah Ellis put it in a *Horn Book* review: "We are swept along by the buoyant and rhythmical recreation of the land, the feel of tall prairie grass tickling the backs of knees, the smell of damp earth, the brilliant prairie light."

The Blackfoot families spend the winter in isolation. Food begins to run scarce, so Shabby Bull goes on a hunting trip into the snow-filled plains. Sweetgrass is alone with her twelve-year-old brother, Otter, two babies, and a demanding stepmother. It is then that smallpox strikes, killing the babies. Then her stepmother and Otter are struck with the disease, and she alone must nurse them. The description of this winter is "graphic and powerfully written," according to a *Publishers Weekly* reviewer. And by saving what is left of her family, Sweetgrass proves to her father that she is a woman. With the return of spring, the reader understands that Sweetgrass and Eagle-Sun will marry.

In writing the book, Hudson not only drew on historical records, but also spent time with Native American families as part of her research. In addition, she used records of traders, Blackfoot winter population counts and surviving oral history. "I tried to let the universal shine through a pattern of details of the time," she told Stander. A measure of the success she had in that attempt is witnessed by the awards she won and the continuing popularity of the book. As Kit Pearson put it in her *Christian Science Monitor* review, "Hudson unobtrusively combines historical, feminist, and native Indian themes in a moving account of a prairie Indian woman in the 1800s."

Despite the success of *Sweetgrass,* it did not find a U.S. publisher until 1989, when Philomel Books brought it out: ten years from the time Hudson had completed its first draft. Hudson's second book did not take so long to find a home. In 1990, Philomel also published *Dawn Rider.* In this book, Hudson returned to the familiar ground of the Blackfoot Indians and the trials of one young Indian girl, but this time the epoch is the early 1700s.

Kit Fox, sixteen, like Sweetgrass, has dreams. She is a middle child and "nothing special to anyone," but she desperately wants to ride one of her father's newly won horses. This is a time before the horse was a common commodity for the Blackfoot people, and Kit Fox wants to become the first in her tribe to ride this animal which has come to them through battle with the Snake tribe. Kit Fox must first overcome the prejudice of her tribe, the Blood band, against females, as well as their fear of the horse itself. The guardian of the horse, Found Arrow, and Kit Fox soon become romantically involved. In return for her help with his vision quest, Found Arrow allows her to tame and secretly ride the horse. Kit Fox's riding skills are put to the test when her tribe is attacked by the Snakes, and she must ride to get help from allies, or her tribe will be massacred. As with *Sweetgrass,* Hudson authentically re-creates a lost culture and bygone time in *Dawn Rider.* As *Horn Book*

Hudson's last novel before her death, *Dawn Rider* features an eighteenth-century Blackfoot girl who overcomes tribal prejudices and her own fears to tame a wild horse and help her tribe in battle. (Cover illustration by Jan Spivey Gilchrist.)

reported in its review of the book, "the plot is fast paced and believable. The time and place are well established, and the characters, multidimensional."

Hudson was at work on a third novel for Philomel at the time of her death. She was just thirty-five years old when she died. "Jan was a writer of ideas," according to her publishers. "The idea of carrying out a dream; the idea of knowing somewhere in your soul that you are as capable as anyone, despite the sexism of your culture. Jan's ideas will live on in her books, and we will continue to know her through her writing."

■ Works Cited

Review of *Dawn Rider, Horn Book,* March/April, 1991, pp. 198-199.
Ellis, Sarah, "News From the North," *Horn Book,* September/October, 1986, p. 626.
"Jan Hudson," article provided by Philomel Books, 1990.

Pearson, Kit, "A Harvest of Children's Books from Canada," *Christian Science Monitor,* October 5, 1984, p. B8.

Review of *Sweetgrass, Publishers Weekly,* February 24, 1989, p. 234.

Stander, Bella, "Jan Hudson," *Publishers Weekly,* December 22, 1989.

■ For More Information See

PERIODICALS

The Booktalker, September, 1989, p. 14.
English Journal, December, 1990, pp. 78-79.
Language Arts, April 1, 1990, pp. 425-426.
Publishers Weekly, November 23, 1990, pp. 65-66.*

—*Sketch by J. Sydney Jones*

*   *   *

HUGHES, D. T.
See HUGHES, Dean

*   *   *

HUGHES, Dean 1943-
(D. T. Hughes)

■ Personal

Born August 24, 1943, in Ogden, UT; son of Emery T. (a government worker) and Lorraine (Pierce) Hughes; married Kathleen Hurst (a teacher and educational administrator), November 23, 1966; children: Tom, Amy, Robert. *Education:* Weber State College, B.A. (cum laude), 1967; University of Washington, M.A., 1968, Ph.D., 1972; postdoctoral study at Stanford University, 1975, and Yale University, 1978. *Politics:* Democrat. *Religion:* Mormon.

■ Addresses

Home and office—1466 West 1100 North, Provo, UT 84604. *Agent*—Amy Berkower, Writers House, Inc., 21 West 26th St., New York, NY 10010.

■ Career

Central Missouri State University, Warrensburg, associate professor of English, 1972-80; Brigham Young University, Provo, UT, part-time visiting professor, 1980-82; writer, part-time editor, and consultant, 1980-88; full-time author, 1988—. Guest author, speaker, and workshop leader at writing conferences. *Member:* Children's Literature Association, Society of Children's Book Writers and Illustrators, Authors Guild, Authors League of America.

■ Awards, Honors

National Endowment for the Humanities summer seminar stipend, 1975 and 1978; Outstanding Faculty Achievement award, Central Missouri State University, 1980; *Honestly, Myron* was selected one of the "Best Books for Kids" by Children's Book Committee, *Parent* magazine, 1983; Editor's Choice award, *Booklist,* 1989, for *Family Pose.*

■ Writings

YOUNG ADULT FICTION

Nutty for President, illustrated by Blanche Sims, Atheneum, 1981.
Hooper Haller, Deseret, 1981.
Facing the Enemy, Deseret, 1982.
Honestly, Myron, illustrated by Martha Weston, Atheneum, 1982.
Switching Tracks, Atheneum, 1982.
Jenny Haller, Deseret, 1983.
Millie Willenheimer and the Chestnut Corporation, Atheneum, 1983.
Nutty and the Case of the Mastermind Thief, Atheneum, 1985.
Nutty and the Case of the Ski-Slope Spy, Atheneum, 1985.
Brothers, Deseret, 1986.
Nutty Can't Miss, Atheneum, 1987.
Theo Zephyr, Atheneum, 1987.
Cornbread and Prayer, Deseret, 1988.
Nutty Knows All, Atheneum, 1988.
Family Pose, Atheneum, 1989.
Jelly's Circus, Aladdin, 1989.
Nutty the Movie Star, Atheneum, 1989.
Big Base Hit, illustrated by Dennis Lyall, Knopf, 1990.
Championship Game, illustrated by Lyall, Knopf, 1990.
Line Drive, illustrated by Lyall, Knopf, 1990.
Lucky Breaks Loose, Deseret, 1990.
Lucky's Crash Landing, Deseret, 1990.
Lucky's Gold Mine, Deseret, 1990.
Making the Team, illustrated by Lyall, Knopf, 1990.
Pressure Play, illustrated by Lyall, Knopf, 1990.
Rookie Star, illustrated by Lyall, Knopf, 1990.
What a Catch!, illustrated by Lyall, Knopf, 1990.
Winning Streak, illustrated by Lyall, Knopf, 1990.
All Together Now, illustrated by Lyall, Knopf, 1991.
Defense!, illustrated by Lyall, Knopf, 1991.
Kickoff Time, illustrated by Lyall, Knopf, 1991.
Lucky Fights Back, Deseret, 1991.
Lucky's Mud Festival, Deseret, 1991.
Play-Off, illustrated by Lyall, Knopf, 1991.
Safe at First, illustrated by Lyall, Knopf, 1991.
Stroke of Luck, illustrated by Lyall, Knopf, 1991.
Superstar Team, illustrated by Lyall, Knopf, 1991.
Up to Bat, illustrated by Lyall, Knopf, 1991.
Backup Goalie, illustrated by Lyall, Knopf, 1992.
Lucky the Detective, Deseret, 1992.
Lucky's Tricks, Deseret, 1992.
Nothing But Net, illustrated by Lyall, Knopf, 1992.
Point Guard, illustrated by Lyall, Knopf, 1992.
Psyched!, illustrated by Lyall, Knopf, 1992.
Total Soccer, illustrated by Lyall, Knopf, 1992.
Victory Goal, illustrated by Lyall, Knopf, 1992.
(With Tom Hughes) *Baseball Tips,* illustrated by Lyall, Random House, 1993.
End of the Race, Atheneum, 1993.

DEAN HUGHES

Go to the Hoop!, illustrated by Lyall, Knopf, 1993.
Nutty's Ghost, Atheneum, 1993.
On the Line, illustrated by Lyall, Knopf, 1993.
Quick Moves, illustrated by Lyall, Knopf, 1993.
Shake Up, illustrated by Lyall, Knopf, 1993.
Lucky's Cool Club, Deseret, 1993.
Lucky in Love, Deseret, 1993.
Re-Elect Nutty!, Atheneum, 1994.
One-Man Team, Knopf, 1994.
Second-Team Star, Knopf, 1994.
K-9 Crime Busters, Random House, 1994.
The Trophy, Knopf, 1994.

OTHER

Under the Same Stars (historical novel), Deseret, 1979.
As Wide as the River (historical novel), Deseret, 1980.
Romance and Psychological Realism in William Godwin's Novels, Arno, 1981.
The Mormon Church: A Basic History (nonfiction), Deseret, 1986.
(Under name D. T. Hughes) *Lullaby and Goodnight* (true crime book), Pocket Books, 1993.

Contributor to anthologies, including *Monsters, Ghoulies, and Creepy Creatures,* edited by Lee Bennett Hopkins, A. Whitman, 1977, and *Merrily Comes Our Harvest In,* edited by Hopkins, Harcourt, 1978. Contributor of poetry to periodicals, including *The Friend* and *Cricket.*

■ Work in Progress

"I'm working on a sequel to *Family Pose,* which may be titled *Family Secret.*"

■ Sidelights

Dean Hughes is a prolific and versatile writer who has written nonsense poetry, historical novels, a scholarly monograph, sports novels, children's stories, and young adult novels. Several of Hughes's early published works for young people—*Under the Same Stars, As Wide as the River, Hooper Haller, Facing the Enemy,* and *Jenny Haller*—draw on his background as a Mormon. At the time Hughes wrote these books he was also teaching, first at Central Missouri State University, then at Brigham Young University in Utah. Since 1980, however, Hughes has gradually given up his teaching duties in order to write. He is well known for his sports stories and the series of novels he has written about Frederick "Nutty" Nutsell.

Hughes has written more than twenty sports novels. Most of these are found within three series: "The Angel Park Hoop Stars," the "Angel Park Soccer Stars," and the "Angel Park All-Stars." Critics have noticed that Hughes distinguishes his plots with in-depth characters and realistic descriptions. In two of his baseball books, *Big Base Hit* and *Making the Team,* "readers witness respect, consideration, and personal growth" in the characters, according to Janice C. Hayes in *School Library Journal.*

Nutty Nutshell thought "boy genius" William Bilks was just a nerd until William uses his talents to help elect Nutty as president of his school's student council. (Cover illustration by Blanche Sims.)

Nutty Nutsell is a fifth grader whose hidden talents have been brought out and developed with the help of his classmate and "boy genius," William Bilks. At the beginning of *Nutty for President* the title character is an inarticulate and average student. However, Nutty becomes transformed into a political powerhouse—almost in spite of himself—by William's precocious and savvy advice. As a result, Nutty becomes the first fifth grader ever to be elected president of the student council. William's machinations actually resemble the cynical approach to politics present in adult elections. Indeed, as Hughes once commented, "I try to raise serious questions for young readers, often in the context of a humorous book. How does America elect its leaders? Is honesty really possible?" A critic for *Kirkus Reviews* described *Nutty for President* as "a standout in its class . . . snappy [and] well-grounded." Writing in *School Library Journal,* Steve Matthews commented that "the school setting and student interaction is well portrayed with recognizable character types."

Honestly, Myron examines the honesty issue head-on. Myron is a fifth-grader who takes his teacher's lesson on honesty so seriously he resolves to be completely honest from that day forward. Myron becomes confused when his unvarnished truth-telling provokes hostility in the neighborhood and inadvertently threatens to turn voters against an important school bond issue up for approval. The tension escalates when Myron—despite his support of the bond issue—contradicts Mrs. Kendall, his principal, on the issue during a radio broadcast. "Myron's commentary on her political distortion creates a furor," Carolyn Noah noted in *School Library Journal.* The book ends with children and adults alike chastened by the power of honesty. "If Myron learns that 'everything was so much more complicated than he thought it ought to be,' the grownups also learn a lesson about being upfront with the voters," stated a critic for *Kirkus Reviews.*

Millie Willenheimer and the Chestnut Corporation combines humor with a serious message concerning another institution of American society, capitalism. In the book Millie develops a collection of horse chestnuts into a financial asset, but becomes disillusioned by the seeming necessity for dishonesty in order to achieve success. "Readers will learn a lot about capitalism" and "should enjoy a few laughs along the way," according to a reviewer in *Booklist.*

Hughes Crafts Serious Novels

While the "Nutty" series, *Honestly, Myron,* and *Millie Willenheimer* are basically humorous novels about fundamental American values and institutions, *Switching Tracks, Family Pose,* and *End of the Race* assume a more serious approach. Hughes once told *SATA* that *Switching Tracks* is a story "that deals with certain problems of our time, but I would not call it a 'problem novel.' It's mainly a story—and for me, a touching one—about a scared eighth-grade boy and a scared seventy-eight-year-old man, who find solace and escape in their friendship." The boy is named Mark, and he has moved to a new town with his mother after the suicide

of his father. Sullen and aloof, Mark ignores his schoolwork and alienates his friends and family. However, he eventually accepts an offer from Willard, a retired railroad worker, to help the elderly man work on his complex set of model trains. Through his friendship with Willard, Mark discovers the strength to deal with the traumatic secret he has kept to himself since his father's suicide. A critic in *Kirkus Reviews* described Hughes's treatment of the "guarded relationship" between Willard and Mark as "touching but never sentimental or predictable." In *School Library Journal* Robert Unsworth stated that *Switching Tracks* "is a realistic, absorbing study of a troubled young man."

Hughes's experience as a bellman at a hotel in Seattle, Washington became the basis for his young adult novel *Family Pose.* The book is about David, a runaway orphan who is befriended by Paul, a hotel bellman and recovering alcoholic. Because of his experiences in the foster-care system, David is very reluctant to seek help or tell anyone about himself. A dedicated group of hotel workers, however, gradually helps bring David out of his shell. The novel was praised by a critic for *Kirkus Reviews* as a "moving and memorable story" because of

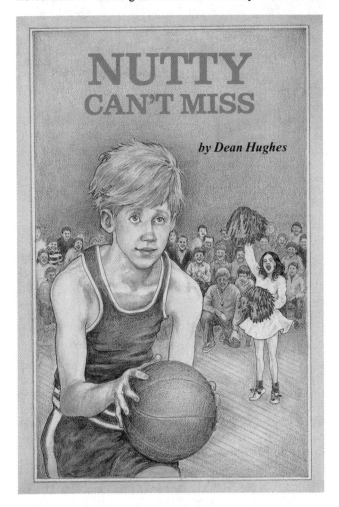

Nutty and William team up again to recue the school basketball team from its humiliating record, but Nutty has second thoughts about Bilks' plan to turn him into a superstar. (Cover illustration by Helen Cogancherry)

Nutty, now a movie star, is threatened by a ghost not to
go to the set where he's working on a feature. Can
Nutty's pal William prove the ghost is a fake? (Cover
illustration by Jacqueline Garrick.)

its "lovingly drawn characters and strong central relationship." These sentiments were echoed in *Horn Book*
by Ethel R. Twichell, who wrote that "the growing
affection between Paul and David [is] well presented
and give[s] the book considerable emotional impact."
And in the *New York Times Book Review,* Betsy Hearne
noted that "the detailed setting and the subtly unfolded
observation of each character in *Family Pose* give
readers the uncanny sense of a life crisis relived."

Hughes once commented, "My goal is to write books
that are truly fine pieces of art. I love writing. I love the
freedom, the creativity and the wonderful feedback I get
from kids, librarians and teachers. I want to make young
people think and feel and care—there are too many
forces pushing them in the opposite directions."

Hughes told *SATA:* "My first home was a trailer house.
It wasn't one of those double-wide mobile homes. This
little thing was smaller than the travel trailers you see on
the highways these days. I have seen the famous log
cabin that Abe Lincoln lived in as a child, and I know
our trailer was smaller. We lived in it longer, too.

"We were poor, I guess. But it didn't seem so to me.
What I remember are the kids in the neighborhood; the
long Utah summers; the timeless days in the vacant lot
we called 'the field.' I remember the smell of the
milkweed, the chattering noise of the flying grasshoppers with red and black wings, the dirt-clod wars,
and the old tire swing in the giant box elder tree.

"One summer when I was restless for something to do,
my mom taught me to embroider. I would sit with my
legs inside a pillowcase and stitch a fancy trim around
the edge. The poor pillowcase would get filthy dirty. If
some guy had called me a sissy, I suppose I would have
had it out with him. But I don't remember feeling any
contradiction. Why couldn't a rough-and-tumble kid
create flowers out of french knots? To me, it was just
one more pleasure in life.

"I really am a collection of contradictions. I write fiction
all day. And yet I'm a deeply practical man. I'm steady
and systematic about my writing—and disciplined. I
don't leap off into some dream world and 'see what
happens.' I brainstorm to develop my idea and characters; I do a thorough outline; I draft and re-draft many
times. And I never miss deadlines.

"My writing career has been evolving lately, pulling me
more and more toward writing about sports. I'm still
doing books about Nutty, however, and I'm still doing
serious, young-adult novels. But the Angel Park series
has proven to me that lots of young people want to read
about sports. Sports provide great action plots and good
entertainment, but they also raise questions about us as
a people, and they bring out traits that are worth
probing seriously. For example, *The Trophy* is about a
fifth-grade boy playing organized basketball for the first
time, but the real issue of the novel is the relationship of
a boy and his alcoholic father. I will not write exclusively about sports in the future, but at least for the present,
they will serve as the setting for many of my books.

"There is one more huge contradiction in my life. My
dad could read a little, but only a little. I don't think he
ever read a book in his whole life. So how did I become
a writer?

"I'm not sure.

"But back in my childhood days, I somehow developed
a sense that I was going to do something interesting with
my life. My teachers told me I was smart—and I *was* a
good student (in spite of talking too much). But it was
really my mother who made me feel I could do whatever
I set my mind to. She read to me and created my first
love for books, and even more importantly, she welcomed me in from catching grasshoppers and taught me
to embroider. Somehow, along with the desire to do
something well, she also gave me the feeling that the
range of joys in this life is very wide.

"I certainly do have a full life."

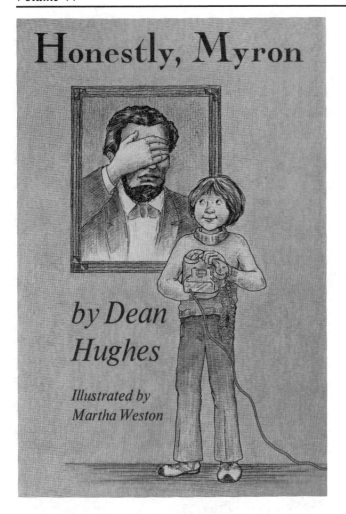

Honesty might not always be the best policy, as Myron learns after he resolves to tell nothing but the truth and winds up making a lot of people angry. (Cover illustration by Martha Weston.)

Hughes used his own experiences as a hotel bellman to write this story about a runaway orphan. (Cover illustration by Mary O'Keefe Young.)

■ Works Cited

Review of *Family Pose, Kirkus Reviews,* April 1, 1989, pp. 547-48.

Hayes, Janice C., review of *Big Base Hit* and *Making the Team, School Library Journal,* June, 1990, p. 122.

Hearne, Betsy, review of *Family Pose, New York Times Book Review,* May 21, 1989.

Review of *Honestly, Myron, Kirkus Reviews,* April 15, 1982, pp. 489-90.

Matthews, Steve, review of *Nutty for President, School Library Journal,* February, 1982, p. 77.

Review of *Millie Willenheimer and the Chestnut Corporation, Booklist,* April 15, 1983, p. 1095.

Noah, Carolyn, review of *Honestly, Myron, School Library Journal,* August, 1982, p. 117.

Review of *Nutty for President, Kirkus Reviews,* May 1, 1981.

Review of *Switching Tracks, Kirkus Reviews,* July 15, 1982, p. 802.

Twichell, Ethel R., review of *Family Pose, Horn Book,* September/October, 1989, p. 621.

Unsworth, Robert, review of *Switching Tracks, School Library Journal,* September, 1982, pp. 139-40.

■ For More Information See

PERIODICALS

Children's Literature in Education, Volume 21, number 3, 1990, p. 193.

Horn Book, June, 1981, p. 302.

Kirkus Reviews, April 1, 1987.

School Library Journal, May, 1983, p. 72; December, 1993, p. 112.

Social Education, April, 1983, p. 252; April/May, 1990, p. 226.

*   *   *

HURMENCE, Belinda 1921-

■ Personal

Surname pronounced *Her*-mence; born August 20, 1921, in Oklahoma; daughter of Warren Coleman (an electrician) and Eula (a homemaker; maiden name, Bonnell) Watson; married Howard Henry Hurmence (a chemical engineer), March 10, 1948; children: Leslie Hurmence Abrams. *Education:* University of Texas,

B.A., 1942; attended Columbia University, 1945-1947. *Politics:* "Moderate to liberal." *Religion:* Episcopalian. *Hobbies and other interests:* Early child development, tennis, gardening, breadmaking.

■ Addresses

Home and office—149 East Water St., Statesville, NC 28677.

■ Career

Writer. *Mademoiselle,* New York City, assistant fiction editor, 1947-48; *Flair,* New York City, executive editor, 1948-49. *Member:* Society of Children's Book Writers and Illustrators, Authors Guild, Authors League of America.

■ Awards, Honors

Work-in-progress grant, Society of Children's Book Writers, 1978-79, for *A Girl Called Boy;* American Library Association (ALA) Notable Children's Book, 1980, and National Council for Social Studies (NCSS) Notable Children's Trade Book in the Field of Social Studies, 1981, both for *Tough Tiffany;* Parents' Choice Award and National Council of Teachers of English Teacher's Choice Award, 1984, for *A Girl Called Boy;* Golden Kite Award, Society of Children's Book Writers, and NCSS Notable Children's Trade Book in the Field of Social Studies, 1984, for *Tancy;* American Association of University Women (NC Division) Award in Juvenile Literature, 1984, for *Tancy,* and 1989, for *The Nightwalker;* North Carolina Writer's Fellowship, 1985; *School Library Journal* Best Adult Book for Young Adults citation, for *My Folks Don't Want Me to Talk about Slavery.*

■ Writings

Tough Tiffany, Doubleday, 1980.
A Girl Called Boy, Clarion, 1982.
Tancy, Clarion, 1984.
My Folks Don't Want Me to Talk about Slavery (slave narratives; also see below), John Blair, 1984.
The Nightwalker, Clarion, 1988.
Before Freedom, When I Just Can Remember: Twenty-seven Oral Histories of Former South Carolina Slaves (slave narratives; also see below), John Blair, 1989.
Before Freedom: Forty-eight Oral Histories of Former North & South Carolina Slaves (combined edition of *Before Freedom, When I Just Can Remember* and *My Folks Don't Want Me to Talk about Slavery*), New American Library-Dutton, 1990.
Dixie in the Big Pasture (historical novel), Clarion, 1994.
We Lived in a Little Cabin in the Yard (Virginia slave narratives), John Blair, 1994.

BELINDA HURMENCE

■ Work in Progress

Two nonfiction titles on working days of a female airline pilot and sports clothes designer and manufacturer; a historical novel about an oil camp child of the 1930s; a volume of slave narratives geared to the juvenile market.

■ Sidelights

Belinda Hurmence is known for her novels written for children and young adults, which are often about the lives of black children, as well as for her editions of slave narratives. Her books are noted for their evocative sense of place; their effective use of dialogue, often in the dialect of the characters; and their strong characterizations. Hurmence's interests, reflected in her work in progress, also include careers for women and the pioneer period in general of American history.

"My parents and both sets of my grandparents homesteaded in the Oklahoma Indian Territory, in the Kiowa-Comanche-Apache lands known among those tribes as the Big Pasture," Hurmence remarked in the *Sixth Book of Junior Authors and Illustrators.* "My mother's people came into the O.T., as it was called, in three covered wagons the year Oklahoma became one of the United States. My father's family also arrived prior to statehood."

Given these facts, it is not surprising that Hurmence has recently completed an historical novel entitled *Dixie in the Big Pasture* which covers the period of early statehood in Oklahoma history. "The central character in the book is based on my aunt, who is 98 now. She was twelve when Oklahoma became a state," the author told *Something about the Author* (*SATA*) in an interview. "My family is very long-lived. My uncle is still alive at 103. All my relatives were very helpful in writing the book. I have one sister. The family has always stayed close to one another except for me, and I left early. *Dixie in the Big Pasture* is the first time I have written about my family, and it's taken me a long time."

Hurmence enjoyed writing from an early age. "School was always very important to me," Hurmence recalled, "for it was in school that I got encouragement to be a writer. In first grade, for example, there was a competition, and I was given a prize of Beatrix Potter's *Peter Rabbit*. In it my teacher had inscribed 'I'm very proud of you. You are a good writer.' I knew from then on that I was going to be a writer."

As she grew older, Hurmence found more public ways to prove her writing talents. "In high school I was always looking for contests to enter, and I actually won a good many of them. When I was a senior, a national essay contest that I entered won me a week in Washington, D.C., and an invitation to the White House, for tea with Mrs. Roosevelt." The author continued pursuing her literary goals after high school. "In college I had a couple of classes with Frank Dobie, the great western regionalist writer. He was also the advisor on the literary magazine. I wrote and did editing and production for the magazine and learned a lot."

After graduating from college, Hurmence moved to New York City. "I'd always wanted to live there, and the end of the war seemed like a good breaking point," she said in her interview. "While I was working on Wall Street, in the insurance industry, I was also going to Columbia School of General Studies at night and studying creative writing under Gladys Tabor and George Davis, who was executive editor of *Mademoiselle*. At first I wanted to be a writer of adult fiction, and I did write a couple of short stories that were published, as well as a novel that wasn't. It was George, my teacher, who bought my first story, and almost immediately after that he asked me if I would be interested in a job working on *Mademoiselle*."

"I worked on *Mademoiselle* for a year or so, and then Cowles Publications started a new publication called *Flair*. It was a bit like *Vanity Fair*, but they didn't get the advertising, so it lasted only a couple of years." During this time the author married Howard Hurmence, and soon after the couple had a baby girl.

"In 1951, when my daughter was two years old, we moved to New Jersey," Hurmence related in her interview. "I belonged to a writer's group and was trying to sell adult stories, but in the 1960s I was also working as a volunteer librarian in a neighborhood house in Morristown. I was really struck with how few books there were for the black children there. I started to write for these children."

Hurmence continued her work reading every day to black children in a day care center after she and her husband moved to North Carolina in 1968. This experience served her well in her writing. "My own knowledge of black dialect I use in my stories comes, I think, because of my close connection with the black community," she explained. "I didn't sell books for a long time, but I did sell some stories to children's magazines."

Still, success did not come easy, Hurmence soon learned. "I discovered that writing for children is even more difficult than writing for adults. You follow the same rules, I suppose—except if you're writing for adults, I think you don't *have* to write as well as you can. You can get away with writing sloppy. Whereas with children you can't because there are too many people keeping up the standards, like the librarians who choose the books. I don't write for those librarians particularly, however. I write what I please, and then I wait to see what my editor thinks about it. I work very closely with my editor at Houghton Mifflin, James Giblin. He has been my editor for four novels, counting *Dixie in the*

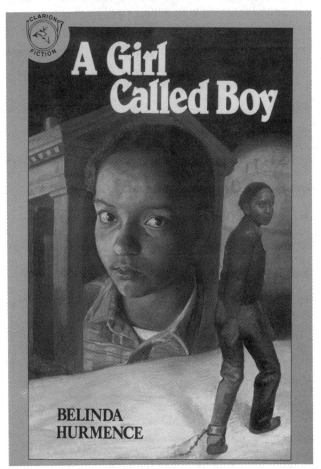

Hurmence conducted in-depth research on the Underground Railroad and slave narratives before writing this tale of a young girl who is transported back in time to the 1850s. (Cover illustration by Steven Assel.)

Pasture. He is a writer himself and is very tactful yet very thorough, too."

It was not until 1980 that Hurmence published her first book for children. In *Tough Tiffany,* a strong yet sensitive eleven-year-old black girl attempts to keep her large and difficult family together in a small North Carolina city. The book won widespread praise for its "natural warmth," as Marilyn Kaye comments in *School Library Journal,* and "sharply drawn" characters, according to *Bulletin of the Center for Children's Books* contributor Zena Sutherland. A *Kirkus Reviews* writer likewise remarks on the main character's "positive, head-on approach to problems." The American Library Association named *Tough Tiffany* a Notable Children's Book in 1980; the book was also named a Notable Trade Book in Social Studies by the National Council for Social Studies.

Although her book was lauded, Hurmence herself was coming under fire, she related. "Some critics started to say that blacks should have their own writers writing about them," Hurmence recalled. "I agree that blacks should be writers, but I do believe it is wrong to say that you should only write about your own culture. I think the important thing is to write a good book. From black children I get no objection. Where I hear an objection is from black scholars. They don't object to my nonfiction, that is, my editing of black slave narratives, but to my fiction. I remember one professor who really pasted *A Girl Called Boy,* and it hit me hard."

Nevertheless, Hurmence continued to focus on black characters in her work. She described the process by which she came to write *A Girl Called Boy:* "After I wrote *Tough Tiffany,* I had an idea for writing a book about the Underground Railroad. I researched the topic and found it was hard to get materials written from the slave's viewpoint. At that point I didn't know about the WPA Works Progress Administration collection of slave narratives. I was visiting an historical museum in Savannah, Georgia, and looking for pictures of slaves. While I was going through their picture collection, my husband said he'd found an interesting book. The book was *Slavery Time,* published by the Beehive Press in 1973. It had excerpts from the WPA collection on Georgia slaves, and I immediately thought, 'That's for me!' So I got in touch with the Library of Congress and they provided me with microfilm of all the slave narratives. And believe me, that's a production—10,000 pages' worth!"

The author continued: "The more I read the more I realized that the Underground Railroad didn't really figure with most slaves in the South. Most slaves did not escape north but rather to someplace closer to home. So that's when I came up with the idea for *A Girl Named Boy.*

Blanche Overtha Yancey—Boy for short—despises her family's slave origins until, in this time travel tale, she finds herself fleeing from slave patrols in the 1850s. She experiences deprivation and fear as a runaway, and

As with *A Girl Called Boy,* Hurmence was inspired by slave narratives to write this tale of one freed slave's search for her mother. (Cover illustration by Charles Lilly.)

security, complacency, and lack of pride as a house slave before returning to the present. In *Horn Book,* Ann A. Flowers says Hurmence's "detailed descriptions of slave life create a memorable picture of an agonizing period." *A Girl Called Boy* received the Parents' Choice Award and the National Council of Teachers of English Teacher's Choice Award in 1984. The Teacher's Choice Committee praised its "vivid picture of . . . plantation slave life" and "compelling fictionalized story," according to *Language Arts.* As Hazel Rochman concludes in *School Library Journal,* readers will enjoy the story "for its adventure and setting and for the universal nightmare it dramatizes."

In an author's note appended to her next book, *Tancy,* Hurmence writes that the idea for the novel, like that of *A Girl Named Boy,* "began among the pages of the slave narratives. . . . *Tancy* is meant to embody the innumerable ex-slaves who set out to find their families after the Civil War. Her yearning and searching parallel what many young people experience even today, looking for some idea, or 'mother,' on the way to discovering themselves." Like her predecessors Tiffany and Boy, *Tancy* is a resourceful, adventurous black girl, this time

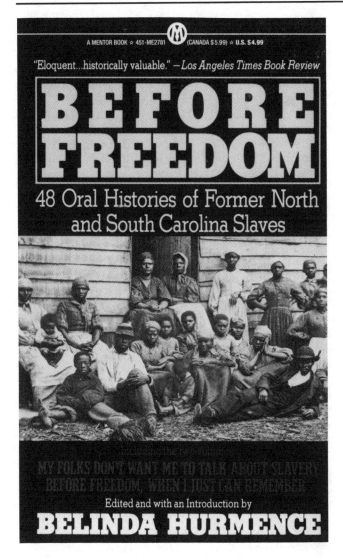

A combination of two previous books, this collection includes narratives on slave life spanning pre- and post-Civil War years.

sixteen. Tancy has been taught to read and write by the plantation owner's son, Billy. She uses these skills to her advantage after escaping, becoming a worker in a Freedman's Bureau center and later a teacher.

"Hurmence's numerous, well-defined characters and realistic atmosphere ... ensure the reader's sympathetic interest," notes a *Publishers Weekly* critic. *Tancy* received the Golden Kite Award and was selected as an NCSS Notable Children's Trade Book in the Field of Social Studies in 1984. Sutherland of the *Bulletin for the Center of Children's Books* praises *Tancy*'s "striving for personal emancipation" as "movingly depicted," and adds that the variety of characters she encounters "dramatizes the suffering of slavery."

My Folks Don't Want Me to Talk About Slavery, a collection of narratives from North Carolina ex-slaves edited by Hurmence, was published in 1984. It is from this book that the author draws some of the ideas and background for both *A Girl Named Boy* and *Tancy*. Slaves could not own land as white homesteaders could,

Hurmence notes in her introduction to *My Folks*. "But in the sense of the self-sufficiency for which Americans admire their forebears—working the land, building houses, growing and preparing food—slaves were genuine homesteaders. They not only did the work; they endured through bondage to freedom. The idea for *My Folks Don't Want Me to Talk About Slavery* grew out of my admiration of those very real pioneers."

Many readers may ask why some of the slaves quoted in the book can speak of their masters with affection. Hurmence reminds her readers that these oral histories were collected during the Depression, a time of "deep poverty for many whites and most blacks. The entire nation looked backward with nostalgia during the 1930s. To an aging, destitute black person, bondage may well have seemed less onerous in retrospect, particularly if coupled with memories of an easygoing master, a full stomach, the energy of childhood." In addition, the author explained, "some of the accounts may have been skewed ... by the subjects' telling what they believed their questioners wanted to hear."

Despite these built-in limitations, *My Folks Don't Want Me to Talk About Slavery* is praised by reviewers like Robert C. Bealer. Writing in *Science Books and Films,* Bealer describes the volume as a "fine little book" and a "useful instrument to better comprehend and learn from history." The author agreed. "I think everybody in the U.S. should read some of those slave narratives," Hurmence said in her interview. "They certainly opened my mind."

In 1988's *The Nightwalker,* Hurmence returns to contemporary America. In this mystery, set in the intriguing background of the Outer Banks of North Carolina, environmental issues and the mind of 12-year-old Savannah are spotlighted. A series of fires has been consuming local fishing shacks. Is the culprit hoping to arouse opposition to the government's attempts to destroy a traditional way of life? Or is the real suspect the nightwalker, subject of an old local Indian legend? In *Horn Book,* Elizabeth S. Watson writes, "While the emphasis is on plot and setting, the characters are realistically drawn and act believably." *The Nightwalker* received the American Association of University Women (NC Division) Award in Juvenile Literature in 1989.

Hurmence returns to her continuing project editing slave narratives in *Before Freedom, When I Can Just Remember: Twenty-seven Oral Histories of Former South Carolina Slaves.* The book was published in 1989. In her introduction Hurmence again describes her first excitement upon discovering "the treasure that lay in the oral histories." She added: "The concept of bondage has always fascinated free Americans. With slavery more than a century behind us, and beyond the recollection of any living person, the fascination still persists. Perhaps the invisible, traumatic ties that bind us evoke a dread empathy with the physically enslaved," the author speculates. Reviewing the book in *School Library Journal,* Alice Conlon writes that "the collection offers students a chance to use readable primary sources" to find out how Southern slaves actually lived.

Hurmence has several works in progress, including two volumes on careers for women in the airline and fashion business, and another historical novel about a child in the oil camps of Texas in the 1930s. But she retains her fascination with the slave narratives that she first read over twenty years ago. "My main aim is to tell both black and white children their history and to give black kids a sense of self through literature," she said in her interview. "While I've written mainly for middle school readers, I wish I could write books for younger readers. There are more books for the youngest black readers than there used to be, but there are still not enough."

She concluded: "I like the kids that I'm writing for. The middle grades are my favorite age. They're still unspoiled, and there's an innocence about them as well as a certain sophistication.

"When the kids that I talk to ask me how they could become writers, I tell them that they are writers right now, that writing is something they're going to be doing all their lives, and the writing they do will make a difference in the jobs they fill. I'm very strict with them!

"If kids ask me how to become fiction writers, I tell them to learn to write a lot of dialogue. Last spring a boy in a gifted class said that the dialogue he wrote was never as good as he expected. I told him, that's a condition of writing!"

■ Works Cited

Review of *A Girl Called Boy, Language Arts,* April, 1983.

Bealer, Robert C., review of *My Folks Don't Want Me to Talk about Slavery, Science Books and Films,* March-April, 1986, p. 206.

Conlon, Alice, review of *Before Freedom, School Library Journal,* September, 1989, p. 287.

Flowers, Ann A., review of *A Girl Called Boy, Horn Book,* August, 1982, p. 404.

Holtze, Sally Holmes, editor, *Sixth Book of Junior Authors and Illustrators,* H. W. Wilson, 1989, pp. 143-144.

Hurmence, Belinda, author's note to *Tancy,* Clarion, 1984.

Hurmence, Belinda, introduction to *My Folks Don't Want Me to Talk about Slavery,* John Blair, 1984.

Hurmence, Belinda, introduction to *Before Freedom, When I Just Can Remember,* John Blair, 1989.

Hurmence, Belinda, interview with Scott Gillam for *Something about the Author,* conducted August, 1993.

Kaye, Marilyn, review of *Tough Tiffany, School Library Journal,* February, 1980, pp. 56-57.

Rochman, Hazel, review of *A Girl Called Boy, School Library Journal,* May, 1982, p. 62.

Sutherland, Zena, review of *Tough Tiffany, Bulletin of the Center for Children's Books,* March, 1980, p. 135.

Sutherland, Zena, review of *Tancy, Bulletin of the Center for Children's Books,* June, 1984, p. 187.

Review of *Tancy, Publishers Weekly,* March 30, 1984.

Review of *Tough Tiffany, Kirkus Reviews,* March 1, 1980, p. 289.

Watson, Elizabeth S., review of *The Nightwalker, Horn Book,* January-February, 1989.

■ For More Information See

BOOKS

Children's Literature Review, Volume 25, Gale, 1991, pp. 92-97.

Killion, Ronald G., compiler, *Slavery Time When I was Chillun Down on Marster's Farm,* Beehive Press, 1973.

PERIODICALS

Bulletin of the Center for Children's Books, September, 1982.

Kirkus Reviews, April 15, 1982.

Social Education, April, 1981; April, 1985.

Washington Post Book World, July 15, 1990.

—Sketch by Scott Gillam

I

IKEDA, Daisaku 1928-

■ Personal

Born January 2, 1928, in Tokyo, Japan; son of Nenokichi and Ichi Ikeda; married Kaneko Shiraki, May 3, 1952; children: Hiromasa, Takahiro. *Education:* Fuji Junior College.

■ Addresses

Office—c/o Soka Gakkai, 32 Shinanomachi, Shinjuku-ku, Tokyo 160, Japan.

■ Career

Soka Gakkai, Tokyo, Japan, president, 1960-79, honorary president, 1979—; Soka Gakkai International, Tokyo, president, 1975—. Seikyo Press, honorary president. Founder of schools, including Soka Junior and Senior High Schools, Tokyo, 1968, and Kansai, 1973; Soka University, 1971; Sapporo Soka Kindergarten, 1976; Soka Elementary School, Tokyo, 1978, and Kansai, 1982; and Soka Women's Junior College, 1985. Also founder of Institute of Oriental Philosophy, 1962, Min-On Concert Association, 1963, Komeito Party, 1964, Fuji Art Museum, 1973, and Tokyo Fuji Art Museum, 1983. *Member:* Kenya Oral Literature Association, Brazilian Academy of Letters.

■ Awards, Honors

Poet Laureate, World Academy of Arts and Culture, 1981; United Nations Peace Award, 1983; Order of the Sun of Peru in the Grade of Grand Cross, 1984; Glorious Order of Christopher Columbus in the Grade of Grand Cross, Dominican Republic, 1987; Order of Vasco Nunez de Balboa in the Grade of Grand Official, Panama, 1987; United Nations Honorable Award, 1988; United States Congressional Award for Peace through Youth, 1988; Contribution to Chinese Art Award, Chinese Ministry of Culture, 1989; Grand Cross of the National Order of Merit, Colombia, 1989; UNHCR Humanitarian Award, 1989; Commemorative Order of the Centenary of Turkish-Japanese Friendship, Turkey, 1990; National Order of the Southern Cross, Brazil, 1990; Order of Merit of May, the Grade of the Grand Cross, Argentina, 1990; International Eminent Poet, International Poets Academy, 1991; Knight Grand Cross of the Most Noble Order of the Crown, Thailand, 1991; Honorary Cross of Science and the Arts, Austria, 1992; Honorary membership, Austrian artists' association, Kunstlerhaus, 1992; Medal of the Grand Officer of the Order of Arts and Letters, France, 1992; International Tolerance Award, Simon Wiesenthal Center; Rosa Parks Humanitarian Award.

Honorary doctoral degrees from numerous universities, including Moscow State University 1975; University of Buenos Aires, 1990; University of Guanajuato, 1990; University of Philippines, 1991; Ankara University, 1992; University of Nairobi, 1992; and National University of Cordoba (Argentina), 1993. Honorary professorships awarded from numerous universities, including Beijing University, 1984; Wuhan University, China, 1990; and University of East Asia, Macao, 1991.

■ Writings

JUVENILE FICTION; IN ENGLISH TRANSLATION

Collected Stories for Children, Foundation for Children/Santi Pracha Dhamma Institute, 1989.
The Snow Country Prince, illustrated by Brian Wildsmith, translated by Geraldine McCaughrean, Knopf, 1991 (published in Japan by Rakuda Shuppan, 1990).
The Cherry Tree, illustrated by Wildsmith, translated by McCaughrean, Knopf, 1992 (published in Japan by Rakuda Shuppan, 1991).
The Princess and the Moon, illustrated by Wildsmith, translated by McCaughrean, Knopf, 1992 (published in Japan by Rakuda Shuppan, 1991).
Over the Deep Blue Sea, illustrated by Wildsmith, translated by McCaughrean, Knopf, 1992 (published in Japan by Rakuda Shuppan, 1992).
Princess in the Desert Country, Gakken, 1992.

DAISAKU IKEDA

YOUNG ADULT FICTION; IN ENGLISH TRANSLATION

Alexander's Decision, Shuei-sha, 1987.
Fireflies Glow, Shogaku-kan, 1987.
Hiroshima Story, Shuei-sha, 1987.
Rainbow over the Pacific Ocean, Kin-no-Hoshi-sha, 1987.
Star Park, Gakken, 1988.
Kanta and the Deer, Akane-shobo, 1989.
Dawn of Revolution, Shuei-sha, 1990.
Peace River, Poplar-sha, 1990.
Winds Rustling in the Fields, Sheui-sha, 1990.

YOUNG ADULT ESSAYS; IN ENGLISH TRANSLATION

Talking to Boys, Poplar-sha, 1971.
Essays on Boyhood, Seikyo Press, 1972.
To You Who Will Pioneer the Future, Kin-no-Hoshi-sha, 1972.
Advice to Young People, translated by Robert Epp, World Tribune Press, 1976 (published in Japan as *Mirai o Hiraku Kimitachi e,* 1972).
Words for 365 Days, Poplar-sha, 1974.
On Youth, Seikyo Press, 1975.
The Human Revolution—A Revised Version for Young Readers, five volumes, Seikyo Press, 1983-85.

FOR ADULTS; IN ENGLISH TRANSLATION

Lectures on Buddhism, translated by Takeo Kamio, Seikyo Press, 1962.
Science and Religion, Soka Gakkai, 1965 (originally published in Japan as *Kagaku to Shukyo,* 1965).

The Human Revolution, twelve volumes, Seikyo Press, 1965, abridged three volume edition, Weatherhill, 1972 (originally published in Japan as *Ningen Kakumei,* 1966).
Guidance Memo, translated by George M. Williams, World Tribune Press, 1975 (published in Japan under same title by Seikyo Press, 1966).
The Family Revolution, World Tribune Press, 1970 (originally published in Japan as *Katei Kakumei,* 1967).
Complete Works, Seikyo Press, 1968.
The People: A Collection of Poetry, translated by Robert Epp, World Tribune Press, 1972.
Buddhism: The First Millenium, Kodansha International, 1977 (published in Japan as *Watakushi no Bukkyo Kan,* 1974).
Buddhism: The Living Philosophy, East Publications, 1974.
The Tide Toward the Twenty-First Century: Addresses, Soka University Student International Center, c. 1975.
The Living Buddha: An Interpretive Biography, Weatherhill, 1976 (published in Japan as *Watakushi no Shakuson Kan,* 1975).
(With Arnold J. Toynbee) *Choose Life,* Oxford University Press, 1976 (published in Tokyo as *The Toynbee-Ikeda Dialogue,* Kodansha International, 1976).
Hopes and Dreams, translated by Epp, World Tribune Press, 1976.
Yesterday, Today, and Tomorrow (essays), translated by Epp, World Tribune Press, 1976.
Songs from My Heart, Weatherhill, 1978.

Also author of (with Aurelio Peccei) *Before It Is Too Late;* (with Rene Huyghe) *Dawn after Dark;* (with Bryan Wilson) *Human Values in a Changing World;* (with Karan Singh) *Humanity at the Crossroads;* (with Joseph Derbolav) *Search for a New Humanity;* (with Anatoli A. Logunov) *The Third Rainbow Bridge;* (with Chang Shuhong) *Brilliance of Dunhuang;* (with Linus Pauling) *A Lifelong Quest for Peace;* (with Norman Cousins) *A Dialogue between World Citizens;* (with Chingiz Aitmatov) *Ode to the Grand Spirit;* (with Chandra Wickramasinghe) *The Year 2000—Emergent Perspective;* (with Richard Nicolaus Garf von Coudenhove-Kalergi) *Civilization—the West and the East;* (with Yasushi Inoue) *Letters of Four Seasons;* (with Nemoto Makoto) *On the Japanese Classics; The Flower of Chinese Buddhism; Life: An Enigma, A Precious Jewel; Buddhism and the Cosmos; Unlocking the Mysteries of Birth and Death: Buddhism in the Contemporary World; A Lasting Peace—Collected Addresses of Daisaku Ikeda; A Lasting Peace; Glass Children and Other Essays; My Personal History; On Women; Selected Writings; On Historical Personalities and Society; Eiji Yoshikawa—His Personality and His World; Bouquet of Daily Life;* and *Songs of Victory.*

Ikeda's works have been translated into numerous languages, including Chinese, French, Spanish, German and Italian.

■ Sidelights

Daisaku Ikeda is a world-renowned poet, educator, philosopher, peace activist, photographer, and children's book author. His prodigious literary and philosophical output is devoted to the principles of Soka Gakkai ("Value-creating Association"), an international organization based on the principles of Mahayana Buddhism as taught by Nichiren Shoshu, a thirteenth-century monk. The stated goal of Soka Gakkai, whose membership worldwide exceeds ten million, is the promotion of peace, education, and culture.

Ikeda was the fifth of eight children born to a poor family engaged in the production of edible seaweeds in Tokyo. Ikeda was often ill as a child, but helped in the family business and even took on a paper route when he was in sixth grade to contribute to the family resources. Of this experience, Ikeda told *Something about the Author* (*SATA*): "Every day, when I finished my route, I felt exhilarated by a sense of having accomplished something. I refused to feel sorry for myself and tried always to face and overcome whatever obstacles arose. As young as I was, hurrying along dawn-lit streets in all kinds of weather, I knew that my experiences would stand me in good stead one day." The young Ikeda enjoyed reading and hoped to become a journalist, but when the Second World War started, he was required to work in an ironworks (a job that exacerbated his chronic respiratory problems and eventually caused tuberculosis).

After the war, Ikeda met Josei Toda, the owner of a publishing house called Nihon Shogakken. Ikeda became Toda'a pupil, eventually becoming editor in chief of a magazine called *Boken Shonen* ("Boys' Adventures"). "With the fire of youth, I dashed about striving to make our magazine more popular than any other," Ikeda told *SATA* of his early days at the publication, adding that "In railway stations, at bus stops, on the street, I was always thinking about what children were reading. In front of schools, I stopped pupils to ask what kinds of books they liked."

Ikeda's children's book exemplify the virtues of hope and perserverence in times of difficulty that their author embraces. In *The Cherry Tree,* for example, a little boy and his younger sister carefully wrap the trunk of an old cherry tree that has not bloomed since the war in order to protect it during the winter. When all the other people in the village have given up hope that the tree will ever bloom again, it does. *The Snow Country Prince* has a similar theme. Two children separated from their parents by the illness of their father during a long, harsh winter rescue and care for an injured swan, and are rewarded by the appearance of the Snow Country Prince. As the swan recovers and prepares to fly away, the children's father begins to get well and makes plans to return to his family. Of *The Snow Country Prince,* a *Publishers Weekly* reviewer commented: "The universal

When their father is stricken by a long illness, Mariko and Kazuo find courage by nursing an injured swan back to health. (Cover illustration by Brian Wildsmith.)

message of this Japanese folktale is well suited to young readers grappling with their burgeoning independence and responsibility," while a commentator for *Junior Bookshelf* concluded that Ikeda'a work is "a most beautiful book which manages to make its best effects by understatement."

Ikeda summed up his his hopes for his young readers by noting that he wants "to help create an age when smiling, playing children can experience happiness to the full. On the pure white canvas of the childish mind, we must project beautiful pictures filled with love, fantasy, and creativity. My decision to take up the writing of juvenile literature reflects my wish to achieve this end."

■ Works Cited

Review of *The Snow Country Prince, Junior Bookshelf,* February, 1991, p. 16.
Review of *The Snow Country Prince, Publishers Weekly,* September 13, 1991, p. 79.

■ For More Information See

PERIODICALS

School Library Journal, May, 1991, p. 57.
Wilson Library Bulletin, March, 1992, p. 93.*

J

JACOBS, Shannon K. 1947-

■ Personal

Born June 19, 1947, in Butte, MT; daughter of Dale F. (a geologist) and Virginia (a homemaker; maiden name, Slocum) Kittel; married George E. Jackson (an employee relations consultant), January 14, 1977. *Education:* Regina School of Nursing, R.N., 1967; University of Colorado, B.A., 1982. *Hobbies and other interests:* Traveling, painting, learning Spanish.

■ Addresses

Home and office—422 Cook Street, Denver, CO 80206.

■ Career

Worked as a registered nurse, various cities, 1967-78; University of California, Los Angeles, senior editor, 1978; Jeppesen Sanderson, Englewood, CO, technical writer, 1979-81; *Colorado Business,* Denver, CO, news and feature writer, 1981-82; United Cable Television, Denver, proposal writer, 1981-82; freelance writer, 1982-83, and 1987—; Craig Hospital, Englewood, CO, writer, 1983-85, patient-staff education coordinator, 1985-87. Denver Public Schools, volunteer tutor for Indian Education program, 1993—. *Member:* International Council for Bird Preservation, Society of Children's Book Writers and Illustrators, Cultural Survival, Sierra Club, Audubon Society, Nature Conservancy, Greenpeace, National Wildlife Federation, Cousteau Society, Defenders of Wildlife.

■ Writings

Next of Kin (a trilogy of one-act plays, comprised of *Birds of a Feather, Cross My Heart,* and *Finders and Keepers*), produced by the University of Colorado at Denver Department of Theatre, 1986.
Song of the Giraffe, Little, Brown, 1991.
The Boy Who Loved Morning, Little, Brown, 1993.

SHANNON K. JACOBS

Contributor of articles to *Colorado Offices & Design, Colorado Homes & Lifestyles, Frontier, Colorado Business,* and *National Observer.* Contributor of poetry to the "Poetry Forum" in the *Denver Post.* Author of children's plays, including *Sweet William the First,* produced by Goddard Middle School, 1983.

■ **Work in Progress**

Australian Stories, based on the author's travels to Australia. Research on the ways of life, traditions, and social structures of Native Americans, Bushmen, and Aborigines; on the Pygmies of Central Africa; and on regional wildlife rehabilitators and rescuers.

■ **Sidelights**

Shannon K. Jacobs told *SATA:* "I began writing when I was about nine or ten. At first I tried to write novels and short stories, then I settled on poetry, which became my main mode of writing during my teenage and young adult years. Because I was very shy and had a hard time talking with people, poetry helped me learn who I really was by discovering how I really felt. In school, other kids thought I was 'stuck-up' because I wasn't warm and friendly on the outside. But I knew I was caring and sensitive on the inside. I just didn't know how to express that part of myself.

"Gradually, by expressing my thoughts, feelings, and opinions in writing, I discovered more about who I was. And it helped me learn to express what was inside. I developed a sense of pride because I was creating something *and* it was a reflection of my inner self. It was important also that I kept these works private, only showing them to very close friends, until I felt strong enough and wanted to share them with others. Poetry is such a private expression. If I hadn't been a writer, I don't know how I would have discovered that person locked up inside. I'm very grateful for the therapeutic effects of writing.

"I grew up in New Mexico, living for three years on the Laguna Indian Reservation when I was seven to ten years old. That time left a definite impression on me and my writing. It taught me the deepest respect and gratitude for Native people and their profound love of Earth and of all life. What I would most like to achieve through my works is the creation of stories that allow others to experience the richness of indigenous peoples' ways of life—their love of family, social harmony, and ongoing care of and respect for the natural world. We have so much to learn from their ways, developed over thousands of years.

"The most important advice I can give to other writers, based on my own experience, is: *write about that which you love.* Then the research, writing, editing, and submitting is ALL WORTH IT, even if it doesn't get published. Also, write every day, pretend you are in training, for that is exactly what it is. Save your everyday writing because sometimes that's where the best ideas come from. And, finally, I would tell aspiring writers to plan on rewriting and editing what they do many, many times. They need to learn to enjoy this process, this refinement, as a sculptor polishes his work, as a painter layers her works, as any artist must perfect his/her work, to make it the very best."

CHARLOTTE FOLTZ JONES

JONES, Charlotte Foltz 1945-

■ **Personal**

Born November 1, 1945, in Boulder, CO; daughter of Forrest C. (an aeronautical technician) and Mildred E. (an office manager; maiden name, Deibert) Foltz; married William C. R. Jones (a carpet installer and builder), April 17, 1971; children: John Paul. *Education:* Central Business College, received advanced secretarial degree, 1964; attended University of Colorado. *Religion:* Roman Catholic. *Hobbies and other interests:* Needlework, railroading, hiking.

■ **Addresses**

Home—1620 Quince Avenue, Boulder, CO 80304.

■ **Career**

Boulder Valley Public Schools, Boulder, CO, secretary, 1966-1975; free-lance writer, 1976—. Writing instructor, Boulder Valley Schools Lifelong Learning, 1990-93, and Boulder Senior Center, 1991. *Member:* Society of Children's Book Writers and Illustrators (Rocky Mountain Division President, 1989-90), National Writers Club, Colorado Authors League.

■ **Awards, Honors**

Distinguished Achievement Award, Educational Press Association of America, 1984, for an article published in *Growing Parent/Growing Child;* first place in essay category, Mentor Magazine Contest, 1990; finalist, Colorado Authors League/Colorado Center for the Book Contest, 1991, for *Mistakes That Worked;* Top Hand Award in children's non-fiction book category, Colorado Authors League, 1992, for *Mistakes That Worked.*

■ Writings

Only Child: Clues for Coping, Westminster, 1984.
Mistakes That Worked, illustrated by John O'Brien, Doubleday, 1991.

Contributor to magazines.

■ Sidelights

"There must be no greater accomplishment than to touch a child's life in a positive way," Charlotte Foltz Jones told *SATA.* "And the greatest reward is to have a child say, 'I read *all* your book and I liked it. I really did!'"

Jones's first book for children, *Only Child: Clues for Coping,* was the product of her experiences as an only child and as the mother of an only child. The book offers advice to children with no brothers and sisters, intended to help them deal with the expectations of those from larger families. In a *School Library Journal* review, Phyllis K. Kennemer found that the book offered sound advice regarding "making and keeping friends, coming to terms with feelings, and avoiding boredom." Anne Raymer, reviewing the book in *Voice of Youth Advocates,* praised *Only Child* for the way that it "disputes the old myths characterizing only children as lonely, spoiled, or maladjusted."

Jones approached a different topic for her second book, *Mistakes That Worked.* This book, illustrated by John O'Brien, describes inventions and discoveries that were made unintentionally. "In fact," observes Cathryn A. Camper in a *School Library Journal* review, "some of the inventors had no idea they'd stumbled on something useful until years later." Several brand-name products, such as Coca-Cola, which was originally concocted as a headache remedy, are included in the collection.

Commenting on her reasons for writing, Jones told *SATA:* "When I sit down to write, I don't think in terms that I am writing for children. I write for myself— maybe for the part of me that never grew up, the part that still wonders and looks about in amazement. There is so much I don't know so I look for answers that satisfy the child I used to be."

■ Works Cited

Camper, Cathryn A., review of *Mistakes That Worked, School Library Journal,* October, 1991, p. 139.
Kennemer, Phyllis K., review of *Only Child: Clues for Coping, School Library Journal,* February, 1985, p. 76.
Raymer, Anne, review of *Only Child: Clues for Coping, Voice of Youth Advocates,* June, 1985, p. 146.

■ For More Information See

PERIODICALS

Booklist, October 15, 1991, p. 437.
Bulletin of the Center for Children's Books, October, 1991, p. 41.

K

KAHL, Jonathan (D.) 1959-

■ Personal

Born May 7, 1959, in Shirley, MA; son of Richard and Roslyn Kahl; married Carol Jean Waldvogel (a music teacher), 1987; children: Joseph James and Samantha Rose. *Education:* University of Michigan, B.A., 1981, M.S., 1983, Ph.D., 1987.

■ Addresses

Home—4762 North Elkhart Ave., Whitefish Bay, WI 53211.

■ Career

National Oceanic and Atmospheric Administration, Boulder, CO, research associate, 1987-89; University of Wisconsin—Milwaukee, Milwaukee, WI, professor of atmospheric science, 1990—. *Member:* American Meteorological Society.

■ Writings

Weatherwise: Learning about the Weather, Lerner, 1992.
Wet Weather: Rain Showers and Snowfall, Lerner, 1992.
The Power of Tornadoes and Hurricanes, Lerner, 1993.
Thunder and Lightning, Lerner, 1993.

■ Sidelights

"I'm very excited about the weather," Jonathan Kahl told *SATA.* "One of my biggest goals as a meteorologist, educator and author is to share this interest with others, especially kids. There's a lot of raw beauty in the sky and in the clouds—you just have to get used to looking for it."

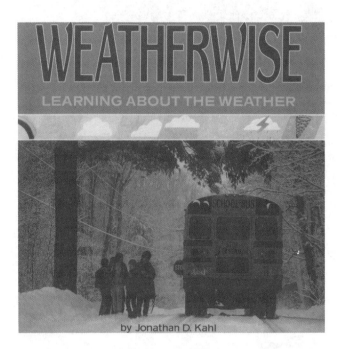

Young readers can learn all about what causes different kinds of weather in Kahl's informative introduction to meteorology.

KERR, Tom 1950-

■ Personal

Born June 1, 1950, in Plainfield, NJ; son of Robert Corry Kerr II (a manufacturers representative) and Florence Kerr (a homemaker; maiden name, Bigelow); married Heather Ritchie, December 29, 1974 (divorced August 28, 1986); married Mary Isabelle Marshall (in advertising sales), September 20, 1986; children: Emily French. *Education:* Williams College, B.A., 1972; State College of Victoria, Hawthorn, Australia, diploma of education, 1974. *Religion:* Episcopalian. *Hobbies and other interests:* Guitar, photography.

TOM KERR

■ **Addresses**

Home—125 Bamm Hollow Rd., Middletown, NJ 07748. *Office*—*Asbury Park Press,* 3601 Highway 66, Neptune, NJ 07754.

■ **Career**

Education Department of Victoria, Victoria, Australia, teacher-artist and consultant, 1973-77. *Melbourne Sun,* Melbourne, Australia, artist, 1977-84; *Asbury Park Press,* Neptune, NJ, news artist, 1986—. Christ Church, youth group advisor, 1990—, member of choir, 1992—. *Member:* American Association of Editorial Cartoonists, Society of Newspaper Design, National Cartoonists Society.

■ **Awards, Honors**

Award of Excellence, Society of Newspaper Design, 1993, for page design and illustration; First Place award for color illustration, NJPA, 1993.

■ **Illustrator**

Tova Navarra, *Playing It Smart: What to Do When You're on Your Own,* Barron's, 1989.
Wayne Eldridge, *Best Pet Name Book Ever,* Barron's, 1990.
"Whiz Quiz" series, eight books, Barron's, 1990-92.

Michele A. Paige, *After the SAT's: An Insider's Guide to Freshman Year,* Barron's, 1991.
Andy Seamans, *Who, What, When, Where, Why in the World of World History,* Barron's, 1991.
Seamans, *Who, What, When, Where, Why in the World of Nature,* Barron's, 1992.
Navarra, *On My Own: Helping Kids Help Themselves,* Barron's, 1993.

■ **Work in Progress**

Children's books entitled *George the Upside-Down Dog* and *Lester the Fire-Breathing Dragon;* a picture book of beach activities titled *At the Beach.*

■ **Sidelights**

Tom Kerr told *SATA:* "I began my illustrating career on the beaches of Maine when I was a child. The first drawing I remember was a Bugs Bunny of which I was very proud. Hauling my mother down to the very site the next day, I was to discover that the tides have the soul of an editor—the drawing was washed away. I have drawn all my life and dreamed of drawing for and about children even as a child. I have never had any real art training per se, but simply love to draw. My first story was a special project taken on in college. It was a story about a young boy and a pirate which I both wrote and illustrated. It turned out badly, but underlined the deep interest I have in the genre. I never thought, however, that I could make a living as an illustrator until I was asked at age twenty-four what I wanted to do 'when I grew up.' It was then that I said I wanted to draw for a living. Freelancing from the house after school (I was a teacher at that time), I submitted to every newspaper, magazine and publisher I could find.

"I hope to re-create the sense of fun, playfulness, curiosity, energy and honesty that all children possess. Add to that the gift of humor and you've got me pegged.

"Since I work for a newspaper during the day, I work on my illustrations early in the morning before everyone gets up. I feel fresher and more energetic in the morning, although deadlines have a way of making the morning last for 24 hours.

"I always feel I am working for the child, not the publisher, when I draw. In *Playing It Smart,* this was especially true, when my drawings were meant to show kids how to cope on their own when parents aren't around.

"My real favorites have been the great pen-and-ink artists of the last century. A. B. Frost is an absolute favorite, with Edward W. Kemble, Gustave Dore, Norman Lindsay and others being part of the group. I also love the innocent simplicity of E. H. Shepard. It is difficult to point to specific contemporary illustrators and writers. The market has grown so significantly that there is a huge pool of talent now in print.

"My advice is simple: Anyone who can't take rejection should not be in the business. It takes persistence, patience and very thick skin. If you believe in your work and work to improve, then there is a future."

*   *   *

KNIGHT, Theodore O. 1946-

■ Personal

Born October 14, 1946, in Providence, RI; son of Monroe O. (an electrician) and Lilla (a librarian; maiden name, Taudvin) Knight; married Norma Aldrich (a special education teacher), August 10, 1968, children: Matthew Monroe, Anne Aldrich. *Education:* Brown University, B.A. (with honors), 1968; State University of New York at Buffalo, Ph.D., 1975; further study at Rhode Island College, and Roger Williams College. *Politics:* Independent. *Religion:* "Varies." *Hobbies and other interests:* Hiking, canoeing, family, travel, music, reading.

■ Addresses

Home and office—89 Johnson Rd., Foster, RI 02825.

THEODORE O. KNIGHT

■ Career

College Hill Book Store, Providence, RI, manager, 1975-81; Jamestown Publishers, Providence, RI, senior editor, 1982-88; freelance writer/editor, 1989—. Instructor in literature and writing at various colleges and universities, 1971—.

■ Writings

(Editor) Jerry Silbert, Douglas Carnine, and Marcy Stein, *Direct Instruction Mathematics* (textbook), Charles E. Merrill/Custom Publishing, 1989.
(Editor) Deborah Greh, *Computers in the Artroom,* Davis Publications, 1989.
Silver Burdett and Ginn Social Studies—World Cultures (teacher's edition), Silver Burdett/Ginn-Mazer, 1990.
Heath Composition and Grammar, Grade 12 (teacher's edition), D. C. Heath/Boultinghouse & Boultinghouse, 1990.
The Olympic Games, Lucent Books-Greenhaven Press, 1991.
(Editor) *Glencoe English, Grade 12* (teacher's edition), Glencoe/Ligature, 1991.
(Editor) *Macmillan Reading, Grade 8* (teacher's edition), Macmillan, 1991.
Study Strategies for Career Programs (textbook), Richard D. Irwin, 1993.
Study Strategies for College Programs (textbook), Richard D. Irwin, 1993.

Also editor of *ACTION Anthology* series of remedial reading anthologies, Scholastic, Inc. Book review columnist for *Buffalo Spree* magazine, 1972—; reviewer for *Magill's Book Reviews* (online service), 1991—.

■ Work in Progress

College level reading skills textbook, publication expected in 1994; a young adult biography of former President Jimmy Carter; a history of the Olympic Games for adults.

■ Sidelights

Theodore O. Knight told *SATA:* "As a freelance writer who works in several areas, I'm constantly trying to combine my knowledge and background with my interests and the need to earn a living. I enjoy doing young adult non-fiction, because it gives me an opportunity to learn more about all sorts of subjects that excite my interest. Writing about things so that they are clear to young adult readers is a great exercise in really learning a subject."

L

LAIRD, Elizabeth 1943-

■ Personal

Born October 21, 1943, in Wellington, New Zealand; daughter of John MacLelland (a general secretary) and Florence Marion (a homemaker; maiden name, Thomson) Laird; married David Buchanan McDowall (a writer), April 19, 1975; children: Angus John, William Alistair Somerled. *Education:* University of Bristol, B.A. (with honors), 1966; London University, Certificate of Education, 1967; Edinburgh University, M.Litt., 1971. *Religion:* Church of England. *Hobbies and other interests:* Chamber music, gardening.

■ Addresses

Home—31 Cambrian Rd., Richmond, Surrey TW10 6JQ, England.

■ Career

Writer, 1980—. Bede Mariam School, Addis Ababa, Ethiopia, teacher, 1967-69; Pathway Further Education Centre, Southall, London, England, lecturer, 1972-77. *Member:* Society of Authors and Illustrators, Anglo-Ethiopian Society.

■ Awards, Honors

Carnegie Award runner-up, and Burnley Express Book Award, both 1988, both for *Red Sky in the Morning;* Children's Book Award, 1992; Sheffield Children's Book Award, 1992; Glazen Globe prize, Royal Dutch Geographical Society, 1993, all for *Kiss the Dust.*

■ Writings

Anna and the Fighter, illustrated by Gay Galsworthy, Heinemann Educational, 1977.
The House on the Hill, illustrated by Galsworthy, Heinemann Educational, 1978.
The Garden, illustrated by Peter Dennis, Heinemann Educational, 1979.

ELIZABETH LAIRD

The Big Green Star, illustrated by Leslie Smith, Collins, 1982.
The Blanket House, illustrated by Smith, Collins, 1982.
The Doctor's Bag, illustrated by Smith, Collins, 1982.
Jumper, illustrated by Smith, Collins, 1982.
(With Abba Aregawi Wolde Gabriel) *The Miracle Child: A Story from Ethiopia,* Holt, 1985.
The Dark Forest, illustrated by John Richardson, Collins, 1986.

The Long House in Danger, illustrated by Richardson, Collins, 1986.

Henry and the Birthday Surprise, illustrated by Mike Hibbert, photographs by Robert Hill, BBC, 1986.

The Road to Bethlehem: An Ethiopian Nativity, foreward by Terry Waite, Holt, 1987.

Prayers for Children, illustrated by Margaret Tempest, Collins, 1987.

Wet and Dry, Pan Books, 1987.

Hot and Cold, Pan Books, 1987.

Light and Dark, Pan Books, 1987.

Heavy and Light, Pan Books, 1987.

Busy Day, illustrated by Carolyn Scrace, Children's Press Choice, 1987.

Happy Birthday! A Book of Birthday Celebrations, illustrated by Satomi Ichikawa, Collins, 1987.

Hymns for Children, illustrated by Tempest, Collins, 1988.

Sid and Sadie, illustrated by Alan Marks, Collins, 1988.

(With Olivia Madden) *The Inside Outing,* illustrated by Deborah Ward, Barron, 1988.

Red Sky in the Morning, Heinemann, 1988, published as *Loving Ben,* Delacorte, 1989.

Crackers, Heinemann, 1989.

Rosy's Garden: A Child's Keepsake of Flowers, illustrated by Ichikawa, Philomel, 1990.

Kiss the Dust, Dutton, 1991.

The Pink Ghost of Lamont, Heinemann, 1991.

Hiding Out, Heinemann, 1993.

THE CUBBY BEARS BOOKS

The Cubby Bears' Birthday Party, illustrated by Scrace, Collins, 1985.

The Cubby Bears Go Camping, illustrated by Scrace, Collins, 1985.

The Cubby Bears Go on the River, illustrated by Scrace, Collins, 1985.

The Cubby Bears Go Shopping, illustrated by Scrace, Collins, 1985.

LITTLE RED TRACTOR BOOKS

The Day The Ducks Went Skating, illustrated by Colin Reeder, Tambourine Books, 1991.

The Day Veronica Was Nosy, illustrated by Reeder, Tambourine Books, 1991.

The Day Sidney Ran Off, illustrated by Reeder, Tambourine Books, 1991.

The Day Patch Stood Guard, illustrated by Reeder, Tambourine Books, 1991.

TOUCAN 'TECS SERIES

The Grand Ostrich Ball, illustrated by Peter Lawson, Heinemann, 1989.

Artic Blues, illustrated by Lawson, Heinemann, 1989.

Gopher Gold, illustrated by Lawson, Heinemann, 1989.

High Flyers, illustrated by Lawson, Heinemann, 1989.

Going Cuckoo, illustrated by Lawson, Heinemann, 1989.

Fine Feathered Friends, illustrated by Lawson, Heinemann, 1989.

Kookaburra Cackles, illustrated by Lawson, Heinemann, 1989.

Peacock Palace Scoop, illustrated by Lawson, Heinemann, 1989.

Highland Fling, illustrated by County Studio, Buzz Books, 1991.

The Big Drip, illustrated by County Studio, Buzz Books, 1991.

Desert Island Ducks, illustrated by County Studio, Buzz Books, 1991.

The Snail's Tale, illustrated by County Studio, Buzz Books, 1991.

FOR ADULTS

English in Education, Oxford University Press, 1977.

Welcome: To Great Britain and the U.S.A., Longman, 1983.

Faces of Britain, Longman, 1986.

Faces of U.S.A., photographs by Darryl Williams, Longman, 1987.

Arcadia, Macmillan, 1990.

■ Work in Progress

A novel for adults based on the life of the Russian mathematician Sonia Kovalevsky; screenplays for *The Bible, the Animated Version,* made in Russia and Britain in association with the British Broadcasting Corporation, and S4C, Channel 4 Wales.

■ Sidelights

A linguistics expert with a passion for travel, Elizabeth Laird has written on a wide range of subjects for young adult readers, including Christian folklore from Africa, the Kurdish rebellion in Iraq, and the death of a younger sibling. Laird has been inspired by her experiences as a traveller and teacher, and was particularly motivated to adapt Ethiopian Christian folklore for a European audience after spending two years in Ethiopia. "I always had a burning desire to travel," Laird told *SATA,* "and as soon as I possibly could, at the age of eighteen, I took off from home (with my parents blessing!) and went to Malaysia where I spent a year as a teacher's aide in a boarding school for Malay girls. That experience only gave me a taste for more, so after I had graduated in French (which involved a wonderful spell as a student in Paris) I headed off to Ethiopia, and worked for two years in a school in Addis Ababa. In those days the country was at peace, and it was possible to travel to the remotest parts by bus and on horseback."

Exploring Foreign Lands

That experience provided the background for *The Miracle Child: A Story from Ethiopia,* which was written in collaboration with Abba Aregawi Wolde Gabrie. The book recounts the life of Takla Haymanot, a thirteenth-century Ethiopian saint revered for the miracles of healing the sick and raising the dead. The text is accompanied by reproductions of eighteenth-century paintings by Ethiopian Monks. Vincent Crapanzano of the *New York Times Book Review,* asserted that the reproductions are "informative and explain many of the artistic conventions of Ethiopian painting in a manner so simple as to be understandable to a child, yet interesting to an adult."

Laird's second adaptation of Ethiopian religious folklore followed the same format. *The Road to Bethlehem: An Ethiopian Nativity,* is an Ethiopian account of the events surrounding the birth of Jesus. The tale presents a more earthly account of the nativity than the standard Christian version, and credits Mary with an active role as a healer and saint. "Mary is no ordinary woman in these stories, and not just because she is the mother of Jesus," observes Rosemary L. Bray of the *New York Times Book Review.* "As the Holy Family flees Herod into Egypt, Mary embarks on a ministry of healing: 'The dumb spoke, the lame ran, the deaf heard, and the blind could see.'" A reviewer from the *Bulletin of the Center for Children's Books* concluded that *The Road to Bethlehem* combines familiar themes of the New Testament "with popular legends and miracles into a cohesive narrative."

Laird's interest in foreign places inspired another novel, *Kiss the Dust.* Set in Iraq, the novel tells the story of Tara Khan, a twelve-year-old Kurdish girl, whose family is forced to relocate as the result of the Iraqi govern-

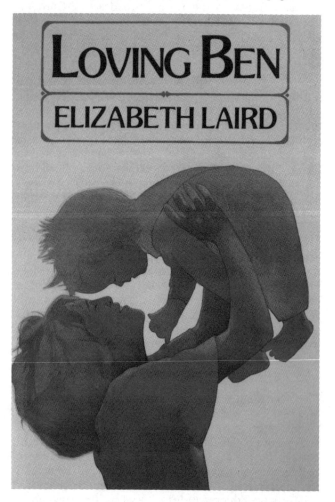

Laird's own personal tragedy inspired this heartwarming tale about Anna and her handicapped brother Ben. (Cover illustration by Neil Waldman.)

ment's attempts to suppress the Kurds. Tara's family escapes first to Iran, where she is forced to adopt a highly conservative Muslim lifestyle, and finally to England, where she must confront the shock of an entirely new, secular culture. Critics have commented on the graphic depiction of violence in the story, and although some find the detail unnecessary, others find it appropriate to, and accurate for, the wartime situations in which Tara is embroiled and is fleeing. "*Kiss the Dust* is filled with wonderfully researched ethnographic details about both Kurdish and refugee culture, and opens a door to a foreign world," writes Elizabeth Cohen of the *New York Times Book Review.* This is particularly the case, observes Cohen, when Tara makes comparisons between her journey's beginning in urban Sulaimaniya and its end in a working-class neighborhood in London.

Using Family Experiences

Laird's first novel for young adults was inspired by the birth and death of a younger brother. *Red Sky in the Morning* (released as *Loving Ben* in the U.S.) tells the story of Anna, the twelve-year-old narrator, whose brother, Ben, is born brain damaged. Through Anna, Laird recreates the family struggle of raising a handicapped child, and the confusing feelings of pain and release experienced when the child dies. "Anna's voice rings true throughout as she moves from awkwardness and judgmental statements to a more mature empathy," writes Barbara Chatton in a *School Library Journal* review. Critics also praised the author's rendering of the adult characters outside Anna's family. The adults who help Anna understand new aspects of human nature "are sufficiently real, and the story homely and natural enough for the wisdom of the moral lessons conveyed to be palatable," writes a *Junior Bookshelf* reviewer.

Laird has also written for younger children. Her book *Rosy's Garden: A Child's Keepsake of Flowers,* is a collection of flower lore and legend dispensed within the framework of Rosy's visits to her garden-loving grandmother's house. In addition to the story-telling, Rosy's grandmother teaches her to make such garden trifles as rose water, potpourri, and herb sandwiches. *Rosy's Garden* is an "unusual treasury of flower lore" according to Carolyn Phelan's review in *Booklist.*

Laird has also written the text for several picture books, including the *Cubby Bears* and *Little Red Tractor* books. In the latter, a tractor and its driver, Stan, come to the rescue of farmers and livestock in need of assistance. While Duncan, the tractor, is never given human thoughts or actions, it still becomes "a character in the gentle stories," commented Carolyn Phelan in a *Booklist* review. And according to *School Library Journal's* Nancy Seiner "child appeal is assured by the winning personalities of the animals and the major role played by the tractor."

Commenting on her work for *SATA,* Laird wrote: "I started writing when the children were small, though I had written a detailed diary since I was a child. For a

In one of the Little Red Tractor books, a piglet named Sidney leads Duncan and Stan on a merry chase. (Cover illustration by Colin Reeder.)

long time I stuck to familiar themes, close to home, or wrote about important events in my childhood, like the death of my younger brother, which I drew upon in *Loving Ben.* Now, however I feel I can mine those years of travel, and I made a start with *Kiss the Dust.*

"I feel immensely privileged to be able to earn my living as a writer. I cherish the freedom. I enjoy working on my own thing in my own time. I also love the unexpectedness. I never know where the inspiration will strike next, or into what exciting byways it will lead me."

■ **Works Cited**

Bray, Rosemary L., review of *The Road to Bethlehem, New York Times Book Review,* December 6, 1987, p. 80.

Chatton, Barbara, review of *Loving Ben, School Library Journal,* September, 1989, p. 252.

Cohen, Elizabeth, review of *Kiss the Dust, New York Times Book Review,* October 4, 1992, p. 22.

Crapazano, Vincent, "Tekla the Wonderworker," *New York Times Book Review,* November 10, 1985, p. 38.

Phelan, Carolyn, review of *Rosy's Garden, Booklist,* March 15, 1990, p. 1446.

Review of *Red Sky in the Morning, Junior Bookshelf,* August, 1988, p. 197.

Review of *The Road to Bethlehem, Bulletin of the Centre for Children's Books,* January, 1988.

Seiner, Nancy, review of *The Day Patch Stood Guard* and *The Day Sidney Ran Off, School Library Journal,* September, 1991, p. 236.

■ **For More Information See**

PERIODICALS

Booklist, June 1, 1991, p. 1879.
Bulletin of the Centre for Children's Books, October, 1989, p. 36.
Kirkus Reviews, October 1, 1989, p. 1476.
Publishers Weekly, October 27, 1989, p. 70.
School Library Journal, July, 1990, p. 61; July, 1992, p. 90.
Washington Post Book World, February 11, 1990, p. 6.

*   *   *

LANKFORD, Mary D. 1932-

■ **Personal**

Born December 7, 1932, in Denton, TX; divorced, 1983; children: four. *Education:* University of North Texas, B.A., 1952; Texas Woman's University, M.L.S., 1982; graduate study at Eastern New Mexico State University. *Hobbies and other interests:* Gardening, travel, piano, reading.

MARY D. LANKFORD

■ Addresses

Home—500 Kosstre, Irving, TX 75061. *Office*—820 O'Connor Rd., Irving, TX 75061.

■ Career

Dover, DE, elementary school librarian, 1962-63; Walker Air Force Base, Roswell, NM, media services librarian, 1965-66; Irving Independent School District, Irving, TX, director of library and media services, 1966—. Adjunct professor, University of North Texas and Texas Woman's University, School of Library and Information Studies. Member of advisory committee, Elementary School Library Collection, Brodart Foundation, 1977—; member of Teacher Education Advisory Committee, University of Dallas, 1980-88; member of advisory committee, University of North Texas, School of Library Science, 1981-83; chair, advisory committee, Texas Woman's University, School of Library and Information Studies, 1984-91. *Member:* International Reading Association, American Library Association, Texas Library Association, Phi Delta Kappa.

■ Awards, Honors

Texas Association of School Librarians distinguished library service award for school administrators, 1984; University of North Texas School of Library and Information Science distinguished alumnus award, 1984; Texas Library Association distinguished service award, 1985; inducted into University of North Texas School of Library and Information Science Hall of Fame, 1989; Media Program of the Year Award, American Association of School Librarians, 1991; University of North Texas distinguished alumni award, 1992.

■ Writings

Is it Dark? Is it Light?, Knopf, 1991.
Hopscotch Around the World, Morrow, 1992.
Films for Learning, Thinking, and Doing, Libraries Unlimited, 1992.
Educational Fieldtrips, ABC-CLIO, 1992
Christmas Customs Around the World, Morrow, 1993.
The Quinceanera, Millbrook Press, 1993.

OTHER

Contributor to *School Library Journal, Texas School Business, Texas Library Journal, Booklist,* and other publications. Member of editorial advisory board, *Booklist,* 1979-83, and *Book Links,* 1993; consultant, *Children's Catalog,* 15th edition, H. W. Wilson, 1986. Newsletter editor, Texas Association of School Library Administrators, 1985-87.

■ Sidelights

"Books and writing have been a part of my life since childhood," Mary D. Lankford told *Something about the Author* (*SATA*). "My decision to become a librarian was made in the fourth grade. I loved the librarian; I loved the way the library smelled (she used lacquer on the books); I loved to read; and I knew I would be happy doing something with books and reading.

"*Is It Dark? Is It Light?* is the result of an idea I got while driving. The road looked as if it could drive into a full moon. As clouds moved across the moon, it began to look square, not round. I started playing with opposites about the moon, putting some of those words on a post-it note on my steering wheel. *Hopscotch Around the World* was a result of curiosity. I read that this game was etched in the Forum in Rome, and was considered one of the oldest games. I began checking the indexes of game books, looking for the word 'hopscotch'. I made copies of these games. I then started interviewing people about how they played hopscotch in their state or country.

"I am delighted that the books I have written have been so well received by teachers, librarians, and young people."

*   *   *

LEVINE, Evan 1962-

■ Personal

Born June 15, 1962, in Chicago, IL; daughter of Paul and Phyllis Levine; married Robert Levy (an editor and writer), December 2, 1990. *Education:* Swarthmore College, B.A.; New York University, M.A.

■ Career

Author of books for children. Metropolitan Museum of Art, New York, writer/editor for children's publications; Marymount Manhattan College, New York, instructor in writing for children. *Member:* Society of Children's Book Writers and Illustrators.

EVAN LEVINE

■ Writings

Not the Piano, Mrs. Medley!, illustrated by S. D. Schindler, Orchard, 1991.
Kids Pick the 200 Best Videos for Kids, Phoros/St. Martin's Press, 1993.
What's Black and White and Came to Visit?, illustrated by Betsy Lewin, Orchard, 1994.

Also author of "Children's Guide to T.V." (weekly newspaper column), distributed by United Feature Syndicate.

■ Work in Progress

"Working on a new picture book."

■ Sidelights

Evan Levine told *SATA:* "I've always loved children's books, and feel great pleasure that I can 'give something back' to a field that has given me so much pleasure. I've written two picture books and hope to write many more. I love it, but I write very slowly, and I go through many, many drafts.

"So far, everything I've written has come out of my own experience—events that mattered to me, that were important. I especially like to write about role reversals and everyday events that become wildly exaggerated.

"I like to read quirky authors for kids. Some of my favorites are William Steig, Arthur Yorinks, and Russell Hoban.

"My advice to aspiring writers is not original, but it's true: keep at it no matter what! Writing for kids may look easy, but it's hard work. Write about things you really care about—always know why you're writing about that subject, what it is that drew you, that demands to be told. And read a lot of children's books!"

*   *   *

LINDENBAUM, Pija 1955-

■ Personal

Born April 27, 1955, in Sundsvall, Sweden; daughter of Gosta Lindenbaum (a director) and Barbro Kalin Olsson (a teacher); married Mikael Nilsson (an artist), May 18, 1989; children: Alva. *Education:* Konstfackskolan, 1975-79.

■ Addresses

Home—Sulitelmav 13, 161 33 Bromma, Sweden. *Office*—Nipfjallsv 1, 161 33 Bromma, Sweden.

■ Career

Writer and illustrator.

PIJA LINDENBAUM

■ Awards, Honors

Boodil My Dog was named one of the best illustrated books of 1992 by the *New York Times.*

■ Writings

(And illustrator) *Else-Marie and Her Seven Little Daddies,* Henry Holt, 1991.
(And illustrator) *Boodil My Dog,* translated by Gabrielle Charbonnet, Henry Holt, 1992.

■ Work in Progress

Illustrating a children's book by Swedish author Lennart Hagefors.

■ Sidelights

Pija Lindenbaum told *SATA:* "When my first manuscript with illustrations, *Else-Marie and Her Seven Daddies,* was completed, wrapped in a parcel and on its way to being published, I didn't realize that the book would be given such a reception, or that it would arouse such feeling in readers from different countries. I only thought that I had written a fairy tale, an unbelievable story to laugh at.

"But people wanted to know who the author was, and how I really felt. It was quite amusing to me that people talked more about me than about the book. During the Book Fair in Bologna that year, a German publisher asked my publisher for a copy of the book to bring to her psychiatrist. Some people didn't think it was possible to publish it. But there were many who dared, and that has made me very happy and grateful. In Sweden, *Else-Marie and Her Seven Daddies* was awarded three literary prizes and grants; it was also dramatized for a production in Amsterdam."*

Puzzles, colorful illustrations and photos, and a fold-out clockface are included in this instructive book.

LLEWELLYN, Claire 1954-

■ Personal

Born in 1954 in Great Britain; married, 1979; children: one daughter and one son.

■ Addresses

Home and office—27 North Road Ave., Hertford, Herts SG14 2BT, England.

■ Career

Longman Publishers, editor, 1978-84; Macdonald Children's Books, commissioning editor, 1984—. Writer of children's books.

■ Writings

My First Book of Time, illustrated by Julie Carpenter, photographs by Paul Bricknell, Dorling Kindersley, 1992.

"FIRST LOOK" SERIES

First Look at Clothes, Gareth Stevens Children's Books, 1991.
First Look in the Air, Gareth Stevens Children's Books, 1991.

First Look at Growing Food, Gareth Stevens Children's Books, 1991.
First Look under the Sea, Gareth Stevens Children's Books, 1991.

"TAKE ONE" SERIES

Changing Clothes, Simon & Schuster, 1990.
Growing Food, Simon & Schuster, 1990.
Under the Sea, Simon & Schuster, 1990.
In the Air, Simon & Schuster, 1990.
Rubbish Simon & Schuster, 1990.
Bridges, Simon & Schuster, 1990.
Winter, Simon & Schuster, 1991.
Spring, Simon & Schuster, 1991.
Summer, Simon & Schuster, 1991.
Autumn, Simon & Schuster, 1991.

■ For More Information See

PERIODICALS

Booklist, October 15, 1991, p. 441.
Bulletin of the Center for Children's Books, July, 1992, p. 299.
Horn Book, July, 1992, p. 468.
Junior Bookshelf, June, 1992, pp. 112-113.
Kirkus Reviews, May 1, 1992, p. 613.
Publishers Weekly, May 4, 1992, p. 55.
School Library Journal, August, 1992, p. 152.*

*   *   *

LLOYD, Megan 1958-

■ Personal

Born November 5, 1958, in Harrisburg, PA; daughter of Warren (a history teacher) and Lois (a kindergarten teacher; maiden name Hughes) Lloyd; married Thomas Thompson (an antiques dealer). *Education:* Attended Pennsylvania State University, 1976-78; Parsons School of Design, B.F.A., 1981. *Politics:* Independent. *Religion:* Presbyterian.

■ Career

Free-lance illustrator of children's books, 1982—. Harper Junior Books, New York City, assistant to the art director, 1981-82; worked in restoration of American antique furniture, 1983-88. Founding member and art director for the Children's Literature Council of Pennsylvania, 1985—; former president and founding member of Citizens for Responsible Development (a local community group working for sound planning of growth), 1986-87.

■ Writings

SELF-ILLUSTRATED

Chicken Tricks, Harper, 1983.

ILLUSTRATOR

Lee Bennett Hopkins, *Surprises,* Harper, 1984.
Ida Luttrell, *Lonesome Lester,* Harper, 1984.

Victoria Sherrow, *There Goes the Ghost*, Harper, 1985.

Norma Farber, *All Those Mothers at the Manger*, Harper, 1985.

Thom Roberts, *The Atlantic Free Balloon Race*, Avon Books, 1986.

Tony Johnston, *Farmer Mack Measures His Pig*, Harper, 1986.

Linda Williams, *The Little Old Lady Who Was Not Afraid of Anything*, Crowell, 1986.

Hopkins, *More Surprises*, Harper, 1987.

Nancy MacArthur, *Megan Gets a Dollhouse*, Scholastic, 1988.

Carolyn Otto, *That Sky, That Rain*, HarperCollins, 1990.

Patricia Lauber, *How We Learned the Earth Is Round*, HarperCollins, 1990.

Brenda Guiberson, *Cactus Hotel*, Holt, 1991.

Jane and Robert O'Connor, *Super Cluck*, HarperCollins, 1991.

Eric Kimmel, *Baba Yaga*, Holiday House, 1991.

Paul Showers, *How You Talk*, HarperCollins, 1992.

Guiberson, *Spoonbill Swamp*, Holt, 1992.

Melvin Berger, *Look Out for Turtles!*, HarperCollins, 1992.

Mary Neville, *The Christmas Tree Ride*, Holiday House, 1992.

Guiberson, *Lobster Boat*, Holt, 1993.

Kimmel, *The Gingerbread Man*, Holiday House, 1993.

Neville, *The Gingerbread Doll*, Clarion, 1993.

MEGAN LLOYD

Tom Birdseye, *A Regular Flood of Mishap*, Holiday House, 1994.

Ellen McKenzie, *The Perfectly Orderly House*, Holt, 1994.

■ Sidelights

"I was born and raised in south-central Pennsylvania," Megan Lloyd told *Something about the Author* (SATA), "growing up with my parents, one older sister, a cat, and a dog. Both my sister and I began taking ballet lessons when we were young, but my sister did not show any great love for that particular art form and stopped dancing shortly thereafter. I fell in love with ballet and pursued it with all that I had. For many years I was convinced that it would be my career—so convinced that I didn't really give a great deal of thought to anything else. Because ballet was 'my thing,' I wasn't allowed to take horse riding lessons when my sister and mother did, mainly because my sister fell off a horse and broke her arm while my mother fell off and broke her knee. Surely this was too risky a sport for an aspiring dancer!

"At fifteen the terrible blow fell. I discovered that there were practically NO five-foot-one-inch dancers with short legs, no matter how good they were at jumping and stretching and pirouette-ing. I was crushed. In my despair—and it truly felt like the world was crumbling—I decided that I would transfer my creative efforts to the visual arts, and I began to think of myself as an 'artist.' Fortunately, the high school I attended had an excellent art department, with very talented and supportive teachers. Things seemed to run smoothly until it was time for the big college decision.

"When I began to think seriously about colleges I was visiting my aunt and uncle in the Boston area, and they took me to see Harvard. I fell in love with the law school there; and determined that art was simply no way to make a living, and what I really wanted to do was become an attorney. Secretly, I just wanted to attend Harvard Law School. Why, I don't know now, but it seemed important at the time.

"I began my college career at Pennsylvania State University in the pre-law program. That lasted for all of two semesters at which time I felt miserable, missed my art work, and was totally confused. I didn't want to be a fine artist; I didn't like to 'make pictures up from scratch'! But I didn't want to be a lawyer. What to do, what to do.

Becomes a Book Illustrator

"My mother, understanding my confusion, suggested that I might like to illustrate picture books. And to sweeten the suggestion, she showed me a copy of Brian Wildsmith's book *Circus*. That was all it took. I had never seen a book like that before. It was wonderful.

"I went to the Parsons School of Design and studied illustration. And I continue to work and work and work at learning, growing, and developing. The more I learn

Lloyd at first planned to be a ballet dancer before choosing a career to illustrate books like Jane and Robert O'Connor's *Super Cluck.*

about illustrating books, the more I discover all that I don't know! That's great—it keeps illustrating a stimulating career. Each book presents a new puzzle to solve. Who could ask for more?

"Many of my early books are fiction. Recently, I have done a number of non-fiction books. I do a great deal of research for both types of story. With fictional pieces, I explore settings and characters, costumes and lighting, all of which make the illustration process interesting to me. With non-fiction books, I carry my research even further, usually traveling to the geographical location in which the book is set.

"In *Cactus Hotel,* for example, I did all of the research at the Saguaro National Monument in Tucson, Arizona. For *Lobster Boat,* I traveled to Maine and found a lobsterman to take me out on his boat with him while he pulled his lobster traps. And for *Winter Wheat,* a story about a farmer growing winter wheat in the state of Washington, I drove clear across the country to photograph the wheat farm belonging to the author's father and mother! If I can't see what it is I am to draw, I simply can't make successful illustrations.

"When not working, I spend a great deal of time with my two Belgian Sheepdogs, Abel and Yonder. Both dogs are learning how to herd sheep and to be sled dogs, too. Most of the sheepherding involves my trying not to be run over by a stampeding flock of sheep. Most of the sledding involves me running alongside the dogs, encouraging them onward! It's good fun."

LoFARO, Jerry 1959-

■ Personal

Born September 3, 1959, in Bethpage, NY; son of Hector LoFaro (a roofing mechanic) and Matilda Scavone (a secretary); married Kathleen La Bonte (a singer, actress, and office manager) September 8, 1990. *Education:* Attended State University of New York at New Paltz, NY, 1980-81. *Politics:* Democrat. *Religion:* Catholic.

■ Addresses

Home and office—57 Laight St., 4th floor, New York, NY 10013. *Agent*—American Artists, 353 West 53rd St., 1W, New York, NY 10019.

■ Career

Freelance illustrator, 1985—. Art instructor for *Airbrush Action* Magazine Seminars, 1989—; *Fashion Institute of Technology,* New York City, art instructor, 1990—. Lecturer at colleges, including Adelphi University and the School of Visual Arts. *Exhibitions:* Exhibitor in various worldwide traveling exhibitions sponsored by the Society of Illustrators and the Image Bank.

■ Illustrator

Melvin Berger, *How Life Began,* Doubleday, 1991.

Also illustrator of book covers for publishers such as Doubleday, Bantam, Random House, Scribner, and Viking Penguin. Contributor to *Hot Air 1,* 1990, *Society of Illustrators Annual,* and *Communication Arts Annual.*

■ Sidelights

"The first things I drew were dinosaurs. It's interesting how things come around," LoFaro told *Airbrush Action*'s Bettie Johnson, discussing the 24 original paintings he created for *How Life Began.* "I accessed how I felt as a kid, and I got as excited as the first time. I hope I conveyed those feelings."

LoFaro studied fine art, art history, and English for a year and a half at the State University of New York in New Paltz before focusing on figure drawing and anatomy at the Art Students' League of New York. After years of persistent contact with publishers, LoFaro illustrated his first book cover, *Life Is Elsewhere,* by Milan Kundera. According to Johnson, this illustration "won him a second-place spot in *Airbrush Action*'s First Airbrush Excellence Competition." LoFaro was on his way to success.

After completing the illustrations for *How Life Began,* LoFaro told Johnson, "what I do now took a long time to learn . . . . Now that I definitely know how to paint, my work is gaining the fearless edge again."

■ Works Cited

Johnson, Bettie, "Jerry Lofaro: Looking Forward into
        His Past," *Airbrush Action,* January-February, 1991,
        pp. 8-15.

M

MADENSKI, Melissa (Ann) 1949-

■ Personal

Born August 31, 1949 in Portland, OR; daughter of Harold M. (in sales) and Florence (a homemaker; maiden name, Stavseth) Hegge; married Mark Madenski (a cabinetmaker), June 9, 1979 (died 1987); children: Dylan, Hallie. *Education:* Portland State University, B.A., 1971; attended Breadloaf School of English M.A. Program, Middlebury College, 1990, and 1992. *Hobbies and other interests:* Gardening, bicycling, hiking.

■ Addresses

Home—9990 Slab Creek Rd., Neskowin, OR 97149.

■ Career

Clackamas and Oceanlake Elementary Schools, Lincoln City, OR, teacher, 1972-77; Neskowin Valley School, Neskowin, OR, language arts instructor, 1984-85; freelance writer/editor. Teacher of writing workshops; teacher of English as a Second Language. Co-manager in Bowsprit and Allegory bookshops, Lincoln city, OR, and affiliated with Canyon Way Bookstore, Newport, OR, and Cafe Roma Books, Lincoln City, OR, 1972-85. Intern at Northwest Writing Institute, Lewis and Clark College, Portland, OR, 1994—. *Member:* Society of Children's Book Writers.

■ Awards, Honors

American Library Association Notable Book Award in social studies, 1991, for *Some of the Pieces.*

■ Writings

Some of the Pieces, illustrated by Deborah Kogan Ray, Little, Brown, 1991.

Contributor of non-fiction articles and essays to periodicals, including *Oregon Coast, Oregonian Daily, Practical*

MELISSA MADENSKI

Homeowner, Christian Science Monitor, and *National Geographic Traveller.*

■ Work in Progress

In My Mother's Garden, illustrated by Sandra Speidel, Little, Brown, publication expected 1995. Continued work on essays, collection of essays on travel; researching non-fiction for periodicals, including the effect of "natural" areas in urban settings and "restoration" projects in natural areas.

■ Sidelights

Melissa Madenski told *SATA:* "I didn't 'always want to be a writer.' When I was in grade school, I had to write at least ten versions of 'What I Did This Summer,' but beyond that I kept only a diary with the briefest of entries. I did, however, love to read above all else. I read when I was and wasn't supposed to. I read sitting in a chair, in bed, and while walking to school—until my mother, afraid I might get hit by a car, threatened to take my books away. Then I hid my book under my coat and began to read as soon as I was out of her sight. I was the only student in class to have my Scholastic book order delivered in a box or sack because of the number of titles. There was nothing I liked more than the cover of a new book that held the promise of taking me on some new adventure.

"We still read a great deal in our family. We have no TV and visit four different libraries on a regular basis. My son, Dylan, who is twelve, loves humor books and reads to us at night. My daughter, Hallie, wants to be a biologist and likes the *Eyewitness* books on animals. I still love E. B. White's books and like nothing better than to spend an evening reading his essays. Right now I'm reading *Amy's Eyes,* a story by Richard Kennedy, to my children.

"I began to write as much as I read when I taught language arts to third-through fifth-graders in a small school on the Oregon coast. We became a community of writers. We wrote every day—in journals, in notebooks, and on pieces of paper that might one day be turned into finished stories and essays. I became fascinated with people's stories, both made-up and real. I learned a great deal about the writing process from these students, some of whom still visit with me, even though they're now in college!

"I began to write essays about things that had happened to me. I would love to say I had a plan for each piece of writing, but oftentimes an idea would be in my head for months or even years until it was put on paper. I didn't write a story for children until I felt a story 'pushing' at me. Watching my son grieve over the death of his father reminded me of some of the myths I'd read as a child. I thought he was a bit of a hero, at least to me. That is when I began *Some of the Pieces.*

"Real life doesn't often fit into the confines of a book, thank heavens. But I think a story is a little like clay. You get to mold the details into something that makes a reader keep turning the pages to 'see what happens.' Some of those details really happened and some things may be made up, but what is important is that you put things together in a way that serves the story you're telling. So when people ask me if a story is true, I always feel slightly dishonest saying yes or no, because so much of truth is in fiction and so much of fiction can be in a true story that the division isn't always clear to me.

"Some people say it is important to write what you know. I know one author who says that's rubbish, that it's important to explore what you don't know. But I think the only rule to follow is to write what you're compelled to tell. Even if it's a story that's been told before, your view of the world will make it unique. I've never been good at giving advice. I think what has most often worked for me in pursuing anything is to do it, even when I'm tired, discouraged, and feeling like a failure. I get up every morning before my children, before the sun—and sometimes before the birds—because I'm compelled to tell stories, even if those words never reach anyone but my own family.

"I still learn the most by studying and reading good writing. I admire the work of Barry Lopez, Terry Tempest Williams, Rainer Maria Rilke, and Sigurd Olson, among others. I've read and reread fiction by Barbara Kingsolver, David James Duncan, Susan Kenney, Anne Tyler, Ursula Hegi, and Maura Stanton. Everyone in our family has enjoyed the work of Jerry Spinelli, E. B. White, Richard Kennedy, Tom Birdseye, Jane Yolen, Daniel Manus Pinkwater and Beverly Cleary. We've read *Owl Moon, Where the Wild Things Are,* and *Sophie and Lou* too many times to be counted.

"The measure of a good story is that it can be read or told again and again and again. It simply becomes richer and more loved with each retelling."

■ For More Information See

PERIODICALS

Booklist, October 15, 1991.
Kirkus Reviews, October 1, 1991.
Philadelphia Inquirer, February 9, 1992.

*   *   *

MAGNUS, Erica 1946-

■ Personal

Born August 14, 1946, in Waterbury, CT; daughter of Paul Gerhard (a self-employed inventor) and Hermine Adelaide (an artist and teacher; maiden name, Magnus) Magnus; married David Owen Thomas (director of the Ohio University School of Film), August 12, 1972; children: Peter David (deceased), Krista Mary, Karen Roslyn. *Education:* Attended Sticting Academe Atelier '63, Haarlem, The Netherlands, 1966-68; Minneapolis College of Art and Design, B.F.A., 1970; Southern Illinois University School of Art, M.F.A., 1974. *Politics:* "Independent (Leaning Democrat)." *Religion:* "For me religions are meant to be 'vessels of the Spirit,' and I believe in Spirit, whenever and however in shows itself. I don't believe it is confined to or defined by any one 'vessel.'" *Hobbies and other interests:* "Walking, walking, walking, especially along the Atlantic Ocean; if Ohio had enough snow, I would cross-country ski; if time would allow, I would love to turn pots on a wheel."

◼ Addresses

Office—The Studio, 7181 Whitlind Lane, Athens, OH 45701.

◼ Career

Free-lance artist, painter, and teacher of art education at the college and adult education level, and to gifted children, 1972—. *Great River Review,* contributing artist, 1976-77, and art director, 1977-79. Member of the Illustrators Art Steering Committee, Dairy Barn Cultural Center, 1992. *Exhibitions:* The Dean Gallery, Minneapolis, MN, 1970; Art Gallery, St. Mary's College, Winona, MN, 1975; Biennale Illustracionne Bratislava, Czechoslovakia, 1985; Master Eagle Gallery, New York City, 1987; Art Open, The Dairy Barn, Southeastern Ohio Cultural Arts Center, Athens, OH, 1988 and 1989; The Illustrator's Art, The Dairy Barn, Athens, 1990 and 1993; Buckeye Book Fair Illustrator's Exhibition, Wayne Center for the Arts, Wooster, OH, 1992. *Member:* Society of Children's Book Writers and Illustrators, Authors Guild, Authors League of America.

◼ Awards, Honors

Parents Choice Award for Illustration, 1984, for *Old Lars;* Reading Round Table of Chicago Books, 1984, 1986, and 1992; Ohio Citizen Award for Author/Artist, 1988.

◼ Writings

AND ILLUSTRATOR

Old Lars, Carolrhoda Books, 1984.
The Boy and the Devil, Carolrhoda Books, 1986.
Around Me, Lothrop, Lee & Shephard, 1992.
My Secret Place, Lothrop, Lee & Shephard, 1994.

◼ Work in Progress

Developing a story "based on my mother's family coming to America from Norway on a tramp steamer in 1923."

◼ Sidelights

Erica Magnus told *SATA:* "I am a painter who one day went looking for a small illustration job to help meet my expenses and ended up being 'recruited' by an excellent and determined editor into the world of children's picture books. She was then, and now continues to be, the single most important influence in this direction I've taken. To whatever extent I find myself writing, it is Susan Pearson who has evoked it. She elicited without encroaching. She writes beautifully herself, addressing her intended audience directly with clarity, simplicity, and always, *the magic!*"

Magnus strived to create her own brand of magic in picture books, and to get her start, she relied on stories she was familiar with. "My first two books were adapted from Norwegian folk tales," the author told *SATA,*

ERICA MAGNUS

"which was a wonderful way to begin, for the stories were already time-proven, and I had vivid images etched in my mind from years of hearing them told." Her first book, *Old Lars,* tells the story of an old man who goes out to gather wood. Once Lars fills the cart, however, he cannot move it, so he empties the cart and goes home, satisfied with a good day's work. A *Publishers Weekly* review of *Old Lars* noted that Magnus had visited Norway, the setting for the book, and that her pictures show that she had "'memorized' the mountains and valleys, the country dwellers and their tots." A reviewer for *Booklist* noted the "droll and economic" style of the book and praised *Old Lars* as "a rich bit of humor for younger children." Magnus also produced a second folk tale adaptation, *The Boy and the Devil.* The book tells the story of a boy who discovers how he can outsmart an inventive devil who plays tricks on people.

As Magnus related to *SATA,* she attempts to use elements of her own life to create pictures that are drawn from nature. "I now see myself as quite fortunate to have had an uninterrupted relationship with nature for so many of my childhood years. For me a one-to-one encounter with the natural world was so affirming that I sometimes feel very concerned that most children today have so little access to it. In my books I try to show children experiencing their own environments directly through their use of play and imagination."

Magnus's approach to depicting nature was next presented in the book *Around Me,* which a *Publishers Weekly* reviewer described as "a happy hymn to nature as well as an enlightening consideration of perspective." The book utilizes cutout pages to make children realize the way a picture can be seen in different ways. A picture of flames, for instance, appears to be a large forest fire when viewed through a two inch cutout, but when the page is turned, the picture is expanded, and the flames are revealed as a part of a living room with a comfortable fireplace. *School Library Journal* reviewer Joyce Richards found *Around Me* "a nice addition for times of quiet reflection and thought," and Linda Hanson, in the *Duluth News-Tribune,* praised the way *Around Me* "brings nature down to child-sized level."

Learning from Others

Discussing those artists and writers that have influenced her, Magnus finds that she has learned from several different sources. "Of those who make the pictures as well as the stories, there are many whose craft I admire," she told *SATA.* "What Maurice Sendak achieved in *Where the Wild Things Are,* or how Chris Van Allsburg wove magic into *The Polar Express,* opened my eyes to the many ways stories and pictures can support and amplify each other. But it is painters, past and present, who have influenced me the most. Among them, and perhaps the strongest influence, is my mother, Hermine Magnus. I respect her knowledge of color, the force and honesty of her work, and the undercurrent of joy she finds in nature and which permeates each painting's structure."

Magnus also finds that her parents were good role models in regards to achieving her goals. "I have always known that art was my way of being in the world," she

Magnus combines text and cut-out pages to bring the vast world of nature within a child's grasp in this self-illustrated book.

explained to *SATA.* "My mother paints and my father is an inventor, and neither one of them ever gave me the impression that you abandoned your 'work of love.' On the contrary, my parents raised five of us and my mother never gave up on her painting, even when for years she could only do it in her mind. Consequently, I had no illusions about it being easy or that one had to wait around for an 'inspiration.' Like anything else worthwhile, it is mostly work, but if you love it, you cannot give it less than your best, no matter what price you pay in human terms.

"From the little I've done so far, I would say to others wishing to write and/or illustrate children's books that they should work from their own experience in a way best suited to their natural style. Children are instinctively drawn to things that ring 'true' and are quick to see 'when the emperor has no clothes.' As editors will tell you, it is important to know your audience. I would add, listen to *all* feedback, because even rejection letters can help steer you in the right direction. I was advised to share, not lecture. I think it's good advice.

"In addition to my work with children's books, I continue to develop my painting ideas, mostly in large pastel on paper pieces. Like most other professional women I know, a lot of energy must go into balancing and juggling the needs of family members, parenting, and the demands of my art. In this I am one of the many who do the best they can with their chosen circumstances."

■ Works Cited

Review of *Around Me, Publishers Weekly,* May 11, 1992, p. 71.
Hanson, Linda, "On the Bookshelf/Children's Books," *Duluth News-Tribune,* Sunday, May 24, 1992, p. 3E.
Review of *Old Lars, Booklist,* October 15, 1984.
Review of *Old Lars, Publishers Weekly,* July 20, 1984, p. 81.
Richards, Joyce, review of *Around Me, School Library Journal,* August, 1992, p. 144.

■ For More Information See

PERIODICALS

Bulletin of the Center for Children's Books, October, 1984.
Children's Book Review Service, September, 1984; April, 1987.
Library Materials Guide, fall, 1985.
Library Services Journal, April-June, 1985.
Minneapolis Star Tribune, October 15, 1984.

*   *   *

MARKS, Alan 1957-

■ Personal

Born October 19, 1957, in London, England; married Jenny Walker (a psychologist); children: Charlotte,

ALAN MARKS

Elisabeth. *Education:* Attended Medway College of Design, England, 1976-77; Bath Academy of Art, England, B.A. (with first-class honors), 1977-80. *Hobbies and other interests:* Music, opera, gardening.

■ Addresses

Home—Padbrook, Mill Lane, Elmstone, Canterbury, Kent CT3 1HE, England.

■ Career

Freelance illustrator. Neugebauer Press, Salzburg, Austria, illustrator, 1988—; has worked as an illustrator for Simon and Schuster, Heinemann, Hamish Hamilton, and Oxford University Press.

■ Awards, Honors

Carnegie Medal (with Kevin Crossley-Holland), Library Association, London, England, 1985, for *Storm;* UNICEF Illustrators of the Year Award, Bologna, 1992.

■ Writings

SELF-ILLUSTRATED

Adaptor, *Childe Roland: An English Folk Tale* (part of "Folk Tales of the World" series), Blackie, 1988.
Nowhere to Be Found, Picture Book Studio, 1988.
Compiler, *Ring-a-Ring O'Roses and a Ding, Dong, Bell: A Book of Nursery Rhymes,* Picture Book Studio, 1991.
The Thief's Daughter, Simon & Schuster, 1993.
Over the Hills and Far Away, Picture Book Studio, 1993.

ILLUSTRATOR

Kevin Crossley-Holland, *Storm,* Heinemann, 1985.
Fiona Waters, *Golden Apples,* Heinemann, 1985.

Rosemary Sutcliffe, *Roundabout Horse,* Hamish Hamilton, 1986.
Eleanor Fargeon, *Something I Remember,* Blackie, 1987.
Jacob and Wilhelm Grimm, *The Fisherman and His Wife,* Picture Book Studio, 1989.
Jill Paton Walsh, *Birdy and the Ghosties,* Simon and Schuster, 1989.
Hans Christian Andersen, *The Ugly Duckling,* Picture Book Studio, 1990.
Joan Aiken, *The Shoemaker's Boy,* Simon and Schuster, 1991.
Andrew Clements, *Temple Cat,* Picture Book Studio, 1991.
Jill Paton Walsh, *Matthew and the Sea Singer,* Simon and Schuster, 1992.
Chris Powling, *It's That Dragon Again,* Hamish Hamilton, 1993.
Chris Powling, *A Razzle Dazzle Rainbow,* Viking, 1993.
Kevin Crossley-Holland, *The Green Children,* Oxford University Press, in press.

■ Sidelights

Alan Marks told *SATA:* "Drawing was important to me as a child. I can't remember a time when I didn't draw. I guess there is still a part of me that loves to hold up a drawing and say, 'Look what I've done.' There is something very magical about drawing—starting with a blank page and filling it with movement, depth, colour, light, and atmosphere." And, according to *Financial Times* contributor Michael Glover, Marks does appear to create movement in his illustrations. In his review of Marks's *Ring-a-Ring O'Roses and a Ding, Dong, Bell: A Book of Nursery Rhymes,* Glover stressed that "animals leap, jump, fly, skedaddle off the edge of the page, leaving the eye breathless with excitement."

Marks acknowledged the latitude that he has been given with his work when he told *SATA:* "Michael Neugebauer (from Picture Book Studio) has given me great scope to choose and illustrate texts, a freedom used to best effect in my first nursery rhyme book, *Ring-a-Ring O'Roses and a Ding, Dong, Bell.* I'm not sure that an English publisher would have allowed me such freedom. But, as Glover suggested in *Financial Times,* the result was a 'zestfulness and an edge of originality.'" Rachel Fox, in her *School Library Journal* review of the volume, called the drawings "refreshing" and "eye-catching." Marks told *SATA* that he's working on a second nursery rhyme book, which he hopes "will be different again."

"Largely with the wish to make whole books, and perhaps to explore my own childhood," Marks continued, "I have written my own texts on occasions. *Nowhere to Be Found,* published in 1988, was my first book with Neugebauer and a turning point in my career."

Nowhere to Be Found is the story of a boy who loses his temper, then disobeys his mother's instructions by straying into "The Land of Nowhere," where everyone is continuously lost. In this imaginative world, many adults have lost their sense of smell and their memories; some are lost in thought, and one elderly woman has lost a stitch from her knitting. A *Growing Point* reviewer noted that the young boy embarks on a "journey very familiar to children working their way through a tantrum." Another critic, Leigh Dean in *Bulletin of the Center for Children's Books,* called *Nowhere to Be Found* "a charming, light-hearted cautionary tale."

Reveals Influences on His Work

Marks also told *SATA:* "I have more recently written a story for seven- to nine-year-olds called *The Thief's Daughter,* which has been published by Simon and Schuster in England. I love to write, but it takes me a long time. Again, I'm inspired by other writers: Jill Paton Walsh, Kevin Crossley-Holland, Alan Garner, Lawrence Durrell, and J. D. Salinger, to name a few. My influences are wide—Auguste Rodin to Arthur Rackham, you might say—but they can all draw. Others include Edgar Degas, Jim Dine, Ralph Steadman, Alan Lee, and Edmund Dulac. My work has also been coloured, I think, by my early childhood in the docklands of London and a very contrasting move to the Kent countryside."

Marks's other self-illustrated work is *Childe Roland,* a folk tale he adapted which revolves around a courageous prince who embarks on a dangerous quest. Commentator Betsy Hearne, reviewing the title in *Bulletin of the Center for Children's Books,* especially praised Marks's illustrations, noting that his watercolor paintings are "openly imagined and well composed, with good drafting and subtle color blends." A contributor to *Publishers Weekly* commended the artwork as well, calling the pictures "well-executed and appropriately eerie." Throughout his career Marks has also illustrated several books for other authors, including Fiona Waters's *Golden Apples,* Jill Paton Walsh's *Birdy and the Ghosties,* Joan Aiken's *Shoemaker's Boy,* and Andrew Clements's *Temple Cat.*

Marks admitted to *SATA:* "I wouldn't go so far as to say that I couldn't do anything else, but I feel privileged to find work as an illustrator. Watching my own children with books has reinforced my belief that books and reading have a universal and instinctive appeal, and that writing and drawing are important to the human spirit."

■ Works Cited

Review of *Childe Roland: An English Folk Tale, Publishers Weekly,* May 12, 1989, p. 291.

Dean, Leigh, review of *Nowhere to Be Found, Bulletin of the Center for Children's Books,* July, 1988, p. 143.

Fox, Rachel, review of *Ring-a-Ring O'Roses and A Ding, Dong, Bell: A Book of Nursery Rhymes, School Library Journal,* March, 1992, p. 232.

Glover, Michael, review of *Ring-a-Ring O'Roses and A Ding, Dong, Bell: A Book of Nursery Rhymes, Financial Times,* December, 1991, p. 16.

Hearne, Betsy, review of *Childe Roland: An English Folk Tale, Bulletin of the Center for Children's Books,* June, 1989, pp. 257-58.

Review of *Nowhere to Be Found, Growing Point,* September, 1988, pp. 5045-46.

■ For More Information See

PERIODICALS

Booklist, June 15, 1989, p. 1824.
Horn Book, May, 1992.
School Library Journal, June-July, 1988, p. 93; September, 1989, p. 242; May, 1992.

*   *   *

MARKS, Peter
See SMITH, Robert Kimmel

*   *   *

MARZOLLO, Jean 1942-

■ Personal

Born June 24, 1942, in Manchester, CT; daughter of Richard (a town manager) and Ruth (a teacher; maiden name, Smith) Martin; married Claudio Marzollo (a sculptor), March, 1969; children: Daniel, David. *Education:* University of Connecticut, B.A., 1964; Harvard University, M.A.T., 1965. *Hobbies and other interests:* Gardening, swimming, reading.

■ Addresses

Home—Cold Spring, NY. *Agent*—Molly Friedrich, Aaron Priest Agency, 708 Third Ave., New York, NY 10168.

■ Career

Teacher in Arlington, MA, 1965-66; Harvard University, Cambridge, MA, assistant director of Project Upward Bound, 1967; affiliated with General Learning Corp., New York City, 1967-69; National Commissional Resources for Youth, New York City, director of publications, 1970-71; Scholastic Magazines, Inc., Englewood Cliffs, NJ, editor of *Let's Find Out* (magazine for kindergarten children), 1971-91; freelance writer, 1972—. Served on the Elementary School Study Group for U.S. Secretary of Education, 1986.

■ Awards, Honors

Close Your Eyes was named a Junior Literary Guild selection, 1978; Best Book for Young Adults citation, American Library Association, 1981, for *Halfway Down Paddy Lane; I Spy Fun House: A Book of Picture Riddles* and *I Spy Mystery: A Book of Picture Riddles* were both named best books of 1993 by *Publishers Weekly.*

■ Writings

FICTION FOR CHILDREN

The House That Dreams Painted, illustrated by Irene Trivas, Macmillan, 1975.

Close Your Eyes, illustrated by Susan Jeffers, Dial, 1978.

Amy Goes Fishing, illustrated by Ann Schweninger, Dial, 1980.

Uproar on Hollercat Hill, illustrated by Steven Kellogg, Dial, 1980.

(With husband, Claudio Marzollo) *Jed's Junior Space Patrol*, Dial, 1982.

(With C. Marzollo) *Robin of Bray*, Dial, 1982.

(With C. Marzollo) *Red Sun Girl*, Dial, 1983.

(With C. Marzollo) *Blue Sun Ben*, Dial, 1984.

(With C. Marzollo) *Ruthie's Rude Friends*, illustrated by Susan Meddaugh, Dial, 1984.

Three Little Kittens, illustrated by Shelley Thornton, Scholastic, 1985.

The Rebus Treasury, illustrated by Carol Devine Carson, Dial, 1986.

(With C. Marzollo) *The Baby Unicorn*, Scholastic, 1987.

Cannonball Chris, illustrated by Blanche Sims, Random House, 1987.

(With C. Marzollo) *Jed and the Space Bandits*, Dial, 1987.

The Silver Bear, illustrated by Susan Meddaugh, Dial, 1987.

Soccer Sam, illustrated by Blanche Sims, Random House, 1987.

Red Ribbon Rosie, illustrated by Blanche Sims, Random House, 1988.

(With C. Marzollo) *The Baby Unicorn and Baby Dragon*, Scholastic, 1989.

The Pizza Pie Slugger, illustrated by Blanche Sims, Random House, 1989.

The Teddy Bear Book, illustrated by Ann Schweninger, Dial, 1989.

Pretend You're A Cat, illustrated by Jerry Pinkney, Dial, 1990.

What Else Can You Do?, illustrated by Jerry Pinkney, Bodley Head, 1990.

In 1492 (biography), illustrated by Steve Bjorkman, Scholastic, 1991.

Slam Dunk Saturday, illustrated by Blanche Sims, Random House, 1992.

Halloween Cats, illustrated by Hans Wilhelm, Scholastic, 1993.

Happy Birthday, Martin Luther King, illustrated by J. Brian Pinkney, Scholastic, 1993.

I'm a Tyrannosaurus: A Book of Dinosaur Rhymes, illustrated by Hans Wilhelm, 1993.

In 1776, illustrated by Steve Bjorkman, Scholastic, 1994.

My First Book of Biographies, illustrated by Irene Trivas, Scholastic, 1994.

Ten Cats Have Hats, illustrated by David McPhail, Scholastic, 1994.

"39 KIDS ON THE BLOCK" SERIES; ILLUSTRATED BY IRENE TRIVAS

The Green Ghost of Appleville, Scholastic, 1989.

The Best Present Ever, Scholastic, 1989.

Roses Are Pink and You Stink, Scholastic, 1990.

The Best Friends Club, Scholastic, 1990.

Chicken Pox Strikes Again, Scholastic, 1990.

My Sister the Blabbermouth, Scholastic, 1990.

"READ-AND-PLAY STORYBOOKS" SERIES

Papa Bear's Party, Scholastic, 1982.

Baxter Bear's Bad Day, Scholastic, 1982.

Doll House Adventure, Scholastic, 1984.

Cinderella, Scholastic, 1985.

Doll House Christmas, Scholastic, 1985.

"I SPY" SERIES; WITH PHOTOGRAPHS BY WALTER WICK

I Spy: A Book of Picture Riddles, Scholastic, 1992.

I Spy Christmas: A Book of Picture Riddles, Scholastic, 1992.

I Spy Fun House: A Book of Picture Riddles, Scholastic, 1993.

I Spy Mystery: A Book of Picture Riddles, Scholastic, 1993.

NONFICTION FOR CHILDREN

Getting Your Period: A Book about Menstruation, illustrated by Kent Williams, Dial, 1989.

(With Patricia Adams) *The Helping Hands Handbook: How Kids Can Help People, Plants and Animals*, illustrated by Jeff Moores, Random House, 1993.

FICTION FOR YOUNG ADULTS

Halfway down Paddy Lane, Dial, 1981.

Do You Love Me, Harvey Burns?, Scholastic, 1983.

JEAN MARZOLLO

NONFICTION FOR ADULTS

(With Janice Lloyd) *Learning through Play,* illustrated by Irene Trivas, Harper, 1972.

Nine Months One Day One Year, Harper, 1975.

Supertot: Creative Learning Activities for Children from One to Three and Sympathetic Advice for Their Parents, illustrated by Irene Trivas, Harper, 1977.

Superkids: Creative Learning Activities for Children Five to Fifteen, illustrated by Irene Trivas, Harper, 1981.

Birthday Parties for Children, Harper, 1983.

The New Kindergarten: Full-Day, Child-Centered, Academic, illustrated by Irene Trivas, Harper, 1987.

Your Maternity Leave: How to Leave Work, Have a Baby, and Go Back to Work without Getting Lost, Trapped, or Sandbagged along the Way, Poseidon Press/Simon & Schuster, 1989.

Fathers and Babies: How Babies Grow and What They Need from You, illustrated by Irene Trivas, Harper-Perennial, 1993.

■ **Work in Progress**

Sun Song, with illustrations by Laura Regan, publication expected by HarperCollins.

■ **Sidelights**

Versatile writer Jean Marzollo has more than sixty books to her credit. She has worked in many different genres, producing rhythmic picture books for children, easy-to-read and chapter books for early readers, nonfiction for middle graders, novels for young adults, and practical nonfiction for parents. She once told *SATA:* "I am interested in children, and I like to write books that support families. Whether I'm writing a picture book, an easy-to-read book, a novel, or a book for parents, I find writing an intriguing challenge. It's a job, a hobby, and a game—all in one."

In an essay for the *Something about the Author Autobiography Series,* (*SAAS*), Marzollo wrote: "I never thought about being an author when I was young, but the pleasure I now take in making books is the same pleasure I took as a child making doll clothes. The creative process is essentially the same. First, you think of something you want to make, next you plan how you'll do it, and then you do it. By the time it's finished, you've usually thought of something else to make! The work is both the challenge and the fun."

Marzollo also wrote in her essay: "When I write books for beginning readers in first grade and novels (or chapter books, as kids like to call them) for second and third graders, I remember what I liked to read at that age—exciting books that made me feel both happy and sad and that taught me something."

Author's Reading Inspires Poems

"In addition to writing early readers and chapter books for beginners, I write picture books. More and more, I enjoy writing picture books that rhyme," she noted in *SAAS.* "One of my favorite books as a child was *A*

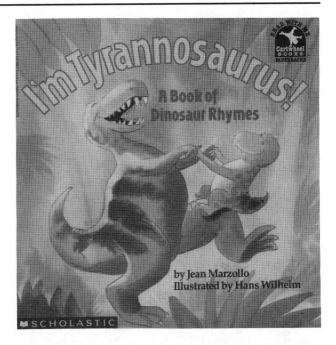

Readers can learn interesting tidbits about dinosaurs while they have fun with Marzollo's peppy rhymes. (Cover illustration by Hans Wilhelm.)

Child's Garden of Verses by Robert Louis Stevenson. Also, my mother had several small poetry books on her bookshelf. With their leather covers and gold titles, they were treasures to me. I liked to hold them and peek through the pages. I still have these books. Rhythm and rhyme are like music; they lure and excite the ear.... Sometimes rhymes and rhythms pop into my head as if I've been singing them."

Marzollo writes down these rhymes as they come to her because ideas don't always reveal themselves when she's at her desk. She has found that if she doesn't write down ideas she forgets them. *Pretend You're a Cat, Close Your Eyes, The Teddy Bear Book,* and *In 1492* are all rhyming books that might have been lost for want of a pencil and a scrap of paper.

Pretend You're a Cat was informed by a setting that Marzollo frequented while growing up. Every year she visited her friend, Martha, whose home was a Connecticut farmhouse. Marzollo has never written about this farm per se, but books with rural settings such as *Pretend You're a Cat* show how Marzollo can draw upon her familiarity with a place without writing about it directly. Even though there were horses on the farm, Marzollo's attempts to write about them have not come to fruition. She has kept all the drafts for a picture book about horses and may still write the book someday.

Ellen Fader in *Horn Book* called *Pretend You're a Cat* "an engaging exploration of imagination, movement, and animal characteristics." With the question "What else can you do...?" at the end of discussions of separate animals, children are expected to make more sounds, actions, and gestures to add to the fun. After reading *Pretend You're a Cat,* a reviewer for *Publishers Weekly* called the verse "vivid and straightforward."

Marzollo has written numerous other works that pair poetry with illustrations. *Close Your Eyes* is a soothing bedtime story with a drowsy rhythm which tells some of the wonderful things one can see with closed eyes. In *The Teddy Bear Book,* a book for young children, Marzollo presents twenty-one rhymes and short poems that deal with the teddy bear world. Another rhyming book, *In 1492,* is an amusing and lighthearted read-aloud which begins with the familiar rhyme, "In fourteen hundred ninety-two, Columbus sailed the ocean blue."

Early Experiences Influence Writing

Marzollo told *SAAS,* "I don't know if people are born creative or taught to be creative. I expect both are true. Having time to explore and make mistakes in a pressure-free environment is important. When I was young, my friends and I had plenty of time on our hands in which to be creative and make mistakes. We didn't have arts and crafts classes nor fancy, expensive materials to work with. But we did have time, and scrap materials."

After college, Marzollo went into teaching, worked at Harvard's Project Upward Bound—a program designed to help academically troubled high school students who were poor—and then decided to enter the field of educational publishing. They were all beneficial choices which advanced her career in writing. The Upward Bound experience made Marzollo realize that even though students under her guidance had a wonderful summer, they had no place to go except back to the schools in which they had failed. One of their problems was that the books they had to read in school were not related to their lives. That was when Marzollo decided to move to New York City. There, she reasoned, was the center of the publishing world. She felt that there was possibly some way she could help,such as publishing educational materials more relevant to kids like those she had known in Upward Bound.

However, her first job in New York was as a preschool researcher in the late 1960s—a time when the United States government was encouraging programs to assist the poor. Many thought that the best way to help the destitute was to aid poor children. Later, when Marzollo started writing, she called upon all of her experiences: researching preschool education, motivating Upward Bound students, teaching English in high school, and growing up in a middle class neighborhood. Her diverse training prepared her to write on many levels. In 1972 she co-authored her first book, *Learning through Play,* using her preschool findings. The same year she became editor of Scholastic's kindergarten magazine, *Let's Find Out.* She guided that publication into its years as an award-winning magazine. Children's books, which grew out of her *Let's Find Out* training, soon followed.

Success With "I Spy" Series

Marzollo's "I Spy" series is an example of a successful effort that grew out of her kindergarten magazine editing experience. Walter Wick shot some photographs for *Let's Find Out,* then continued to collaborate with Marzollo on several books which were successful in the marketplace. With their brightly colored photographs and rhymed riddles, the "I Spy" books provide a visual language game that teachers often use to promote various skills, such as observation, classification, and creativity. Heide Piehler in *School Library Journal* called *I Spy: A Book of Picture Riddles* "an appealing book for children and adults to share and enjoy together."

Marzollo once told *SATA,* "It wasn't until the birth of my children that I began to feel the pull of poetry and fancy as I had felt it once before in my own childhood. I then began to write children's books and later when I gained enough confidence, novels."

Marzollo was inspired to write *Close Your Eyes,* a poem about a drowsy child, while rocking her first-born. Relating the inspiration for the book, Marzollo once told *SATA:* "The first verse of *Close Your Eyes* came to me all of a sudden one evening while I was nursing my first child. I was sitting in a great big old overstuffed

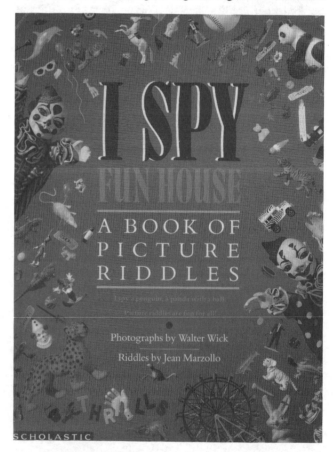

Marzollo's popular "I Spy" books help promote various skills, such as observation, classification, and creativity. (Cover photograph by Walter Wick.)

chair and feeling very relaxed. I looked at my son and wondered what was going on inside his head. He looked so innocent and eager and fresh, and I kept thinking about all the kinds of experiences he might have someday, and how each new mind re-creates the world."

She continued: "So much for inspiration. That was fun, but the rest was hard work. I had help from my editor, Phyllis Fogelman, and my friend, Rosemary Wells. Both kept saying the same thing to me as they read over my drafts of the whole poem: 'Keep it simple. Don't say anything that isn't natural.'... Once the poem was finalized, I was thrilled to find out that Susan Jeffers would illustrate it. Her delicate, imaginative, and beautiful books are like the ones I loved most as a child." The collaboration earned Marzollo and Jeffers praise from commentators such as Harold C. K. Rice of the *New York Times Book Review*, who called *Close Your Eyes* "the most interesting and original picture book to be published in some time."

Later Marzollo wrote the novel *Halfway down Paddy Lane*, which makes use of the author's Irish background and involves time travel. In the book, Kate Calambra, a modern teenager, goes to bed and wakes up in the year 1850 as Kate O'Hara, ready to go to work in a textile mill. She falls in love with Patrick, who is her brother at the time but turns out to be her great-great grandfather. The book gives readers an interesting look at nineteenth-century family life, inhumane working conditions, and immigrant struggles. Catherine Harper in

A family argument turns into uproarious chaos in this humorous picture book. (Cover illustration by Steven Kellogg.)

Voice of Youth Advocates noted that *Halfway down Paddy Lane* is a combination of "enlightening historical fiction ... and entertaining, heart-tugging romance."

Marzollo has also contributed to the genre of science fiction, writing a number of novels with her husband, Claudio, who himself is a science fiction and fantasy fan. Some of the books which they have written together are *Baby Unicorn, Baby Unicorn and Baby Dragon, Jed's Junior Space Patrol, Jed and the Space Bandits, Red Sun Girl, Blue Sun Ben, Ruthie's Rude Friends*, and *Robin of Bray*.

Her sons, Danny and David, have also assisted in their mother's career, not only by proofreading Marzollo's work but by inspiring her to write sport stories, such as *Cannonball Chris, Soccer Sam, The Pizza Pie Slugger, Red Ribbon Rosie*, and the "39 Kids on the Block" series. Marzollo based some of the books in the "39 Kids on the Block" series on real-life situations. "Fizz Eddie" a character in one book was inspired by her sons.

Confronting Problems Objectively

Marzollo likes to indirectly address family problems in her novels. In *The Pizza Pie Slugger*, Billy lives with his father and grandfather over a pizza parlor because his parents are divorced. Billy's problem is that his family annoys him when they come to his baseball games. The social problem, the fact that the parents are divorced, does not become the main point in Marzollo's book. To keep her books from being too moralistic she focuses on characters solving their own problems. Billy's mother seems to solve the dillema when she suggests the family stay away from the games. Billy, however finds a better solution to his problem. A reviewer for *Publishers Weekly* stated, "Families—and baseball—are like pizza, and each person (or piece) helps to make up the whole." All of the books in Marzollo's sports group are light reading with definite appeal to sports-minded youth; at the same time, they reinforce strong family values, struggles of friendship, overcoming fears, and being a good sport.

Marzollo told *SAAS*, "It seems that family problems and solutions have obsessed me in a quiet but persistent way throughout my life. I have written many articles about families for *Parents* magazine and many books for adults about families and children. I think I wrote my picture book *Uproar on Hollercat Hill* as a fantasy of how nice it would be if family fights just blew up and blew away. My family wasn't like that. The fights never blew up and, consequently, never blew away." Written in brief rhymes for young children and with plenty of action and boisterous text, this book has an ambiance quite different from Marzollo's quiet, soothing book, *Close Your Eyes*.

Marzollo also commented in *SAAS*, "Love or lack of love, is a powerful problem to write about. My father inspired my children's books *Cannonball Chris* and *Amy Goes Fishing*." When things got to be too much for Marzollo's father, he went fishing. Therefore, Marzollo called upon that memory when she wrote the latter book, about a little girl who goes fishing with her Dad and discovers it is not boring—as her siblings said it would be. "Both of these books are about the love between child and parent," Marzollo stated.

"Money and acceptance by others are two more universal problems that I like to write about.... Ethnicity can be a character's problem if the character feels unacceptable on the basis of race.... The optimistic and integrated spirit of my middle-class neighborhood is reflected in the six books in my '39 Kids on the Block' series, written for second- and third-grade-readers. The titles of the books in this series are: *The Green Ghost of Appleville, The Best Present Ever, Roses Are Pink and You Stink, Best Friends Club, Chicken Pox Strikes Again,* and *My Sister the Blabbermouth.* In these books I have created an ethnic mix of European Americans, Asians, Hispanics, African Americans, and American Indians. The universal problems in the books are the same ones that always affect children: love, acceptance, embarrassment, loneliness, and competition." In commenting on the series, a reviewer for *Booklist* noted that "fans of Patricia Giff, Judy Delton, and C. S. Adler will welcome Marzollo's appealing neighborhood stories."

Marzollo likes to visit schools, talk about her work, and listen to children tell about the books they have written and "published." Perhaps one reason she likes to be with children is because, as she told *SAAS*, she feels she is "still the child who made doll clothes ... who played Office with Martha on the farm ... and ... who liked the quiet process of making things from beginning to end."

■ Works Cited

Fader, Ellen, review of *Pretend You're a Cat, Horn Book,* July/August, 1990, p. 447.
Review of *The Green Ghost of Appleville, Booklist,* March 15, 1990, p. 1471.
Harper, Catherine, review of *Halfway down Paddy Lane, Voice of Youth Advocates,* December, 1981, p. 33.
Marzollo, Jean, *Something about the Author Autobiography Series,* Volume 15, Gale, 1993, pp. 201-213.
Piehler, Heide, review of *I Spy: A Book of Picture Riddles, School Library Journal,* April, 1992, p. 97.
Review of *The Pizza Pie Slugger, Publishers Weekly,* July 28, 1989, p. 222.
Review of *Pretend You're a Cat, Publishers Weekly,* April 27, 1990, p. 60.
Rice, Harold C. K., review of *Close Your Eyes, New York Times Book Review,* July 9, 1978, p. 32.

■ For More Information See

PERIODICALS

School Library Journal, July, 1990, p. 62.
Wilson Library Bulletin, December, 1980.

MAYER, Barbara 1939-

■ Personal

Born February 17, 1939, in Oak Park, IL. *Education:* St. Mary of the Woods College, B.A.; Ball State University, M.A. *Hobbies and other interests:* Oriental culture, music, desktop publishing.

■ Addresses

Office—Highland High School, 9135 Erie Street, Highland, IN 46322.

■ Career

Journalism teacher and public relations director for the town of Highland, IN, for twenty years; Mayer Public Relations, owner; writer.

■ Awards, Honors

Wall Street Journal Newspaper Fund Fellowship.

■ Writings

The College Survival Guide: An Insider's Guide to Success, VGM Career Horizons, 1981.
How to Succeed in College, VGM Career Horizons, 1992.
How to Succeed in High School, VGM Career Horizons, 1992.

Also author of *The High School Survival Guide,* VGM Career Horizons.

■ Work in Progress

Living the Gift, "a modern inspirational allegory"; research in oriental thought, Zen, modern spirituality.

■ Sidelights

Barbara Mayer told *SATA:* "In this video age there are more people suddenly rediscovering the printed word. Reading, learning, and enjoying at one's own pace is a new treasure that people, including teenagers, are finding again."

■ For More Information See

PERIODICALS

Book Report, May, 1992, p. 39.
School Library Journal, April, 1992, p. 171.
Voice of Youth Advocates, June, 1992, p. 130.

COLIN McCARTHY

McCARTHY, Colin (John) 1951-

■ Personal

Born February 18, 1951, in Ilford, Essex, England; son of John Oliver (a motor car factory worker) and Betty (maiden name, Parker) McCarthy; married Susan Edwina Davenport (a midday assistant at special school), September 16, 1972; children: Keith John, James Kieran. *Education:* Birkbeck College, University of London, B.Sc., 1976; City of London Polytechnic, Ph.D., 1982. *Religion:* Roman Catholic. *Hobbies and other interests:* Amateur drama, jazz, general interest in wildlife, family history.

■ Addresses

Home—7 Arlington Gardens, Romford, Essex, England RM3 0EA. *Office*—Natural History Museum, Cromwell Rd., London SW7 5BD, England.

■ Career

Natural History Museum, London, England, assistant scientific officer, 1970-75, scientific officer, 1975-79, higher scientific officer, 1979-89, senior scientific officer (collection manager—lower vertebrates) 1989—. Diocese of Brentwood Pastoral Council, parish representative, 1987—. *Member:* Essex Naturalists Trust, British Herpetological Society (museum representative, 1981—), Guildonian Players Theatre Club.

■ Writings

Poisonous Snakes, F. Watts, 1987.
Reptile, Dorling Kindersley, 1991.

Also author of numerous encyclopedia articles, reviews and scientific papers.

■ Work in Progress

Projects mainly involving systematics and evolution of venomous snakes.

■ Sidelights

Colin McCarthy told *SATA:* "Most of my writing has been in the scientific field—reporting the results of my research on reptiles at the Natural History Museum, London, England. My books for children were written in response to commissions from the publishers concerned, but I have been pleased at their good reception and wide circulation and would welcome the opportunity to write some more.

"In the longer term, I would be interested to link together some of my wildlife, drama, and music activities. It would be particularly exciting to exploit the possibilities of new computer-based technology in publishing."

■ For More Information See

BOOKS

Children's Books of the Year 1988, Andersen Press, 1988.
Children's Books of the Year 1992, Andersen Press, 1992.

*   *   *

McHARGUE, Georgess 1941-
(Alice Chase, Margo Scegge Usher)

■ Personal

Born in 1941, in Norwalk, CT; daughter of W. R. (in advertising) and Georgess (Boomhower) McHargue; married Michael E. Roberts; children: Mairi Kathleen; (stepchildren) Traci A. Roberts, Kelly Roberts Richardson. *Education:* Radcliffe College, B.A., 1963. *Politics:* Radical-Independent. *Religion:* None.

■ Addresses

Home and office—51 Hollis St., Groton, MA 01450.

■ Career

Golden Press, New York City, various staff positions, 1963-65; Doubleday & Co., Inc., New York City, associate editor, 1965-68, editor, 1968-70; free-lance writer, 1970—. *Member:* American Civil Liberties Union, Amnesty International, Phi Beta Kappa.

GEORGESS McHARGUE

■ Awards, Honors

Book World Spring Festival Award, 1972, and National Book Award nomination, 1973, both for *The Impossible People;* MacDowell Colony fellow, 1984.

■ Writings

JUVENILE NONFICTION

The Beasts of Never: A History Natural and Un-natural of Monsters Mythological and Magical, illustrated by Frank Bozzo, Bobbs-Merrill, 1968, revised edition, Delacorte, 1988.

The Impossible People: A History Natural and Unnatural of Beings Terrible and Wonderful, Holt, 1972.

Facts, Frauds and Phantasms: A Survey of the Spiritualist Movement, Doubleday, 1972.

Mummies, Lippincott, 1972.

Meet the Werewolf, drawings by Stephen Gammell, Lippincott, 1976.

Meet the Vampire, drawings by Stephen Gammell, Lippincott, 1979.

Meet the Witches, Harper, 1983.

JUVENILE FICTION

The Baker and the Basilisk, illustrated by Robert Quackenbush, Bobbs-Merrill, 1970.

The Wonderful Wings of Harold Harrabescu, Delacorte, 1971.

Elidor and the Golden Ball, Dodd, 1973.

The Mermaid and the Whale, Holt, 1973.

Private Zoo, illustrated by Michael Foreman, Viking, 1975.

Stoneflight, Viking, 1975.

Funny Bananas, Holt, 1975.

The Talking Table Mystery, illustrated by Emanuel Schongut, Doubleday, 1977.

The Horseman's Word, Delacorte, 1981.

The Turquoise Toad Mystery, Delacorte, 1982.

See You Later, Crocodile!, Delacorte, 1988.

Beastie, Doubleday, 1992.

OTHER

(Compiler) *The Best of Both Worlds: An Anthology of Short Stories for All Ages,* Doubleday, 1968.

(Compiler) *Little Victories, Big Defeats,* Delacorte, 1974.

(Compiler) *Hot and Cold Running Cities,* Holt, 1974.

(With Michael Roberts) *A Field Guide to Conservation Archaeology in North America,* Lippincott, 1977.

Also author of books for children under the pseudonyms Alice Chase and Margo Scegge Usher.

■ Sidelights

Folklore, the occult, and related subjects are the domain of Georgess McHargue, whose first book, *The Beasts of Never: A History Natural and Un-natural of Monsters Mythological and Magical* explored the probable origins of mythical animals such as the dragon and the unicorn. "She proves that what does not exist can nevertheless seem real," notes Barbara Wersba of the *New York Times Book Review.* "All children know this, of course, but they will never find it more beautifully stated." Her books are populated with lighthearted pixies, mermaids, and brownies, along with murkier creatures such as werewolves, mummies, and vampires. "Miss McHargue does not merely provide us with the flat surface of history . . . ," writes Wersba in a review of *The Impossible People.* "In a cheery, businesslike way, she guides the reader through a veritable labyrinth of detail—simultaneously explaining that myths, and mythical creatures, are but one of humanity's means of coping with the paradoxes and terrors of existence."

"I suppose I write books for children to read because I was a reading child," McHargue once told *SATA.* "For some reason I had more than my share of childhood illnesses, from continuous colds to rheumatic fever, and, sick or well, I read everything I could get my hands on—children's classics, Nancy Drew, comic books, the *Reader's Digest* and *Saturday Evening Post,* Shakespeare, *The Golden Treasury,* my parents' mystery stories, and many supposedly 'adult' books such as *The Once and Future King,* Steinbeck, Hemingway, and a lot of anthropology."

McHargue's ravenous curiosity motivates her interest in everything from art and Renaissance history to gardening and horseback riding. Growing up as the precocious daughter of thoughtful, book-loving parents in New York City, she admits to generally preferring the company of adults to other children. Her father kept a copy of *Webster's New International Dictionary* on a table in the living room, and her mother did the *New York Times* crossword puzzle daily without fail. "Communication was a survival skill in our household," McHargue wrote in *Something about the Author Autobiography Series* (*SAAS*). "Just as the baby bird that does not stimulate its parents by gaping may fail to receive its portion of worms, so the inarticulate in Apartment 15-C would simply fail to have their needs noticed. No good to garble the grammar. 'I don't want no spinach, Daddy,' would get you a large helping and an explication of the hazards of the double negative."

A self-described brainy, bookish "nerd," school was nevertheless a place McHargue described in *SAAS* as "a haven, a place that was safe, interesting, and predictable." She wrote her "first" book with a friend in the fourth grade, *How Not to Eat Lunch*. "By the time I was in junior high school, I was writing so much that I simply didn't think about it often," she wrote in her essay. "I wrote when I was angry; I wrote when I was happy; I wrote in school; I wrote at home. When I wasn't actually writing, I made lists of things I intended to write—still one of my favorite activities in times of stress."

At Radcliffe College, McHargue discovered dozens of fellow "nerds," all yearbook editors, honors students, National Merit finalists, and others to whom she could relate. She considered a career in science until switching her major from microbiology to history and literature. Along with Renaissance studies, she sampled art history,

Many of McHargue's books explore the facts and fiction regarding occult phenomena, including witches, werewolves, and vampires. (Cover illustration by Tony Ratkus.)

Chinese philosophy, German, psychology, and comparative religion. After graduation, McHargue attended secretarial college to make herself "employable."

Publishing Experience with Children's Literature

McHargue's first publishing job was with Golden Press in New York, which publishes mass-market books for children. "When I was looking for my first job with a publishing house," she once told *SATA*, "I suddenly realized that I had a good background for children's books: I had read everything. I also had some strong opinions about what I had *not read* because it wasn't available. Stories that showed families as real people who had problems with anger, jealousy, divorce, and other disruptions were totally non-existent among the books I read and when I turned to adult novels I often came upon things I simply didn't understand. As a result, I am convinced that children should be encouraged to read everything they feel a need for, with no taboos."

McHargue left Golden Press two years later and traveled through Greece and Italy before going to work as an editor for Doubleday in New York. She was active in local and national political campaigns, civil rights organizations, and a variety of peace groups and feminist organizations. Her first book, *The Beasts of Never,* came out of a lunch with a friend who had just become head of Bobbs-Merrill's juvenile book department. The friend had a list of topics she wanted to see written about for children, and McHargue chose "mythical beasts." In 1970 she left Doubleday to become a full-time freelance writer and author, later moving to Cambridge, Massachusetts.

Among McHargue's early works is *The Impossible People: A History Natural and Unnatural of Beings Terrible and Wonderful,* an attempt to determine the origins of the "not-quite-human beings" who populate folklore and myth. It won *Book World*'s Spring Festival Award in 1972 and was a National Book Award nominee in 1973. "Miss McHargue uses her subject with marvelous humor and an unflagging sense of style," writes Jennifer Farley Smith in the *Christian Science Monitor.* "Her imaginative treatment of those who populate our fantasies and folklore is fascinating." A *Kirkus Reviews* critic similarly concludes that the book is "naturally impossible, but terribly wonderful."

In *Facts, Frauds and Phantasms: A Survey of the Spiritualist Movement,* McHargue takes on questionable claims of spiritualism (along with allowances that some phenomena simply cannot be explained) in a book that Michael Cart of *School Library Journal* describes as "a genuine rarity—a juvenile title which can stand with adult books as being as nearly a complete popular introduction to a subject as one might wish." A *Kirkus Reviews* critic likewise calls it "a well researched and intriguing case study in human gullibility ... and invaluable background for would-be investigators of occult phenomena."

Supernatural Creatures Fill Books

McHargue continued to introduce young readers to perversely fascinating topics and characters in *Mummies, Meet the Werewolf, Meet the Vampire,* and *Meet the Witches.* Of *Mummies,* a relatively exhaustive account of both natural and artificial means of mummification, reviewer Paul Heins of *Horn Book* says, "[McHargue] continues to exploit her flair for combining research with an eminently readable style." *Meet the Werewolf,* according to a *Booklist* reviewer, is "especially entertaining for those who wish to know the proper ritual for turning into a werewolf." Various myths and legends of vampire lore are explored in *Meet the Vampire,* including a chapter entitled, "How to Tell a Vampire When You Meet One," and one particularly useful chapter offering advice on the best way to destroy them.

Meet the Witches, said a *Horn Book* critic, answers "an almost insatiable demand among the young for material about witches." The book presents a study of their beginnings, historical influence, and present-day status. Analyzed by type (the primitive witch, the fairy-tale witch, the historical witch, and so on), McHargue ties certain witch characteristics in with classical mythologies, fertility cults, and zombie legends. The concluding chapter outlines doctrines shared by the four schools of modern-day witchcraft, which is distinct from Satanism. The *Horn Book* reviewer notes that due to McHargue's balanced presentation of the history of witchcraft, "the true horror of the book lies not in their doings but in the way these people have been persecuted."

McHargue's juvenile fiction builds as well on folklore and myth, often borrowing from existing legends, embellishing them, and bringing them into the present day. In *Elidor and the Golden Ball,* for example, McHargue retells the story of a twelfth-century Welsh boy who runs away from a cruel teacher and accidentally witnesses the sacred Faery dance. (In the epilogue readers are informed that Elidor was a real person who grew up to become a priest and scholar.) *The Mermaid and the Whale* is based on an old Cape Cod sailors' yarn of the same name; Mary M. Burns, writing in *Horn Book,* calls it a "marvelous blend of the storyteller's art with folklore convention."

The author's real-life penchant for archaeology shows up in *The Turquoise Toad Mystery,* where Ben and Frito (the heroes of a previous novel, *Funny Bananas*) spend Christmas vacation on an archaeological dig. Children team up again in *Beastie,* where Americans Mary, Scott, and Theo are thrown together for the summer when their respective parents come to Scotland to take part in a research team investigating the "beastie" alleged to inhabit the local lake.

A prolific author, McHargue once described her writing life to *SATA:* "I do most of my work at home, but I can write and have written in all sorts of places, from beaches to bus stations. I guess I am blessed with the

Leigh's summer visit to Scotland turns dangerous when she attempts to infiltrate a secret cult restricted to men only. (Cover illustration by Michael Dudash.)

sort of Protestant conscience that won't let me rest until I've accomplished a modicum of work each day."

■ Works Cited

Burns, Mary M., review of *The Mermaid and the Whale, Horn Book,* February, 1974, pp. 46-47.

Cart, Michael, review of *Facts, Frauds and Phantasms, School Library Journal,* October, 1972, p. 130.

Review of *Facts, Frauds, and Phantasms, Kirkus Reviews,* May 1, 1972, p. 545.

Heins, Paul, review of *Mummies, Horn Book,* April, 1973, pp. 152-153.

Review of *The Impossible People, Kirkus Reviews,* December 1, 1971, pp. 1262-1263.

McHargue, Georgess, entry in *Something about the Author Autobiography Series,* Volume 5, Gale, 1988, pp. 237-250.

Review of *Meet the Werewolf, Booklist,* April 15, 1976.

Review of *Meet the Witches, Horn Book,* April, 1984, p. 210.

Smith, Jennifer Farley, review of *The Impossible People, Christian Science Monitor,* May 4, 1972, p. B4.

Something about the Author, Volume 4, Gale, 1973.

Wersba, Barbara, review of *The Beasts of Never, New York Times Book Review,* July 28, 1968, p. 23.

Wersba, Barbara, review of *The Impossible People, New York Times Book Review,* April 2, 1972, p. 8.

■ For More Information See

BOOKS

Children's Literature Review, Gale, 1976, pp. 117-120.

PERIODICALS

Booklist, March 15, 1977, p. 1108; September 1, 1977, p. 43; January 1, 1978, p. 728; November 1, 1979, p. 450; May 1, 1982, p. 1162; September 15, 1984.
Bulletin of the Center for Children's Books, April, 1973, p. 129; November, 1975, p. 50.
Christian Science Monitor, May 7, 1970, p. B3.
Horn Book, August, 1981, p. 43.
New York Times Book Review, May 31, 1970, p. 14; May 25, 1975, p. 10; July 12, 1981, p. 30; January 15, 1989, p. 31.
School Library Journal, January, 1974, p. 41; May, 1982, p. 84; December, 1988, p. 122; July, 1992, p. 74.
Voice of Youth Advocates, June, 1988, p. 102; December, 1988, p. 240.
Washington Post Book World, May 7, 1972, p. 4.*

—*Sketch by Julie Catalano*

*   *   *

MICHAELS, William M. 1917-

■ Personal

Born August 30, 1917, in Washington, DC; son of Manly (a dentist) and Marjorie (a homemaker; maiden name, Newman) Michaels; married Carolyn Clugston (a librarian and author), December 29, 1973; children: R. Patrick, Andrice Jean. *Education:* Attended University of Tennessee, 1935-37; Northwestern University, D.D.S., 1941. *Hobbies and other interests:* Visual arts, travel.

■ Addresses

Home—2 1/2 Orange Street, Charleston, SC 29401; 10401 Grosvenor Place #1101, Rockville, MD 20852.

■ Career

Dental practice, 1941-83. Restaurant owner/operator, 1960-75. *Wartime service:* U.S. Public Health Service, 1943-46. *Member:* American Dental Association (life member), Washington Dental Club (senior member), Washington Print Club, Artist Equity, Print Studio South.

■ Writings

Clare and Her Shadow, self-illustrated, Linnet Books, 1991.

ILLUSTRATIONS

D.A.R. Library Catalog Vol. I (family histories and genealogies), Tidewater Press, 1982.
Carolyn Michaels, *Library Literacy Means Lifelong Learning,* Scarecrow Press, 1985.

Also illustrator of *Children's Book Collecting* by Carolyn Michaels, 1993.

■ Work in Progress

Sculpture bust, woodcuts and etchings.

■ Sidelights

Clare and Her Shadow was inspired when Dr. William Michaels, a retired dentist, took his three-year-old granddaughter, Clare, for a walk one fall afternoon. The sun was shining, and Clare suddenly noticed something she had never noticed before—her shadow.

The book was created totally in woodcuts; the pictures and text are printed from photographs made from woodcut prints created by Dr. Michaels. The lines and whorls in the pictures show the grains of the blocks of wood Dr. Michaels used to make the prints, including a block made from a 260-year-old wooden beam.

*   *   *

MILLAIS, Raoul 1901-

■ Personal

Born October 4, 1901, in Horsham, Sussex, England; son of John Guille (an explorer, writer, and painter) and Francis (Skipwith) Millais; married Katherine Bibby, 1950 (died, 1982); children: John, Hugh, Hesketh. *Education:* Attended Winchester College and Royal Academy School of Art. *Politics:* "Disgusted with all politicians." *Religion:* Church of England.

■ Addresses

Home—Westcote Manor, Kingham, Oxon, England.

■ Career

Writer and illustrator.

■ Writings

Elijah and Pin-Pin, self-illustrated, Simon & Schuster Books for Young Readers, 1991.

■ For More Information See

PERIODICALS

Publishers Weekly, June 8, 1992, p. 62.
School Library Journal, July, 1992, p. 62.

BEN P. MILLSPAUGH

MILLSPAUGH, Ben P. 1936-

■ Personal

Born February 18, 1936, in Cherokee, OK; son of John Franklin (a cattle rancher and farmer) and Ruth Powell (a teacher) Millspaugh; married Karen Ann (a middle school principal), August 14, 1982; children: John Franklin, Linda Shawn. *Education:* Northwestern Oklahoma State University, B.S., 1959; University of Northern Colorado, M.A., 1972, Ph.D., 1981. *Hobbies and other interests:* Travel ("have plans of spending time in England, Australia and New Zealand"), "building a larger, more powerful biplane and spending more time flying the one I now have."

■ Addresses

Home and office—6334 South Jay Way, Littleton, CO 80123.

■ Career

Author. Science teacher at Julesburg High School, Julesburg, CO, and Euclid Junior High School, Littleton, CO, 1960-67; flight operations instructor for United Airlines, 1967-69; Littleton High School, Littleton,

CO, director of aviation and aerospace, 1969-91. Sightseeing and charter pilot, 1967-90. *Member:* Experimental Aircraft Association, Aircraft Owners and Pilots Association, Antique Aircraft Association, Wings of FAME.

■ Awards, Honors

Aerospace Teacher of the Year, National Congress on Aviation and Space Education, 1989; Christa McCauliffe Award, Aerospace Education Association, 1989, for outstanding achievement in aerospace education; Aviation Educator of the Year, Experimental Aircraft Association, 1990; Crown Circle Award, 1990, for outstanding contributions to aviation education; inducted into Colorado Aviation Hall of Fame, 1991.

■ Writings

Ultralight Airman's Information Manual, UAI, 1981.
Ultralight Airman's Flight Manual, UAI, 1981.
Z Car Enthusiast's Guide, Benton-Cutter Press, 1986.
Private Pilot's License Program, TAB Books, 1986.
Commercial Pilot License Program, TAB Books, 1986.
Ultralight Airman's Manual, TAB Books, 1986.
Z Car, A Legend in Its Own Time, TAB/McGraw-Hill, 1990.
Aviation and Space Science Projects, TAB/McGraw-Hill, 1991.
Aerospace Science Projects, TAB/McGraw-Hill, 1994.

Also contributor of articles to automotive and aviation publications.

■ Work in Progress

Further research on an aerospace science book for TAB/McGraw-Hill.

■ Sidelights

"I started writing professionally in 1963 with contributions to automotive model and racing magazines," Ben Millspaugh told *SATA.* Millspaugh's contributions to magazines are generally "how-to" articles, and his books follow a similar format. As the result of his "how-to" experience as both a pilot and a sports car enthusiast, Millspaugh is considered an expert on aviation and the Datsun/Nissan Z car.

A retired high school teacher, Millspaugh says: "Writing comes easy to me because I have worked closely with secondary students between the ages of 14 and 18, and I write everything to that reading level. My writing is generally easy to read and fast-paced for maximum comprehension.... Writing is like a conversation ... I try to imagine what my reader is thinking as I talk to him. I also realize that the attention span of my reader is limited, and for that reason I tend to keep my work 'on task.'"

PIERR MORGAN

MORGAN, Pierr 1952-

■ Personal

First name is pronounced "peer"; born May 2, 1952, in Seattle, WA; daughter of Arthur (an interior designer) and Ruth (Orbison) Morgan; married Steve Leitz, 1974 (divorced, 1979); children: Aaron Morgan. *Education:* Attended University of Washington, 1970-73; Art Center College of Design, B.F.A. (with distinction), 1987. *Hobbies and other interests:* Sketch-journaling, book-binding, knitting and sewing, bird watching, traveling.

■ Addresses

Home and office—759 Oak St., Port Townsend, WA 98368-5227.

■ Career

Freelance artist, 1973—. Children's Center for Creative Arts, Seattle, WA, visual artist, 1981-82; *Sports Northwest* magazine, Seattle, staff illustrator, 1982-84. Guest lecturer at public schools, libraries, and colleges in Washington, Oregon, and California, 1989—. *Member:* Society of Children's Book Writers and Illustrators.

■ Writings

SELF-ILLUSTRATED

(Reteller) *The Turnip: An Old Russian Folktale,* Philomel Books, 1990.
(Reteller) *Sweet Porridge Pot Cooks: An Old German Folktale,* Philomel Books, 1993.
(Reteller) *Supper for Crow: A Northwest Coast Indian Tale,* Crown Books, 1994.

ILLUSTRATOR

Nellie Edge, *Kids in the Kitchen,* Peninsula Publishing, 1975.
Geoffrey Williams, *Treasures of the Barrier Reef,* Price, Stern, 1988.
Williams, *Adventures beyond the Solar System,* Price, Stern, 1988.
Gus Cazzola, *The Bells of Santa Lucia,* Philomel Books, 1991.
Marilyn Hollinshead, *The Nine Day Wonder,* Philomel Books, 1993.

Also contributor of illustrations to *Ladybug Magazine* and *Sesame Street Magazine.*

■ Work in Progress

Walking Home up the Big Hill on the Lookout for Dogs, an adult novel; a middle-grade fantasy novel, several short stories, a young adult novel and several picture books.

■ Sidelights

Pierr Morgan told *SATA:* "Writing and illustrating children's books has been my focus since I was eleven years old. At seven I wrote in my diary, 'I want to be a famous poet when I grow up.' So I wrote poetry. At nine I knew I would be an artist as well, and so I illustrated my poetry. My sixth grade teacher, Peg Fountain, read Newbery Award books to us, such as *The Bronze Bow* and *Island of the Blue Dolphins.* It was at that point that I knew I wanted to write books that well and illustrate them.

"Real drawing was reserved for school. And even then I dabbled around. Things I did in kindergarten were more profound, perhaps, in terms of 'talent.' I was told I was talented but I never wanted to be singled out for it. Somehow I knew it takes more than talent to be able to really do what you want in life. Children are not idiots. They are very perceptive. And I knew simply from observation that people are ridiculed and beaten and cast out for being 'different,' talented, smarter than the rest.

"I went underground. Subconsciously, of course. I knew it was better to gather information and teach myself than to blossom and die on the bush too quickly. There would be a time for me later.

"For years my goal was to have a children's book that I had written and illustrated published by Harper & Row in New York. So I paid attention to the market, wrote stories and sent them out—bad ones, I admit. But rejection didn't stop me. I tried other publishers and kept tabs on editors and names of favorite authors and illustrators. I had quite a collection of new and old first edition children's books in college. My major, through General Studies at the University of Washington, was 'Writing and Illustrating Children's Books.' I had an instructor as my sponsor and took every related class I could think of: children's dramatics, children's literature, storytelling, short story writing. But I met with a snag in the art department and was told I'd have to become a graphic design major to take the classes I wanted, and that was a five-year program. So I dropped out. I would teach myself, I decided.

"I spent the next two years reading children's books and creating note cards and coloring books to sell in shops and street fairs. I was determined never to have a 9-5 job. I would support myself with my art. This notion was spurred on by so many people, strangers and not, who told me 'You'll regret it for the rest of your life' and 'So you want to be a starving artist, eh?' and 'You can't do that!' I thank them all from the bottom of my heart. And I thank God for giving me just the right streak of stubborn.

"Finally, in 1984, after marriage and divorce, being a mom and then a single mom, after deciding Aaron was happier with his dad and losing him to the gods, I decided to go back to school. Growing up I thought it was 'cool' to be self-taught. Much later I discovered I had a very narrow view of the world because of it. And this passion for art and making books had grown to such a heat that I wanted it bad! So I applied to art school this time, because I didn't want to be limited in executing an idea by my lack of technical knowledge. In 1987 I graduated with a portfolio that spoke for me and the confidence to walk above ground in the thick of this place called Earth.

"And to those who come up to me and say, 'I can't draw a straight line' or 'Do you think this is good?', all I have to say is believe in yourself, educate´ yourself and remember, 'success is the best revenge.' (I don't know who originally said this, but my therapist, Mary Anderson, continues to remind me.)"

■ For More Information See

PERIODICALS

Booklist, April, 1990.
Entertainment Weekly, July 13, 1990, p. 70.
Kirkus Reviews, May 15, 1991.
Martha's Vineyard Times, March 28, 1991.
New York Times Book Review, October 21, 1990.
Publishers Weekly, November 8, 1991, p. 63.

*   *   *

MORRISON, Martha A. 1948-

■ Personal

Born October 16, 1948, in Chelsea, MA; daughter of Charles A. and Dorothy A. (Speirs) Morrison; married Joel L. Uchenick (a management consultant), January 6, 1985; children: Nicholas Morrison. *Education:* Wellesley College, A.B., 1970; Brandeis University, M.A., 1972, Ph.D., 1974. *Hobbies and other interests:* Gardening, travel, museum browsing.

■ Addresses

Home—217 Rowley Bridge Road, Topsfield, MA 01983. *Office*—Theology Department, Boston College, Chestnut Hill, MA 02167.

■ Career

Brandeis University, Waltham, MA, assistant professor, 1974-86; Boston College, Chestnut Hill, MA, lecturer, 1987—. Harvard Semitic Museum, Harvard University, visiting specialist, 1974-76; Ben Gurion University Land of Gerar Expedition, area director and director of education, 1982-85; Yale University, visiting lecturer, 1983. Wellesley College Class of 1970, president; Topsfield Town Library, trustee, beginning 1993. *Member:* American Oriental Society, American Schools of Oriental Research, Archaeological Institute of America (president, Boston Society).

■ Awards, Honors

Waltzer Award for Excellence in Teaching, Brandeis University, 1984.

■ Writings

FOR YOUNG READERS

(With Stephen F. Brown), *Judaism,* Facts on File, 1991.

Scholar Martha A. Morrison co-authored a study on the Jewish religion to help students understand how they fit into the pattern of history.

FOR ADULTS

(Editor with D. I. Owen, and contributor) *Studies on the Civilization and Culture of Nuzi and the Hurrians,* Eisenbrauns, Volume 1: *In Honor of Ernest Lacheman,* 1981, Volume 2: *Texts and Studies,* 1985, Volume 4: *The Eastern Archives of Nuzi,* 1992.

Contributor to journals.

■ Work in Progress

A study of Nuzi (a mid-2nd millennium B.C. Mesopotamian city) for a lay audience.

■ Sidelights

Martha Morrison told *SATA:* "My interest in antiquity began with Latin in Junior High School and Bible Sunday School from the time I was quite young. During my college years, I back-pedaled in time to the Bronze Age where the Ancient Near East caught my attention and, coincidentally, where the worlds of the Bible and the Aegean met. I specialized in cuneiform studies, especially the material from the city of Nuzi which offers us extraordinary information about the daily lives and concerns of average people, as well as the larger social, economic, and political history of a thriving civilization.

"All along the way, I had wonderful, challenging teachers who sparked my interest and demanded the best from me. Because of them, I believe that a scholar has a great responsibility not only to teach, but also to inspire interest and wonder about his or her field of expertise. Additionally, the specialist in arcane fields has the responsibility to make information accessible to the layman, without whose interest and support fields become forgotten footnotes of academia. Young people, especially, deserve lucid and accurate material relating to the past so they can better understand how they fit into the stream of culture and history. My participation in the *Judaism* volume came about because I saw the opportunity to contribute to our youth's understanding of the diversity of our culture and the forces that helped shape our society."

■ For More Information See

PERIODICALS

Booklist, April 15, 1992, p. 1520.
School Library Journal, March, 1992, p. 263.

*   *   *

MURPHY, Jim 1947-

■ Personal

Born September 25, 1947, in Newark, NJ; son of James K. (a certified public accountant) and Helen Irene (a bookkeeper and artist; maiden name, Grosso) Murphy; married Elaine A. Kelso (a company president), Decem-

ber 12, 1970. *Education:* Rutgers University, B.A., 1970; graduate study, Radcliffe College, 1970.

■ Addresses

Home and office—138 Wildwood Ave., Upper Montclair, NJ 07043.

■ Career

Seabury Press, Inc. (later Clarion Books), juvenile department, New York City, 1970-77, began as editorial secretary, became managing editor; freelance author and editor, 1977—. *Member:* Asian Night Six Club (founding member).

■ Awards, Honors

Children's Choice, International Reading Association, 1979, for *Weird and Wacky Inventions;* Notable Book, American Library Association, 1982, for *Death Run;* Golden Kite Award for nonfiction, Society of Children's Book Writers and Illustrators, 1992, for *The Long Road to Gettysburg.*

■ Writings

JUVENILE FICTION

Rat's Christmas Party, illustrated by Dick Gackenbach, Prentice-Hall, 1979.
Harold Thinks Big, illustrated by Susanna Natti, Crown, 1980.
Death Run, Clarion Books, 1982.
The Last Dinosaur, illustrated by Mark Alan Weatherby, Scholastic, 1988.
The Call of the Wolves, illustrated by Mark Alan Weatherby, Scholastic, 1989.
Backyard Bear, illustrated by Jeffrey Greene, Scholastic, 1992.
Dinosaur for a Day, illustrated by Mark Alan Weatherby, Scholastic, 1992.
Night Terrors, Scholastic, 1993.

JUVENILE NONFICTION

Weird and Wacky Inventions, Crown, 1978.
Two Hundred Years of Bicycles, Harper, 1983.
The Indy 500, Clarion Books, 1983.
Baseball's All-Time All-Stars, Clarion Books, 1984.
Tractors: From Yesterday's Steam Wagons to Today's Turbo-Charged Giants, Lippincott, 1984.
The Custom Car Book, Clarion Books, 1985.
Guess Again: More Weird and Wacky Inventions, Four Winds Press, 1985.
Custom Car: A Nuts-and-Bolts Guide to Creating One, Clarion Books, 1989.
The Boys' War: Confederate and Union Soldiers Talk about the Civil War, Clarion Books, 1990.
The Long Road to Gettysburg, Clarion Books, 1992.
Across America on an Emigrant Train, Clarion Books, 1993.

Also contributor of articles to *Cricket.*

■ Sidelights

Jim Murphy has written children's picture books and juvenile nonfiction works that have been praised for presenting interesting facts and historical information in an understandable and entertaining fashion. Murphy's success came with the publication of his first book, *Weird and Wacky Inventions,* which eventually led to a sequel entitled *Guess Again: More Weird and Wacky Inventions.* Both works employ a multiple-choice quiz format which invites children to guess a use for an unusual invention. Contraptions featured include a coffin with an escape hatch and a hammock for use on trains. Each is accompanied by a drawing based on an original patent diagram and an invitation for the child to guess its use before being presented with the solution. The books are rounded out with essays on the inventing and patent process. A *Publishers Weekly* critic concluded: "*Guess Again* is just as wacky as its predecessor."

"I was raised in Kearny, New Jersey," Jim Murphy reminisced to *SATA,* "a nice enough suburban town, make up largely of Scots, Irish, and Italians. My friends and I did all the normal things—played baseball and football endlessly, explored abandoned factories, walked the railroad tracks to the vast Jersey Meadowlands, and, in general, cooked up as much mischief as we could. And since Kearny was close to both Newark and New York City, we would often hop a bus or train to these cities. We loved wandering through those places, so much different than our comfortable, tree-lined streets,

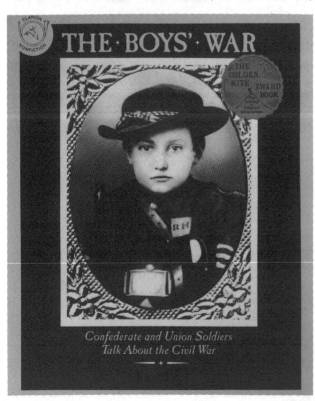

Using the diaries and letters of young boys who fought in the Civil War, Murphy brings wartime living to life in this Golden Kite Award-winner.

watching the people and eating strange and usually greasy foods.

"Oddly enough, I wasn't a very big reader back then. In fact, I hardly cracked a book willingly until a high school teacher announced that we could 'absolutely, positively NOT read' Hemingway's *A Farewell to Arms.* I promptly read it, and every other book I could get a hold of that I felt would shock my teacher. I also began writing, mostly poetry, but with an occasional story or play tossed in there.

"Now this doesn't mean that I abandoned physical activity completely," Murphy continued. "I ran track while in school and was part of national championship teams for the 440 and mile relays. I was also ranked somewhere in the top ten of high school sprinters. In addition, I had a series of strange jobs, including repairing boilers, tarring roofs, putting up chain link fences, operating a mold injection machine, and doing maintenance for two apartment buildings. The highlight, however, was a stint as a tin knocker on several New York City construction jobs.

"It wasn't too long after this that I landed an editorial job in the juvenile department (later named Clarion Books) of Seabury Press. I stayed there seven years, going from editorial secretary to managing editor. It was during this time that I realized that many of my earlier experiences could be of value in my writing."

Achieves Success with Nonfiction Titles

After the publication of *Weird and Wacky Inventions* in 1978, Murphy published a number of other nonfiction titles for juveniles, including *Baseball's All-Time All-Stars,* in which the author presents his ideal players, each accompanied by a short biographical profile. While reviewers were puzzled by the predominance of players from the 1950s and before, others remarked that few lists of this kind, in whatever field, are met with complete agreement by readers. Murphy next employed his talent for presenting nonfiction material in an entertaining fashion in *Tractors: From Yesterday's Steam Wagons to Today's Turbo-Charged Giants.* Here Murphy presents the history of this useful farm machine. Lee Bock in *School Library Journal* remarked that, although other children's tractor books are worthwhile, "none, however, carries the same detailed and readable historical information" as found in Murphy's narrative.

Murphy continued on in the automotive vein with *Custom Car: A Nuts-and-Bolts Guide to Creating One.* The author bought a junked car and, with the help of mechanic Tom Walsh, rebuilt the engine and replaced damaged interior and exterior parts. For the do-it-yourself hobbyist, the book features step-by-step procedures for car repairs, illustrations, explanations and advice, sources for buying parts, and where to find further information. While reviewers cautioned readers that *Custom Car* is not the only source that will be needed to attempt this type of project on their own, the

THE LAST DINOSAUR

by JIM MURPHY   •   Illustrated by MARK ALAN WEATHERBY

LASTIC

Even in his picture books for the very young, Jim Murphy includes a wealth of facts to help his readers learn. (Cover illustration by Mark Alan Weatherby.)

book was praised for its enthusiasm and accessibility. A *Kirkus Reviews* critic summarized: "Despite the fairy-tale quality here ... this makes a breezy first book for both doers and dreamers."

Murphy turned to the American Civil War for his next two major nonfiction titles. In *The Boys' War: Confederate and Union Soldiers Talk about the Civil War,* Murphy utilizes the eyewitness accounts of soldiers age twelve to sixteen to bring to life the battles, living conditions, and psychological impact of combat on the youths who participated. While many reviewers found the book grim, Murphy was praised for bringing home the reality of war for young adult readers. David A. Lindsey, reviewing *The Boys' War* for *School Library Journal,* lauded the book for its sepia-toned photographs which amplify the text. Joanne Johnson in *Voice Of Youth Advocate* pointed to Murphy's use of the boys' own words through their letters and diaries which "makes this war come alive" for the reader. A commentator in *Horn Book* concluded: "This well-researched

and readable account provides fresh insight into the human cost of a pivotal event in United States history."

Murphy's second book for young adults on the Civil War, *The Long Road to Gettysburg,* focuses on two young men—John Dooley, a Confederate soldier, and Thomas Galway, a Union soldier—who were present at one of the war's bloodiest and most famous battles. This personalized view of the fight is augmented with maps, photographs, and the text of Abraham Lincoln's "Gettysburg Address." Anita Silvey, reviewing *The Long Road to Gettysburg* for *Horn Book,* remarked: "Jim Murphy uses all of his fine skills as an information writer ... to frame a well-crafted account of a single battle in the war."

Murphy is also the author of a number of successful picture books for children. Taking on a long-popular subject for young children, *The Last Dinosaur* combines a number of facts about dinosaur life and the factors that probably contributed to their extinction. The story is about a small herd of triceratops and their encounters with a tyrannosaurus rex, with mammals who prey on the triceratops' eggs, and finally with a forest fire which destroys the only remaining nest. Murphy returned to the subject of dinosaurs with the publication of *Dinosaur for a Day,* which dramatizes a day in the life of a vegetarian hypsilophodon and her eight babies as they search for food. While reviewers cautioned readers about the combination of fact and fiction in this work, they also lauded the entertaining format and lifelike illustrations by Mark Alan Weatherby.

Murphy turned to the plight of a modern-day endangered species—the wolf—with *The Call of the Wolves.* When one wolf is separated from his pack during a hunt for caribou, he faces the dangers posed by illegal hunters, other packs of wolves, and sled dogs. In an afterword, Murphy shares further factual information about wolves. Deborah Abbott in her *Booklist* review commented that the "taut story line, [and] compelling illustrations" increases the readers' interest in the account. Betsy Hearne concluded in *Bulletin of the Center for Children's Books* that "the style is straightforward and the dramatically textured paintings ... are so dynamic, this can be read by independent readers older than the picture book listeners for whom it's intended."

"I thoroughly enjoy my work," Murphy once commented to *SATA.* "The nonfiction projects let me research subjects that I'm really interested in; they provide an opportunity to tell kids some unusual bits of information. The fiction lets me get out some of the thoughts and opinions that rattle around in my head."

■ Works Cited

Abbott, Deborah, review of *The Call of the Wolves, Booklist,* January 1, 1990, p. 919.

Bock, Lee, review of *Tractors, School Library Journal,* November, 1984, p. 127.

Review of *The Boys' War: Confederate and Union Soldiers Talk about the Civil War, Horn Book,* January, 1991.

Review of *Custom Car: A Nuts-and-Bolts Guide to Creating One, Kirkus Reviews,* April 1, 1989, pp. 551-52.

Review of *Guess Again: More Weird and Wacky Inventions, Publishers Weekly,* June 27, 1986, p. 97.

Hearne, Betsy, review of *The Boys' War: Confederate and Union Soldiers Talk about the Civil War, Bulletin of the Center for Children's Books,* January, 1991, p. 126.

Hearne, Betsy, review of *The Call of the Wolves, Bulletin of the Center for Children's Books,* September, 1989, p. 13.

Johnson, Joanne, review of *The Boys' War: Confederate and Union Soldiers Talk about the Civil War, Voice Of Youth Advocate,* April, 1991, p. 60.

Lindsey, David A., review of *The Boys' War: Confederate and Union Soldiers Talk about the Civil War, School Library Journal,* January, 1991, p. 120.

Silvey, Anita, review of *The Long Road to Gettysburg, Horn Book,* July, 1992, pp. 469-70.

■ For More Information See

PERIODICALS

Booklist, July, 1986, p. 1615; October 15, 1992, p. 435.
Bulletin of the Center for Children's Books, June, 1988, p. 213.
Kirkus Reviews, May 1, 1992, p. 614.
Publishers Weekly, April 29, 1988, p. 75; September 27, 1991, p. 59; April 20, 1992, p. 58.
School Library Journal, November, 1984, pp. 127, 135; October, 1986, p. 180; September, 1988, p. 184; July, 1989, p. 96; December, 1989, pp. 86-87; June, 1992, p. 146; October, 1992, p. 107.*

N

NEITZEL, Shirley 1941-

■ Personal

Born May 15, 1941, in Ewen, MI; daughter of Theophilus Koehler (a lumberjack) and Ida (Wegner) Koehler (a homemaker); married Eric Neitzel, October 14, 1961; children: Christine. *Education:* Attended Wayne State University, 1958-62; Eastern Michigan University, B.A., 1966; Western Michigan University, M.A., 1979. *Religion:* Lutheran.

■ Addresses

Home—5060 Sequoia Dr. S.E., Grand Rapids, MI 49512.

■ Career

Ypsilanti Public Schools, Ypsilanti, MI, elementary school teacher, 1967-68; Caledonia Community Schools, Caledonia, MI, elementary school teacher, 1969—. *Member:* Peninsula Writers (member of board of directors, 1984—; secretary, 1984-87; vice-president, 1987-89; president, 1989-91).

■ Awards, Honors

Parents' Choice Honor Book, 1992, for *The Dress I'll Wear to the Party.*

■ Writings

ILLUSTRATED BY NANCY WINSLOW PARKER

The Jacket I Wear in the Snow, Greenwillow, 1989.
The Dress I'll Wear to the Party, Greenwillow, 1992.
The Bag I'm Taking to Grandma's, Greenwillow, 1994.

■ Sidelights

Shirley Neitzel told *SATA:* "I am a teacher who writes. I use my writing to teach my students the writing process, and they are often my audience. My first book came about as a result of a lesson I was preparing. Thinking

SHIRLEY NEITZEL

the children would enjoy writing a cumulative tale in the manner of the nursery rhyme 'The House That Jack Built,' my first step was to try it myself.

"When I read my story the children laughed in the right places, and I decided to include it in our classroom anthology. I also showed it to several other teacher-writers. With their encouragement I sent the manuscript to an editor. My students were as excited as I was when the editor decided to make the book *The Jacket I Wear in the Snow.*

"Through my writing I show children that writing includes rethinking and rewriting. They learn that although writing may be difficult at times, it is also rewarding."

■ For More Information See

PERIODICALS

Booklist, September 1, 1989; October 15, 1992.
Horn Book Magazine, September/October, 1989.
Kirkus Reviews, August 15, 1992.
Publishers Weekly, August 24, 1992.
School Library Journal, November, 1989; October, 1992.

* * *

NELSON, Drew 1952-

■ Personal

Born February 11, 1952, in Pittsburgh, PA; son of Andrew L. Nelson (a civil engineer) and Eltheda (Perry) Nelson (a homemaker); married Vaunda Micheaux (an author and librarian) November 18, 1983. *Education:* University of Pittsburgh, B.A., 1974; attended University of Pittsburgh M.F.A. program, 1980-81.

DREW NELSON

■ Addresses

Home—200 Kelly Ave., Apt. 3, Pittsburgh, PA 15221.
Agent—Flannery Literary, 34-40 28th St., No. 6, Long Island City, New York, NY 11106-3516.

■ Career

Leader-Times, Kittanning, PA, journalist, 1977-79; freelance writer, 1974-86; advertising copywriter, 1987-89.
Member: Society of Children's Book Writers and Illustrators; Western Pennsylvania Society of Children's Book Writers and Illustrators.

■ Awards, Honors

Wild Voices was named a Notable Children's Book in the Language Arts by the National Council of Teachers of English, 1991, and a Carolyn W. Field honor book by the Pennsylvania Library Association youth services division, 1992.

■ Writings

Wild Voices, illustrated by John Schoenherr, Philomel Books, 1991.

■ Work in Progress

Books on animals and wildlife: "My lifelong interest in and fascination with wildlife and animals forms the bulk of my research and, obviously, continues on a nearly daily basis."

■ Sidelights

Drew Nelson told *SATA:* "When I'm asked why I became a writer, or even when I became a writer, I find it hard to give a specific answer because writing is something I do, a major part of who I am, not something I like to talk about. I don't know if I actually *became* a writer or if I was born to be a writer. And as to when, I can't remember a time since high school when I didn't write, although I would have to say I wasn't really serious about writing as a career until my sophomore year in college when I changed my major from political science to English and writing. Since then, it's been very hard to think of doing anything else but write and all of my 'professional' employment centered on writing.

"I think my love of writing, and of language, comes from caring parents who took the time—made the time—to read to my brother and me. Some of my earliest memories involve us creeping into our parents' bed early in the morning and begging them to read to us from the copy of *Wind in the Willows* that we'd dragged with us. Our parents were wonderful, enthusiastic readers who created different voices for all the characters and added dramatic emphasis to the stories they read to us.

"I also remember my grandfather, my father's father, as a wonderful storyteller who captivated us with oral histories of his boyhood and of times later, when he worked in and around coal mines in West Virginia. He would tell us about tobacco-chewing mine mules and somehow make his face look just like (what we imagined) the mule's would be. And he would scare us with stories about predatory mine rats that were as big as house cats and make his face into that of a rat's as well. My father continued this storytelling tradition with tales of his youthful adventures, although he isn't nearly the 'facial actor' his father was. So my life was filled with stories from a very young age and the value of reading was instilled through example and practice. It is, perhaps, the greatest gift my parents have given me.

"I wrote *Wild Voices* with several things in mind. First, I wanted these stories to entertain. Then, although the stories are fictive, I hoped I could share something of the lives of real wild animals with the reader. And finally, I felt it was important to portray the animals in these stories as honestly as I could. These animals don't speak with British accents, wear clothes, or inhabit comfortably furnished dens or hollow trees. They live hard lives, real lives, where they are sometimes required to flee or to kill in order to survive. Their lives are filled with natural beauty, but there isn't anything soft or romantic about them. I feel it is important for modern people, most of whom don't come in contact with wild animals, to come to understand the struggle of wild lives, to see wildlife as important, and to support whatever steps are necessary to preserve the wild places that our fellow creatures need in order to continue to live. We are all just tenants of this planet and deserve an equal chance for survival.

"While the influences on my work are too numerous to list, I will say that Jack London, Gary Paulsen, and Farley Mowat are among my favorites. I would recommend Mr. Paulsen's work to anyone—child or adult—who is interested in this field. His writing has such clarity and power that many of his books set the standard for the rest of us.

"My working habits are unusual, I think, and I would not recommend them to anyone as an easy way to go. Generally I find my most productive writing time falls between midnight and about four in the morning. Right now I live in the city and those hours allow me quiet, contemplative, uninterrupted time—no phone calls, no deliveries, little traffic noise. Unlike many writers, I don't actively write every day. I research and observe, then let what I've acquired and experienced 'cook' in my head until it is ready to be written. I find, too, that I cannot talk about works in progress because if I talk about a story it becomes difficult for me to write. It's as though I've already told it and so it doesn't then want to be written. This is a source of frustration for my favorite editor and critic, my wife Vaunda.

"The best advice I can give aspiring writers is to repeat the oldest maxim: write what you know. You must be knowledgeable and comfortable with your subject in order to write about it well. If you sit down and can't write mostly from what is in your head, you need to spend more time researching and observing and digesting. You can't know too much about your subject. You don't have to use everything you know in one story or in one book, but you have to know enough to carry off your intent credibly. The other advice I would give is to read, read, read. Know what's being done in your field and learn about style and technique from the very best writers you can find. And be persistent; *Wild Voices* was rejected initially by the same editor who later published it."

■ For More Information See

PERIODICALS

Kirkus Review, September 1, 1991.
Language Arts, November, 1992.
Publishers Weekly, August 23, 1991.
Scholastic Scope, April 2, 1993.
School Library Journal, November, 1991.
Voice of Youth Advocates, December, 1991.

* * *

NEWTON, Suzanne 1936-

■ Personal

Born October 8, 1936, in Bunnlevel, NC; daughter of Hannis T. and Billie (O'Quinn) Latham; married Carl R. Newton (with North Carolina Employment Security Commission), June 9, 1957; children: Michele, Erin, Heather, Craig. *Education:* Duke University, A.B., 1957.

SUZANNE NEWTON

■ Addresses

Home—841-A Barringer Dr., Raleigh, NC 27606.

■ Career

Novelist, short story writer, and poet. Writer-in-residence at Meredith College. *Member:* Authors Guild, Authors League of America, North Carolina Writer's Conference, North Carolina Writer's Network.

■ Awards, Honors

American Association of University Women (North Carolina chapter) awards for juvenile literature, 1971, for *Purro and the Prattleberries,* 1974, for *Care of Arnold's Corners,* 1977, for *What Are You up to, William Thomas?,* 1978, for *Reubella and the Old Focus Home,* 1981, for *M. V. Sexton Speaking,* and for *Where Are You When I Need You?; I Will Call It Georgie's Blues* was named an American Library Association notable book and best book for young adults, and a *New York Times* and *New York Times Book Review* best book of the year, all in 1983.

■ Writings

Purro and the Prattleberries, Westminster, 1971.
Care of Arnold's Corners, Westminster, 1974.
What Are You up to, William Thomas?, Westminster, 1977.
Reubella and the Old Focus Home, Westminster, 1978.
M. V. Sexton Speaking, Viking, 1983.
I Will Call It Georgie's Blues, Viking, 1983.ʹ
An End to Perfect, Viking, 1984.
A Place Between, Viking, 1986.
Where Are You When I Need You?, Viking, 1991.

Contributor of short stories, poems and articles for adults to magazines, including *Home Life, Parents' Magazine, Human Voice Quarterly, Southern Poetry Review,* and *Long View Journal.*

■ Sidelights

Suzanne Newton describes herself as a writer with "a tendency to create 'heroic' characters." The process of creating characters has changed her personality, she feels. "I have come out of my shy, fearful self and have begun to risk and dare along with" her characters, she once commented. Besides writing, Newton has participated in the Poetry-in-the-Schools project in North Carolina, where poets and writers spend a week in school classrooms helping children to find a voice of their own through poetry. This activity has been as important to Newton as writing, because she feels this is "the business of enabling people to 'become.'"

In line with her belief of the heroic in people, Newton has created a number of characters in her books who stand up to difficult situations and manage to "say all the smart things—although their knees knock." Newton

Taking on the responsibilities of a part-time job gives sixteen-year-old M. V. the independence and self-confidence she needs to confront her aunt about her deceased parents. (Cover illustration by Robert Barrett.)

once confessed that she "used to lie in bed at night and wish I had said" the things she has her characters say.

In *Care of Arnold's Corners,* Newton's heroine, Rosalee, stands up to the narrow-minded attitudes of her parents and neighbors, who are inclined to be suspicious of strangers. Rosalee befriends Raoul King, a longhaired, nonconformist "hippie" who comes to Arnold's Corners in a Volkswagen camper. In a heroic act to warn him of a vigilante raid on his camper, Rosalee suffers a bicycle accident. Among the other people she befriends, in spite of her parents' and neighbors' disapproving attitudes, are Jenny, a seamstress who turns up in town with a baby, and May, a black schoolmate. Rosalee tells her story with a "slightly southern turn of phrase and relaxed, self-deprecatory humor," comments a *Kirkus Reviews* critic. While this reviewer finds the book's tone "entertaining" if "not quite equal to the story's most melodramatic moments," others have had more positive things to say about *Arnold's Corners.* A *Publishers*

Weekly writer notes that "enthusiastic readers of Ms. Newton's clever story will feel the tension ... and sigh with relief" at the ending. "Rosalee is an attractive heroine and her story nicely told," Zena Sutherland similarly comments in the *Bulletin of the Center for Children's Books.*

Similarly, *M. V. Sexton Speaking* is "a wholly satisfying book," M. Jean Greenlaw writes in her *Journal of Reading* review, praising in particular the depth of the characters and their problems. "But best of all, the book makes you laugh." The main character, Martha Venable (M. V.) Sexton, has been living with her Great-aunt Gert since her parents died ten years earlier when she was six. Now a teenager, M. V. is pushed by her strict aunt to find a summer job, which she does at a bakery. The job has a positive effect on the young girl; she becomes self-confident and motivated to confront her aunt for information about her parents' accidental death. The book is not all morals and lessons. It also has its fun side when a "tension-breaking batter-and-frosting-tossing free-for-all in the bakery's back room" breaks out, as a *Kirkus Reviews* writer notes. "There's nothing sugary about it—thanks mostly to M. V.'s fresh, feet-on-the-ground personality." Carolyn Noah in *School Library Journal* likewise finds M. V. to be a "likable, spunky individual." Just as she has done with Rosalee in *Care of Arnold's Corners,* Newton has created in M. V. Sexton another heroic young woman who faces life's challenges with courage.

Family Turmoil Revealed in Novel

Fortitude similarly belongs to the narrator of *I Will Call It Georgie's Blues,* 15-year-old Neal Sloan. The son of a Baptist minister in Gideon, North Carolina, Neal tells the story of the inner turmoil of a family that appears to outsiders to be the perfect American family. But at home, Neal's father is full of anger and his mother is unsuccessful in keeping peace between the father and the children. Neal's sister Aileen is a rebel and his younger brother Georgie is a frightened little boy. Most reviews of *Georgie's Blues* strongly praise the book; for instance, David Gale in *School Library Journal* calls it "an emotionally-charged story of public image versus personal truths."

As Gale continues, the main theme of the story deals with the nature of reality. Georgie, convinced that his parents no longer love him, believes they have been replaced by clones; Neal's love for music becomes his most important reality; the surface appearance of Neal and Georgie's "perfect" family is belied by an overly strict father, a distant mother, and a rebellious sister. "Newton has written a brutal novel of a family in crisis," Gale notes, adding that Newton's story is "grim but gripping, desperate but inherently optimistic."

Anne Tyler in *New York Times Book Review* compares Newton's Georgie to the young John Henry West of Carson McCullers's novel *The Member of the Wedding:* "Seven-year old Georgie is equally touching, but in many ways more fragile, and his presence in this story

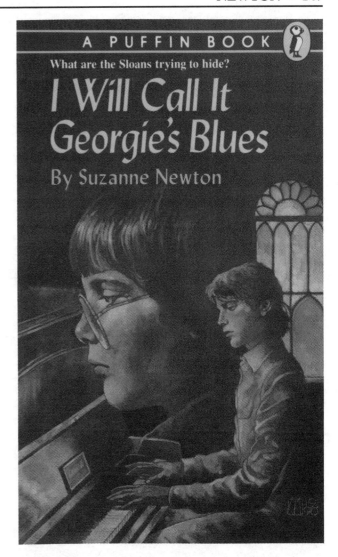

Fifteen-year-old Neal attempts to cope with his dysfunctional family by retreating into his music until tragedy strikes the family in Newton's critically acclaimed novel. (Cover illustration by Stephen Marchesi.)

turns it into something fine and delicate and full of possibility." Tyler thinks Neal's narration of this "sad and wonderful story" effective. Through his telling he is able to show how, as he puts it, "everything is connected, whether I like it or not. Changing one piece means changing all the pieces." Another reviewer, Lisa Fraustino of *Best Sellers,* finds Neal's narration compelling; she compares the vividness of his story to that of Holden Caulfield, the protagonist of J. D. Salinger's *Catcher in the Rye.* "Neal takes us through his story so smoothly, so realistically.... A young audience will find Newton's characters interesting and her story strongly written," the reviewer concludes.

A writer for *Kirkus Reviews,* however, was disappointed in *Georgie's Blues,* calling it "a tired older fiction formula" containing "a dubious psychological grab-bag." But Hazel Rochman, writing in *School Library Journal,* finds the book "improves with rereading.... Newton's strong sense of ugly family secrets beneath a respectable facade [is] a theme which is never lost on teenage readers." The reviewer adds that this story of family tensions "has universal appeal"; her colleagues in the American Library Association agreed, naming the book one of their best books for young adults.

Female Characters Make Difficult Decisions

In *An End to Perfect* Newton explores the struggles of 12-year-old Arden Gifford to deal with the reality of her true feelings when her friend DorJo comes to live with her family. Her difficulties center around DorJo's ties to Arden's mother, which are stronger than her ties to Arden. In this book Newton presents a picture of how deeply a young person experiences pain and suffering. *A Place Between* follows Arden from her old home in Haverlee, a small Southern town, to her new home in Grierson, a more urban area. Arden is between girlhood and her teenage years, as well as between friendships. Arden's grandfather tells her that "We all have times when we leave one place but we don't go right straight to

A PUFFIN BOOK

Where Are You When I Need You?

BY SUZANNE NEWTON

Sometimes your heart can give you the wrong message.

A young woman experiences conflicting emotions when she unexpectedly falls in love with her childhood friend just prior to leaving for college. (Cover illustration by Ellen Thompson.)

another one." He calls this uncertain state "wilderness wandering."

"Arden feels like a displaced person," writes a reviewer in *English Journal*. She is living in a domestic limbo at her grandmother's until her family's house is sold in Haverlee. When she visits her old friends she discovers that she can't just resume old friendships; time and distance have changed Arden and her friends, and even her favorite places no longer seem special. The reviewer feels "young adults who have been upset by family moves and who are in that wilderness between childhood and adulthood" will find comfort in *A Place Between*. A *Horn Book* reviewer likewise comments that "this fresh look at a girl's growth in a caring family that is under stress will provide satisfying reading for the maturing adolescent."

The conflict that Melissa Cord faces in *Where Are You When I Need You?* centers around her plans to go to college against the wishes of her grandmother and an uncle who fiercely disapprove of her leaving home. Melissa's mother had defied family tradition to go to college before her and had gotten pregnant by a fellow student; now Missy faces the same opposition her mother had dealt with earlier. Complicating matters for Missy, who is smart and had always planned to go to college, is when it is time to decide her future, she finds that she has fallen in love with her childhood friend, Jim. Hazel Rochman, writing in *Booklist*, observes that even though Newton once commented that she only knew Missy's choice after finishing the story, "readers will know." Rochman continues, "The pleasant romance and the mild family protest don't stand a chance against the richness of college and the feminist call."

The *Kirkus* reviewer sees Missy working through her confusion and deciding to go, although she leaves open the possibility of returning as a teacher. "Once again," applauds the reviewer, "Newton conveys unexaggerated feelings with rare skill and sympathy, leaving formula romances in the dust." Betsy Hearne in the *Bulletin of the Center for Children's Books* feels that *Where Are You* has a "sure narrative style, natural dialogue, and a realistic situation with which young adult readers can strongly identify." The reviewer from *Publishers Weekly* comments on the "traditions and old-fashioned values permeating Missy's small, conservative town," which the reviewer feels "adds a nostalgic flavor to this contemporary novel." As Carol A. Edwards concludes in *School Library Journal*, Newton's novel "is a quiet, yet exciting and involving, story that shows the everyday continuous choices and emotions that make up young adults' lives and change the way they see themselves and the world."

■ Works Cited

Review of *Care of Arnold's Corners, Kirkus Reviews,* March 15, 1974, p. 301.
Review of *Care of Arnold's Corners, Publishers Weekly,* April 15, 1974, p. 52.

Edwards, Carol A., review of *Where Are You When I Need You?*, *School Library Journal*, March, 1991, pp. 215-216.

Fraustino, Lisa, review of *I Will Call It Georgie's Blues*, *Best Sellers*, December, 1983, p. 348.

Gale, David, review of *I Will Call It Georgie's Blues*, *School Library Journal*, October, 1983, p. 172.

Greenlaw, M. Jean, review of *M. V. Sexton Speaking*, *Journal of Reading*, March, 1982, p. 613.

Hearne, Betsy, review of *Where Are You When I Need You?*, *Bulletin of the Center for Children's Books*, March, 1991, p. 173.

Review of *I Will Call It Georgie's Blues*, *Kirkus Reviews*, September 1, 1983, p. J-177.

Review of *M. V. Sexton Speaking*, *Kirkus Reviews*, December 15, 1981, p. 1524-1525.

Newton, Suzanne, *I Will Call It Georgie's Blues*, Viking, 1983.

Newton, Suzanne, *A Place Between*, Viking, 1986.

Noah, Carolyn, review of *M. V. Sexton Speaking*, *School Library Journal*, December, 1981, p. 72.

Review of *A Place Between*, *English Journal*, October, 1987.

Review of *A Place Between*, *Horn Book*, November/December, 1986, p. 748.

Rochman, Hazel, review of *I Will Call It Georgie's Blues*, *School Library Journal*, October, 1988, p. 40-41.

Rochman, Hazel, review of *Where Are You When I Need You?*, *Booklist*, January 1, 1991, p. 921.

Sutherland, Zena, review of *Care of Arnold's Corners*, *Bulletin of the Center for Children's Books*, November, 1974, p. 50.

Tyler, Anne, review of *I Will Call It Georgie's Blues*, *New York Times Book Review*, November 13, 1983, p. 40.

Review of *Where Are You When I Need You?*, *Kirkus Reviews*, January 15, 1991.

Review of *Where Are You When I Need You?*, *Publishers Weekly*, January 4, 1991, pp. 73-74.

■ For More Information See

BOOKS

Contemporary Literary Criticism, Volume 35, Gale, 1985.

PERIODICALS

Library Journal, April, 1974.
School Library Journal, December, 1978; October, 1984.

—*Sketch by Vita Richman*

*   *   *

NIELSEN, Nancy J. 1951-

■ Personal

Born May 19, 1951, in Sioux Falls, SD; daughter of Merl Dean Luther (a sales representative) and Betty Mylet (a nurse; maiden name, Purcell) Nielsen. *Education:* St.

NANCY J. NIELSEN

Olaf College, B.A., 1973; attended Fuller Seminary, 1977-79; attended California State University, Los Angeles, 1980. *Hobbies and other interests:* Canoeing, bicycling, cross-country skiing, gardening, reading.

■ Addresses

Office—2904 35th Ave. South, Minneapolis, MN 55406.

■ Career

Freelance writer and editor. Elementary school teacher and tutor, CA, 1979-87; communications consultant, 1986—. Guest speaker in schools. *Member:* National Writers' Union, Society of Children's Book Writers and Illustrators, Twin Cities Human Ecology Action League (board member, 1991—), Sierra Club, Kappa Delta Pi.

■ Writings

FOR CHILDREN

Bicycle Racing, Crestwood House, 1987.
Eric Dickerson, Crestwood House, 1987.
Helicopter Pilots, Crestwood House, 1988.
Boundary Waters Canoe Area, Minnesota, Crestwood House/Macmillan, 1989.

Black Widow Spiders, Crestwood House/Macmillan, 1989.
Teen Alcoholism, Lucent Books, 1990.
Animal Migration, F. Watts, 1991.
Carnivorous Plants, F. Watts, 1992.

OTHER

From Freud to Masters and Johnson: The Feminine Psychology of Helene Deutsch, Case Study Insitute, Harvard Business College, 1979.
Timothy Leary and the Psychedelic Drugs, Case Study Institute, Harvard Business College, 1980.

Also contributor to *Family Day Caring, Bridal Fair, Twin Cities, Canoe, Fitness Today,* and other periodicals as well as many educational publications. Editor of educational books, textbooks, and periodicals.

■ Sidelights

Nancy J. Nielsen told *SATA:* "I never dreamed I would become an author when I was a child, but as an adult I began to see more clearly that an author is what I am. I like to write, to be in touch with my creative, intuitive side, and I like the challenge of explaining unusual topics to children.

"All of the books I have written so far are nonfiction books. I use fictional techniques, though, when I write, such as suspense, good descriptive words, and action verbs—anything I can do to 'hook' the reader into wanting to read my books. I want my readers to feel as if they are there, directly experiencing what I'm writing about.

"The more unusual the topics, the better—that's why I enjoyed writing about migrating animals and carnivorous plants. It was easy to make these topics spicy and interesting for kids.

"I need contact with school children to write for them. I go into the schools as a speaker and occasionally teach a writing class for children. I read my books aloud to my niece, Janna, and my nephew, Luke, to get their feedback. When they laugh or ask questions, I know I'm on the right track.

"Most of my best writing takes place after I have written a first draft. I read my manuscripts over carefully and look for improvements. Only when I've done my best job do I send my manuscript to the editor, because I know my name will be on the book.

"Aside from library books, I also write text and curriculum materials. Sometimes I write so first and second graders can read it. Then I might find myself writing something for seventh or eighth graders. I also write for pre-school children, college students, teachers, and parents—and I do some business writing, book editing, and an occasional magazine article.

"I'm not writing a book for kids right now, but I have several ideas in mind. I want to write about successful women and different cultures, and I'm always interested in writing about unusual animals."

■ For More Information See

PERIODICALS

North Crow River News, April 6, 1992, p. 5.
School Library Journal, May, 1991.
Science Books and Films, spring, 1992, p. 179.

P

PACK, Janet 1952-

■ Personal

Born November 5, 1952, in Independence, MO; daughter of A. Neal (a hospital administrator) and Daisy (a homemaker) Deaver; married Gary D. Pack (a computer systems designer), December, 1974. *Education:* University of Missouri—Kansas City, B.A. (music), 1975. *Hobbies and other interests:* Singing, composing and listening to music, reading, collecting books, designing costumes, acting, animals, recreational weight lifting, whitewater rafting, kayaking.

■ Addresses

Home and office—543 Franklin Ave., Lake Geneva, WI 53147.

■ Career

Freelance writer and composer. Occasionally works as a technical writer for Facilitec Controls by Triangle MicroSystems, Raleigh, NC. Worked variously as a fabric-crafts clerk for a Ben Franklin store, a ward clerk for Osteopathic Hospital in Kansas City, MO, an accounts receivable clerk for Herald Publishing House in Independence, MO, an "executive-secretary-receptionist-gofer" for a multi-organization office, a seller of handmade leather items from a booth in a mall in Overland Park, KS, and of hand-crafted pottery from a booth at the Kansas City Renaissance Festival. Designer of costumes and "'practical absurdities' called draft dragons and draft cats." *Member:* Weis and Hickman Traveling Road Show (charter member), Lakeland Animal Shelter Friends.

■ Writings

(With Margaret Weis) *Lost Childhood,* Messner, 1986.
California, Franklin Watts, 1987.
Fueling the Future, Children's Press, 1992.

JANET PACK

Contributor of short stories to anthologies, including "Scourge of the Wicked Kendragon" in *The Dragons of Krynn,* TSR, 1994. Composer and arranger of various musical works for *Leaves from the Inn of the Last Home,* TSR, 1987, and for *Death Gate Cycle* (a seven book series by Margaret Weis and Tracy Hickman), Bantam, 1990-94.

■ Work in Progress

Help Me, a volume of animal rescue stories; a book on microscopes for grade schoolers; a series for upper grades on scientific equipment; a nonfiction book for adults about a friend who started a dog-boarding business in her log cabin; several pieces of fiction; more music (including tapes); fictional or nonfictional descriptions of whitewater rafting and lake kayaking experiences.

■ Sidelights

Janet Pack told *SATA:* "I've always been very curious about nearly everything. This often causes me to over-research nonfiction books, but the information is so fascinating I have difficulty stopping. References culled from dictionaries and encyclopedias always lead to other intriguing revelations or ideas for books.

"My husband Gary and my friend Margaret Weis started my writing career. When the three of us lived in Independence, Missouri, Gary wrote three books with Margaret, two of which were published. Both of them encouraged me to write. It was something I'd always wanted to do but I didn't have the conviction it could be a career.

"Margaret 'gave' me my first book. After moving to Wisconsin she became involved with a book series. Since she could not fulfill the contract for *Lost Childhood,* she offered it to me. I immediately said 'Yes!' and began researching the stories. Margaret and Gary had no doubt I could write that book. Not until the editor accepted the final manuscript did I admit to myself I could really write.

"Reading, cats, exercise, and music are all essential to my well-being, although they compete with each other for attention. Particularly the feline faction. I'm cat-dependent, to the point that while on vacation I stalk the wily beasties and steal hugs that have to last until I get home to my own.

"Cats integrate well with my music. Bast loves to sit close when I practice either piano or voice. She seems particularly fond of singing. She's a critical audience, though—she leaves if I'm doing poorly. Canth seems more attracted to keyboard playing. He'll sit in a chair for hours, ears twitching, while I try to perfect a piece. On an irregular basis, he treats me to his 'cat concertos' which he composes by walking up the piano and trying to grab the keys as they rebound from the pressure of his paws. Canth can be very unsubtle. Three o'clock in the morning is not a good hour for humans to appreciate a cat concerto.

"Both Bast and Canth take advantage of my lap when I'm writing. Bastie usually takes the morning shift. She sits very quietly, sometimes purring, and seldom touches the keys. Canth normally claims the afternoon. He leaps up, flirts for awhile, then settles upside down between my body and the keyboard with paws and tail in midair. This is when I make the most mistakes and his fur gets all over the computer.

"Despite their distractions I'm convinced the cats help me think while I'm writing. Besides, during cold weather they become the best finger-warmers ever made."

■ For More Information See

PERIODICALS

Bulletin of the Center for Children's Books, June, 1986.

*   *   *

PEARSON, Kit 1947-

■ Personal

Born April 30, 1947, in Edmonton, Alberta, Canada; daughter of Hugh and Kay (Hastie) Pearson. *Education:* University of Alberta, B.A., 1969; University of British Columbia, M.L.S., 1976; Simmons College, Center for the Study of Children's Literature, M.A., 1982.

■ Addresses

Home—3888 West 15th Ave., Vancouver, British Columbia V6R 2Z9, Canada. *Agent*—Lee Davis Creal, c/o Lucinda Vardey Agency, 297 Seaton St., Toronto, Ontario M5A 2T6, Canada.

■ Career

Has worked as a children's librarian, and reviewer and teacher of juvenile literature and writing for children.

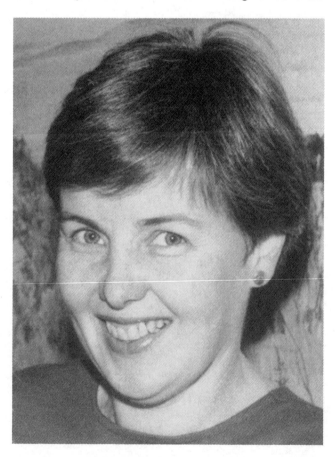

KIT PEARSON

■ Awards, Honors

Book of the Year for Children award, Canadian Library Association, 1988, for *A Handful of Time;* Book of the Year for Children award, Canadian Library Association, 1990, inaugural Mr. Christie Book award, Geoffrey Bilson Award for historical fiction for young people, and Governor General's Award shortlist citation, all for *The Sky Is Falling;* Governor General's Award shortlist citation, for *Looking at the Moon.*

■ Writings

CHILDREN'S NOVELS

The Daring Game, Viking Kestrel, 1986.
A Handful of Time, Viking Kestrel, 1987.
The Sky Is Falling, Viking Kestrel, 1989.
Looking at the Moon, Viking, 1991.
The Lights Go on Again, Viking, 1993.

OTHER

(Reteller) *The Singing Basket,* illustrated by Ann Blades, Firefly Books, 1991.

■ Sidelights

Kit Pearson is an award-winning Canadian writer of novels about the real-life problems of middle graders. She is often praised for her sensitivity in writing about the pain children feel when they are outsiders. Many of her books are about youngsters separated from their homes and families who are trying to get along in new and unfamiliar settings. Her books for middle graders, each set in Canada, are well regarded for their beautiful writing, attention to detail, and emotional power.

Pearson's life and studies have focused on literature, especially children's literature. She graduated in English at the University of Alberta before going on to get her masters of library science at the University of British Columbia. She also received a master of arts in children's literature at the Center for the Study of Children's Literature, Simmons College, in Boston. Pearson has worked as a children's librarian and has published reviews and articles on the subject. She has also taught courses on juvenile literature. One of the characteristics of her writing is to fill her books with references to classic works of children's fiction.

In an interview with Dave Jenkinson, published in *Emergency Librarian,* Pearson talked about her habit of including titles of children's books in her own books. "I have to watch myself," she said. "I'm a former children's librarian, and I love children's books." She goes on to tell how when she was a child she read the books of Edward Eager. Characters in his books were often reading books by another real-life children's author, E. Nesbit, which would inspire their own magical adventures. Once she finished the Eager books, Pearson "rushed out and got the E. Nesbit books and read those and loved them."

In Pearson's first novel, Eliza's first year at boarding school is complicated by a friendship that leads her into trouble. (Cover illustration by Laura Fernandez.)

Pearson's first novel, *The Daring Game,* was published in 1986. It takes place in a girls boarding school in Vancouver, Canada, in 1964. Eleven-year-old Eliza makes friends with Helen, the school rebel, who suggests the "daring game," in which the dorm mates dare each other to break school rules. Eliza lies to cover for Helen when she leaves campus on a dare and jeopardizes her own standing at the school through her loyalty.

Pearson's interest in boarding schools goes back to her own childhood, when she was sent to Crofton House, a boarding school in Vancouver. As she explained in *Emergency Librarian,* "I find it so intriguing that you can take an assortment of kids and put them in a situation where they're almost like a tribe. The adults have nothing to do with them; they're really on their own."

JoAnna Burns Patton, writing in *CM: Canadian Materials for Schools and Libraries,* praises Pearson's "remarkable insight into the emotional growth of young girls." Lorraine M. York states in *Canadian Children's Litera-*

ture that "the pre-adolescent fear which Pearson has best articulated and which many adults will have forgotten or ignored is the most basic: the fear of becoming an adolescent, a teenager." Pearson explains in *Emergency Librarian:* "Eliza is exactly the way I was. In fact, three friends and I made a pact when we were 12 that we would not grow up, and we really thought we didn't have to." Pearson is definitely *not* advocating staying a child. "What Eliza doesn't want to do," she explains, "and I don't blame her, is all the *artificial* stuff about growing up—being a 'feminine' teenager, being an object and all that stuff."

Right after *The Daring Game* Pearson started a new book about two kids who try to conceal the fact that their uncle has quit law school. Pearson says she "knew it was awful after about four chapters. It was so boring." But describing herself as stubborn enough to get through anything, she continued to work on the book for some time: "I thought if I gave it up, maybe it meant I couldn't write another book."

Past Discovered through Magic in *A Handful of Time*

Of course, she could write another book, and her next published book was *A Handful of Time,* which uses the fantasy device of a magic watch and traveling backwards in time to tell a story about mothers and daughters. Twelve-year-old Patricia is sent by her beautiful but cold mother to her family's lakeside cottage. She is being sent to stay with cousins she's never met while her parents are getting divorced.

Patricia, who is shy and unhappy at the cottage, discovers an old watch that transports her back thirty-five years. Made invisible by the powers of the watch, Patricia observes her mother's miserable twelfth summer at the same site. Patricia comes to understand how her mother's difficult childhood affected the woman she has become.

Whereas Patricia's mom had to fight for her freedom growing up, she instead "stifles Patricia by giving her too much freedom," notes Annette Goldsmith in her review in *Books for Young People.* Ultimately, Patricia gains greater strength and self-confidence in the present because of her time travels and the discoveries she has made about her mother.

Yvonne A. Frey, however, writing in *School Library Journal,* faults the portraits of the two mothers as being "wooden and flat." Nevertheless, she notes that the book can reveal to readers how "relationships in the present are often locked into patterns of the past," and that learning family history "often reveals much about oneself." Similarly, *Bulletin of the Center for Children's Books* reviewer Roger Sutton finds the author portrays very well "the tension between family members who are supposed to like each other and don't, and the pain of a child who does not fit in."

In this first volume of a trilogy exploring the lives of English children sent to live in Canada during World War II, Norah finds it difficult to adjust to a new family and a new school. (Cover illustration by Janet Wilson.)

Pearson's third book, published in 1989, is *The Sky Is Falling.* Like her first two books, this one takes place in Canada and focuses on children separated from their families. *The Sky Is Falling,* however, begins in England. It is the summer of 1940, and all of England fears an invasion by Hitler's army. Many parents are sending their children to safety overseas. This exodus comes to include ten-year-old Norah, who has just started a secret club to watch for German planes and spies and has no desire whatsoever to be sent away. But despite Norah's protests, she and her little brother Gavin are evacuated to be "war guests" of a wealthy widow, Mrs. Ogilvie, in Toronto.

This book, the first of a proposed trilogy, was inspired by storyteller Alice Kane's memory of telling stories to evacuee children in Canada. Pearson explains in *Emergency Librarian* that "I have also heard about the war all my life from my parents. My mother used to tell me how 'adorable' the little English evacuees were. I got the feeling that some of these children were treated almost like little pets." This is not at all the case for Norah, however. Mrs. Ogilvie lavishes all her affection on Gavin, the children at her new school taunt her, and as the news from England becomes worse, she is filled with homesickness. Norah runs away after clashing with Mrs. Ogilvie, but returns to resolve her problems and discovers a surprising responsibility that helps her to accept her new country. Denise Wilms, writing in *Booklist*, calls the book a "compelling, sensitive study of children traumatized by separation. Its strength is in its particularly well realized characterizations."

Similarly, Annette Goldsmith, writing in *Quill & Quire*, points out that it is "Pearson's attention to detail both funny and sad that makes this book so engaging." She feels that readers "will appreciate Norah's feelings of homesickness and isolation in a strange country and be cheered by her hard-won ability to cope." Louise L. Sherman similarly observes in *School Library Journal* that "there is plenty of conflict and action to hold young readers' interest in Norah's struggles with her new family and school." *The Sky Is Falling* won the Canadian Library Association Book of the Year Award for Children, the first Mr. Christie's Book Award, and the Geoffrey Bilson Award for Historical Fiction for Young People, which was named after the writer whose nonfiction study of English evacuees in Canada, *The Guest Children*, was published shortly after *The Sky Is Falling*.

Trilogy Examines Wartime Life of Young People

Pearson's next book, *Looking at the Moon*, is the second book in her trilogy about "war guests" in Canada. Like *The Sky Is Falling*, this book continues the story of Norah, who is now thirteen and still living in Toronto with Mrs. Ogilvie. She hasn't seen her parents in three years, and sometimes she isn't even sure if she can remember what they look like. Like Pearson's second book, *A Handful of Time*, *Looking at the Moon* takes place at a lakeside cottage. When Norah meets nineteen-year-old Andrew, she thinks she may be falling in love for the first time. But Andrew has his own problems: he doesn't want to fight in the war, and yet he knows it's what his family expects. What the two of them learn from each other makes for a gentle and moving story of first loves and growing up.

Until *Looking at the Moon* Pearson had always written about preteen girls. "That was my favorite age and still is," she says in *Emergency Librarian*. "I think about age 11 and 12, just before adolescence, you have a kind of 'power', especially girls for some reason .... You have all the freedoms of being a child but you have all the faculties of an adult." Pearson continues, "I have such clear memories of being that age—and of the shock of it all ending at 13."

The story of Norah in *Looking at the Moon* is Pearson's first try at writing about that shocking age. "Norah will be 13 in the second book because I've always wanted to write about the trials of being 13." The last book in the trilogy, *The Lights Go on Again*, is about Norah's younger brother, Gavin, at age ten—Pearson's first book with a boy as the main character. The story is set in 1945, as the war is ending. After the death of his

parents, and Aunt Florence's offer to adopt him, Gavin must decide whether to stay with the family and country he loves, or to go back to England with Norah. This is the author's most serious work, with the tragedy of war conflicting with a young boy's innocence.

Pearson is constantly working, but she can be a tough critic of her own books. She says that *The Daring Game* "doesn't have enough plot. I think it's got great details, ... but if I wrote it again, I would make it a lot tighter. *Handful of Time* had plenty of plot—too much plot—and the trouble was the characters. *Handful* I had to rewrite a lot more than *Daring*."

Pearson's usual writing process begins with a central idea, for example, a girl going back to her mother's past. "I do the whole first draft from beginning to end and *then* I make an outline," she explains. Then she writes her second draft, straight through. "I always have to do it in order—I can't work on this bit and that bit." She finds that dialogue is the easiest part to write but her descriptions and characters always need more work. She also notes that "characters do take over, and I've never known whether that's good or bad."

For example, Eliza and Helen weren't supposed to become friends until the end of *The Daring Game*. "And lo and behold, they made friends at Christmas, and I didn't know what to do about it," Pearson explains. Likewise, Pearson thought *The Sky Is Falling* "would cover the whole war, but when I finished it, it was only Christmas, 1940." This is what ultimately led Pearson to the idea of writing a trilogy covering the entire war.

There is something in the gentleness and warmth of Pearson's characters that makes readers long to reencounter them in new books, to see how they are getting along, how they are changing. A line from Goldsmith's review of *A Handful of Time* encapsulates one of the distinctive qualities of Kit Pearson's writing: "No high dramatics here! This is a subtle and memorable book with a Canadian context and universal appeal."

■ Works Cited

Frey, Yvonne A., review of *A Handful of Time, School Library Journal*, May, 1988, p. 100.

Goldsmith, Annette, review of *A Handful of Time, Books for Young People*, April, 1987, p. 10.

Goldsmith, Annette, review of *The Sky Is Falling, Quill and Quire*, November, 1989, p. 14.

Jenkinson, Dave, "Kit Pearson: Boarding Schools, Beaches and Bombs," *Emergency Librarian*, September-October, 1989, pp. 65-69.

Patton, JoAnna Burns, review of *The Daring Game, CM: Canadian Materials for Schools and Libraries*, July, 1986, p. 167.

Sherman, Louise L., review of *The Sky Is Falling, School Library Journal*, June, 1990, p. 125.

Sutton, Roger, review of *A Handful of Time, Bulletin of the Center for Children's Books*, May, 1988, p. 186.

Wilms, Denise, review of *The Sky Is Falling, Booklist*, May 15, 1990, p. 1805.

York, Lorraine M., review of *The Daring Game, Canadian Children's Literature,* Number 46, 1987, pp. 79-81.

■ For More Information See

BOOKS

Children's Literature Review, Volume 26, Gale, 1992, pp. 172-78.

PERIODICALS

Books in Canada, June-July, 1987, pp. 35-37.
Bulletin of the Center for Children's Books, January, 1987, p. 95.
Canadian Children's Literature, Number 49, 1988, pp. 53-55; Number 69, 1993, pp. 42-43.
CANSCAIP News, summer, 1990, pp. 1-3.

—*Sketch by Ira Brodsky*

*   *   *

STELLA PEVSNER

PEVSNER, Stella

■ Personal

Born in Lincoln, IL; married; children: four. *Education:* Attended Illinois University and Northwestern University.

■ Addresses

Home—Chicago, IL.

■ Career

Writer. Has worked as a teacher; has written advertising copy for a drugstore chain and for various advertising agencies; former promotion director, Dana Perfumes; freelance writer of articles, commercial film strips, and reading texts. *Member:* Authors Guild, Society of Children's Book Writers and Illustrators, Children's Reading Round Table, Society of Midland Authors.

■ Awards, Honors

Chicago Women in Publishing first annual award for children's literature, 1973, for *Call Me Heller, That's My Name;* Dorothy Canfield Fisher award, Vermont Congress of Parents and Teachers, 1977, and Junior Literary Guild outstanding book, both for *A Smart Kid Like You;* Notable Children's Trade Book in the field of Social Studies, 1977, for *Keep Stompin' till the Music Stops;* Golden Kite Award, Society of Children's Book Writers, Clara Ingram Judson award, Society of Midland Authors, and Omar's Award, all 1978, all for *And You Give Me a Pain, Elaine;* Carl Sandburg award, Friends of the Chicago Public Library, 1980, for *Cute Is a Four-Letter Word;* American Library Association Best Books for Young Adults list, 1989, for *How Could You Do It, Diane?*

■ Writings

YOUNG ADULT FICTION

The Young Brontes (one-act play), Baker, 1967.
Break a Leg!, illustrated by Barbara Seuling, Crown, 1969, published as *New Girl,* Scholastic, 1983.
Footsteps on the Stairs, illustrated by Seuling, Crown, 1970.
Call Me Heller, That's My Name, illustrated by Richard Cuffari, Seabury, 1973.
A Smart Kid Like You, Seabury, 1975.
Keep Stompin' till the Music Stops, Seabury, 1977.
And You Give Me a Pain, Elaine, Seabury, 1978.
Cute Is a Four-Letter Word, Clarion, 1980.
I'll Always Remember You ... Maybe, Clarion, 1981.
Lindsay, Lindsay, Fly Away Home, Clarion, 1983.
Me, My Goat, and My Sister's Wedding, Clarion, 1985.
Sister of the Quints, Clarion, 1987.
How Could You Do It, Diane?, Clarion, 1989.
The Night the Whole Class Slept Over, Clarion, 1991.
I'm Emma, I'm A Quint, Clarion, 1993.
Jon, Flora, and the Odd-Eyed Cat, Clarion, 1994.

■ Adaptations

A Smart Kid Like You was made into an ABC "After School Special" starring Kristy McNichol.

Pevsner gets inspiration from family, newspapers, and her own imagination to produce stories such as this tale of a young girl's coming of age. (Cover illustration by Richard Cuffari.)

■ Sidelights

Stella Pevsner has written several successful novels for both children and young adults. Yet she never thought of becoming a children's writer until she herself was a mother of four children. True, as a high school student, she was asked by her English teacher to write a humor column for the school magazine. Later she took a couple of creative writing classes for pure enjoyment. She planned to be a teacher, however, not a writer. When she was growing up, young people, and especially girls, did not think of writing as a career. As Pevsner writes in *Something about the Author Autobiography Series* (*SAAS*), "When I was a child growing up in the small town of Lincoln, Illinois, the career choices for a girl were pretty well limited to teacher, secretary, nurse."

As a child with three brothers and two older sisters, Pevsner amused herself and her siblings by singing, tapdancing, and doing impersonations. She never thought, however, that creative arts like acting, drawing, or writing could actually be jobs that one could do as a adult. "Those were kid things you did in school," she commented. "When you grew up you got a job ... *a real job.*"

"Today my own offspring marvel at how I made it through childhood without TV, cassette player, microwave popcorn, or shopping malls," the author remarked. In fact, the big event of the week for the author was walking to the local library, coming home with as many books as were allowed, and reading for hours under the tree in the front yard. At other times she remembers being a tomboy, playing baseball and getting into "occasional mischief." She also loved dolls and even today still keeps one of her childhood favorites while collecting others as a hobby.

As a young woman she worked in advertising, beginning with writing ads for a drug store chain, advancing to the pots and pans division of a local store, and eventually writing high fashion copy and becoming promotion director of Dana Perfumes. After her marriage she wrote freelance articles until "one fateful day" sometime after the birth of her fourth child.

One of her sons had read every book by his favorite children's author. "One day he wrote to the author and gently chided her for not writing faster. She answered, very nicely, and revealed that she was writing as fast as she could." Her son concluded that since his mother could "do everything else," she should be able to "write a funny book that kids can enjoy." Pevsner took on that

Nina's difficulties in accepting her parents' divorce are compounded when she discovers her math teacher is her father's new wife. (Cover illustration by Gail Owens.)

challenge and has been writing children's books ever since.

Children's Request Begins Writing Career

Her first book, *Break a Leg!*, was the initial result of that challenge, and her children were her most enthusiastic first readers and critics. In the story, a young girl overcomes her shyness by participating in a play and also learns that kids who march to their own drummer have something to contribute. This novel was soon followed by *Footsteps on the Stairs,* a mystery in which a young boy learns to overcome his fear.

Pevsner compares the writing of a book to the making of a collage. In each art form, she once told *SATA,* "the artist/author takes bits of this and that, scraps and dreams and memories and weaves them into a design which is new and strange and yet somehow familiar." In *Call Me Heller, That's My Name,* for example, "the town is imaginary, the railroad is real, the trestle is from a newspaper clipping of a real tragedy." The setting is

Sibling rivalry provides the conflict in this award-winning novel by Pevsner. (Cover illustration by Maria Jimenez.)

the Roaring Twenties, and Heller tries to prove she is as bold as the boys. The theme is, "There is a time for letting go and moving on."

"My very early books," Pevsner explains in her *SAAS* entry, "written as they were, at the behest of my children, were fairly light. Gradually, I found myself exploring deeper themes, in situations which seemed to trouble and bewilder many children." *A Smart Kid Like You,* for example, deals with divorce. Nina, who is starting junior high as one of the few students from a private school, must make a double adjustment when she finds out that her new math teacher is also her father's new wife. Gradually she learns to accept her new stepmother both in and out of the classroom. Nina also realizes that both her parents are happier in their new situations, and this insight helps her make new friends at school. The *Bulletin of the Center for Children's Books* described the book as having "a serious theme," "convincing" characterization, and "logical changes and developments" in Nina. In 1977 *A Smart Kid Like You* won the Dorothy Canfield Fisher Award from the Vermont Congress of Parents and Teachers and was chosen an outstanding book by the Junior Literary Guild; it was later made into an ABC "After School Special."

And You Give Me a Pain, Elaine, originally written for grades six and up, features disruptive behavior from an older sibling. Andrea's older sister constantly steals attention from her, causing Andrea to feel excluded. Andrea had found the support she needed from her brother Joe. When Joe is killed, Andrea must learn to find the strength to go on from within herself. *Elaine* won the Golden Kite Award from the Society of Children's Book Writers, the Clara Ingram Judson Award from the Society of Midland Authors, and the Omar's Award in 1978.

Pevsner reminds us in *SAAS* that "not all of my themes are heavy ones. *Cute Is a Four-Letter Word* is something of a popularity romp." Determined to be the most popular girl in eighth grade, Clara achieves her goal through perseverance, though not without paying a price. In the end she realizes the value of true friends over sycophants. *Cute* was praised in the *Bulletin of the Center for Children's Books* for treating "the maturation of a young adolescent ... with sympathy and insight." Originally published for grades three through six, the book won the Carl Sandburg Award from the Friends of the Chicago Public Library.

Stories Combine Memories and Imagination

"Little bits of remembrance or reality creep into my books," Pevsner notes in her autobiographical entry, "as they do in most writers'. The biggest part of the stories, however, are huge leaps into what-never-was." In *Me, My Goat, and My Sister's Wedding,* for example, the goat is based on a real one that the author had met once and posed for photographs with. In the story, Doug and his friends must figure out how to board a goat for a friend on vacation without Doug's parents finding out.

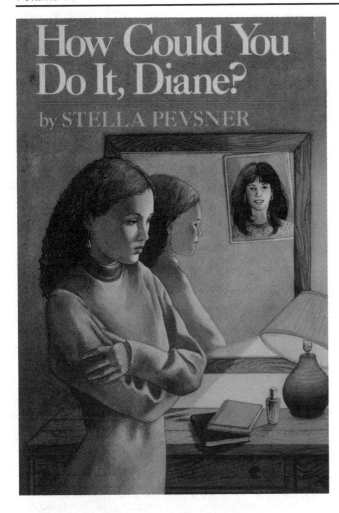

The author was inspired by her readers' questions to write this examination of a teen's suicide. (Cover illustration by Meg Kelleher Aubrey.)

Doug is pretty sure they'd disapprove, and besides they're busy planning his older sister's wedding. With these ingredients, according to *Booklist*, Pevsner writes a "well-crafted comedy that is bound to be popular."

Where does Stella Pevsner get her ideas for writing? "Well," she reveals in *SAAS*, "not at the supermarket. Everyone has ideas, notions, stray thoughts. The only difference is ... writers recognize these mind-wanderings as portions of potential plots and hang onto them and develop them." For example, the idea for *Sister of the Quints* "came from nothing more than reading about a multiple birth and wondering what the siblings in the family thought of this sudden celebrity status thrust upon them. I wondered if they welcomed it or resented it." In the finished novel, the teen heroine, Natalie, thinks about moving to Colorado to be with her mother, because life with her father, her stepmother, and their quintuplets has become very difficult. Writing in *Book Links*, Deborah Abbott described *Sister* as a "thoughtful, entertaining story."

Once after giving a speech to a group of young teenagers, Pevsner asked the group what topics they'd like to read about. Surprisingly, one girl said, "Suicide." At first

taken aback, Pevsner later found herself haunted by the girl's request. One day the title *How Could You Do It, Diane?* came into her head, and eventually Pevsner "began writing down things she said and did, and stuck them away in a folder.... I knew it wouldn't be a book leading to her eventual suicide, but rather about the bafflement of friends and family. How could a seemingly popular, happy girl do this to herself? Still, in the sadness of the story, there is an affirmation of life. The various people in the book mourn Diane, but eventually turn to the continuation of their own lives." *How Could You Do It, Diane?* is praised by Zena Sutherland in the *Bulletin of the Center for Children's Books* who says: "The author has done an impressive job of sustaining interest, displaying insight and sympathy."

The Night the Whole Class Slept Over, as the author describes it in *SAAS*, "details the turmoil of a boy who's trying to tame his eccentric parents, get his baby sister to talk and then shut up, and win the admiration of the sixth-grade class-act beauty." Writing in *School Library Journal*, reviewer Cindy Darling Codell finds that Pevsner "is at her best here, telling an entertaining story while subtly scoring thematic points."

Pevsner summarizes her thoughts and hopes about her readers in her *SAAS* autobiography: "It isn't important to me whether or not a child remembers a book I've written. What I do hope is that I've helped him or her to realize that reading is one of the greatest enjoyments of this world. I would like readers to know that the world itself holds endless possibilities for them. And above all, I would like them to believe that within those possibilities lies the chance to create for themselves the kind of life that will bring them joy, wonder, and satisfaction."

■ Works Cited

Abbott, Deborah, "Families: Who They Are and What They Mean," *Book Links*, February 15, 1991, p. 1217.

Codell, Cindy Darling, review of *The Night the Whole Class Slept Over*, *School Library Journal*, November, 1991, p. 124.

Review of *Cute Is a Four-Letter Word*, *Bulletin of the Center for Children's Books*, September, 1980, p. 18.

Review of *Me, My Goat, and My Sister's Wedding*, *Booklist*, April 15, 1985, p. 1199.

Pevsner, Stella, entry in *Something about the Author Autobiography Series*, Volume 14, Gale, 1992, pp. 183-193.

Review of *A Smart Kid Like You*, *Bulletin of the Center for Children's Books*, September, 1975, p. 17.

Sutherland, Zena, review of *How Could You Do It, Diane?*, *Bulletin of the Center for Children's Books*, September, 1989, p. 14.

■ For More Information See

PERIODICALS

Booklist, October 1, 1991.

Bulletin of the Center for Children's Books, November, 1991, p. 72; November 29, 1993, p. 94.

Horn Book, August, 1980, pp. 410-411.
School Library Journal, August, 1980, p. 78; October, 1989, p. 136; December, 1993, p. 116.

—*Sketch by Scott Gillam*

*   *   *

POLICOFF, Stephen Phillip 1948-

■ Personal

Born April 27, 1948, in Richmond, VA; son of Leonard David (a physician) and Naomi (an artist and printmaker; maiden name, Lewis) Policoff; married Kathleen Mary Beck (a sales manager), April 29, 1989. *Education:* Wesleyan University, B.A., 1970.

■ Addresses

Home—5 West 87th Street, New York, NY 10024. *Office*—Center for Creative Youth, Wesleyan University, Middletown, CT 06459.

■ Career

Center for Creative Youth, Middletown, CT, director of creative writing, 1978—; New York University, New York City, adjunct assistant professor of creative writing, 1986—. Medicine Show Theater Ensemble, literary manager, 1979-86; freelance writer. *Member:* Dramatists Guild, American Society of Composers, Authors, and Publishers (ASCAP).

■ Awards, Honors

Commission from Lincoln Center to write libretto; NEA grant to write libretto for *Bound to Rise.*

■ Writings

Bound to Rise (musical libretto), based on the writings of Horatio Alger, music by Robert Dennis, produced New York City, 1984-85.
East of the Sun, West of the Moon (opera libretto for children), music by Robert Dennis, produced New York City and at the Lincoln Center Institute in New York, 1990.
(With Jeffrey Skinner) *Real Toads in Imaginary Gardens: Suggestions and Starting Points for Young Creative Writers,* Chicago Review Press, 1992.

Contributor to periodicals, including *Seventeen, Parents,* and *Ladies Home Journal.*

■ Work in Progress

An untitled novel for adults, completion expected by autumn 1994; research for a young adult book on dreams—how to think about them and make creative use of them.

■ Sidelights

Stephen Policoff, along with coauthor Jeffrey Skinner, has written *Real Toads in Imaginary Gardens: Suggestions and Starting Points for Young Creative Writers,* a guide for teenage writers seeking insight into the creative process. The text is based on material drawn from the writing classes taught by Skinner and Policoff, both award-winning writers. Discussions on writing poems and plays are included, as well as suggestions on fiction writing. The text includes suggestions on specific topics such as character development, plot, and voice, as well as on manuscript revision.

Though the book is designed for aspiring writers in approximately the eighth to twelfth grades, reviewers have found it a useful and valuable guide for readers of all ages. *Bloomsbury Review* writer Pat Wagner found the book to be a "great gift for anyone struggling to release their literary muse," while Susan H. Patron in *School Library Journal* wrote that "this handbook speaks directly to the experiences and viewpoints of Y[oung] A[dult]s."

The text is organized in two main categories. Skinner focuses on poetry while Policoff enlightens the students on fiction. These teachers insist on hard work to help their young authors-to-be grasp the basic concepts of writing. These concepts are reinforced through examples that were written by young students Skinner and Policoff have had in their classes.

Stephen Policoff told *SATA:* "Writing a book about writing was never one of my dreams, but my coauthor

STEPHEN PHILLIP POLICOFF

and I have had great success exhorting teens to channel their incredible creative drive in our work at the Center for Creative Youth (and elsewhere), and it seemed to us that we could capture the immediacy of our teaching experiences by writing the book as if we were simply having a lengthy chat with the kids, and by making use of the wonderful writing we have managed to squeeze out of our students over the years, as examples of how to make use of our advice. The response to the book has been gratifying. I remember well feeling the yearning to write but being unsure how to begin. *Real Toads in Imaginary Gardens,* we hope, lights the path."

■ Works Cited

Patron, Susan H., review of *Real Toads in Imaginary Gardens, School Library Journal,* April, 1992, p. 158.

Wagner, Pat, review of *Real Toads in Imaginary Gardens, Bloomsbury Review,* March, 1992, p. 14.

■ For More Information See

PERIODICALS

Booklist, June, 1992, p. 1753.
San Antonio Express News, August 16, 1992.

*   *   *

POLIKOFF, Barbara G(arland) 1929-

■ Personal

Born May 13, 1929; daughter of Joseph M. Garland and Julia Garland (a homemaker); married Alexander Polikoff (a lawyer), June 28, 1951; children: Deborah, Daniel, Joan. *Education:* University of Michigan, B.A., 1950; University of Chicago, M.A., 1952. *Hobbies and other interests:* Back-packing, gardening, photography.

■ Addresses

Home and office—848 Broadview Ave., Highland Park, IL 60035. *Agent*—Jane Jordan Browne, 410 South Michigan, Chicago, IL 60605.

■ Career

Von Steuben Public High School, Chicago, IL, teacher, 1951-52; Chicago Natural History Museum, Chicago, associate editor of the *Bulletin,* 1952-55. Sullivan House (alternative school for poor and troubled inner-city kids), board member, 1970-90; Chicago Public Schools, volunteer teacher for writing workshops, 1973-93. *Member:* Society of Midland Authors, Amnesty International, American Civil Liberties Union (ACLU), Sierra Club, Nature Conservancy.

■ Awards, Honors

Best Books citation, *School Library Journal,* 1992, for *Life's a Funny Proposition, Horatio;* Carl Sandburg Award for best children's book, Friends of the Chicago

BARBARA G. POLIKOFF

Public Library, 1993; Notable Book citation, American Library Association.

■ Writings

(And photographer) *My Parrot Eats Baked Beans,* Albert Whitman, 1987.
James Madison (biography), Garrett Publishing Company, 1988.
Herbert C. Hoover: Thirty-first President of the United States (biography), Garrett Publishing Company, 1990.
Life's a Funny Proposition, Horatio (novel), Henry Holt, 1992.

■ Work in Progress

Faithfully Yours, Jane Addams: An Affectionate Chronicle; Time Will Tell, Angie A., a companion novel to *Life's a Funny Proposition, Horatio.*

■ Sidelights

Barbara G. Polikoff told *SATA:* "I've always loved language. When I was very young I collected pretty words the way some children collect rocks or shells. I remember thinking that 'chartreuse' was a particularly beautiful word and that 'porch' was quite an ugly one. As I grew older I collected funny names—a dairy bar called 'The Udder End' and a florist called 'Plant Parenthood.' I began spoken wordplay with my children when they were three years old. By the time they were five, they began putting words on paper. They haven't stopped. Each of them, two daughters and a son, went on to college and earned degrees in literature. My youngest daughter, upon completing a poem, confided that the only feeling comparable to the pleasure of writing a good poem is falling in love. 'Or writing a book that comes out the way you wanted it to,' I responded.

"I can't remember a time that I wasn't writing something: poetry, articles, stories, or memoirs. I have been happiest writing books, and though my first book wasn't published until 1987, I have had three published since then. I've already drafted the first chapter of another book, but have filed it away for the time being. My latest title is a double biography—*Faithfully Yours, Jane Addams: An Affectionate Chronicle*. The book is about Sadie Garland Dreikers, my ninety-three-year-old aunt who first went to Hull House as an eleven-year-old child of poor immigrant parents to take painting lessons. She remained at the settlement house, training in social work under Jane Addams until Addams's death in 1935. With the training she received at Hull House as an artist and social worker, she went on to pioneer the field of art therapy worldwide. Much of the book is based on recorded memories of my aunt that I made over an eight-year period.

"After teaching English in a Chicago high school for a year, it became clear that if I were to be the kind of teacher that I wanted to be, I would never have time for my own writing. I resigned as a teacher and did editorial work for awhile, and then I began working as a volunteer in a Chicago public elementary school, teaching writing one day a week. I've been doing this for twenty years. At first, I taught because I loved it, but during the last decade an urgency has been added to that love and now I teach because I want to help inner-city children gain the full and exciting use of language. In so doing, I want to help them find the key to who they are, and also to help them become literate, productive adults.

"I write books that I hope children will want to read because they will involve them emotionally in things that matter to them: family relationships, the struggle to find and be oneself in spite of social pressures, and love and respect for the natural world and for each other.

Creates the Character of Horatio

"*Life's a Funny Proposition, Horatio* grew out of a conversation I had with my neighbor in the tiny town of Palmyra, Wisconsin. My husband and I have backpacked in the wilderness with our children since they were very young. Five years ago, we built a house in the Wisconsin woods, just one hour and forty-five minutes from our Chicago suburban home, so that we can enjoy living out in nature every weekend. Horatio lives in a town patterned after Palmyra, and the woods he loves are the woods I love. He has a beloved Siberian husky, Silver Chief, and I also have two of those dogs. Horatio's father died when Horatio was very young, as did my father when I was young. Part of his struggle is to accept death and move on with an open heart to what lies in the future. I understand his struggle and I wrote about it because I feel that many children today have to learn to live with loss and grief. The book is serious, but

Polikoff uses humor to lighten this tale of a boy dealing with a move to a small town shortly after his father's death. (Cover illustration by Robert Bender.)

filled with humor, because I believe humor is one of our best tools for survival. Laughter is a great healer.

"Some people ask when I'm going to write a novel for adults, as if books for children were not as important or as difficult to write. Right now, I know that I derive great pleasure from writing for children. Who loves their favorite books the way children do, hiding them under their pillows and re-reading them? Who lives with the characters in books as passionately as children? When my grown daughters come home to visit, they will often pull a book off the shelf that they loved as children and read it from cover to cover. If grown children do that with my books, I will be content."

■ For More Information See

PERIODICALS

Booklist, September 15, 1988, p. 164; June 15, 1992, p. 1826.

Bulletin of the Center for Children's Books, November, 1988, p. 82; September, 1992, p. 21.

Kirkus Reviews, August 1, 1988, p. 1155; July 1, 1992, p. 853.

Publishers Weekly, June 22, 1992, p. 62.

School Library Journal, November, 1988, p. 121; August, 1992, p. 156.

* * *

POLISAR, Barry Louis 1954-

■ Personal

Born November 18, 1954, in Brooklyn, NY; son of Max Polisar (a teacher) and Anita Buchalter (a homemaker); married Roni Lynn Prusky (an art conservator), October 31, 1981; children: Evan Nathan and Sierra Hannah (twins). *Education:* University of Maryland, B.A. (magna cum laude), 1977. *Politics:* "Yes." *Religion:* Jewish. *Hobbies and other interests:* Reading, film, and music.

■ Addresses

Home and office—2121 Fairland Rd., Silver Spring, MD 20904.

■ Career

Musician, singer, and writer. Owner of Rainbow Morning Music (publishing company). Gives workshops and concerts in schools, libraries and museums throughout the United States, Canada, and Europe.

■ Awards, Honors

Parents Choice Honors, 1989, for video, *I'm a 3-Toed, Triple-Eyed, Double-Jointed Dinosaur and Other Songs for Young Children;* Maryland Library Association Award, 1991, in recognition of Polisar's "ability to communicate with and excite children to read."

■ Writings

JUVENILE

Noises from under the Rug, Rainbow Morning Music (RMM), 1986.
Dinosaurs I Have Known, RMM, 1987.
Don't Do That: A Child's Guide to Bad Manners, RMM, 1987.
The Haunted House Party, RMM, 1987.
Snakes! and the Boy Who Was Afraid of Them, RMM, 1988.
The Snake Who Was Afraid of People, RMM, 1988.
The Trouble with Ben, RMM, 1992.
Peculiar Zoo, RMM, 1993.

JUVENILE RECORDINGS

I Eat Kids and Other Songs, RMM, 1975.
My Brother Thinks He's a Banana, RMM, 1977.
Naughty Songs for Boys and Girls, RMM, 1978.
Captured Live and in the Act, RMM, 1979.
Songs for Well-Behaved Children, RMM, 1979.
Stanley Stole My Shoelace and Rubbed It in His Armpit, and Other Songs My Parents Won't Let Me Sing, RMM, 1980.
Off-Color Songs for Kids, RMM, 1981.
Juggling Babies, RMM, 1989.

Old Dog, New Tricks, RMM, 1993.
Teacher's Favorites, RMM, 1993.
Family Trip, RMM, 1993.

Has also recorded *Family Concert,* RMM.

JUVENILE VIDEOS

I'm a 3-Toed, Triple-Eyed, Double-Jointed Dinosaur and Other Songs for Young Children, RMM, 1988.
My Brother Threw up on My Stuffed Toy Bunny and Other Songs for Older Children, RMM, 1988.

Has also recorded *Barry's Scrapbook,* 1993.

■ Sidelights

Barry Louis Polisar taps into the humor of children with his enthusiastic songs, poems, and stories. Steve McKerrow in the *Baltimore Sun* declared that Polisar is someone "who knows what it is like to *be* a kid. You can't sing such lyrics as ... 'underwear is everywhere' without having a vivid memory of the world from a pint-sized perspective." Polisar's "tell-it-like-it-is" style of kids' entertainment is heard in all of his lyrics and stories. His first album, *I Eat Kids and Other Songs,* contains such songs as "I Don't Brush My Teeth and I Never Comb My Hair" and "He Eats Asparagus, Why Can't You Be That Way?" Polisar's off-the-wall humor has prompted folksinger Tom Lehrer, as quoted by McKerrow, to describe him as "a delightfully subversive antidote to Mister Rogers."

"Polisar talks to children about things they know in a language they understand," wrote Matt Seiden in a

BARRY LOUIS POLISAR

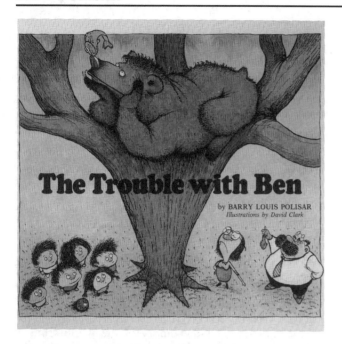

The Trouble with Ben

by BARRY LOUIS POLISAR
Illustrations by David Clark

Children's entertainer Polisar brings his off-the-wall humor to this tale of a bear who gets into trouble for being himself. (Cover illustration by David Clark.)

Baltimore Sun article. Responding to Seiden's question of how he learned the language of kids, before he and his wife had any of their own, Polisar talked about growing up in a large family "filled with eccentrics and funny people." Although Polisar planned to be a teacher, majoring in literature and film in college, he began to give concerts of his music in elementary schools, invited by teacher friends who heard him perform. He considered such performances "an anti-profit enterprise" and as he told McKerrow, he recorded his first two albums without any intention of making such activities the focus of his career.

Since those first efforts Polisar has been singing and writing for children and, without much fanfare or publicity, his songs and books have become popular across the country with children and their parents. He has written songs for the television series *Sesame Street* and performed at the White House, the Kennedy Center, and the Smithsonian. Polisar's books, written for primary to middle-grade audiences, include works such as 1987's *The Haunted House Party* and *The Trouble with Ben*, published in 1992. *The Haunted*

House Party, told in verse, tells of a boy who invites friends to his house for an impromptu Halloween party, while his parents are away for the evening. "This book is good Halloween fun as the boy and his friends watch in amazement as goblins, witches, ghosts, etc., crash the party, then help clean up afterwards before the parents come home," commented Alice Cronin in *School Library Journal.* In *The Trouble with Ben,* Polisar looks at the difficulty of being different from one's peers. Ben is a bear attending a human elementary school and having trouble fitting in. His bear-like behavior is not acceptable with teacher and pupils, but try as he might, he cannot imitate the actions of students around him. He eventually learns to be himself and have fun in the process.

Polisar also includes workshops and concerts in elementary schools in his schedule. When performing at a school he will present one or two 35- or 45-minute concerts, along with a series of "meet-the-writer" workshops during the rest of the day. "These workshops are designed to interest children in becoming better writers and readers," Polisar told *SATA.*

"In my work—my songwriting, my poems, and my books for children, I always try to use humor as a way of both diffusing an otherwise uncomfortable situation as well as a way of showing how so many of our feelings and experiences are universal," Polisar stated. "When I work with children in the schools, I try to present the craft of writing—though hard work—as fun. I think children learn best when they are having fun. And cherish that knowledge—and love of knowledge—forever."

■ Works Cited

Cronin, Alice, review of *The Haunted House Party,* *School Library Journal,* March, 1988, p. 200.
McKerrow, Steve, "He Plays to a Young Crowd," *Baltimore Sun,* May, 1988.
Seiden, Matt, "Poetry Your Kids Will Love—and You, Too," *Baltimore Sun,* May 25, 1988.

■ For More Information See

PERIODICALS

Booklist, June 1, 1992, p. 1766.
Publishers Weekly, June 8, 1992, p. 62; August 2, 1993.
School Library Journal, July, 1992, p. 63.

R

RABE, Berniece (Louise) 1928-

■ Personal

Surname rhymes with "Abe"; born January 11, 1928, in Parma, MO; daughter of Grover Cleveland (a farmer) and Martha (Green) Bagby; married Walter Henry Rabe (vice-president of Precision Diamond Tool Co.), July 30, 1946; children: Alan Walter, Brian Cleve, Clay Victor, Dara Mari. *Education:* National-Louis University, B.A., 1963; Columbia University, M.A., 1989.

■ Addresses

Home—860 Willow Lane, Sleepy Hollow, IL 60118. *Agent*—McIntosh & Otis, Inc., 310 Madison Ave., New York, NY 10017.

■ Career

Model with Patricia Stevens Model Agency, Chicago, IL, 1945-46; teacher and tutor in special education, Elgin, IL, 1963-67; freelance writer, 1968—. *Member:* Children's Reading Roundtable, Fox Valley Writers (member of executive board), Off Campus Writers (member of executive board).

■ Awards, Honors

Naomi named *School Library Journal's* one of 150 "best of the best" children's books published 1965-1978; Golden Kite Award, Society of Children's Book Writers, for *The Girl Who Had No Name;* best book of the year citation, Society of Midland Authors, for *The Orphans;* ALA Notable Children's Book citation, for *The Balancing Girl.*

■ Writings

FOR CHILDREN

Two Peas in a Pod (picture book), Whitman-Racine, 1974.
Can They See Me? (picture book), Whitman-Racine, 1976.

BERNIECE RABE

The Balancing Girl (picture book), illustrated by Lillian Hoban, Dutton, 1981.
Margaret's Moves, illustrated by Julie Downing, Dutton, 1987.
A Smooth Move (picture book), illustrated by Linda Shute, Albert Whitman, 1987.
Where's Chimpy? (picture book), photographs by Diane Schmidt, Albert Whitman, 1988.
Magic Comes in Its Time, Simon & Schuster, 1993.
The First Christmas Candy Canes: A Legend, Longmeadow Press, in press.

FOR YOUNG ADULTS

Rass, Thomas Nelson, 1973.
Naomi, Thomas Nelson, 1975.
The Girl Who Had No Name, Dutton, 1977.
The Orphans, Dutton, 1978.
Who's Afraid?, illustrated by Maribeth Olson, Dutton, 1980.

Rabe's own demanding childhood is reflected in this novel of a young girl living in Missouri during the Great Depression of the 1930s.

Love Reigns, Book Lures, 1986.
Rehearsal for the Bigtime, illustrated by Diane de Groat, Franklin Watts, 1988.
Tall Enough to Own the World, Franklin Watts, 1989.

Contributor of short stories to children's magazines, including *Friend, Ensign, Cricket,* and *Childcraft,* and to adult quarterlies; contributor of articles to *World Book* and *Encyclopedia Britannica.* Author of *Whillie the Masseuse* (novella), published in *Mid-American Review,* 1988.

■ Work in Progress

An Indian ghost story titled *Keeping the World in Balance;* a story with a racial theme tentatively titled *Pave the Way.*

■ Sidelights

Berniece Rabe grew up in a large, poor family in rural Missouri during the Depression. She later raised four children of her own and has lived a comfortable suburban life in Illinois. Out of these two very different experiences, Rabe has created over a dozen novels and picture books, several of them written for specific children and grandchildren, and numerous short stories

for both children and young adults. Her novels have been described by such adjectives as "vivid," "true-to-life," and "attractive," which suggest the powerful impact her work can have.

"I was born the twelfth child, one deceased before my birth," Rabe related in *Something about the Author Autobiography Series* (*SAAS*). "My parents were poor farmers in southeast Missouri. Nineteen twenty-nine, a year after my birth, the stock market crashed and the bank foreclosed on Dad's farm to make good a note he'd signed for a cousin. Thereafter, we lived at poverty level, Dad sharing the proceeds of his farming, fifty-fifty, with the landowner." To make matters worse, Rabe's mother died the year before Berniece turned two, leaving her father with eleven children and a farm to run. In desperation, he agreed to marry a thirty-six-year-old woman with seven children of her own whose father had deserted them. "Many men did that during those severe hard times," Rabe explained. "There was not government aid for all the people in need."

Since the Bagbys and Daniels were very different families, "the normal quarreling within a household was amplified," the author recalled. "My older sisters and stepsisters immediately fled the home for very young marriages, leaving me the remaining Bagby female in the house. I became the whipping girl when my stepmother was angry with my father—whom she dared not offend. Whippings were the accepted form of child discipline. All the children got more than their share of them. But I was an outspoken child and mine were almost daily, and sometimes, if my stepmother was very distraught, her whippings extracted blood—leaving scars, physical and psychological."

Despite these hardships, Rabe found solace in her large family, for there was always a sibling with whom she could sympathize. She also was a superior student whose teachers often became "surrogate" parents. Like many children growing up in the country at the time, Rabe attended a one-room school. She recalled, "I always did all things my teacher asked of me and never said No. I was proud of that record."

When Rabe reached third grade, however, the school district lines changed and she had to attend a large brick school in town. Entering a new school was intimidating, especially since there were many more students, some of them town children from well-off families. "I was no longer just Berniece Bagby with a mind and will of her own," Rabe remembered, but "was known as one of the poor Bagby kids.... I had never before considered myself poor, or considered my economic status at all. I was simply me, or so I'd thought before. This loss of identity kept my mouth closed for some time." But after she overheard her teacher describe her to another teacher as "bright enough," she once again felt comfortable participating in class.

After eighth grade, Rabe was "farmed out to older siblings so I could attend high school piecemeal until [age] sixteen." One of these schools was in Venice,

California, where her sister Virginia lived. At Venice High she was amazed to discover that art was a required subject. One of the proudest moments in her life was having a sculpture of a woman that she had created, after much advice and helpful (however difficult to accept) criticism from her teacher, chosen for a Greater Los Angeles school-art exhibit. Rabe likens the creation of that sculpture to the process of developing a book. "I write in about the same fashion. Only now, it's editors and friends instead of teachers who send me back again and again until I'm almost ready to chuck the whole thing. Almost. I can't say I'm a self-made woman. Others have made me do it."

Having fulfilled virtually all the requirements for high school graduation by the time she was sixteen, Rabe bravely ventured to Chicago with a friend and inquired at Chicago University about the cost of tuition. Having found the figure beyond her means, she simply put the thought aside (she finally received a degree in 1963 after three of four children were in school) and began looking for a job. She soon found work as a professional model, and at seventeen travelled overseas on assignment. There she met her future husband, Walter Rabe, who was stationed in the army. "He seemed so refreshing to me," the author noted. "None of the smooth lines men usually handed models. I could tell he really liked me. Above all else I needed to be safe, loved, and feel I belonged—start a home."

Class Assignment Yields Germ of Novel

For the next seventeen years, Rabe was "busy being a housewife and homebuilder and decorator," she remembered in *SAAS.* "I do mean home builder. My husband and I built two houses with our own hands with occasional help." After the birth of her last child in 1964, at her husband's suggestion, Rabe took a creative writing course at the local community college. When her instructor assigned everyone to bring in a manuscript for the next meeting, Rabe didn't know what to write about. When the teacher suggested a fight scene, Rabe at first resisted. "But desperation always produces, and the night before the manuscript was due, inspiration hit. I saw, in my mind's eye, this great, long farm table with all my brothers and sisters seated around it. Standing at the end of that table was my stepbrother, shouting, 'I hate cabbage. I will not eat cabbage! It makes me puke!'" Rabe was nervous about returning to class with the finished story, but she courageously handed it in. When the teacher finished reading it to the class she announced, "'Now, you've heard an author. Where's the rest of the book?'"

From this beginning, Rabe's first novel, *Rass,* gradually grew—but not before about two-thirds of the author's only copy of the manuscript was accidentally discarded and had to be produced again. Finally, after numerous rejections, Rabe received a letter from her agent on Christmas Eve, informing her that *Rass* had been sold. The story of a young boy—one of ten children—and his attempts to win his father's notice performed well, and

After her mother dies and she is passed from sister to sister, Girlie begins a quest to find a real home and discover why her father didn't want her. (Cover illustration by Muriel Wood.)

soon Rabe's editor asked her to write another book. Rabe has been writing ever since.

Rabe's second novel, *Naomi,* also features a single member of a large, poor Missouri farm family. The eleven-year-old protagonist must cope with her mother's lack of support and her own superstitious belief, acquired from a fortune-teller, that she will not live beyond her fourteenth birthday. A local nurse, however, proves more helpful to the doubtful child, and by the end of the story Naomi, now fourteen (and still alive), has grown and learned to live with her mother. A reviewer for the *Bulletin of the Center for Children's Books* gives *Naomi* a starred review and praises the book as a "discerning portrait of a young adolescent" and a "vivid portrait of a place and a time and a way of life."

In 1977's *The Girl Who Had No Name,* Rabe continues exploring family life in rural southeast Missouri during the Depression. Girlie (short for "Girl Baby") is the youngest of ten girls, and is passed from one sister to another after the death of her mother. Girlie attempts to find out why her father gave her such a generic name, and in the process finds out much about herself and her family. Rabe's novel shows the family dealing with difficult times "on its own terms, caring for each other in a way that arouses admiration," writes Ruth M. Stein in *Language Arts*. "What might seem depressing is relieved by Girlie's lively spunkiness, honesty, and courage," Virginia Haviland similarly comments in *Horn Book. The Girl Who Had No Name* won the Golden Kite Award for fiction in 1977.

In Rabe's next book, *The Orphans,* twins Adam and Eva are already orphans when the death of their two uncles in a car accident leaves them homeless as well. Feeling very protective of his twin, who feels fearful and insecure, Adam resolves to get her legally adopted so that she will be part of a family. Both twins want to live with their step-grandmother, G-Mama, but the law of that time does not allow single women to adopt. After a series of bluffs and close calls, Adam and Eva find a way around the law and end up being adopted by the sheriff herself. A *Kirkus Reviews* critic observes that "the children's plight and their fears will win them allies," while a *Bulletin of the Center for Children's Books* reviewer notes that "the characterization and dialogue are colorful ... and the story well constructed."

Grandchildren Inspire Books

One of Rabe's most popular books, *The Balancing Girl,* grew out of a later personal experience. Her first granddaughter, Rochelle, was born with spina bifida, a congenital condition which caused her to be paralyzed from the waist down. "We had our season of mourning for her loss," the author noted in *SAAS,* "but soon were captured by her personality and all the many things she *could* do." When Rochelle's mother noted the lack of

Inspired by a grandchild with spina bifida, *The Balancing Girl* was one of the first about a handicapped child to focus on personality, not disability. (Cover illustration by Lillian Hoban.)

appropriate books about handicapped children, Rabe responded by writing *The Balancing Girl.* The book is praised in the *Bulletin of the Center for Children's Books* as "just the sort that's needed to fill a gap..., for it focuses on Margaret and not on her physical condition."

When *The Balancing Girl* was such a success, Rabe recalled in her essay, "my other grandchildren, later on, started demanding *their* book. And I was forced into writing *Margaret's Moves,* which has a lot of Justin in it." About this sequel, in which Margaret tries to raise money for a new wheelchair, a *Booklist* critic remarks: "Rabe has done an excellent job of creating a down-to-earth, believable young girl in Margaret.... A nice reprise for this most likable heroine."

A Smooth Move (1987), a picture book which tells things from grandchild Chad's point of view, is about a family that must move from Oregon to Washington, D.C. The moving van's ill-timed arrival, the last night in the old house, and the problems of adjusting to a new school may all sound familiar to families who have undergone this experience. *A Smooth Move* is described in *Kirkus Reviews* as "an eventful, true-to-life story that should appeal to families involved with a move."

With granddaughter Rebecca in mind, Rabe wrote *Rehearsal for the Bigtime,* in which four sixth-graders organize a musical performing group supervised by a stern but supportive teenager. Their hard work is recognized when the group wins a prize at a Halloween parade and the father of one member changes his mind about the shortcomings of his daughter. A *Kirkus Reviews* critic hails the book as "a cheerfully vigorous ... lively, realistic story that kids should enjoy."

Rabe has also drawn inspiration outside of her own family, however. She described the genesis of 1988's *Where's Chimpy?* in *SAAS:* "I looked out my window one day to see little Misty Spurlock running around playing with her daddy and dragging with her a toy monkey. Misty is a cutie, a delight, and [has] Down syndrome. I had to do a book for her to star in. I just had to." Working with her editor and a photographer, Rabe did just that. Preschoolers will see themselves in Misty, a young child who must have her favorite stuffed animal in order to go to bed. *Where's Chimpy* is "an upbeat, attractive concept book with a charming little star," according to a *Kirkus Reviews* critic.

Rabe feels strongly about the theme of her next book, *Tall Enough to Own the World.* "It's about a good boy, a fifth grader, who does a lot of acting-out because he is too different to be happy; he can't read," the author described in her autobiographical entry. "I feel it is one of the biggest tragedies in this world that any child be denied the joy of reading." Rabe remembers having a stepmother who "believed that books complicate life, especially for women, and [who] once pulled a book from my hand and threw it in the heater. After that I hid to read, inside a huge old wardrobe during the winter and in the top of a tree during the summer." The result "is a lively, involving story with well-drawn characters and a believable family situation," states another *Kirkus Reviews* writer.

Rabe describes her 1993 book *Magic Comes in Its Time* as a friendship story inspired by her own love for storks. Jonathan's family likes to say that he was "brought by storks" because the day they adopted him a family of storks began nesting on their roof. When Jonathan's family returns to the German town where he was born, Jonathan looks forward to seeing his good-luck birds—which he hopes will bring him a baby brother. But changes in the town have driven the storks away; only after Jonathan and his new friend Robert work to build a nest in an empty field does Jonathan begin to see his dreams come true. "Fascinating information about storks keeps the plot anchored," writes Stephanie Zvirin of *Booklist*, who calls the novel a "pleasant, upbeat tale." A *Kirkus Reviews* critic likewise finds the story "heartwarming," and adds that in the portrayal of Jonathan and Robert's growing friendship, "the interaction of the boys is healthy and believable."

Rabe summarizes her life as an author like this: "I've lived in two very different cultures and very different books come out of them. The material determines my style. Some people find it difficult to imagine that the same woman who wrote *Naomi* also wrote *Where's Chimpy?* There's no mystery to it, I'm simply a diverse woman. My husband says there's never a dull moment. He's never known what to expect next from me."

■ Works Cited

Review of *The Balancing Girl, Bulletin of the Center for Children's Books,* February, 1982, p. 114.

Haviland, Virginia, review of *The Girl Who Had No Name, Horn Book,* October, 1977, pp. 533-534.

Review of *Magic Comes in Its Time, Kirkus Reviews,* October 15, 1993.

Review of *Margaret's Moves, Booklist,* February 15, 1987, p. 903.

Review of *Naomi, Bulletin of the Center for Children's Books,* December, 1975, p. 69.

Review of *The Orphans, Bulletin of the Center for Children's Books,* February, 1979, p. 104.

Review of *The Orphans, Kirkus Reviews,* October 15, 1978, p. 1139.

Rabe, Berniece, entry in *Something about the Author Autobiography Series,* Volume 10, Gale, 1990, pp. 261-275.

Review of *Rehearsal for the Big Time, Kirkus Reviews,* January 1, 1988, p. 59.

Review of *A Smooth Move, Kirkus Reviews,* July 1, 1987, p. 998.

Stein, Ruth M., review of *The Girl Who Had No Name, Language Arts,* April, 1978, p. 523.

Review of *Tall Enough to Own the World, Kirkus Reviews,* March 1, 1989, p. 382.

Review of *Where's Chimpy?, Kirkus Reviews,* June 15, 1988, p. 902.

Zvirin, Stephanie, review of *Magic Comes in Its Time, Booklist,* October 1, 1993.

■ For More Information See

PERIODICALS

Bulletin of the Center for Children's Books, January, 1974; January, 1978, p. 85; October, 1988, p. 51; May, 1989, p. 234.

Horn Book, February, 1982, p. 36.

New York Times Book Review, August 12, 1973, p. 8; June 22, 1975, p. 8.

School Library Journal, December, 1979; October, 1981, p. 134; December, 1988, p. 92; May, 1989, p. 111; October, 1989, p. 47; October, 1993, p. 128.

* * *

RAVILIOUS, Robin 1944-

■ Personal

Born November 15, 1944, in Torrington, England; daughter of Laurence (an author and glass engraver) and Jill (an actress; maiden name, Furse) Whistler; married James Ravilious (a photographer), September 1, 1970; children: Ben, Ella. *Education:* Lady Margaret Hall, Oxford University, B.A., 1966. *Religion:* Church of England. *Hobbies and other interests:* Local history, gardening, natural history, music.

Robin Ravilious's love of nature is demonstrated in the soft pictures and gentle stories she creates for young readers. (Illustration by the author from *The Runaway Chick.*)

■ Addresses

Home—Western House, New Street, Chulmliegh, Devon EX18 7DB, England. *Agent*—Gina Pollinger and Murray Pollinger, Literary Agents, 222 Old Brompton Road, London SW5 0BZ, England.

■ Career

Several secretarial posts, including Principal's secretary, Newnham College, Cambridge, England; writer and illustrator.

■ Awards, Honors

Sunday Times/Kenneth Allsop Essay Prize, 1976.

■ Writings

FOR CHILDREN

(And illustrator) *The Runaway Chick,* Methuen Books, 1987.
(And illustrator) *Two in a Pocket,* Heinemann, 1991.
(Illustrator) Jenni Fleetwood, *The Story Tree,* Dent Children's Books, 1992.

FOR ADULTS

(With James Ravilious) *The Heart of the Country,* Scolar Press, 1980.

■ Work in Progress

Several stories for children.

■ Sidelights

Robin Ravilious told *SATA:* "I have spent a large part of my life in this very rural and unspoiled countryside, absorbing its landscape, its wildlife and its changing moods. I shared my love of it with my own two children, taking them for walks and drawing while they played. It then seemed logical to use those drawings to make books that could reach a wider audience of children who also loved nature, or who would if they had the chance to learn about it. Although my stories are partly fantasy, they are always based on natural fact, and I illustrate them with naturalistic pictures."

■ For More Information See

PERIODICALS

Booklist, October 15, 1987, p. 399.
Children's Book Review Service, January, 1988, p. 50; July, 1991, p. 148.
Kirkus Reviews, April 15, 1991, p. 545.
Publishers Weekly, September 25, 1987, p. 107.
School Library Journal, July, 1991.

REAVER, Chap 1935-1993

OBITUARY NOTICE—See index for *SATA* sketch: Given name Herbert R. Reaver; born June 10, 1935, in Cincinnati, OH; died January 11, 1993, in Marietta, GA. Medical practitioner, educator, and author. Reaver is best remembered for his 1990 young adult mystery, *Mote,* which won the Edgar Allan Poe Award for that classification. Reaver began a career in chiropractic medicine in Ohio in 1957, continuing his practice in Georgia after his family's move there in 1980. After his relocation Reaver also began dabbling in writing, penning *Mote* and contributing articles and short stories to periodicals. In addition, he found time to teach writing classes at Marietta Junior High School. In 1992, he saw publication of his young adult western *A Little Bit Dead.* He had completed a third novel, entitled *Bill,* before his death.

OBITUARIES AND OTHER SOURCES:

PERIODICALS

School Library Journal, May, 1993, p. 20.

* * *

REMKIEWICZ, Frank 1939-

■ Personal

Born April 14, 1939, in Rockville, CT; son of Frank Remkiewicz (a tool designer) and Clara (Hyjek) Remkiewicz; married Sylvia Nissley (an art consultant); children: Sarah, Jessica, Madeleine. *Education:* Art Center College of Design, B.P.A. (with honors), 1965.

FRANK REMKIEWICZ

■ Addresses

Home and office—15960 Drake Rd., Guerneville, CA 95446. *Agent*—Kendra Marcus, 67 Meadow View Rd., Orinda, CA 94563.

■ Career

Norcross Greeting Cards, New York City, staff illustrator, 1968-73; freelance author and illustrator, 1973-92.

■ Awards, Honors

New York Times Ten Best of the Season citation, 1991, for *The Last Time I Saw Harris; I Hate Camping* was named a Children's Book of the Year by Bank Street College; Children's Choice Award, National Council for Reading, 1992.

■ Writings

SELF-ILLUSTRATED

The Last Time I Saw Harris, Lothrop, 1991.
Greedyanna, Lothrop, 1992.
Final Exit for Cats: A Feline Suicide Guide, HarperCollins, 1992.
There's Only One Harris, Lothrop, 1993.

Illustrator and writer of over one thousand greeting cards and several hundred single-panel cartoons for various northern California newspapers.

Author's works have been translated into French, Japanese, Chinese, and Korean.

ILLUSTRATOR; BOOKS BY SUZY KLINE

Horrible Harry in Room 2B, Viking, 1988.
Horrible Harry and the Ant Invasion, Puffin Books, 1989.
Horrible Harry and the Green Slime, Puffin Books, 1989.
Horrible Harry's Secret, Puffin Books, 1990.
Horrible Harry and the Christmas Surprise, Viking, 1991.
Horrible Harry and the Kickball Wedding, Viking, 1992.
Song Lee in Room Two B, Viking, 1993.

ILLUSTRATOR; OTHER

Jean Fisher, editor, *Manuscript Writing,* Western Publishing, 1984.
Sarah Leslie, *The Saggy Baggy Elephant and the New Dance,* Golden Books, 1985.
Lada J. Kratky, *En Chivo en la Huerta,* Hampton-Brown, 1988.
Jean Langerman, *No Carrots for Harry!,* Parents Magazine Press, 1989.
Alma F. Ada, *Una Semilla Nada Mas,* Hampton-Brown, 1990.
Ellen Jackson, *Ants Can't Dance,* Macmillan, 1991.
P. J. Petersen, *I Hate Camping,* Dutton, 1991.
Patricia R. Giff, *I Love Saturday,* Puffin Books, 1991.
Jonathan London, *Froggy Gets Dressed,* Viking, 1992.

The constant "Mine!" of a youngest child taxes her family's patience in this light-hearted picture book. (Cover illustration by the author.)

Nancy Lamb, *The Great Mosquito, Bull and Coffin Caper,* Lothrop, 1992.
Jonathan London, *Let's Go Froggy,* Viking, 1994.

■ Work in Progress

The Bone Ranger, a story about dogs in the Old West, publication expected in 1994; *Fiona, Fletcher and Floyd,* telling of "a fractured flamingo family searching for their lost father."

■ Sidelights

Frank Remkiewicz has served as illustrator for several children's books. His drawings are described by Diane Roback of *Publishers Weekly* as "bold swatches of color crisply outlined." Remkiewicz has also written and illustrated several of his own children's books, including *The Last Time I Saw Harris,* which tells the story of Edmund and his best friend, Harris, a parrot. Harris can perform a number of unusual tricks, including identifying colors. When Edmund is about to teach Harris the color purple, a strong wind blows the parrot away, and Edmund and a chauffeur set out to find him. While some reviewers felt that younger readers might be alarmed about the temporary loss of Harris, most complimented the story. *Booklist* contributor Ilene Cooper found "most of the humor coming from the brightly colored, cartoon-style illustrations," while Martha V. Parravano concluded in *Horn Book* that the "flat, spacious pictures ... match the droll, understated—though utterly absurd—tale. A delightful concoction."

Remkiewicz's next work shares with *The Last Time I Saw Harris* a plot that relies on a common situation taken to the extreme for comic effect. Narrated by Anna's brother, Eddie, *Greedyanna* is about a demanding girl whose parents indulge her wishes by believing that her behavior only is a passing phase. Anna eventually has her parents sleeping on the ground and eating lima beans during a family camping trip because she wants the tent to herself and she hates lima beans. Virginia E. Jeschelnig remarked in *School Library Journal* that "the watercolor cartoons nicely convey the humor of Eddie's predicament and carry the story for pre-readers. Anna's antics will surely amuse, and may even encourage an errant child to share."

Remkiewicz told *SATA:* "I was that kind of kid who was always reading or drawing. Since I was drawing well before I started school, I always considered art to have seniority over the likes of long division or medieval history. This attitude got me into difficulties more than once. My favorite subjects were horses, cartoons, wildlife, and contraptions that rolled, floated, tooted, or flew. My heroes of the day were illustrators like Bill Peet, Robert Lawson, and Kurt Weiss. They provided me with a screen-full of imagery that I'll never forget.

"Winter in kindergarten found us all painting Santa. Mine came out so well that I was to do it over again on a huge piece of brown paper that covered the chalkboard. Santa was bigger than me. I was excused from the regular stuff, given bigger brushes, more paint and sure enough ... here came Santa. Other teachers saw the mural sized figure and 'borrowed' me to do the same for their classrooms. Flattered but embarrassed, I took heart since these gigs were getting me out of a lot of tedious activities like nap time, scissors, yarn, and flash cards. 'All I ever needed to know, I learned in kindergarten' may be true. Twenty years later I found myself on Madison Avenue at Norcross Greeting Cards ... yes, drawing Santa Claus.

"I've always been drawn to the field of humor. Since I'm writing and illustrating my own stories now, I try to make them funny in an outrageous or off-the-wall way. During classroom presentations, again ... I find myself by the chalkboard in front of the kids. Now we are seeking ways to write and draw those ideas that squeeze their way through the every day chores of our minds. It's a thrill to watch my own book being read by a group of children and I like it when they smile, but I love it when they laugh."

■ Works Cited

Cooper, Ilene, review of *The Last Time I Saw Harris, Booklist,* November 15, 1991, p. 631.
Jeschelnig, Virginia E., review of *Greedyanna, School Library Journal,* November, 1991, p. 107; July, 1992, p. 63.
Parravano, Martha V., review of *The Last Time I Saw Harris, Horn Book,* September/October, 1991, p. 588.
Roback, Diane, review of *Greedyanna, Publishers Weekly,* March 16, 1992, p. 79.

■ For More Information See

PERIODICALS

Children's Book Review Service, February, 1992, p. 76; July, 1992, p. 149.
Kirkus Reviews, May 1, 1992, p. 620.
Publishers Weekly, October 18, 1991, p. 61.
School Library Journal, November, 1991, p. 107.

* * *

RICHARDSON, Judith Benet 1941-

■ Personal

Born November 26, 1941, in New York, NY; daughter of James (a journalist) and Mary (Liles) Benet; married Phillip L. Richardson (an oceanographer), 1966; children: Arthur, Mary. *Education:* New York University, B.A.; Boston University, M.A.

■ Career

Writer. Instructor at various institutions, including Sea Education Association, Woods Hole, MA, and Parents' Cooperative School, RI. President, Woods Hole Library. *Member:* Society of Children's Book Writers and Illustrators.

JUDITH BENET RICHARDSON

■ Writings

"MAUSHOPE'S LANDING" SERIES

David's Landing, Woods Hole Historical Collection, 1985.
Mirrors are Lonely, Woods Hole Historical Collection, 1992.

PICTURE BOOKS

(With Sally Mavor) *The Way Home,* Macmillan, 1991.
(With Mavor) *Come to My Party,* Macmillan, 1993.

■ Work in Progress

A picture book entitled *Old Winter,* in which the season is represented as a person; the third novel in the "Maushope's Landing" series, tentatively titled *First Came the Owl,* which will feature a half-Thai heroine.

■ Sidelights

Judith Benet Richardson has enjoyed a productive collaboration with illustrator Sally Mavor for several years. The duo's first book, *The Way Home,* tells the tale of Savi, a baby elephant, who refuses to go home after a day at the beach. Although Savi's mother leaves her behind, she lays down a trail of banana leaves to lead Savi safely home.

*   *   *

ROBINSON, Aminah Brenda Lynn 1940-

■ Personal

Born February 18, 1940, in Columbus, OH; daughter of Leroy William Edward Robinson (a custodian and artist) and Helen Elizabeth Zimmerman-Robinson (an artist and homemaker); married Clarence Adrian Robinson, September 24, 1964 (divorced, January 10, 1981); children: Sydney Edward.

■ Addresses

Home and office—Columbus, OH.

■ Career

Ohio Public Library, Columbus, OH, assistant librarian, 1958-64; Mountain States Telephone Company, Boise, ID, draftsperson, 1964-66; illustrator at television station in Mississippi, 1966-67; North American Rockwell Corporation, Columbus, senior illustrator, 1968; City Recreation and Parks Department, Columbus, arts specialist, 1972-91. Lecturer and visiting artist; freelance artist. *Exhibitions:* Work exhibited at numerous institutions, including Main Library, Ohio University, 1979; Pan American Institute, Kent State University, 1982; Collectors Gallery, Columbus Museum of Art, Columbus, OH, 1983 and 1990; Carl Solway Gallery, Cincinnati, OH; Esther Saks Gallery, Chicago, IL, 1984; Kathryn Markel Gallery, New York City, 1985; Jamaica Arts Center, Jamaica, 1993; Columbus Foundation, Columbus, 1993; and Performing Arts Center, Springfield, OH, 1993.

■ Awards, Honors

Outstanding Citizen in the Community, National Epicureans, 1974; Kumba Black Liberation Award, 1978; travel grant, Art for Community Expression, 1979; Aid to Individual Artist Fellowship awards, Ohio Arts Council, 1979-80, 1986-87, 1988-89; Columbus Star, 1980, for outstanding service to the quality of life in Columbus, OH; Governor's Award for Visual Arts in Ohio, 1984; Salute to Black Women Award, Eta Phi Beta, 1984; Certificate of Appreciation, Martin Luther King, Jr. Center for Performing Arts, 1989; National Jewish Book Award, 1993, for *Elijah's Angel;* honorary degree from Columbus College of Art and Design, 1991.

■ Writings

(Illustrator) Michael J. Rosen, *Elijah's Angel: A Story for Chanukah and Christmas,* Harcourt Brace Jovanovich, 1992.
The Teachings: Drawn from African-American Spirituals, Harcourt Brace Jovanovich, 1992.
(Illustrator) Mem Fox, *Sophie,* Harcourt Brace Jovanovich, in press.

Contributor to journals, including *Ohio* magazine, *Chicago Tribune, Columbus Homes and Lifestyles,* and *Artspace.*

■ Work in Progress

Blackberry Patch and *Uncle Alvin's Hand-Me-Downs,* both books of stories and illustrations, and *Operatta,* a symphonic poem.

AMINAH BRENDA LYNN ROBINSON

■ Sidelights

Aminah Brenda Lynn Robinson is an accomplished artist who has exhibited her work widely in Ohio and other parts of the United States. In 1992 she illustrated *Elijah's Angel: A Story for Chanukah and Christmas,* a book by Michael J. Rosen. *Elijah's Angel* is a story about the friendship that forms between Michael, a Jewish boy, and Elijah, an elderly Christian man. The story turns on the conflict within Michael when Elijah gives him an angel he has carved from wood. Michael fears that having a Christian angel in a Jewish home is a desecration, until his parents reassure him that angels are for everyone.

Ari L. Goldman noted in the *New York Times Book Review* that often stories attempting to resolve Christian and Jewish differences fail to ring true. However, he called *Elijah's Angel* a "finely done" book and attributed the effectiveness of the book to its basis on a real-life barber and woodcarver in the Columbus, Ohio neighborhood where the artist and author once lived. While a *Publishers Weekly* reviewer found Robinson's illustrations geared more to adult tastes, Ilene Cooper, reviewing *Elijah's Angel* for *Booklist,* remarked that "the naive-style paintings, done in house paint on scrap rags, boldly simulate woodcuts, and though the artwork is not pretty, it ... has the feel of reality. In a time of so much dissension, stories like this one ... are hopeful guideposts to the way people can live together."

■ Works Cited

Cooper, Ilene, review of *Elijah's Angel: A Story for Chanukah and Christmas, Booklist,* August, 1992, p. 2013.

Review of *Elijah's Angel: A Story for Chanukah and Christmas, Publishers Weekly,* September 7, 1992, p. 62.

Goldman, Ari L., review of *Elijah's Angel: A Story for Chanukah and Christmas, New York Times Book Review,* December 13, 1992, p. 35.

■ For More Information See

PERIODICALS

Columbus Alive!, December 10-24, 1992, pp. 1, 14-16.

*   *   *

RODOWSKY, Colby 1932-

■ Personal

Born February 26, 1932, in Baltimore, MD; daughter of Frank M. Fossett and Mary C. Fitz-Townsend; married Lawrence Rodowsky (a judge on the Maryland Court of Appeals), August 7, 1954; children: Laurie, Alice, Emily, Sarah, Gregory, Katherine. *Education:* College of Notre Dame of Maryland, B.A., 1953. *Religion:* Roman Catholic.

COLBY RODOWSKY

■ Addresses

Home and office—4306 Norwood Rd., Baltimore, MD 21218. *Agent*—Gail Hochman, Brandt & Brandt, 1501 Broadway, NY 10036.

■ Career

Teacher in public schools in Baltimore, MD, 1953-55, and in a school for special education, 1955-56.

■ Awards, Honors

American Library Association Notable Book citation for *The Gathering Room,* and Best Books for Young Adults citation for *Julie's Daughter;* Hedda Seisler Mason Award, Enoch Pratt Library, for *Fitchett's Folly;* School Library Journal "Best Books of the Year" citations for *The Gathering Room, Julie's Daughter,* and *Sydney, Herself.*

■ Writings

FOR CHILDREN

Dog Days, illustrated by Kathleen Collins Howell, Farrar, Straus, 1990.

Jenny and the Old Great-Aunts, illustrated by Barbara Roman, Macmillan, 1992.

FOR MIDDLE GRADES

What about Me?, F. Watts, 1976.

P.S. Write Soon, F. Watts, 1978.

Evy-Ivy-Over, F. Watts, 1978.

A Summer's Worth of Shame, F. Watts, 1980.

The Gathering Room, Farrar, Straus, 1981.

H, My Name Is Henley, Farrar, Straus, 1982.

Keeping Time, Farrar, Straus, 1983.

Fitchett's Folly, Farrar, Straus, 1987.

Hannah in Between, Farrar, Straus, 1994.

FOR YOUNG ADULTS

Julie's Daughter (sequel to *Evy-Ivy-Over*), Farrar, Straus,
  1985.
Sydney, Herself, Farrar, Straus, 1989.
Lucy Peale, Farrar, Straus, 1992.

OTHER

Also author of reviews for the *Baltimore Sun;* contributor to *Christian Science Monitor, New York Times Book
Review, Washington Post, McCall's* and *Good Housekeeping.* Young adult short stories have been antholo-
gized in *Visions,* edited by Donald Gallo, Delacorte,
1987, and in *Connections,* edited by Gallo, Delacorte,
1989.

■ **Work in Progress**

A sequel to *Sydney, Herself;* a novel; short stories.

■ **Sidelights**

The characters in Colby Rodowsky's award-winning
books live in a tough world, often marked by unpredict-
able events and undependable authority figures. These
children and teenagers must contend with such issues as
parental abandonment, poverty, and death. Not all is
bleak in Rodowsky's world, however; warm and loving
people exist. Reviewers frequently praise her ability to
create interesting and likeable characters.

Rodowsky was born in Baltimore, Maryland. As a child
she wanted to become a writer, and her mother encouraged her. "I don't know whether it was because she was
a doting mother or she really thought I could write, but
she was very supportive," the author told *Contemporary
Authors New Revision Series* (*CANR*). Rodowsky spent
many summers on Virginia's eastern shore with her
grandmother, and the area became the setting of several
of her books. She majored in English in college and
edited the literary magazine. After receiving her B.A.,
she married and had six children. The family lived in "a
very noisy house" she once commented in *SATA*. It
contained her husband, five children (one had married),
two dogs, and two cats. "The house is quiet now—the
children grown up and moved away," she later told
SATA. "But the family now includes four sons-in-law,
one daughter-in-law, and *many* grandchildren, who all
visit often (and only one dog and one cat)."

Rodowsky started her writing career through a casual
visit to one of her former teachers from Notre Dame.
"We weren't talking about writing; we were just talking
about books," she told *CANR*. Her former teacher
"finally stopped what she was saying and looked at me
and said, 'Just think; you have all your writing still
ahead of you.' It really kind of gives me cold chills even
now when I think about it. I did not go home and write a
book, but I went home thinking maybe I hadn't missed
the boat on what I'd really wanted to do." She added, "I
was about forty, and at that time I thought if you hadn't
done anything by forty, you never would. Now I know a
lot better."

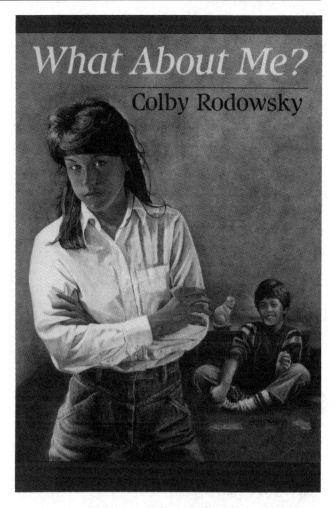

Drawing from her experience with teaching retarded
children, Rodowsky shows how having a child with
Down's Syndrome in the family can bring both
heartache and joy. (Cover illustration by Diana
Deutermann.)

Characters Come to Terms with Feelings

Many of Rodowsky's books show characters struggling
with ambivalent feelings toward family members. In her
first book, *What about Me?*, a fifteen-year-old girl
resents her brother "Fredlet," who has Down's syndrome. While Rodowsky taught retarded children, she
told *CANR*, "I kind of backed into it because I wanted
to write about a child who had a younger brother or
sister with a handicap . . . . I didn't set out to write about
a retarded child." Although Rodowsky generally knows
how a book will end, and often writes the last page first,
what happens to Fredlet took her by surprise. *P.S. Write
Soon* concerns crippled Tanner McClean, who writes an
idealized version of her life to her pen-pal Jessie Lee.
She glosses over her handicap and the unexpected
marriage of her older brother. But although she dislikes
her new sister-in-law, Cheryl, the older girl teaches
Tanner how to face life.

Rodowsky's fifth book, *The Gathering Room,* an American Library Association Notable Book, "takes place in
an old cemetery in Baltimore," she said to *CANR*. When

his friend is assassinated, Mudge's father, Ned, moves his family from the city and takes a job as the cemetery caretaker. Ned teaches nine-year-old Mudge in the room where the mourners used to congregate, and the boy befriends the spirits of the dead, who "provide this simple, well-wrought story with a pleasant, if melancholy sense of time and mortality," writes Jane Langton in the *New York Times Book Review. School Library Journal* contributor Elizabeth Holtze says "the author writes clear narrative and convincing dialogue.... Despite the cemetery setting and the problem posed ... this is a happy book."

In another unusual story, *Keeping Time,* street performer Drew escapes to sixteenth-century London to avoid his strained family relationships. When he hears the music "Greensleeves," he slips back in time. "I didn't quite know when I started that book where it was going," she explained to *CANR.* "I knew I wanted to go back in time, and I knew it had to have a musical connection because Drew is a musician. Oddly enough, I

felt kind of spooky about the book.... I guess it started when I asked my son one night at dinner about a song that people would know today that was also known a long time ago. He suggested 'Greensleeves.'" While some critics found the switches from one era to another too abrupt, Rodowsky again received praise for her dialogue and characterization. Mary M. Burns in the *Horn Book* calls it "an intriguing novel of adolescence." She continues, "what makes the novel impelling is the author's ability to develop distinctive characters through subtle imagery and plausible conversation." *School Library Journal* contributor Barbara Jo McKee says, "This is a well-written novel packed with history as well as much meaning between the lines."

Slugfest: *Evy-Ivy-Over, H, My Name Is Henley,* and *Julie's Daughter*

The young girl with the unusual name of Slug connects three of Rodowsky's books. In *Evy-Ivy-Over,* she lives a carefree, if unorthodox, life with her grandmother. But as Slug matures, she realizes her hand-me-down clothes are funny-looking and that Gussie herself is an odd character. She learns through contact with "normal" families, however, to appreciate Gussie. "I was very close to both of my grandmothers," Rodowsky told *CANR.* "In *Evy-Ivy-Over* ... I tried to describe the grandmother-grandchild relationship, though I must say neither of my grandmothers was at all like Gussie."

While not the main character, Slug also appears in *H, My Name Is Henley,* which deals with the plight of a young girl and her restless mother, Patti. Patti is unable to stay in any one place for long: she stays until she quits her job and moves to another city. "Henley is probably the most mature and perceptive 12-year-old I've met in YA literature," states *Voice of Youth Advocates* contributor Barbara Lenchitz Gottesman. "Rodowsky has created a masterpiece." And while other reviewers have pointed to some weak characterization, "The tension and conflict between mother and daughter, the strain on a child forced into adult responsibilities, and the characterization of Patti are intensely real," writes Nancy C. Hammond in *Horn Book.*

Julie's Daughter, which won a Best Books for Young Adults award, unites Slug and her mother Julie, who abandoned her infant daughter at the bus station. Slug and Julie are brought together in caring for their neighbor, the artist Harper Tegges, who is dying of cancer. The story is seen through their three viewpoints. *Voice of Youth Advocates* contributor Debbie Earl says "the differing narrations help us develop sympathy and understanding for the main characters," and finds the book "sensitively done and surprisingly humorous." Christine Jenkins in *Interracial Books for Children Bulletin* says "*Julie's Daughter* succeeds in portraying strong women, both old and young."

More Family Matters

"Rodowsky deftly balances adventure, pathos and surprising comedy in a tale about early days" on the eastern shore of Maryland in the book *Fitchett's Folly,* writes a

COLBY RODOWSKY

Julie's Daughter

aerial fiction

Slug meets the mother who abandoned her seventeen years ago and the two try to reconcile by caring for a terminally ill neighbor. (Cover illustration by Elaine Norman.)

Publishers Weekly reviewer. *Fitchett's Folly* focuses on a motherless girl, Sarey-Ann, whose father drowns when he rescues another child. Sarey-Ann has to deal with her feelings of resentment toward the foundling, Faith, who comes to live with the girl, her little brother, and her aunt. A *Horn Book* contributor says, "Sarey's prickly dislike is convincingly portrayed in her first-person recounting.... Scrapes and adventures add to the story of Sarey's eventual acceptance of Faith."

Sydney, Herself features another child who has lost a parent. Sydney's Australian father died a month before she was born. But through an English assignment, Sydney decides she is the daughter of a rock singer, a member of the group the Boomerangs. When Sydney gives her story to a local newspaper, events snowball. A *Horn Book* reviewer states that "The story is fresh, humorous, and believable. Sydney is interesting— bright, gritty, and sometimes sulky." Carol Edwards writes in the *School Library Journal* that "Rodowsky makes her readers work, never patronizing or condescending, yet always revealing inner layers that poke through the surface," and adds that the book is "funny, poignant, and appealing."

Dog Days is written for a younger audience than *Sydney, Herself.* The author of the heroine's favorite dog stories, and her famous dog, move in next door. A *Publishers Weekly* writer finds that the book "lacks the depth of some of Rodowsky's earlier works," but it provides "plenty of humor, numerous ironic twists and memorable characters." And a *Horn Book* contributor says, "Rodowsky is understanding of human nature and adept at dialogue and story structure." *Jenny and the Grand Old Great-Aunts* is aimed at an even younger audience. In what *School Library Journal* reviewer Anna DeWind calls an "appealing cross-generational story," Jenny is dropped off by herself to spend the afternoon with her great aunts in their terrifyingly still Victorian home. But one aunt introduces the little girl to a treasure cache in the attic. "This comforting story deftly conveys the strength of the bond that can exist between the old and the young," writes a *Publishers Weekly* contributor.

In *Lucy Peale,* a love story for teens, a girl from a strict pastor's family is date-raped. Her father condemns her and she runs away to Ocean City, where she meets Jake, a kind young man, who invites her to stay with him. They fall in love, but Lucy must find her own destiny. Rodowsky alternated the story between Lucy's viewpoint and a narrator's, which some reviewers found awkward. But in a starred review *Publishers Weekly* applauded the author's use of plot twists which keep Lucy's and Jake's attention focused on their developing relationship, rather than on sex. And Jacqueline Rose in the *School Library Journal* appreciates "the moods created by descriptions of the sea town's atmosphere that mirror the characters' feelings."

Rodowsky is perplexed by comments that imply that writing for children is easier than writing for adults. "I don't think when you write for children that you ever consciously decide you're going to make something

·COLBY RODOWSKY·

What has four paws and a nose for adventure?

The prospects for Rosie's summer brighten when a neighbor with a golden retriever moves in next door in this gentle story for children. (Cover illustration by Eric Jon Nones.)

simpler, that you ever write down in any way," she told *CANR.* "It's a challenge—a kind of balancing act," she explained to *SATA,* "and I get irritated by people who think you write for children because that's where you start, and then you work up to writing for grownups. I don't think it's any easier to write for children than for adults, but the rewards are great—particularly when I get a letter from a child whose life has been touched by a book of mine."

■ Works Cited

Burns, Mary M., review of *Keeping Time, Horn Book,* April, 1984, p. 203.

DeWind, Anna, review of *Jenny and the Grand Old Great-Aunts, School Library Journal,* April, 1992, p. 99.

Review of *Dog Days, Horn Book,* March/April, 1991, p. 202.

Review of *Dog Days, Publishers Weekly,* November 23, 1990, p. 65.

Earl, Debbie, review of *Julie's Daughter, Voice of Youth Advocates,* April, 1986, p. 34.

Edwards, Carol A., review of *Sidney, Herself, School Library Journal,* July, 1989, p. 92.

Review of *Fitchett's Folly, Horn Book,* July/August, 1987, p. 473.

Review of *Fitchett's Folly, Publishers Weekly,* April 24, 1987, p. 70.

Gottesman, Barbara Lenchitz, review of *H, My Name Is Henley, Voice of Youth Advocates,* April, 1983, p. 41.

Hammond, Nancy C., review of *H, My Name Is Henley,* April, 1983, p. 167.

Holtze, Elizabeth, review of *The Gathering Room, School Library Journal,* October, 1981, p. 146.

Jenkins, Christine, *Interracial Books for Children Bulletin,* Volume 17, number 1, 1986, p. 7.

Review of *Jenny and the Grand Old Great-Aunts, Publishers Weekly,* January 6, 1992, p. 66.

Langton, Jane, review of *The Gathering Room, New York Times Book Review,* October 25, 1981, p. 47.

Review of *Lucy Peale, Publishers Weekly,* May 4, 1992, p. 57.

McKee, Barbara Jo, review of *Keeping Time, School Library Journal,* January, 1985, p. 88.

Rodowsky, Colby, essay in *Contemporary Authors New Revision Series,* Volume 23, Gale, 1988, pp. 340-44.

Rose, Jacqueline, review of *Lucy Peale, School Library Journal,* July, 1992, p. 91.

Review of *Sidney, Herself, Horn Book,* September/October, 1989, p. 631.

■ For More Information See

PERIODICALS

Booklist, July, 1992, p. 1933.

Bulletin of the Center for Children's Books, February, 1984, p. 116.

Horn Book, October, 1981, p. 537; May/June, 1992, p. 338.

Publishers Weekly, June 9, 1989, p. 70.

School Library Journal, January, 1983, p. 87; September, 1985, p. 148.

Wilson Library Bulletin, February, 1990, p. 84; May, 1990, p. 58.

—Sketch by Jani Prescott

*   *   *

ROOS, Stephen 1945-

■ Personal

Born February 9, 1945, in New York, NY; son of William Ernest (a writer) and Audrey (a writer; maiden name, Kelley) Roos. *Education:* Yale University, A.B., 1967. *Politics:* Democrat.

■ Addresses

Home—RR2, Box 706, Banks Hill Rd., Pawling, NY 12564. *Agent*—Writers House, 21 West 26th Street, New York, NY 10010.

STEPHEN ROOS

■ Career

Harper & Row Publishers (now HarperCollins), New York City, copywriter in marketing department for children's books, 1968-76, junior editor of adult trade fiction, 1976-80; writer, 1980—. Institute for Children's Literature, Redding Ridge, CT, instructor, 1983-89.

■ Awards, Honors

Charlie May Simon Award, 1986, for *My Horrible Secret.*

■ Writings

My Horrible Secret, Delacorte, 1983.

My Terrible Truth, Delacorte, 1983.

My Secret Admirer, Delacorte, 1984.

(With parents, who write under the joint pseudonym Kelley Roos) *The Incredible Cat Caper,* Delacorte, 1985.

Confessions of a Wayward Preppie, Delacorte, 1986.

The Fair-Weather Friends, Atheneum, 1987.

Thirteenth Summer, Atheneum, 1987.

My Favorite Ghost, Atheneum, 1988.

You'll Miss Me When I'm Gone, Delacorte, 1988.

And the Winner Is..., Atheneum, 1989.

Twelve-Year-Old Vows Revenge after Being Dumped by Extraterrestrial on First Date, Delacorte, 1990.

A Young Person's Guide to the Twelve Steps (nonfiction), Hazelden, 1992.

Never Trust a Sister over Twelve, Delacorte, 1993.

"MAPLE STREET KIDS" SERIES

Silver Secrets, Hazelden, 1991.
Leave It to Augie, Hazelden, 1991.
My Blue Tongue, Hazelden, 1991.
Dear Santa: Make Me a Star, Hazelden, 1991.

"PET LOVERS CLUB" SERIES

Love Me, Love My Werewolf, Delacorte, 1991.
The Cottontail Caper, Delacorte, 1992.
Crocodile Christmas, Delacorte, 1992.

■ Work in Progress

Bird Boy of Fair Street, completed manuscript of a chapter book about a boy whose best friend moves away; writing a book about a decaying neighborhood in Connecticut, tentatively titled *Mrs. Constable, My Darling.*

■ Sidelights

"I don't think I ever decided to be a writer as a child," Stephen Roos said in an interview with *Something about the Author* (*SATA*), "I just wrote." And when he began to write professionally, he wasn't sure he wanted to write books for children. But that's what happened. His first published book, *My Horrible Secret,* won the Charlie May Simon Medallion (which was presented to him by then-governor Bill Clinton, of Arkansas) and launched the New Eden books, which have sold hundreds of thousands of copies. After the 1987 publication of his novel about a teenage alcoholic, *You'll Miss Me When I'm Gone,* Roos turned to a series of four novels about children growing up in alcoholic or other dysfunctional homes, and a nonfiction guide to the Twelve Steps of Alcoholics Anonymous. Roos is particularly noted for his range in handling young people's problems, from school bullies to teen suicide. In her *Horn Book* review of *My Terrible Truth,* Kate M. Flanagan observes that the humor in Roos's writing "stems from the wry characterizations of a group of typical middle-school students with their not-so-earth-shattering concerns and dilemmas."

The son of two writers, Roos grew up on the Upper East Side of New York City and in the small town of New Canaan, Connecticut. He also lived and traveled in Europe for several years. In New York he was surrounded by the theatrical and literary people who were friends and colleagues of his parents. In New Canaan, where his parents moved when he was five, he discovered the gentle and affluent small-town life which figures prominently in many of his books.

Roos termed his parents "bourgeois hippies." They were free-spirited and nontraditional people, but they had a taste for the good life as it could be lived in a New York City brownstone or an old country farmhouse. He remembered them in his interview as "wonderful and interesting and *difficult* people. I am very grateful to them," he added, "but they were not very parental."

His parents collaborated on tens of mystery novels under the joint pseudonym Kelley Roos, and his father also wrote plays and the books for musicals. Roos feels lucky to have been exposed to professional writers so early in life. "It was very exciting to read wonderful books," he explained, "and then meet the men and women who wrote them." Around age ten, he started reading his parents' books, which he loved. He also was stagestruck from an early age.

Early Writing Reflects Childhood Concerns

Around fifth or sixth grade, his parents "started really vagabonding" around Europe with Roos in tow, and he found "this was not so hot for me." He decided to express his unhappiness by writing a story about a family that moved around too much. He gave it to his parents, and their reaction was not what he hoped for. He wanted them to settle down and lead a normal life, but they responded to his talent with comments like, "What a good writer you are! You should submit this to your school magazine." Roos thought this was "a very frustrating connection emotionally, but as a young writer I was always encouraged."

Ultimately, though, writing the story was an affirming experience. Roos explained, "I was able to say 'this is too much' by writing the story, and I did get my point across." Roos returned to live in the United States at a prep school in Connecticut while his parents stayed in Europe—where they remained until after Roos graduated from college.

Loomis School was a mixed bag for Roos. He got to live in one place, "but not as I would have wanted," he explained, "with my parents in a nice suburban house." However, prep school did provide some of the stability he craved. Roos's experiences at the Loomis School became the basis for his first book for older kids, *Confessions of a Wayward Preppie.* His first books were generally light comic novels, and Roos wanted a slightly darker tone, which Mary M. Burns of *Horn Book* calls "wryly touching, sometimes humorous." The story is about what Roos calls an "intellectual crime," that is, an instance of cheating, and he feels the ultimate theme of the book is about responsibility. Burns concurs, noting that while the book is "readable and fast-moving" it also works as "a fascinating consideration of responsibility—to oneself, one's friends, and to the larger community."

Roos went on from Loomis School to study at Yale University; he changed majors frequently before settling on a degree in history. He says he was "not a wonderful student," but he loved going to school. At this time, he noted, "I had no idea what I was going to do with any of it." A great pleasure for him at this time was writing the book and lyrics to two college musicals. As for a career as a writer, Roos believes he "probably had a sense of competition" with his parents about writing. This took the guise of Roos telling himself that while he liked to write, he really didn't have a "message to convey, no point to make."

As a result, after graduation Roos went on to the Radcliffe Publishing Procedures course and then spent more time in Europe, studying in Stockholm and traveling in Greece and Eastern Europe. When he returned home, he found a job writing ad copy for the marketing department of Harper & Row. "That was really my introduction to children's books," he remarked in his interview. At Harper Roos began to read all the books from their children's list. "The most creative writers," he noted, "were on the children's list—E. B. White, Maurice Sendak." Harper's had an enormous list of books, and Roos read "hundreds and hundreds" of them for fun.

Drawn to Reading—and Writing—Children's Books

The author's love of reading children's books led him to try his hand at writing them. Occasionally, he'd read a book and think, "I can do better than that." So, as he recounted, he would "try to write a good version of a bad book." But the results were not successful—he described these early attempts as "terribly embarrassing, horrible, horrible things." In retrospect, Roos thinks it would have made better sense to emulate good writers

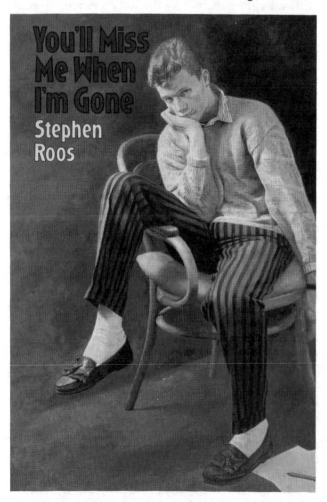

Roos turned from comedy to realism in this powerful story of a teenager coming to terms with his alcoholism. (Cover illustration by Allan Manham.)

who he admired. And, of course, later on he was influenced by writers whose work he liked very much. He feels, however, that the most important thing for new writers is "just trying, starting wherever you can. Any beginning," he said, "is a good beginning."

After eight years in the marketing department, Roos moved to a junior editor position. He had wanted to be an editor for some time, but there weren't any openings in the children's division, so he accepted a position in the adult trade department. But after four years, he felt he wasn't going where he wanted to in his career. "I just knew I had to take a chance," he related. "That's when I made the break for it—to write."

He quit his job with the idea that he would try writing for a year. He had enough money to last a year, a small house in upstate New York, and a place to stay in Key West for the winter. "I gave myself a year," he reported, "to get one nice word, from anybody, about my writing, and then I would continue." Roos's first project was to write an adult novel. He found an agent, but the manuscript was never published. He also started a book for teenagers called *My Horrible Secret.* He spent three months on it, "but nothing happened," Roos said; "it just didn't come alive." So he put the project aside, and all he had left was a title that he liked very much. Then he came up with the idea of a book about a boy who can't throw a baseball. Despite his doubts about whether throwing a ball was a worthy enough subject, Roos went ahead and started putting it together. In three or four months, he finished the manuscript.

Around that time, Roos was walking down 57th Street in New York when he ran into George Nicholson, then head of Delacorte. Nicholson asked Roos what he was doing, and Roos told him about the manuscript. Nicholson's response, according to Roos, was "Well, if you send it to us, at least we'll give you a quick rejection." Roos had been in publishing long enough to know this wasn't a bad offer. He also knew Delacorte's list and thought he might be a likely candidate for them. About five days before Roos's one-year deadline, Delacorte accepted the book for publication.

My Horrible Secret turned out to be a very successful book for the first-time author. It sold well in cloth and paperback, was picked up by a book club, and won Roos the Charlie May Simon Award. However there was a downside to this success, Roos explained: "I tried to turn everything I learned from writing the book into a formula for how to write a book. But as you move along, everything's different, and I got a little stuck in it. Recovering from the success of that book is part of the trick because its still the most successful book I've done."

Roos also had a strong reaction to the publication of the book. When first reading the galleys, he felt terribly exposed by the book he had written. "I felt so bad," he says, "that if I could have I would have said, 'Stop the presses and I'll give the money back.' I had no intention of revealing who I was in a book for ten year olds. Even though it's a giddy book, there's more of me than I meant to reveal." In the story fifth-grader Warren not only must face his fear of playing ball, but also his comparisons to his popular and athletic older brother Roger. In his efforts to come up with an alternative to baseball, Warren further embarrasses himself by falling off a horse; he redeems himself, however, by arranging a charity all-star baseball game and overcoming his fear to make a game-saving catch.

Small-Town Life Provides Lessons and Laughs

Roos immediately started on a sequel, *My Terrible Truth,* which takes place in the same town. The focus is on Shirley, Roger's sixth-grade classmate, who is tormented by the bossy Claire and worried about her social life. Roos considers the book his most satiric and comic look at the white-picket-fence small-town life featured in many of his stories. For example, one girl in the book has a nervous breakdown when the stripes on her sheets aren't straight. *My Terrible Truth* is one of Roos's personal favorites. "I was very happy writing that book," he noted. "It's wonderful when something comic is working." He was even amused by what he calls "the first really stinko review" he ever got. It was from a paper in Virginia, and Roos recalled a putdown to the effect that "the kids in this book are so petty than any fifth grader who reads it will not want to become a sixth grader."

After the second book, Roos says, he felt like a professional writer. Beginning with *My Secret Admirer,* his third novel, Roos would sell books to publishers on the basis of an outline. After the outline was accepted, he would write the book. After doing many books this way, Roos is returning to his original method. He feels that some of the creativity is taken away by selling an outline. "I'm going through a period now of loosening up and changing my ways," he said in his interview.

For the first five or so years of his writing career, Roos would write a book and a half each year. Most of the books were humorous in tone, and Roos wanted to make a change by writing about teen depression and suicide in *You'll Miss Me When I'm Gone.* Sixteen-year-old Marcus, the protagonist of the novel, seems to have it all: he gets along at school, with an enjoyable position on the school newspaper, and he has a girlfriend and a car. After wrecking his car, however, and facing the loss of his friends, Marcus must come to terms with his drinking. With the aid of an understanding school psychologist, Marcus accepts that he is an alcoholic and begins to move forward with his life. In *Voice of Youth Advocates,* Becki George commends the author for creating "a very believable character and plot.... Readers will recognize the excuses and rationalizing Marcus uses to justify why and when he drinks." *Horn Book* contributor Elizabeth S. Watson similarly observes that Marcus's problems "are real ones for today's adolescent and believable as part of the plot."

The publication of *You'll Miss Me When I'm Gone,* and Roos's personal experiences growing up, led to his writing a series of books for children living in alcoholic and other dysfunctional families. Roos pitched the idea to a couple of mainstream editors, but they weren't interested "because it smacked of bibliotherapy," he related. So Roos put the idea aside and continued working on more commercial projects.

Children of Problem Families Featured in Series

A few years later, he got a call from an editor at Hazelden, a publisher of educational materials, who wanted to pick up the Dell edition of *You'll Miss Me When I'm Gone* for their catalogue. While talking, Roos was reminded of his children of alcoholics idea, and he suggested it to the editor at Hazelden. The editor loved the idea, and Roos began to write the four-book "Maple Street Kids" series. Tara's parents in *Dear Santa: Make Me a Star* are recovering alcoholics, and Tara, in response, becomes the "perfect daughter." Rooney in *My Blue Tongue* is always playing outrageous pranks and telling huge lies to distract herself and everyone else from her father's gambling addiction. Families in the other books include a mother addicted to prescription drugs and a boy whose much-loved uncle is alcoholic.

Susan Hogan/Albach writes in the *Duluth News-Tribune* that "the impact of addictions on families isn't a subject typically tackled in children's books," making Roos's books "terrific tools of understanding and reassurance." *School Library Journal* contributor Kenneth E. Kowen calls *My Blue Tongue* "a commendable undertaking," but feels that Roos "takes the easy way out" since problems are resolved "with speed and ease." In contrast, Pamela K. Bomboy, also writing in *School Library Journal* describes the books as "written with a great deal of warmth and care."

After a particularly busy and productive period when Roos was writing three books of his "Pet Lovers Club" series in addition to the Hazelden books, Roos found himself physically and spiritually depleted. There was a year when he found himself totally blocked and unable to write, and Roos noted "I haven't been a good sport about it."

But this period of quiet seems to be leading Roos in new directions as a writer. His current project takes place in a very different setting from the idyllic small towns he usually writes about. This book is about a decaying neighborhood of Victorian homes along the Old Post Road in Connecticut. What had once been a genteel neighborhood of elegant Victorian houses is now a mix of strip malls and rundown apartments, Jiffy Lubes, and funeral homes. Roos commented, "The book seems to be about a kid who wants to be an artist, to draw. I wonder," he asked aloud, "whether I'm going to deal with this writer's block problem through this kid?"

"What I want to relearn," he said in his interview, "is just to enjoy the writing more." For Roos the creative act seems to be the most important thing. As he said in his acceptance speech for the Charlie May Simon

Medallion, "As I move along in my writing, I find I'm grateful for the surprises and for the arduousness. It makes my work a challenge; it makes my life interesting to me."

■ Works Cited

Bomboy, Pamela K., review of the "Maple Street Kids" series, *School Library Journal,* June, 1992, pp. 124.

Burns, Mary M., review of *Confessions of a Wayward Preppie, Horn Book,* September/October, 1986, p. 593.

Flanagan, Kate M., review of *My Terrible Truth, Horn Book,* February, 1984, p. 55.

George, Becki, review of *You'll Miss Me When I'm Gone, Voice of Youth Advocates,* April, 1988, p. 29.

Hogan/Albach, Susan, "Hazelden Books Help Children of Addicts," *Duluth News-Tribune,* December 29, 1991.

Kowen, Kenneth, review of *My Blue Tongue, School Library Journal,* June, 1992, pp. 124-25.

Roos, Stephen, interview with Ira Brodsky for *Something about the Author,* conducted on July 28, 1993, in New York City.

Watson, Elizabeth S., review of *You'll Miss Me When I'm Gone, Horn Book,* March/April, 1988, p. 211.

■ For More Information See

PERIODICALS

Bulletin of the Center for Children's Books, March, 1983, p. 132.

Center City Review, Special Edition 1991, p. 3.

Publishers Weekly, September 20, 1991; October 18, 1993, p. 73.

School Library Journal, May, 1983, p. 76; January, 1984, p. 80; July, 1992.

—Sketch by Ira Brodsky

S

SALASSI, Otto R(ussell) 1939-1993

OBITUARY NOTICE—See index for *SATA* sketch: Born October 2, 1939, in Vicksburg, MS; died of liver disease, February 10, 1993, in Fayetteville, AR. Librarian and writer. Salassi is remembered for his young adult literature, particularly his 1987 novel *Jimmy D, Sidewinder, and Me,* which received a notable book citation from the American Library Association. Salassi began his career working as a mathematician with Douglas Aircraft Company after serving with the U.S. Air Force. He received his master's degree in library science in 1968, then began a series of library-related jobs at schools such as Bemidji State College, Motlow State Community College, and the University of Arkansas. Turning to writing full time, Salassi also found time to teach at the University of Arkansas, William Smith College, and Hobart College. His other young adult novels include *On the Ropes* and *And Nobody Knew They Were There.* He also contributed stories to periodicals such as *Boys' Life* and *Southern Humanities Review.*

OBITUARIES AND OTHER SOURCES:

BOOKS

Sixth Book of Junior Authors, H. W. Wilson, 1989, pp. 259-260.

PERIODICALS

New York Times, February 12, 1993, p. B7.
School Library Journal, April, 1993, p. 24.

*   *   *

SALZMAN, Marian 1959-

■ Personal

Born February 15, 1959, in New York, NY; daughter of Norman (a business executive) and Ruby (a consultant; maiden name, Freeman) Salzman; *Education:* Brown University, B.A., 1980; attended Harvard University Graduate School of Arts and Sciences.

MARIAN SALZMAN

■ Addresses

Home—666 Greenwich Street, Apartment 1103, New York, NY 10014. *Office*—BKG Youth, 79 Fifth Ave., New York, NY 10003.

■ Career

Career Insights Magazine, Providence, RI, editor, 1981-83; freelance writer, 1983-86; *Management Review Magazine,* New York City, editor, 1984-85; Kehoe, White, Savage & Company, New York City, director of media relations, 1986-88; *CV: The College Magazine,* editor-in-chief, 1988-89; BKG Youth Inc., New York City, president and creative director, 1989—. Brown University Club, director, 1986-89.

■ Awards, Honors

Susan Colver Rosenberger Prize in sociology, Brown University, 1980; Dorot Foundation fellowship, 1980; New York Public Library "Best Book for the Teenage" Award, 1992.

■ Writings

(With Deidre Sullivan) *Inside Management Training,* NAL/Plum, 1985.
(With Nancy Marx) *MBA Jobs!,* AMACOM, 1986.
(With Nancy Marx Better) *Wanted: Liberal Arts Graduates,* Doubleday/Anchor, 1987.
(With Ann O'Reilly) *War and Peace in the Persian Gulf: What Teenagers Want to Know,* Peterson's Guides, 1991.
(With Teresa Reisgies) *Greetings from High School,* Peterson's Guides, 1991.
(With Teresa Reisgies) *150 Ways Teens Can Make a Difference,* Peterson's Guides, 1991.
(With Deidre Sullivan) *Kids Can Do,* William Morrow/Avon, 1994.

Contributor to *Beauty Handbook, The Brown University Family Therapy Letter, Forbes,* and *Self.*

■ Work in Progress

Generation Rap, a book for parents about the generation gap between them and their teens; broad-based research on twentysomethings; on teen culture, especially a day in the lives of teens; and on family life in America.

■ Sidelights

Marian Salzman told *SATA:* "About my life: It's probably not all that surprising that I have made my professional career an extension of high school and college—both times were remarkably happy for me. I have always been over-committed. By day I work in an office and fly around the country. By night I am a book addict, reading, writing, and thinking about book ideas. I have also been both sociable and something of a loner. When I was in junior high, I clearly remember deciding to write a book documenting the perils of growing up in suburbia, of growing up as the oldest of three sisters who are all born within thirty-two months, and of fighting the stereotype of being a giggly blonde. Recently I found some of my notes and, while they are funny, they never would have cut it as a book. But, not surprisingly, I did author a book for teenagers about making the transition from junior high to high school, and I did get the opportunity to rag on things like zits, the long wait for a driver's license, and the anticlimactic prom.

"I spent a very happy, stimulating three years at Brown University just as it was emerging as the hot school. This dramatically altered my thinking: what college taught me was that, provided you could maintain the stamina to last through the all-nighters, everything is possible. You just have to dream and persevere. After Brown I floated for a while, tried graduate school, and then helped found a career magazine for college students. For three years I was an editor, a typist, an advertising salesperson, and a work junkie. That experience helped to shape my future professional expectations since I learned how to stay enthusiastic and interested for fifty, sixty, seventy hours a week.

"Now, more that ten years later, life is simpler. The good news is that I can still roam the country, looking for the next story or trend, counseling clients that want to touch young markets; the bad news is that no one asks me for identification when I sit down at a bar or cocktail lounge. Thus, for me, the last rite of passage is behind me: I am truly an adult whose professional role model is 'Harriet the Spy.' That's what I expected to be at fifteen and what I am at thirty-three. I am also the proud owner of a bloodhound named Sam, and a golden retriever named Tyler. For now, the pups (all two hundred pounds of them) and I are happily living in Greenwich Village, thinking about the day when we could move, for weekends at the very least, to a place where there is green grass and clean air. Fat chance that day will ever come!

"About my company: BKG Youth formulates, executes, and analyzes custom and syndicated youth research. We serve as a direct link between marketers and young people ages four to thirty. We are a recognized leader in identifying youth trends, attitudes, and consumer behavior. I founded the company in the winter of 1989-90 and have expanded it rapidly since then, thanks primarily to the high-quality colleagues I have assembled in offices in New York City and Los Angeles. Our clients have included Cosmepak, Espirit, *Esquire,* Mastercard, Nintendo, *Rolling Stone, Teen,* and the United States Post Office. We produce the National Teen Summit, an annual meeting of student leaders sponsored by corporations which wish to impact high school students and publish *nachur ov realitees,* a bi-monthly trend-analysis report created to give subscribers—which include DDB Needham, *Details,* K-Mart, Nike, and more than fifty others—a new perspective on youth culture.

"What BKG Youth is best known for is its ability to reach young people across America and to speak to these kids, teens, and young adults in their own language, relating to them in terms of their own attitudes, interests, and needs. Sometimes we find out the zaniest things; for example: a survey that BKG Youth conducted for *Esquire* magazine interviewed one thousand college students in the United States. The results, among other items, showed that seventy-three percent of the students believe in God, ten percent have had sex in a school library, and fifty-two percent stated a belief that they had done something in college that would disqualify them from political office. On a more serious note, citing one of BKG Youth's recent surveys of young people, the author of 'Green Teens,' an article in *New York Times Magazine* on March 8, 1992, noted that 'more than seventy-five percent championed the environment as their favorite cause—over homelessness, AIDS, illiteracy, and drug abuse.'"

One of Salzman's many books, *150 Ways Teens Can Make a Difference* (for grades eight to twelve), offers quick and easy information for young adults who want to know the practical aspects of volunteer work. One important concept reported in the book is how to match one's personality and talents to a job. Pat Braun in *Booklist* says, "it clearly demonstrates that teen volunteers feel good about themselves and the jobs they accomplish." At the end of the book is a list of groups, organized state by state, that teens can contact. About Salzman's *Greetings from High School,* written with the help of Teresa Reisgies and several thousand teenage contributors, *Booklist* summarizes the book as "an upbeat catchall geared to the college-bound teen [that] contains advice on everything from getting along in school to dating and stress." *School Library Journal* contributor Dona Weisman notes that the book is "well organized and ... easy-to-read" and comments that *Greetings from High School* should be a "popular and useful book."

■ Works Cited

Braun, Pat, review of *150 Ways Teens Can Make a Difference, Booklist,* February 1, 1992, p. 1019.
Review of *Greetings from High School, Booklist,* June 1, 1992, p. 1727.
Weisman, Dona, *School Library Journal,* November, 1991, pp. 143-44.

■ For More Information See

PERIODICALS

New York Post, March 12, 1992.
School Library Journal, April, 1992, p. 161.
Wilson Library Bulletin, June, 1991, pp. 113-14.

*   *   *

SCAMELL, Ragnhild 1940-

■ Personal

Given name pronounced "roundhill"; born March 20, 1940, in Copenhagen, Denmark; daughter of Viggo (in business) and Karin Marie (a homemaker; maiden name, Bennedsen) Holdt; married Ernest Harold Scamell (an attorney), September 11, 1977; children: Cleere; stepchildren: Grant, Adrian, Joanna, Amanda. *Education:* Educated in Denmark to A-level standard, followed by commercial college; Institute of Linguists, London, 1985. *Politics:* Conservative. *Religion:* Church of England. *Hobbies and other interests:* Painting, reading, classical music.

■ Addresses

Home and office—Woodsdale Farmhouse, Pope Street, Godmersham, Kent CT4 7DN, England.

■ Career

Freelance translator, 1985—; author of books for children. *Member:* Institute of Linguists (London), Ashford Art Society.

■ Writings

Solo Plus One, illustrated by Elizabeth Martland, Little, Brown, 1992.
Buster's Echo, HarperCollins, 1993.
Three Bags Full, Orchard Books, 1993.

■ Work in Progress

More books involving animals.

■ Sidelights

Ragnhild Scamell told *SATA:* "Although my first book was published only in 1992, I have, in fact, always been writing for children. Short stories published in magazines and longer stories clutter every drawer in my study. I was born in Denmark, the first of four daughters, into a huge and very close family, but I soon found my way across the North Sea to my adopted country, England.

"*Solo Plus One,* was inspired by my own Siamese cat, whose ferocious behavior belies his need for unconditional tenderness and who takes cover under our labrador dog when all else fails. The story was based on the

A generous sheep is left in the cold after she donates her wool to her friends in Ragnhild Scamell's picture book. (Cover illustration by Sally Hobson.)

findings of Konrad Lorenz, whose theory of imprinting states that a newly hatched gosling will follow the first object it sees, be it a cardboard box, a man, or a balloon—or a bad cat? I turned the gosling into a duckling, and the story began."

Solo Plus One is the story of a cat who likes to eat eggs until he finds one that is not raw. A duckling pops out, mistakes the cat for its mother, and proceeds to follow the cat everywhere. Eventually the cat is able to return the baby duck to its real mother. *Horn Book* says, "Bold illustrations of the substantial black cat and the little, misinformed duckling lend color to an amusing story."

Scamell also told *SATA:* "I live with my husband, three cats, and a dog in a large rambling house surrounded by fields full of sheep and cattle. We live in the heart of Kent's most beautiful countryside, a few miles from Canterbury. Naturally, it is here that I find my inspiration, and my next three books, are set in the surrounding area. They all involve animals going about their important daily business. I hope they are humorous."

■ Works Cited

Horn Book, May, 1992, p. 334.

■ For More Information See

PERIODICALS

Kirkus Reviews, March 15, 1992, p. 398.
Publishers Weekly, May 11, 1992, p. 71.

*   *   *

SCHANZER, Ros
  See SCHANZER, Rosalyn

*   *   *

SCHANZER, Rosalyn 1942-
  (Ros Schanzer, Roz Schanzer)

■ Personal

Born November 26, 1942, in Knoxville, TN; daughter of Sam Good (an architectural engineer) and Bess (Mark) Good Hazelwood (a homemaker); married Steve Schanzer (director, Intelligence Systems Secretariat), July 24, 1966; children: Adam, Kim. *Education:* University of Cincinnati, B.F.A. and B.S., 1964. *Religion:* Jewish. *Hobbies and other interests:* Travel, swimming, photography, soccer.

■ Addresses

Home and office—11630 Havenner Rd., Fairfax Station, VA 22039.

ROSALYN SCHANZER

■ Career

Hallmark Cards, Kansas City, MO, designer, 1964-71; freelance illustrator of books, magazines, posters, and filmstrips, 1971—. George Washington University, assistant professorial lecturer in art, 1984-89. *Member:* Children's Book Guild of Washington.

■ Awards, Honors

The Golden Happy Birthday Book was listed as one of the twenty-five best picture books of the year by *Saturday Review of Books,* 1976; Best in Show and Dukane Gold Camera Award, International Film Festival, 1980, for *Comparing Sizes* (filmstrip); *All about Hanukkah* was voted one of the three best Jewish picture books of the year by the Jewish Book Council, 1989.

■ Writings

SELF-ILLUSTRATED

The Beggar's Treasure, Holt, 1973.
(Under name Roz Schanzer) *My First Jewish Word Book,* Kar-Ben, 1992.
Ezra in Pursuit, Doubleday, 1993.
Ezra's Quest, Doubleday, in press.

ILLUSTRATOR UNDER NAME ROZ SCHANZER, EXCEPT WHERE INDICATED

(Under name Rosalyn Schanzer) Barbara Shook Hazen, *The Golden Happy Birthday Book,* Western Golden Press, 1976.
Ranger's Rick's Surprise Book, National Wildlife Federation, 1979.
Animal Architects, National Geographic Society Books for Young Readers, 1987.
Wendy Lewison, *When an Elephant Goes Shopping,* Marvel Monkey Tales, 1988.
Harriet K. Feder, *It Happened in Shushan,* Kar-Ben, 1988.
Jean Waricha, *Ben's Three Wishes,* Marvel Monkey Tales, 1988.
Judye Groner and Madeline Wikler, *All about Hanukkah,* Kar-Ben, 1988.
Where Is the Afikomen?, Kar-Ben, 1989.
Susan Remick Topek, *Ten Good Rules,* Kar-Ben, 1991.
In the Synagogue, Kar-Ben, 1991.
Judy Nayer, compiler, *My First Picture Dictionary,* McClanahan Book Co., 1992.
(Under name Ros Schanzer) Muff Singer, *Puppy Says 1, 2, 3,* Joshua Morris, 1993.

Also illustrator, sometimes under name Roz Schanzer, of several hundred books, posters, magazine articles, games, and filmstrips for children, including the filmstrip *Comparing Sizes,* Harcourt, 1980, and a series of eight books by Dr. Lawrence Balter, *Dr. Balter's Stepping Stone Stories,* Barrons, 1989 and 1990.

■ Work in Progress

Researching material for a third *Ezra* book; six squeeze-and-squeak board books for Joshua Morris.

■ Sidelights

Rosalyn Schanzer told *SATA,* "I made my debut on Thanksgiving Day, 1942, with a paintbrush in one fist and a Crayola in the other, and I have been coloring ever since. So far, I have colored about three hundred books for kids and an untold number of magazine illustrations, filmstrips, posters, and other items too numerous and sundry to mention.

"Here are some interesting things I have done when I was not chained to my desk watching pictures fall out of my fingers: I have helped sail a very famous sailboat over eight hundred miles from Bermuda to Boston with five men. I have had my dislocated ankle repaired in the jungles of Ecuador by an illiterate peasant who wielded a five-foot machete and told me not to dance for a week. I have flown in a tiny plane through a storm over the ruins of Tikal in Guatemala and have swum past sharks in the reefs of Belize. I have taught illustration to graduate students at George Washington University and have been a very good lap swimmer, a pretty good photographer, and a not-too-great karate doer (might for right!).

"I have been married to my husband, Steve, since 1966, and we have two great kids whom we adopted in El Salvador and Ecuador; Adam, born in 1975, who plays a mean game of soccer, and Kim, born in 1980, who is a real beauty. We also have a dog named Jones.

"In addition to my regular work, I have just finished spending a gigantic portion of the last five years researching, writing, and illustrating two books for Doubleday, *Ezra in Pursuit* and *Ezra's Quest.* These books represent a real breakthrough for me. They attempt to put the reader right into each painting, sort of like Alice in *Through the Looking Glass.* The text and art are funny, historically accurate, and full of outrageous characters, authentic detail, and surprising twists and turns. I have also tried extremely hard to make these books different from anything that's been done before, and I hope I have succeeded, because these are the books for which I would prefer to be known."

*   *   *

SCHANZER, Roz
See SCHANZER, Rosalyn

*   *   *

SCHELLER, Melanie 1953-

■ Personal

Born February 2, 1953. *Education:* University of North Carolina at Greensboro, B.S., 1975; University of North Carolina at Chapel Hill, Master of Public Health, 1977, Master of Education, 1991. *Hobbies and other interests:* Aerobic dancing and reading mystery novels.

■ Addresses

Home and office—819 Demerius St., Apt. N3, Durham, NC 27701.

■ Career

Author of children's books and freelance health writer. Health and Safety Office, University of North Carolina at Chapel Hill, information and communication specialist, 1982-84; *Medical Self-Care,* contributing editor, 1986-90; Design and Technology Center of the School of Nursing, University of North Carolina at Chapel Hill, educational media specialist, 1991 and 1992. Scheller has utilized her writing skills and knowledge of health-related concerns as a volunteer for such organizations as the Durham, North Carolina Arts Council, the American Red Cross, YWCA, and VISTA.

■ Awards, Honors

Creative Journalism Competition winner, North Carolina Writer's Network, 1989; New Books of Merit citation, *Five Owls,* 1992, for *My Grandfather's Hat.*

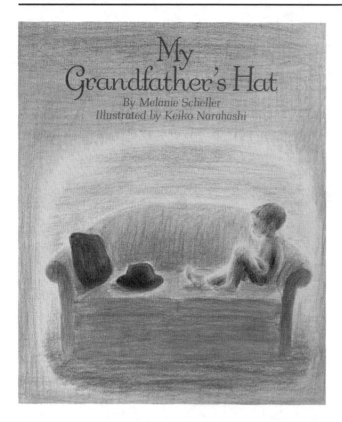

Melanie Scheller debuted as a children's author with this 1992 picture book. (Cover illustration by Keiko Narahashi.)

■ Writings

My Grandfather's Hat, illustrated by Keiko Narahaski, Macmillan/Margaret K. McElderry, 1992.

Scheller has also published a number of articles on health-related issues in such periodicals as *Medical Self-Care, American Baby, The Independent Weekly,* and *Woman's World.*

■ Work in Progress

Several picture books and one nonfiction book for middle school readers.

*   *   *

SCHINDEL, John 1955-

■ Personal

Born July 20, 1955, in Norwalk, CT; son of Morton Schindel (a children's film producer) and Ellen (an early childhood education specialist; maiden name, Bamberger) DeFranco; married Linda Fogel (a technical writer and editor); children: Celia. *Education:* New School for Social Research, B.A., 1981. *Hobbies and other interests:* Cooking, sight-seeing, walking, going to parks and the zoo.

■ Addresses

Home—4335 Everett Ave., Oakland, CA 94602.

■ Career

Weston Woods Studios, Weston, CT, voice editor and filmmaker, 1973-82; Magic Lantern Productions and Jester Inc., Asheville, NC, filmmaker, 1983-87; picture book writer, 1988—; University of California, Berkeley Extension, instructor in children's picture book writing, 1992—. *Member:* Author's Guild, California Academy of Sciences, Oakland Museum, Oakland Zoo.

■ Awards, Honors

Children's Choice Award, International Reading Association, 1992, for *"Who Are You?"*

■ Writings

"Who Are You?", illustrated by James Watts, Margaret K. McElderry Books, 1991.
I'll Meet You Halfway, illustrated by James Watts, Margaret K. McElderry Books, 1993.
Something's Fishy, illustrated by Maryann Cocca-Leffler, Simon & Schuster, 1993.

Also author of screenplays for children's films, including *Paper Wings,* Churchill Films, 1985, and *Waffles,* Churchill Films, 1986.

■ Work in Progress

Two picture book manuscripts: *Dear Papa,* for Albert Whitman and Company; and *What's for Lunch?,* for Lothrop, Lee, and Shepard Books.

JOHN SCHINDEL

■ Sidelights

John Schindel told *SATA:* "I came to write picture books from being a filmmaker. I once worked at Weston Woods Studios, producers of book-based films for children, where I was surrounded by some of the best children's books ever written. It was there that I learned what makes a picture book tick.

"I admire the work of many picture book writers: William Steig, Tomi Ungerer, Ruth Krauss, Robert McCloskey, Beatrix Potter, and Arnold Lobel, to name a few. Their stories are timeless and speak to everyone, not just to children. They grab hold of us. Their voices are strong, vibrant, and clear. They are wonderful storytellers and masters of the picture book form.

"When I write, images and scenes appear in my mind as though I am watching a movie. I strive to find just the right words to express what I see and feel, to make my story and characters come alive. When my story is done I tape-record what I've written, then close my eyes and listen. Hopefully the images and scenes will come flowing back to me with the story in focus."

■ For More Information See

PERIODICALS

Booklist, February 15, 1993, p. 1068.
Kirkus Review, July 15, 1991, p. 935.
Publishers Weekly, March 1, 1993, p. 55; April 12, 1993, p. 61.
Sacramento Bee, March 7, 1992.
San Francisco Examiner, December 10, 1991.
School Library Journal, February, 1992, p. 78.

*   *   *

SCHLEICHERT, Elizabeth 1945-

■ Personal

Surname is pronounced "shly kurt"; born October 30, 1945, in Boston, MA; daughter of William James (a management consultant) and Lucia (a homemaker; maiden name, Woodworth) Parker; married Robert Schleichert (a general contractor), September 18, 1982; children: one son. *Education:* Smith College, B.A., 1967; attended University of Vienna, Austria, 1968-69; Rutgers University, M.A., 1970; Loyola College, graduate study, 1986-87. *Hobbies and other interests:* Running, biking, photography, gardening.

■ Addresses

Home—Suburban Washington, DC.

■ Career

Rye Country Day School, Rye, NY, social studies teacher, 1970-73; St. Agnes School, Alexandria, VA, history and psychology teacher, 1979-81; freelance editor for publications, including *National Geographic Traveler* and *Smithsonian,* 1981-83; *National Geographic Traveler,* Washington, DC, regional editor, 1983-88; freelance writer, 1988—. Open University, adult education teacher, 1981-82; United Church of Christ, Seneca Valley, head of adult education, 1987-89.

■ Writings

The Life of Elizabeth Blackwell, Twenty-first Century Books, 1991.
The Life of Dorothea Dix, Twenty-first Century Books, 1991.

Contributor to books, including *Treasures of the Smithsonian,* Smithsonian Books, 1983; *Crimes and Punishments* (part of the "Library of Curious & Unusual Facts" series), Time-Life Books, 1991; and *Ecology* (part of the "Understanding Science & Nature" series), Time-Life Books, 1992. Writer of educational filmstrips for the National Geographic Society, including *The GeoTrek,* 1992, and *A First Look at Energy,* 1993. Contributor to numerous magazines, including *Cat Fancy* and *AAA World.*

■ Work in Progress

Concentrating on writing filmstrips and magazine articles, and working on a museum exhibit.

ELIZABETH SCHLEICHERT

■ Sidelights

Elizabeth Schleichert told *SATA:* "How I got to write two books for Twenty-first Century publishers is an interesting story. I had answered an ad that appeared in the Sunday edition of the *Washington Post* which read something like this: 'Local publisher seeks authors for children's book series of biographies. Send resume and cover letter to . . . .' So I dutifully followed the instructions and never heard a word. Since that has been my experience in answering classifieds through the paper, I didn't give it much thought.

"But then about two months later, I was again perusing the Sunday classifieds under 'W' for writers when I recognized the same ad with the same address. I realized I felt frustrated and didn't know how to proceed. If I were to send them a frustrated and sassy note, that would doom my chances, yet I felt a strong urge to try again. Something told me I was suited to this job, whatever it was, so I sat down at my computer and dashed off a limerick about a freelance writer who kept answering ads but nothing ever came of it, and me oh my, what was I to do (all in verse, of course). Well, within two days the phone rang, and it was Twenty-first Century Books saying they liked my poem and could I come have a chat with them?

"While I didn't expect this approach to work, it was the instinct that this was something I could do that drove me to keep at it. And to me that's the key in this freelance writing business. For every rejection letter I get from a publisher, whether it be for an article or for a book idea, I figure there is someone out there who will say yes. One article I wrote, about a beautiful part of West Virginia, was submitted to about ten or twelve newspapers, Middle Atlantic magazines, and airline and auto travel magazines, and every one wrote back 'no thanks, doesn't suit our editorial needs.' Finally, on the thirteenth or fourteenth try, I got a 'yes.'

"It's a crazy business, but my intention is to hang in there with it. I have to bring in a certain income every month to make ends meet in the family, so much of my writing time is taken up with contract projects which I do on a regular basis for area publishers. These are fun, but time-consuming, leaving me less time than I would like for doing my own research and proposals for new books. Having an active six-year-old at home, while being a wonderful source of fun and inspiration, also limits the time I can spend on projects.

"In what other profession is the world of the past and the fascinating people and places of then and now one's oyster?"

CAROL SCHWARTZ

SCHWARTZ, Carol 1954-

■ Personal

Born April 3, 1954, in Kansas City, MO; daughter of John (a railroad employee) and Mary (an insurance office manager; maiden name, Cedarland) Mullenix; married Robert Schwartz (executive director of Industrial Designers Society of America), July 27, 1975; children: Zachary, Allison. *Education:* Attended Rhode Island School of Design (mobility program), 1975-76; Kansas City Art Institute, B.F.A., 1976. *Hobbies and other interests:* Gardening.

■ Addresses

Home—8311 Frontwell Circle, Gaithersburg, MD 20879. *Agent*—Dilys Evans, P.O. Box 400, Norfolk, CT 06058.

■ Career

Kircher and Associates, Washington, DC, designer/illustrator, 1976-77; Wickham and Associates, Washington, designer/illustrator, 1977-78; Graphichouse Ltd., Washington, designer/illustrator, 1978-79; Stansbury, Ronsaville Wood, Inc., Annapolis, MD, staff illustrator, 1979-81; freelance illustrator, 1981-89; freelance illustrator of children's books, 1989—. *Exhibitions:* Society of Illustrators Original Art Exhibition, 1991; Illustrators' Club Second, Fifth, and Sixth Annual Exhibitions. *Member:* Society of Children's Book Writers and Illustrators, Illustrators' Club of Washington, DC, Virginia, and Maryland, Children's Book Guild (Washington, DC).

■ Awards, Honors

Outstanding Science Trade Book for Children, National Science Teachers Association/Children's Book Council Joint Committee, 1991, and Best of Category Award, Illustrators' Club Fifth Annual Exhibition, both for *Sea Squares;* Best of Category Award, Illustrators' Club Sixth Annual Exhibition, for *Good Night to Annie.*

■ Illustrator

Deborah Moss, *Lee, the Rabbit with Epilepsy,* Woodbine House, 1989.
Moss, *Shelly, the Hyperactive Turtle,* Woodbine House, 1989.
The Nutcracker, Dial, 1991.
The Twelve Days of Christmas, Dial, 1991.
Joy Hulme, *Sea Squares,* Hyperion, 1991.
Eve Merriam, *Good Night to Annie,* Hyperion, 1992.
Where's That Insect, Scholastic, 1993.
Where's That Reptile, Scholatic, 1993.
Joanne Ryder, *One Small Fish,* William Morrow, 1993.
Margaret Wise Brown, *Animals in the Snow,* Hyperion, 1994.
Where's That Fish, Scholastic, 1994.
Where's That Cat, Scholastic, 1994.
Elizabeth Lee O'Donnell, *Winter Visitors,* Morrow, in press.
Hulme, *A B Sea,* Hyperion, in press.

■ Sidelights

"Ever since I can remember I've enjoyed art and wanted to be an artist," Carol Schwartz told *SATA.* "My mother says that when I was two-and-a half, I drew a picture of Mickey Mouse and it actually looked like Mickey. My parents encouraged me to draw and when I was twelve I began taking private oil painting lessons. The dream of going to a college that specialized in art became a reality." After college Schwartz worked as an illustrator in several Washington, DC, design studios before she realized that she wanted to illustrate children's books.

"I remember how entertaining and magical books were to me as a child," Schwartz commented. "I hope I can bring some of that to children through my illustrations. My own family has enriched my work. They help me by modeling and by expressing their opinions. I learn from every book I illustrate. Each one is like a new challenge, a new adventure."

MARIE-LOUISE SCULL

SCULL, Marie-Louise 1943-1993

■ Personal

Born April 4, 1943, in Stockholm, Sweden; died September 9, 1993; daughter of Joseph Hilding (a mechanical engineer) and Martha Noren Walter; married George Glenn Rodgers, April, 1978 (marriage ended, May, 1980); married Lynn Corson Scull (typesetter and vice-president, Mim-G Studios, Inc.), September 18, 1980; children: Kristina Louise Dent (deceased). *Education:* Middletown High School, H.S. diploma. *Politics:* Independent. *Religion:* Protestant. *Hobbies and other interests:* Painting, antiques, doll collecting, gardening, and golf.

■ Career

Mim-G Studios, Inc., West Mystic, CT, president and commercial artist, 1972-93. Co-founder of "Cancer and Beyond" (self-help cancer support group for patients and their partners/caregivers serving southeastern Connecticut). *Member:* Mystic Garden Club (garden therapy chair, 1990-92).

■ Illustrator

Margaret Read McDonald, *The Skit Book,* Shoe String Press, 1990.
Connie Colom, editor, *Mystic Seaport's Holiday Cookbook for Children,* Mystic Seaport Museum Stores, 1990.

Bernadine Cook, *Looking for Susie,* Shoe String Press, 1991.

Also illustrator of numerous book cover/jacket designs for Mystic Seaport Museum and Shoe String Press.

■ Work in Progress

Dinosaur research.

■ Sidelights

Marie-Louise Scull told *SATA,* "Many people have commented that my illustrations of children, whether rendered realistically as in 'Susie' or as cartoon characters as in 'The Cookbook,' possess a troll-like quality. This may be due to spending my early years in my homeland, Sweden, where 'Trolls' and 'Tomtes' are very prominent in folklore.

"Early preference for the myriad of fairy tales, Hans Christian Andersen, the Brothers Grimm, Aesop's Fables, and Disney's animations may subconsciously have triggered a desire to write stories with a subtle moral or a positive message.

"Drawing began as soon as I realized the pencil was a magical tool capable of depicting what was in my head. As a teenager the dream was to become a commercial artist, work for Disney and to eventually freelance—write and/or illustrate children's books.

"Derailment and detours along the way have prevented some of this, but the taste has been peaked by the few projects to date. The hope of allocating more time toward the realization of the dream has been fueled, and a couple of projects are on the drawing board.

"Writing and illustrating for today's children offers tremendous challenge. Due to the amount of information targeted at them on a daily basis coupled with the decline of the traditional family (and its values) which forces them to become self-sufficient at a much earlier age, today's children seem far more sophisticated than past generations. It is, at least for me, a challenge both feared and welcomed."

[Sketch reviewed by husband, Lynn Scull]

*   *   *

SHEA, Pegi Deitz 1960-

■ Personal

Born September 22, 1960, in Matawan, NJ; daughter of George A. Deitz (a high school teacher and coach) and Margaret J. (a legal secretary) Devlin; married Thomas F. Shea (a professor of English), July 19, 1986; children: Deirdre Vincena, Thomas Sullivan. *Education:* Graduated from Rutgers College, Rutgers University, 1982. *Politics:* Democrat. *Religion:* Catholic.

PEGI DEITZ SHEA

■ Addresses

Home and office—27 Fox Hill Drive, Rockville, CT 06066.

■ Career

Pegi Deitz Public Relations, president and freelance writer, 1986—. Children's book writer and poet. *Member:* St. Bernard's Christian Service Committee, Society of Children's Book Writers and Illustrators (New England SCBWI Conference Planning Committee member, 1992-93).

■ Awards, Honors

Evelyn Hamilton Award for Creative Writing, Rutgers College, 1982.

■ Writings

Bungalow Fungalow, Clarion, 1991.
Stitches, Boyds Mills, in press.

Pegi Deitz has written promotional materials for companies in the film, video and audio industries. She also writes travel, op-ed, and humorous pieces. Her poetry for adults has appeared in publications including *Dan River Anthology, Connecticut Writer, College Composition and Communications, The Aquarian, Tunxix Review, Connecticut River Review.*

■ Work in Progress

Children's books *Canning Day, Seeing through the Shadows, Walks in France with Uncle Pierre, Romps in Ireland with Cousin Colin, Pierre's Resistance, In the New Moon's Arm, Wonder in My Window, Bumble into Everything, Bumble Everywhere,* and others.

■ Sidelights

Pegi Deitz Shea told *SATA,* "Although I have been writing since I was able to write, I feel it's never too late for anyone to start writing. My first efforts were little poems that I wrote on construction paper for holidays and birthdays. The sight of those cards up on the mantlepiece, quite a place of honor in our home, inspired me to continue. I won two dollars in a poetry contest when I was in fifth grade and thought, 'Wow, this writing business pays!' While it may not have made me wealthy, writing has certainly enriched my life. Writing has opened me up to new lands, new people, new ways of thinking.

"For me, the act of writing melds experience with imagination. A book or poem may be inspired by something I have read, seen, heard, lived. But once I have the kernel of thought, the heat of my imagination makes it explode in unknown directions. Call it 'Shea's Popcorn Theory' of writing. The process is exciting; the result is delicious—most of the time. I have been known to 'burn' a batch now and then.

"To extend my popcorn metaphor a bit, it's extremely important to have other people 'taste' your writing and tell you not only IF it's good or bad, but especially WHY it's good or bad. It may hurt at times to hear that your story needs more work. But keep in mind that you are writing it because you want people to read it, enjoy it. You want your writing to be the best it can be.

"Speaking of reading, I feel that to be a good writer, you have to read a lot and read well. Reading well doesn't mean reading fast or pronouncing words correctly. It means looking for, AND appreciating, all the different meanings words have. Ask yourself, 'Why or how is this sentence funny or sad? What images does the writer use to make me feel a certain way?' By understanding how a story succeeds, you will understand how to make your writing succeed."

*   *   *

SHEEHAN, Patty 1945-

■ Personal

Full name, Patricia Lynne Sheehan; born November 11, 1945, in Montclair, NJ; daughter of William P. Sheehan (an advertising executive) and Louise M. Sheehan (a homemaker). *Education:* Florida Atlantic University, B.A. (magna cum laude), 1967, M.Ed., 1972. *Politics:* Liberal. *Religion:* "Belief in benevolent higher power." *Hobbies and other interests:* Hiking, skiing, acting, singing, dancing, traveling.

■ Addresses

Home and office—3501 Juan Tabo NE, G-10, Albuquerque, NM 87111.

■ Career

Teacher of English as a second language in Spain and Central America, 1969-73; Opportunity Industrialization Center, Albuquerque, NM, adult education teacher and counselor, 1973-75; Albuquerque Public Schools, Albuquerque, elementary teacher, 1975-85; Counseling and Psychotherapy Institute, Albuquerque, counselor and psychotherapist, 1985—. Consultant to schools in New Mexico, and conductor of personal growth seminars, 1992—. Motivational speaker. *Member:* Southwest Writers, Society of Children's Bookwriters, American Association of Counseling and Development, Commission for the Status of Women (board member).

■ Awards, Honors

Kylie's Song selected for Coors National Literacy Campaign, 1990.

■ Writings

Kylie's Song, Advocacy Press, 1988.
Albuquerque Then and Now, Sandia Publishing, 1989.
Gwendolyn's Gift, University of New Mexico, 1989, Pelican, 1991.
Kylie's Concert, Marsh Media, 1993.

PATTY SHEEHAN

Gwendolyn's Gifts

By Patty Sheehan
Illustrated by Claudia Bumgarner-Kirby

Only after trying to make things for herself does Queen Gwendolyn overcome her boredom in Patty Sheehan's story of going against tradition. (Cover illustration by Claudia Bumgarner-Kirby.)

Also senior editor of *Families in Recovery Parenting* magazine, 1989-91.

■ Adaptations

Kylie's Song and *Kylie's Concert* have been recorded on videotape by Marsh Media, 1993.

■ Work in Progress

Another children's story for Advocacy Press, and researching "wildlife in Glacier National Park for *Kylie's Concert* teachers' guide."

■ Sidelights

"As a child," Patty Sheehan told *SATA,* "I loved creating fantasy characters and writing stories. I laughed a lot and made other kids laugh too. I always got us doing dramatic plays, and to this day am involved with my friends in fun and funny activities. I love to draw but haven't yet developed that talent well enough to illustrate my own books.

"I've always been very sensitive to my own and others' feelings and have been interested in why people behave as they do. I remember a play I was part of while in third grade. I had a small singing part and was teased about not singing as well as I could have. Then the teacher reprimanded me for not singing out. My first book, *Kylie's Song,* is about a singing koala, and it reflects the

pain I experienced. Except for drawing and occasional creative writing assignments, very few things I enjoyed were offered at school. I often got bored and would write cartoons and stories for my own amusement as well as for family and friends. They enjoyed the stories, and occasionally, even a teacher would laugh.

"In college I realized that school could be exciting. I studied psychology, sociology, and many other subjects which helped me understand why people acted as they do. I loved discussions with my friends and writing term papers, and became an honor student. It was then that I realized how important it is to get involved in the things you enjoy. Today I have a private practice as a psychotherapist and my stories help children understand their own and others' behavior. As a psychotherapist, trainer, and author of children's books, I work with parent groups, children, and teachers, helping them to build their self-esteem, creativity, and writing skills. All of my work is aimed at helping each of us to trust our own natures to guide us in developing our own uniqueness.

"Now I am writing a lot of songs and taking singing lessons. This is a very exciting challenge, and I am beginning to 'sing out' to small groups."

*   *   *

SILVERSTEIN, Robert Alan 1959-

■ Personal

Born May 17, 1959, in Brooklyn, NY; son of Alvin (a professor and writer) and Virginia B. (a translator and writer; maiden name, Opshelor) Silverstein; married Linda Rose Babeu (a social worker), June 19, 1987; children: Emily Rachel, Jamey David. *Education:* Rut-

Robert Alan Silverstein and daughter Emily.

gers University, B.A., 1982. *Politics:* Democrat. *Hobbies and other interests:* Painting, photography, drawing, fiction writing, song writing, movie watching.

■ Addresses

Office—Avstar Publishing Corp., P.O. Box 537, Lebanon, NJ 08833.

■ Career

Avstar Publishing, Lebanon, NJ, managing editor, 1988—.

■ Writings

WITH PARENTS, ALVIN AND VIRGINIA B. SILVERSTEIN

John, Your Name Is Famous, Avstar, 1989.
Overcoming Acne, Morrow, 1990.
(And illustrator) *Lyme Disease: The Great Imitator,* Avstar, 1990.
Michael: Fun and Facts about a Popular Name, Avstar, 1990.
John: Fun and Facts about a Popular Name, Avstar, 1990.
So You Think You're Fat, Harper, 1991.
Addictions Handbook, Enslow, 1991.
Steroids: Big Muscles, Big Problems, Enslow, 1992.
Smell: The Subtle Sense, Morrow, 1992.
Recycling: Meeting the Challenge of the Trash Crisis, Putnam, 1992.
Food Power!: Proteins, Millbrook, 1992.
Food Power!: Fats, Millbrook, 1992.
Food Power!: Carbohydrates, Millbrook, 1992.
Food Power!: Vitamins and Minerals, Millbrook, 1992.
Saving Endangered Animals, Enslow, 1993.

ILLUSTRATOR

Mice: All about Them, Lippincott, 1980.
Futurelife, Prentice-Hall, 1982.
World of the Brain, Morrow, 1986.

■ Work in Progress

Some Ants Are Farmers, Lothrop; *Eagles, Hawks and Owls,* Golden Press.

■ Sidelights

Robert Alan Silverstein told *SATA:* "I've always wanted to be a writer as far back as I can remember. It's not that surprising since both my parents are writers. (And yet I'm the only one of six children to follow in their footsteps.) A few years ago, when I was offered the opportunity to join my parents in writing children's science books, I jumped at the chance. (I'd much rather write fiction but I have a family to feed!)

"Writing is an extremely fulfilling occupation. Unlike previous paper-pushing office jobs, writing produces a finished product that I can be proud of, and one that I know will help expand and enrich people's minds.

"Recently I fulfilled a lifelong literary ambition. I've been writing short stories since grade school, but I always wanted to write a novel. Over the past year I wrote not one, but three! (Admittedly, two are rather short.) I also wrote and illustrated two picture books. Although I haven't yet placed these projects, I must admit that this accomplishment—even more than the twenty-five children's nonfiction books that I co-authored with my parents—has given me the satisfaction of finally feeling that I've fulfilled my childhood dream to be a writer."

*   *   *

SINCLAIR, Jeff 1958-

■ Personal

Born April 1, 1958, in Toronto, Ontario, Canada; son of Keith (a sales manager) and Kaye (a homemaker) Sinclair; married July 24, 1982; wife's name, Karen (a certified general accountant); children: Brennan, Conner.

■ Addresses

Home—33152 Edgewood Ave., Abbotsford, British Columbia V25 4N5, Canada.

■ Career

Creative director for an international giftwares company, 1984-93; freelance illustrator.

■ Awards, Honors

First Prize, Original Comic Feature, *Vancouver Sun* Newspaper Comic Talent Contest, 1988; First Prize,

Jeff Sinclair and his children

Commercial Cartoon Illustration, International Cartoon Festival, 1991.

■ Illustrator

Raymond Blum, *Mathemagic,* Sterling Publishing, 1991.
Martha Bolton, *TV Jokes and Riddles,* Sterling Publishing, 1992.
George Shea, *On the Road: Fun Travel Games and Activities,* Sterling Publishing, 1992.
Meredith Berk, *Go Ahead—Make Me Laugh,* Sterling Publishing, 1993.
James D. Ertner, *Super Silly Animal Riddles,* Sterling Publishing, 1993.
Raymond Blum, *Math Tricks, Puzzles and Games,* Sterling Publishing, 1993.

■ Work in Progress

On the Plane, an activity book.

■ Sidelights

Jeff Sinclair told *SATA:* "I remember visiting my grandparents in Toronto when I was seven years old. We had moved to Vancouver when I was a baby and didn't get to see them as much as any of us would have liked. My mother and grandmother sent letters back and forth and I would always include a few pieces of artwork. Cartoons of dogs and cats, fishermen and frogs, speedboats and bats. Nana wrote about how talented I was and how I did such nice, neat work. The natural response to such accolades would no doubt generate many more scribbles and scratches and bits of paper sent from afar.

"One Christmas, as we arrived for the holidays on Webb Avenue, while everyone was getting reacquainted and catching up on the family news, Papa called me aside, telling me that he had something special he's like me to see. As he walked me through the dining room and into the kitchen, I was thrilled to find that every scrap of work I had ever sent had found its way onto the wall above the kitchen table.

"Papa told me that art should be put on display for everyone to see and enjoy. He said that every time he sat down at breakfast and looked up at that wall, he would think of me. 'People who have a talent should make use of it. Most people only dream about doing such things.' He said that I was lucky to find something I really liked doing.

"My grandparents have both gone now, but the memories of that place, and the gallery they hung so proudly above the kitchen table, stay with me in my thoughts and dreams. They remind me that I'm very fortunate to possess such a special gift. I'm reminded every time I pick up my pen, living the dream again."

ROBERT KIMMEL SMITH

SMITH, Robert Kimmel 1930-
(Peter Marks)

■ Personal

Born July 31, 1930, in Brooklyn, NY; son of Theodore (in civil service) and Sally (Kimmel) Smith; married Claire Medney (a literary agent), September 4, 1954; children: Heidi, Roger. *Education:* Attended Brooklyn College (now Brooklyn College of the City University of New York), 1947-48.

■ Addresses

Home—Brooklyn, NY. *Agent*—(literary) Claire Smith, Harold Ober Associates, 425 Madison Ave., New York, NY 10017; (television/plays) Lois Berman, WB Agency, 156 East 52 Street, New York, NY.

■ Career

Doyle, Dane, Bernbach (advertising agency), New York City, copywriter, 1957-61; Grey Advertising, New York City, copy chief, 1963-65; Smith & Toback (advertising agency), New York City, partner and writer, 1967-70; full-time writer, 1970—. *Military service:* U.S. Army, 1951-53. *Member:* Authors Guild, Authors League of

America, Dramatists Guild, Eugene O'Neill Theatre Center, Eugene O'Neill Playwrights (co-chair, 1974-75), Kayoodle Club (president, 1969), Society of Children's Book Writers and Illustrators, Writers Guild.

■ Awards, Honors

Named Eugene O'Neill Playwright, 1971, for *A Little Singing, A Little Dancing;* Massachusetts Children's Book Award, 1980, for *Chocolate Fever;* American Library Association Best Book Award, 1983, for *Jane's House;* Dorothy Canfield Fisher Award, 1986, William Allen White Award, 1987, and Mark Twain Award, 1987, all for *The War with Grandpa.*

■ Writings

JUVENILE

Chocolate Fever, illustrated by Gioia Fiammenghi, Coward, 1972.
Jelly Belly, Delacorte, 1981.
The War with Grandpa, illustrated by Richard Lauter, Delacorte, 1984.
Mostly Michael, illustrated by Katherine Coville, Delacorte, 1987.
Bobby Baseball, illustrated by Alan Tiegreen, Delacorte, 1989.
The Squeaky Wheel, Dell, 1992.

"SADIE SHAPIRO" SERIES

Sadie Shapiro's Knitting Book, Simon & Schuster, 1973.
Sadie Shapiro in Miami, Simon & Schuster, 1977.
Sadie Shapiro, Matchmaker, Simon & Schuster, 1979.

NOVELS

Ransom, McKay, 1971.
Jane's House, Morrow, 1982.

OTHER

A Little Singing, A Little Dancing (play; produced at O'Neill Memorial Theatre, July, 1971), published as *A Little Dancing* in *Best Short Plays of 1975,* edited by Stanley Richards, Chilton, 1975.

Also author of several plays and television scripts. Contributor of short fiction to periodicals, writing under pseudonym Peter Marks prior to 1970.

■ Adaptations

Chocolate Fever was adapted for *CBS Story Break,* CBS-TV, 1983; *Jane's House* was filmed for television and aired on CBS-TV during the 1993-94 season.

■ Sidelights

"My philosophy is to write funny about serious things," said Robert Kimmel Smith, summing up his approach to writing for children in an interview with *Something about the Author* (*SATA*). "Underneath the humor there's serious stuff. I just don't let it get too close to the surface." Some of Smith's more memorable heroes include a boy battling weight problems, another at odds

with his grandfather over "territorial rights," and yet another caught in the middle of his parents' divorce. Humor is a key ingredient in all of the author's juvenile books, an ingredient Smith feels works in getting children to open a book in the first place and stay with it until the end. "In addition to being a writer and getting kicks that way," he said to *SATA*, "you also get the feeling that you're doing something worthwhile, and that you're enticing kids to read." While Smith admitted in his interview that that is a peripheral goal ("I'm in this for creative expression, to get stories that are in me down on paper"), he also allowed that it is a rewarding endeavor to give young readers something entertaining: "I've kept various letters, from boys usually, who say to me that they never used to like to read until they read one of my books."

An aversion to reading was never one of Smith's problems; he grew up devouring tales of the Wild West, pioneers, and pirates. Instead of wanting to follow in the characters' footsteps, however, Smith became fascinated with their creators. "I loved reading so much that writers became my heroes," he recalled for *SATA*. Smith's "first flourishing" as a writer began in grammar school, when he started writing short pieces aided by a favorite teacher, Philip Gross. By junior high school, Smith had been put in an accelerated class. He noted that he "did grades seven and eight in a year and a half. I wasn't writing much. I was just trying to keep up with the work." But the compulsion to write was never far away.

At fourteen, Smith had a crucial confrontation with his parents over his choice of career. "I told my parents I wanted to be a writer and they said, quote, 'There's no way you can ever make a living,'" he related to *SATA*. Smith was crushed, but in retrospect understands the reason for their reaction. The Smiths had raised their son during the Depression and viewed a career as good for only one thing—generating income. "Money was a very big thing to them," said Smith. "They told me I had to be self-supporting because there was no family fortune, which I could tell, anyway." Nevertheless, his parents decree "made sense. They thought I should have something to fall back on." Ever practical, Smith told *SATA*, "I immediately thought of going underground. I would work at anything and make a living, but at nights and on weekends I would be a writer and someday I would get my work published and someday I would make a living at it."

As uncomplicated as this plan sounded, the path to Smith's ultimate success as an author was somewhat circuitous. He told *SATA* that "in the next couple of years my parents had convinced me that I should become—a *doctor!*" Resigned, he went off to Brooklyn College ("the only college I could go to because it was free"), where he announced a pre-med major. "I must say I was totally unprepared," Smith admitted in his interview. "I took chemistry, and it was terribly difficult, because math is just anathema to me. To make a long story short, I got an 'A' in English, and I don't even want to tell you what I got in the other things. My heart wasn't in it, and my mind certainly was not." Convinced that the college was going to put him on academic suspension, Smith practiced a "protective move," and left on his own: "I was not yet nineteen years old and I thought I was washed up. My life was over. I was terribly down on myself."

Soon after, Smith had his life changed by an event responsible for redirecting many a young man's life—the United States Army draft. "Luckily for me, they sent me to Germany, where there was a very fine post library," he recalled. Smith read all the books, and then, with other soldiers, started to write musical revues for the service clubs. "I could sing in those days," he added, "and we had a barbershop quartet. I had a lot of things trying to get out of me at that time."

Early Career Provides Lessons in Writing

The next key event in the author's life came when he was discharged from the Army in 1953 and he returned to New York. "I met a young woman who was five feet tall and weighed 98 pounds and loved books and reading as much as I did," Smith reminisced to *SATA*. Set up on a blind date with Claire Medney, Smith remembered that they "went dancing, then to a friend's house, and then talked books and writing until 3 a.m. I went home and told my mother that this was the kind of girl I could marry. And Claire did the same thing! I always say that she was the first person I could tell my dreams to."

Smith and his fellow book-lover were married the following year. In 1957, Smith was hired by New York advertising agency Doyle, Dane, Bernbach. "That's where my education in writing really began," he said in his interview. "I was a copywriter and had to turn out my little pieces of work. Those were very hard but very heady years." Of his beginnings in advertising, Smith recalled: "I found that having a deadline ... is a jolly good idea. It makes you stick-to-it and not dream your day away. So, that sort of discipline has stood me in good stead. You don't write a book in one day. In fact, the mere thought of writing a whole book is sort of staggering. But, if you can write five good pages a day (and you can), then pretty soon you have a book." It was during this time that Smith first saw his name in print—sort of. "I wrote several short stories and even had a few of them published in second rate magazines," he reminisced to *SATA*. Smith took his early pseudonym—Peter Marks—from two nephews named Peter and Mark.

From Doyle, Dane, Bernbach, Smith went on to Grey Advertising in New York as copy chief, writing print and broadcast ads for major clients selling jewelry, fragrances, cruise lines, beers, and many other products. In 1967, he formed Smith & Toback with partner Harvard Toback, but the writing bug had taken hold and this time there was no putting it off. "I really had the feeling that if I broke away and had the time on my hands and worked every day at it, I could write a novel," Smith remarked. "I knew about narrative and could tell

a story. I'm sure now that I was never destined to be a short story writer, where you have to leave a lot of it to the imagination and let the reader fill in. I wanted to tell everything."

By this time, Smith's wife Claire had gone to work as a literary agent for Harold Ober Associates. "She has been the other side of me," acknowledged Smith. "My best editor, the best person to judge whether what I'm writing is any good, and to see some things that I haven't seen in my work."

Appropriately enough, Smith began his new life as a full time writer on New Year's Day, 1970. "I brought my typewriter home from the office, and with fear and trembling set up my desk on the other side of the bed in the corner of the room," he told *SATA*. His first manuscript was based on a story he used to tell his seven-year-old daughter, Heidi, about a boy who loved chocolate more than any other thing. "Actually, the boy was me," Smith admitted. "I have been a chocolate-lover since I was knee-high to a Hershey bar." Every night, Smith would tell Heidi about five minutes' worth of the story. After a couple of weeks, the story was done, but Heidi wanted to hear it again. "I had almost

Robert Kimmel Smith uses humor to deal with the real-life problems kids face—in this case, a boy who is forced to give up his room when his grandfather moves in. (Cover illustration by Richard Lauter.)

forgotten how it went," Smith said, "so, on Heidi's suggestion, I wrote it all out."

Smith's original dream of writing novels began to take shape; eventually he wrote the first hundred pages and outline of a suspense story about a group of affluent children captured by a terrorist organization while being chauffeured by limousine to an exclusive school. "My wife sold that on the first submission to a house called David McKay, who offered me a contract," Smith related to *SATA*. "I never worked as well, as seriously, or to such good effect as I did then. It was a golden time."

Smith spent the rest of that year writing *Ransom,* while *Chocolate Fever* was accepted by Coward. At the time, however, the author was also concentrating on adult novels, especially the "Sadie Shapiro" stories. Sadie is a spry, pink-sneakered septuagenarian—world famous for knitting and jogging—who contributes the royalties from the publication of her knitting book to worthy causes. The series, noted Smith, "did not start out as a trilogy. It started out as one funny book." Of *Sadie Shapiro in Miami,* Jakki Savan of the *St. Louis Post-Dispatch* wrote that the book "is a veritable fairy tale for adults ... reminiscent of old-fashioned stories in which literary heroes are not existential, no social commentary is made and the 'good guys' always triumph in the end."

Books Explore Humorous and Serious Topics

Despite Sadie's success, Smith went back to the juvenile genre at the urging of both his wife and editor, fellow author Ferdinand Monjo. "Ferdinand said, in so many words, that since *Chocolate Fever* was selling so well I was a fool if I didn't write another children's book. I liked and respected him, and at that time, I was having trouble writing the second Sadie book."

The result of Monjo's prodding became *Jelly Belly,* a book that drew, like many of Smith's stories, on personal experience. "I was a fat kid," said Smith in his interview. "And I was fat until I went into the Army. I remember all the names that kids called me." Unlike the book's hero, Smith never went to diet camp, but he did share the character's feelings of low self-esteem. Smith called it his "funniest book. I get mail from kids who say it's the funniest book they've ever read."

Smith's writing took a decidedly serious turn with his next novel, *Jane's House,* the story of a family trying to heal itself after the untimely death of a vivacious wife and mother. When the father remarries a young advertising executive, ten-year-old Bobby and sixteen-year-old Hilary struggle with the newcomer in their mother's house. Jane Briggs-Bunting, writing in the *Detroit Free Press,* claimed that *Jane's House* "is a stunning novel that makes you grin idiotically at one moment and shed silent tears the next." In *The War with Grandpa,* Smith built his story around a comment from his young son Roger, who said he loved his room and never wanted to live anywhere else. "It made me think about how kids make sanctuaries out of their rooms," said Smith in his

SATA interview. In the book, Peter wages "warfare" against a widowed grandfather who comes to live with the family—and takes Peter's bedroom. *The War With Grandpa* was called "an honest tale of a painful family adjustment process" by a *The Baltimore Sun* contributor.

Smith's next book, *Mostly Michael,* is the author's personal favorite. "I don't think it's my best work," he commented. "This book has some rough edges and I kind of like that." Written in diary format covering a one-year period, Smith admitted the book "was very difficult to do. It's a long book, with thousands of scenes. It gives you a feeling of being in a loving family for this one year. They fight with each other, have ups and downs. It's real life."

A diehard baseball fan (with a preference for the New York Mets), Smith used his five years of experience coaching his son's Little League team to write *Bobby Baseball,* a book dedicated to sportscaster Red Barber: "In the book, I became the manager, and my son sort of became the player who dreamed of glory, but we changed it so it's not really about us. I was very happy to be able to drop in some real facts about baseball."

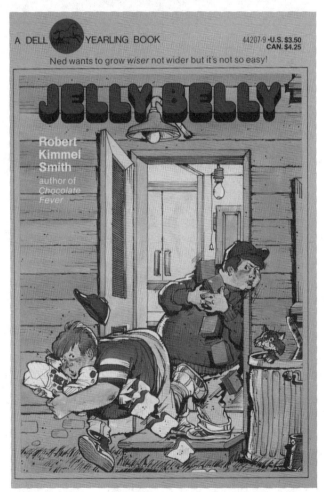

Smith drew on his own experiences as an overweight child to create this funny account of a boy's attempts to slim down. (Cover illustration by Bob Jones.)

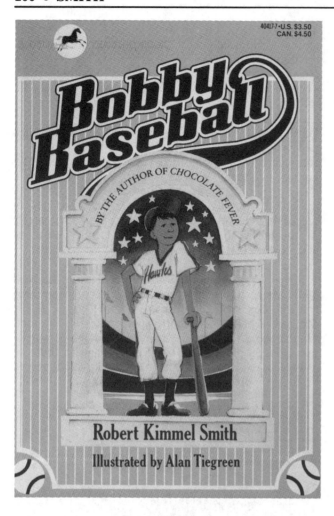

Bobby loves everything about baseball until being on a Little League team coached by his dad puts too much pressure on him. (Cover illustration by Alan Tiegreen.)

Barbara S. McGinn of *School Library Journal* wrote, "Tight writing, humor, and good character development lift this book well above the average for the sports fiction genre." Carolyn Phelan, commenting on *Bobby Baseball* for *Booklist,* said that Smith "delivers his most satisfying performance to date."

A contemporary problem takes center stage in *The Squeaky Wheel,* which was Smith's way of letting kids know "that there is life even after their parents are divorced, and that they must speak up for their rights." The book is told in the first person by sixth-grader Mark Baker, who is struggling to make the transition from his old life to a new one. Denise Wilms, in her review for *Booklist,* noted, "Smith captures well the emotional pain of children in the throes of adjusting to the new and painful changes of divorce."

In his *SATA* interview, Smith observed that his characters are not based on real people (with the exception of Sadie Shapiro, modeled after his wife's aunt). Smith explained for *SATA,* "When I write, I create my own special world. The people I make up—and my writing is all people—are mine. I tell them what to say, what to do, and no one else can do it. If the book or play I'm writing is really working well, then the people I've created start to speak and act for themselves. That's always the best part for me."

Smith said that his writing "has evolved from a carefree, think-of-an-idea and then go to work on it" approach to a more thoughtful and studied one. "I feel more children sitting and looking over my shoulder than I did before. And I've had a couple of run-ins with censorship. Luckily, it seems to be in localized areas, but I see a political movement of certain people wanting to get themselves on school boards, who would like to control what children read and what they think. That's what this is all about, controlling them so they don't question authority."

Of the parents who made the fortunately mistaken prediction that their son would "never make a living writing," Smith said their support of his subsequent career was unflagging; "My father was one of my greatest fans. My parents were absolutely thrilled that I dedicated books to them. There was a literary luncheon held in Fort Lauderdale and I was one of three writers brought in as a main speaker. I would say that that was a high point of their later lives."

■ Works Cited

Briggs-Bunting, Jane, "A Family's Grief," *Detroit Free Press,* November 14, 1982.

McGinn, Barbara S., review of *Bobby Baseball, School Library Journal,* December, 1989, p. 103.

Phelan, Carolyn, review of *Bobby Baseball, Booklist,* November 15, 1989, p. 676.

Savan, Jakki, review of *Sadie Shapiro in Miami, St. Louis Post-Dispatch,* November 6, 1977.

Smith, Robert Kimmel, telephone interview with Julie Catalano for *Something about the Author,* conducted August 6, 1993.

Review of *The War with Grandpa, Baltimore Sun,* August 5, 1984.

Wilms, Denise, review of *The Squeaky Wheel, Booklist,* September 15, 1990, p. 164.

■ For More Information See

PERIODICALS

Booklist, August, 1982, p. 1484.

Horn Book, January/February 1990, pp. 66-67.

Los Angeles Times, November 13, 1977.

Miami Herald, August 7, 1977, p. 7-E.

New York Times Book Review, May 13, 1984.

Publishers Weekly, April 24, 1987; October 27, 1989.

School Library Journal, August, 1982; April, 1984, p. 119; July, 1987; October, 1990.

—Sketch by Julie Catalano

HENRI SORENSEN

SORENSEN, Henri 1950-

■ Personal

Born February 18, 1950, in Aarhus, Denmark; son of Svend Aage (a glazier) and Maren Marie (Jensen) Sorensen; married Lise Winther (a college teacher); children: Mathilde Therese, Alexandra Beatrice. *Education:* Attended University of Aarhus, 1974-80; The Academy of Fine Arts in Aarhus, 1980-83.

■ Addresses

Home—640 Broadway, New York, NY, 10012. *Agent*—Evelyne Johnson Assoc., 201 East 28th Street, New York, NY 10016.

■ Career

Freelance illustrator, 1985—. Worked as a glazier and at a film company making graphics and models.

■ Illustrator

Alvin Tresselt, *Sun Up*, Lothrop, 1991.
Sheila Cole, *When the Rain Stops*, Lothrop, 1991.
Alvin Tresselt, *The Gift of the Tree*, Lothrop, 1992.
Ann W. Dodd, *Footprints and Shadows*, Simon & Schuster, 1992.
Harriet Diller, *Granddaddy's Highway*, Boyds Mills Press, 1992.
Ruth Horowitz, *Mommy's Lap*, Lothrop, 1992.

Nancy W. Carlstrom, *What Does the Rain Play*, Macmillan Children's Book Group, 1993.
Jeff Shepard, *I Know a Bridge*, Macmillan Children's Book Group, 1993.
Laura K. Melmed, *I Love You As Much ...*, Lothrop, 1993.
Jane B. Mason, *River Day*, Macmillan, 1994.
Elaine Moore, *Deep River*, Simon and Schuster, 1994.
Robert Frost Poetry for Young People, edited by Gary D. Schmidt, Magnolia, 1994.

■ Work in Progress

Illustrating *Prince Nautilus*, by Laura K. Melmed, for Lothrop.

■ Sidelights

Henri Sorensen told *SATA:* "As a child I lived near the Art Museum in Aarhus. I went there once or twice a week to look at the paintings from the golden age of Danish painting, which I admired very much. I think that my interest in naturalism and impressionism was formed at that time. When I was a teenager, I was more interested in the non-figurative, abstract expression, but later my interest in naturalism reappeared.

"I knew that I couldn't live as a naturalistic artist in Denmark because it was considered very old fashioned. So after school I was educated as a glazier in my father's company, and later I worked in another company for some years. In my spare time, I always painted. I decided to study art history and went to college and university. During my studies at the university, I found more and more pleasure in painting and less in the theoretical studies, so I decided to study art at the Academy. I had a lot of pleasure painting every day for the next three years. My main interest then, as now, was the impressionistic painting. After finishing the Academy, I worked in a film company where I made graphics and models, but mostly studied lighting. I then discovered that there was a market for my kind of art in advertising and publishing and started working as a freelance illustrator in 1985.

"The thing that means most to me when I read a manuscript is the mood. I always see the mood of the pictures in my head before I start illustrating. Moods are difficult to show in lay-outs. Therefore I prefer to do the finished illustrations at once—and change or re-do them if necessary—rather than be stuck with a lay-out that might hinder the creativity and inspiration, resulting in lifeless illustrations.

"When I illustrate a book, I always hope that my illustrations will appeal both to grown-ups and to children. I'm often surprised to see how much children notice and how important colors are to them. They themselves are extremely good narrative illustrators. Therefore, I disagree with those who think that you have to simplify the mode of expression when illustrating children's books."

STAHL, Hilda 1938-1993

OBITUARY NOTICE—See index for *SATA* sketch: Born September 13, 1938, in Chadron, NE; died March 28, 1993. Author. A prolific writer of books for children and adults, Stahl penned several adventure, romance, mystery, and detective series. She turned to writing after completing a correspondence course in the field and then selling one of her stories to a periodical in the late 1960s. In 1972 she published *Tina's First Love* as part of the "Tina" series and went on in the next two decades to pen more than ninety titles. Among her works are *Undercover* and *Blackmail,* both part of the "Amber Ainslie" detective series; *The Inheritance* and *The Covenant,* both part of "The White Pine Chronicles" series, which she wrote for adults; *Sadie Rose and the Daring Escape,* the first book in her "Sadie Rose" adventure series; and *Disappearance of Amos Pike,* part of the "Wren House" mystery series.

[Date of death provided by free-lance writer Carol Farley.]

* * *

STEFFENS, Bradley 1955-

■ Personal

Born February 10, 1955, in Waterloo, IA; son of Henry Wallace (a machinist) and Marcella Rose (a switchboard operator; maiden name, Krueger) Steffens; married Bonnie Rose Szumski (an editor), July 5, 1980,(marriage ended); children: Ezekiel, Tessa Rose. *Education:* Attended Macalester College, St. Paul, MN, 1973-74. *Religion:* Lutheran. *Hobbies and other interests:* Racquetball, golf, aerobics.

■ Addresses

Home—13628 Pomerado Rd., No. 36, Poway, CA 92064-3539. *Office*—c/o Mitchell International, 9889 Willow Creek Rd., San Diego, CA 92131-1119.

■ Career

Deluxe Check Printers, Inc., St. Paul, MN, copywriter, 1982-87; Gelbach Lee, St. Paul, copywriter, 1987-88; Mitchell International, San Diego, CA, copywriter, 1989-94. *Member:* Society of Children's Book Writers and Illustrators.

■ Awards, Honors

Contemporary Writers Series awards, Depot Arts Center, Duluth, MN, 1985 and 1987; winner of Emerging Voices Competition, The Loft, Minneapolis, MN, 1987; recipient of poetry prizes from *Artemis, New Worlds Unlimited,* the St. Paul Chapter of the American Association of University Women, and the White Bears Arts Council.

BRADLEY STEFFENS

■ Writings

NONFICTION

(With Harry Nickelson) *Vietnam,* Lucent Books, 1989.
(With James House) *The San Francisco Earthquake,* Lucent Books, 1989.
Working Mothers, Greenhaven Press, 1989.
Animal Rights, Greenhaven Press, 1989.
Printing Press: Ideas into Type, Lucent Books, 1990.
The Children's Crusade, Lucent Books, 1991.
Photography: Preserving the Past, Lucent Books, 1991.
Free Speech: Identifying Propaganda Techniques, Greenhaven Press, 1992.
Phonograph: Sound on Disk, Lucent Books, 1992.
The Fall of the Roman Empire, Greenhaven Press, 1994.
Addiction: Distinguishing between Fact and Opinion, Greenhaven Press, 1994.
Censorship, Lucent Books, 1994.
Loch Ness Monster, Greenhaven Press, in press.

PLAYS

Pageant of the Masters, produced in Minneapolis, MN, by KFAI Radio Players, 1979.
Last Stand, produced in Minneapolis, at Playwrights' Center, 1979.
Virodha-Bhakti: A Sequence of Pageants, produced in Minneapolis, by Olympia Arts Ensemble, 1980.

The Cursing of the Fig Tree, produced in Minneapolis, at Augsburg College Chapel, 1982.

OTHER

Contributor of poetry to periodicals, including *Crosscurrents, Bellingham Review, Stone Country, Bellowing Ark,* and *Loonfeather.* Contributor of commentaries and opinion pieces to periodicals, including *Los Angeles Times, Minnesota Literature,* and *San Diego Writer's Monthly.*

■ Work in Progress

Auriga and Other Poems; The Right of the State (adult), an examination of First Amendment controversies.

■ Sidelights

Bradley Steffens told *SATA:* "I first thought about being a writer in eleventh grade. My creative writing teacher, James Malone, told our class to write something about the automobile culture of Los Angeles, where we lived. It could be anything, Malone said—an essay, a poem, a short story, the first chapter of a novel. Wanting to avoid homework, I dashed off a twenty-line poem in class and turned it in. The next day, Malone sat on the corner of his desk with a piece of paper in his hand. 'Someone has turned in the first assignment,' he said, 'and I want to share it with you.' He began to read my poem aloud. A trained actor, he read with sensitivity and passion. When he finished, the room was silent. He looked up from the page. 'That, boys and girls, is poetry,' he said. He walked over to my desk and laid the paper in front of me. 'Publish it this semester, and I'll give you an "A" in the course,' he promised. 'You won't have to do another thing.' That morning changed my life. I changed my high school major. I changed the college I planned to attend. I began to write in earnest. I sent the poem out, and kept sending it out after it was rejected. Two years later, that poem, 'Automobile,' was accepted by the editor of *River Bottom,* a small literary journal published in Eau Claire, Wisconsin. After that, I never considered doing anything but writing."

■ For More Information See

PERIODICALS

School Library Journal, May, 1992, p. 128; May, 1993, p. 135.

*   *   *

STEIN, Wendy 1951-

■ Personal

Born November 11, 1951, in Boston, MA; daughter of Harold (a physician) and Doris (a mother and homemaker; maiden name, Domroe) Stein. *Education:* Received B.A. from Trinity College and M.A. from Syracuse University. *Politics:* "Independently radical." *Hobbies and other interests:* Camping, canoeing, reading,

whale-watching ("not too convenient in central New York, though"), working with stained glass.

■ Addresses

Home and office—1909 Collins Rd., LaFayette, NY 13084.

■ Career

Syracuse Herald-Journal, Syracuse, NY, reporter, 1974-75; New Readers Press, Syracuse, NY, worked as managing editor of periodicals department and senior editor; freelance writer and editor, 1983—. Contact Hotline, telephone counselor; Burnet Park Zoo, education volunteer.

■ Writings

Atlantis: Opposing Viewpoints, Greenhaven Press, 1989.
Shamans: Opposing Viewpoints, Greenhaven Press, 1991.
Communication Skills That Work (workbook), Contemporary Books, 1991.
Dinosaurs: Opposing Viewpoints, Greenhaven Press, 1994.

Also author of workbook *Ready, Set Study!,* Contemporary Books, and driver education book *Taking the Wheel,* New Readers Press; author of several other books on consumer and coping skills. *Lake Effect,* fiction editor.

■ Work in Progress

A book of humorous essays; a stress management kit.

■ Sidelights

Wendy Stein told *SATA:* "In both published and unpublished works, I like to question reality a bit. I ask readers to suspend what they think, forget their assumptions, and look at life from another angle. I am fascinated by what we can't see. That's why writing three books for Greenhaven Press's 'Great Mysteries' series has been so much fun and so challenging. While these books are nonfiction, there is a lot of room to let imagination soar. *Shamans: Opposing Viewpoints* was especially interesting because the shamans see and travel to a world that is invisible to most of us most of the time, except perhaps occasionally when we are falling asleep, dreaming, or just waking. The shamans' vision challenges the 'reality' that is sponsored by science and reason. The shamans perceive this world *and* the spirit world, and in reading about them, we have to wonder why we have chosen to believe only our physical senses to the exclusion of our intuition and spirituality.

"In my writing for young children as well as for adults, I love to give voices and personalities to animals, trees, sneezes, garbage pails, and anything else that doesn't usually get a chance to be heard. Maybe that is why I was so fascinated by the shamans—they too believe in the spirits and voices of 'inanimate' things.

"In writing that is as yet unpublished, I tend to look at the world with an eye for the absurd and my tongue often planted in my cheek. I think I owe my sense of the absurd to my mother and my tongue-in-cheekness to my father. To my grandmother I owe my fascination with eccentric families, because when I was a kid, she entertained me for hours with tales of my own strange relatives.

"It is always amazing to me how many people have some fantasy of writing a book—or at least having a book out there with their name on it. I encourage anyone who dares to think it to do it, but that sometimes gets me in trouble because they then ask if I will a) edit it, b) ghostwrite it, c) co-write it, or d) write it for them! Actually, I do enjoy doing editing work too, and I would like to do more collaborative work either with another writer or an illustrator. I wish I could draw because I love creating visual puns but cannot express them graphically. (Yes, *Airplane* is one of my favorite movies.)

"I don't know what I would do if I weren't a writer. I've been writing since I was a kid, and I think I always took it for granted that I would do something in the writing field, even though my parents kept pleading with me to do something 'more practical.' Translation: Find a job that offers health insurance coverage!

"When I finished graduate school, I did get a job, and there was health insurance. I worked as a writer and editor for New Readers Press, the publishing division of Laubach Literacy International. But the absurdity of that job finally hit me after many years—I was writing for people who couldn't read! Could any writer be more insecure than that? Truthfully, though, I learned a lot and I am proud of the work that I did. Writing for newly literate people required me to write tightly and clearly; the message had to be well thought out and presented with an economy of words. I use those skills in everything else I write, but I have to admit that it certainly is a relief to stretch out a bit when I am writing for a more literate reader and use a few fancy words and phrases now and then."

*   *   *

STIRLING, Ian 1941-

■ Personal

Born in 1941, in Zambia; *Education:* University of British Columbia, B.S., 1963, M.S., 1965; University of Canterbury, Ph.D., 1968. *Hobbies and other interests:* Hiking, photography, cross-country skiing.

IAN STIRLING

■ Addresses

Home—7811 144 St., Edmonton, Alberta T5R 0R1, Canada. *Office*—c/o Publicity Director, Sierra Club Books, 100 Bush St., San Francisco, CA 94104.

■ Career

Canadian Wildlife Service, Edmonton, Alberta, Canada, research scientist, 1970—; University of Alberta, Edmonton, adjunct professor of zoology, 1979—. *Member:* Canadian Society of Zoologists, American Society of Mammalogists, Arctic Institute of North America, Marine Mammal Society.

■ Writings

Polar Bears, University of Michigan Press, 1988.
Bears, Sierra Club, 1992.
(Editor) *Bears, Majestic Creatures of the Wild,* Rohdahl Press, 1993.

■ Work in Progress

Researching the ecology of polar bears and Arctic seals.

■ Sidelights

Ian Stirling told *SATA:* "I always had an interest in the outdoors, wildlife and polar regions. Through many years of research on polar bears and seals, I have developed a keen interest in the conservation and biology of polar oceans.

"Although I have written many scientific papers over the years, I have long been concerned about the limited amount of technically-accurate information about bears that is available for the public, particularly children. Hence, I wrote this children's book, *Bears,* and the earlier book, *Polar Bears,* both of which are aimed at libraries.

"On a broader scale, I am interested in science education for the public at large and about the rapidly declining state of the globe in an ecological sense."

* * *

STRAUSS, Gwen 1963-

■ Personal

Born May 19, 1963, in Deschappelles, Haiti; daughter of Julian Max (a veterinarian) and Kate Cowles Nichols Rummel (a politician) Strauss. *Education:* Attended Friends World College (Kyoto), 1985; Hampshire College, B.A., 1986; Wheelock College, M.S., 1987. *Politics:* Democrat. *Religion:* Buddhist. *Hobbies and other interests:* Sailing, reading, films, painting, dance, the circus.

■ Addresses

Home—2, rue Veron 75018 Paris, France; 1682 Ocean-view Dr., Tierra Verde, FL 33715. *Office*—c/o Publicity Director, Alfred Knopf, 201 E. 50th St., New York, NY 10022. *Agent*—Geri Thoma, Elaine Markson Agency, 44 Greenwich Ave., New York, NY 10011.

■ Career

Writer. Park School, Boston, MA, creative writing teacher, 1986-87; Frank Books, Paris, France, editorial assistant, 1992. *Member:* Authors Guild, Authors League, Nature Conservancy, Writers Union, American Academy of Poets.

■ Awards, Honors

Grolier Poetry Prize nomination.

■ Writings

Trail of Stones (poems), illustrated by Anthony Browne, Knopf, 1989.
The Night Shimmy (children's book), illustrated by Browne, Knopf, 1991.

Contributor of poems, articles and short stories to *Kenyon Review, Frank, Poetry Northwest, New Republic,*

GWEN STRAUSS

Manhattan Poetry Review, Antioch Review, and *Paris Transcontinental.*

■ Work in Progress

Two novels, *The Guru* and *The Strongman,* and a collection of short stories.

■ Sidelights

Gwen Strauss told *SATA:* "My family moved around a lot when I was growing up, and so I seem to have grown gypsy feet. When I was seventeen, after graduating from high school, I lived on a small 26-foot sailboat with my boyfriend. We sailed all through the Caribbean, Mexico, Guatemala, and up the east coast of America. Then I finally realized it would be a good idea to go back to school. I studied poetry in college. And in order to keep moving and to write my senior thesis on Japanese women poets of the eleventh century, I went to live in Kyoto, Japan. During that year, I traveled to China, Taiwan, Hong Kong, and Korea, where I became interested in Buddhism.

"After graduating, I moved to Boston and started teaching fourth grade, while going to school myself for my Master's degree in education. During this period I discovered children's literature. I met Anthony Browne, a great British author/illustrator, at a seminar in 1987.

We decided to work together on a book of poems based on fairy tale characters. And that was how I got my first book published.

"I always wrote, and will probably always write, but it helped immensely to share my work and to get some encouragement. And it helped me to learn how important it is to always try to make your work that thing that makes you happiest in your life.

"For the last three years I have been living in Paris, in a sunny apartment with my two cats. I have been working on a novel and short stories, and, of course, traveling. My last big trip was a long journey through Russia, Khazakstan, Ukraine, and Uzbekistan. I am planning soon to move onto a barge so I can take my cats and books with me, while exploring the canals of Europe."

*   *   *

SYMES, R. F.

■ Addresses

Office—Department of Mineralogy, Natural History Museum, Cromwell Road, London SW7 5BD, England.

■ Career

Head of department of mineralogy at Natural History Museum, London, England.

■ Writings

(With others) *Rocks and Minerals* (part of "Eyewitness" series), photographs by Colin Keates and Andreas Einsiedel, Knopf, 1988.
(With R. R. Harding) *Crystal and Gem* (part of "Eyewitness" series), Knopf, 1991.

Also author of *Rocks and Minerals of Cornwall,* Natural History Museum Publications.

■ Sidelights

The head of mineralogy at London's Natural History Museum, R. F. Symes has cowritten *Crystal and Gem* and *Rocks and Minerals,* both of which are part of the "Eyewitness" series, which provides young readers with information on a variety of topics. In the latter title, written collectively by the staff of the Natural History Museum, the authors explain such subjects as the creation and uses of rocks and the various classes of rocks. They also discuss how to collect and cut rocks and provide insight into such subjects as mining and the role of erosion in rock formation. Reviewing the "Eyewitness" series in *School Library Journal,* Joy Daentl especially noted the illustrations, pointing out that "brilliantly photographed museum specimens provide the visual framework for these informative mini-tours of the natural world." The critic added that in *Rocks*

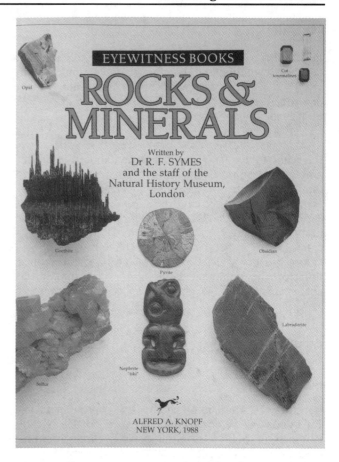

Introducing readers to the world of geology, R. F. Symes' book covers everything from how fossils and stalactites are formed to how gems are mined and cut.

and Minerals, "one can identify specimens from the seashore and from space." Zena Sutherland in *Bulletin of the Center for Children's Books* praised the text of *Rocks and Minerals,* stating that "the descriptive material is accurate, authoritative, and clear." Robert D. Hale in *Horn Book* commended the prose as well, concluding that "basic information is related in a succinct and highly satisfactory style."

■ Works Cited

Daentl, Joy, review of *Rocks and Minerals, School Library Journal,* May, 1989, pp. 23-24.
Hale, Robert D., "Musings," *Horn Book,* May-June, 1992, pp. 369-70.
Sutherland, Zena, review of *Rocks and Minerals, Bulletin of the Center for Children's Books,* July, 1988, p. 240.

■ For More Information See

PERIODICALS

Booklist, August, 1988, p. 1921.
School Library Journal, July, 1991, p. 76.
Washington Post Book World, April 14, 1991, p. 10.

T–U

TARG BRILL, Marlene
See BRILL, Marlene Targ

* * *

TERRIS, Susan 1937-

■ Personal

Born May 6, 1937, in St. Louis, MO; daughter of Harold W. (a realtor) and Myra (Friedman) Dubinsky; married David Warren Terris (a stockbroker), August 31, 1958; children: Daniel, Michael, Amy. *Education:* Wellesley College, B.A., 1959; San Francisco State College (now University), M.A., 1966. *Politics:* Democrat. *Religion:* Jewish. *Hobbies and other interests:* Sewing, knitting, needlepoint work, cooking, hiking.

■ Addresses

Home—11 Jordan Ave., San Francisco, CA 94118. *Agent*—Marilyn Marlow, Curtis Brown Ltd., 10 Astor Pl., New York, NY 10003.

■ Career

Novelist and poet. University of California Extension, San Francisco, CA, teacher of "Writing for Children" course and writing workshops. Has done tutoring, library work, and research. Lecturer on children's books to schools and libraries. *Member:* Authors Guild, Society of Children's Book Writers and Illustrators, Academy of American Poets, PEN, Poetry Society of America.

■ Awards, Honors

New York Times Outstanding Children's Book citation, 1973, for *Plague of Frogs;* Children's Book of the Year citation, Library of Congress, 1981, for *No Scarlet Ribbons;* Junior Literary Guild Selection, 1982, for *Wings and Roots;* Notable Best Book for Young Adults citation, American Library Association, 1987, Silver Medalist, Commonwealth Club of California Book

SUSAN TERRIS

Awards, 1987, and Feminist Fortnight, British Booksellers, 1988, all for *Nell's Quilt.*

■ Writings

The Upstairs Witch and the Downstairs Witch, Doubleday, 1970.
The Backwards Boots, Doubleday, 1971.
On Fire, Doubleday, 1972.

The Drowning Boy, Doubleday, 1972.
Pickle, Four Winds Press, 1973.
Plague of Frogs, Doubleday, 1973.
Whirling Rainbows, Doubleday, 1974.
The Pencil Families, Greenwillow, 1975.
Amanda, the Panda, and the Redhead, Doubleday, 1975.
No Boys Allowed, Doubleday, 1976.
The Chicken Pox Papers, F. Watts, 1976.
Two Ps in a Pod, Greenwillow, 1977.
Tucker and the Horse Thief, Four Winds Press, 1979.
Stage Brat, Four Winds Press, 1980.
No Scarlet Ribbons, Farrar, Straus, 1981.
Wings and Roots, Farrar, Straus, 1982.
Octopus Pie, Farrar, Straus, 1983.
Baby-Snatcher, Farrar, Straus, 1984.
The Latchkey Kids, Farrar, Straus, 1986.
Nell's Quilt, Farrar, Straus, 1987.
Author! Author!, Farrar, Straus, 1990.

Also contributor to a series of elementary school texts. Contributor of stories, poems and articles to magazines, and of book reviews to *New York Times* and *San Francisco Chronicle.*

■ Adaptations

Tucker and the Horse Thief was adapted into a movie by Home Box Office (HBO) in 1982.

■ Work in Progress

Beany's Baby, a novel about a girl who plays on a boys baseball team, for Farrar, Straus.

■ Sidelights

"One of my young fans once told her mother, 'Mrs. Terris is one of the safest people I know, but her books are *so* dangerous,'" Susan Terris recalled in an interview for *SATA.* It is this borderland between safety and danger that Terris has been exploring since 1970 in the more than twenty books she has written for juveniles and young adults. In award-winning books such as *Plague of Frogs, Wings and Roots,* and *Nell's Quilt,* Terris has explored the "pivotal moments" of young women's lives. "I have never lost my fascination with the experiences of children and young adults," Terris told *SATA.* "The years between ten and fourteen were of particular importance in my life. They were difficult yet exciting; and I remember them with great clarity. Most of all I remember the fear—fear of new people, fear of new situations, and the fear of wondering how a person can ever find safety in such an unsafe world. To me these fears are connected to turning points which affect what we do with our lives. If we hope to change and work through unhappiness, we need to confront our fears and act decisively."

Overcoming fear and challenges have been major themes in Terris's life off the written page, as well, though there would seem to be little fearful in her childhood. "I had—for a writer—an uncommonly happy childhood," Terris remarked in her interview. "I was born in St. Louis, Missouri, and grew up in the country with devoted parents who both prized me as a daughter. I have none of those complaints women often speak of, for my father encouraged me in all ways." Both parents were avid readers and Terris spent most of her childhood "reading, writing, and climbing trees." She was a competitive athlete as a youngster, swimming the freestyle in relays, participating in field hockey, and studying modern dance.

But books and story-telling were her twin passions. "In ways I had a solitary childhood. My brother is four years younger than I and my sister ten, so they really weren't companions for me. When I got home from school, I read. And played with dolls, I must confess, until the absurd age of twelve, because they offered an opportunity for story play." Far more than dressing up her dolls and playing mommy, Terris created elaborate stories around them, stories resembling her favorites of the time, *The Secret Garden, The Box Car Children,* and *Little Women*—all stories with secret places.

Terris began writing down stories at an early age, selling her first at age 12 to *Calling All Girls* and earning 25 dollars for it. With this first story, about a young girl walking home alone in a park after dark and meeting a man who turns out to be deaf, Terris already had her territory of overcoming fear mapped out. Terris's parents were as supportive about her writing as the athletics. Her father had wanted to be a writer himself and had started a novel, but after graduating from college in 1929, in the beginning of the Great Depression, he went to work in the family real estate business instead. His love of writing was passed on to his oldest daughter. Her early work also appeared in the school paper at the girls school, Mary Institute in St. Louis, where she attended elementary and high school. "School liked me a lot, I was a good student," she recalled for *SATA.* "My years there were very fortunate, because they helped create a positive self-image for myself. They allowed me later in life to stand up to rejection and criticism, two essentials for any writer."

Through her teenage years Terris continued her love for reading and writing. "My parents never censored my reading. I read what they were reading. My favorites authors became—and continue to be—Dickens, Hardy and Eliot, the great nineteenth-century writers." She had what she terms "typical" teenage experiences with friends, dates and books, and then went to college at Wellesley College in Massachusetts, where she earned her B.A. in English literature. "College was okay," Terris said. "But it wasn't the kind of incredible experience my earlier schooling was." She took creative writing courses and was editor of the literary magazine at Wellesley. It was there she studied with Philip Booth, the poet, who further encouraged her writing by telling her she had to "broaden her vision." "Looking back," Terris said, "I think that he was saying I needed to grow up. The stories I was writing then were about children and adolescents. Now, many years later, I am still writing about the same subjects."

Creating Textbooks Leads to Other Writing Ventures

It was when Terris was a freshman that she met her future husband. They were married in 1958 and Terris graduated the next year. In 1960 they moved to San Francisco, where they have lived ever since. In the fall of 1960 Terris entered graduate school at then-San Francisco State College (now University), and had three children in diapers during her Masters program. Not long after earning her M.A., Terris was offered a job writing textbooks for Chandler Publishing Company. "It was great fun," Terris told *SATA*. "I got to write about volcanoes, disasters, dinosaurs. Anything I wanted." It was this job which gave Terris the courage and confidence to try and sell picture books to New York publishers. "I was very methodical," Terris said, "and spent six months doing six picture book stories." Then she met the well-known children's author Marilyn Sachs, who encouraged her to submit one to Doubleday. After revision, the book, *The Upstairs Witch and the Downstairs Witch,* was accepted. There soon followed *The Backwards Boots,* which according to Terris has "taken on a separate life of its own," being a favorite of storytellers across the United States.

"I had a very easy beginning with publishing, but soon discovered that Doubleday would take only one picture book a year, so I decided to write a novel. I had never done one before and my years as a researcher paid off." Terris chose several of her favorite children's books, including *Charlotte's Web* and *Where the Lilies Bloom,* and dissected them chapter by chapter to see how they were constructed. Her own first novella, *Pickle,* was rejected by Doubleday, but her next one, *On Fire,* was accepted. The story of the strange friendship between a girl and a 15-year-old boy who helps her come into her own, *On Fire* won praise from *Publishers Weekly:* "Susan Terris's characters are well-developed; her understanding of their problems and emotions is keenly expressed."

Terris followed this with *The Drowning Boy,* about a young boy who, through his devotion to an autistic child, begins to find his own center. After revision, her novella, *Pickle,* was published by Four Winds Press. It is the story of a ten-year-old young girl trying to make it in a new environment, and of the lessons she learns about herself in the process. Then came the publication of *Plague of Frogs* in 1973, a book which won Terris her first real recognition when it was named a *New York Times* Outstanding Children's Book of 1973. A 14-year-old girl's smug life is disrupted when her mother brings an unwed, pregnant 16-year-old into the home. Again, there are lessons to be learned for Terris's protagonists at the most difficult of times. "Marcella [the pregnant girl] was really drawn from a young woman who took care of my sister," Terris told *SATA*. "But the main character is in no way my sister. I use bits and pieces of my own experiences in the books. *Plague of Frogs* is set in suburban St. Louis, for instance. Where I grew up. *Pickle* takes place in San Francisco. But the stories are not mere autobiography."

Linnett Purcell discovers that her natural talent as a young stage actress can win her the attention—and sometimes resentment—of her friends and family. (Jacket design by Susan Gaber.)

Terris was productive during the 1970s, publishing almost a book a year, experimenting in new forms such as journal entry and dual narration. "I never think of audience when I'm writing," Terris told *SATA*. "I leave that for my editor to decide. I don't worry about language, degree of difficulty or subject matter. I have an enormous amount of respect for young readers and think they can understand all sorts of issues and problems. Children, I find, respect people who are honest with them, who don't talk down to them. I try to write about things that I find are important and have no time for books with no intense feeling. I am definitely not a Minimalist."

The books Terris wrote in the 1970s continued to explore turning points, epiphanies in the lives of children. In *Whirling Rainbows,* a "fat, blue-eyed Jewish Indian" looks for acceptance and provides, according to *Library Journal,* "good bibliotherapy for young adolescents striving for peer acceptance." Sibling rivalry and parental acceptance provide the backdrop for *The Pencil Families* and *Amanda, the Panda, and the Redhead.* Sickness, mistaken identity, and shifting realities are at the core of *The Chicken Pox Papers, Two Ps in a Pod,* and *Stage Brat. Tucker and the Horse Thief* marked a turning point for the author herself, being her first historical novel, a story about a Jewish family in the Gold Country whose son befriends a newly arrived boy only to discover he is really a girl. "This is a sort of typical Shakespearean pants part," Terris explained. "My take on *As You Like It*." The book not only broke new ground for Terris as a writer, but also was adapted for an HBO movie. But to get it published, she had to leave the publishing house she had been with since 1970.

Young Adult Challenges Addressed in Historical and Mystery Novels

With her next book, *No Scarlet Ribbons,* a story describing the difficulties of a blended family, Terris moved to Farrar, Straus & Giroux, where she has been since 1981. "I am an intensely loyal person," Terris said to *SATA*. "I have been married to the same person all these years; I have the same agent I started with. But editors seem to come and go. Every time they turn thirty-four they go off to write novels or translate Russian or get arrested for shoplifting." She has been working with the same editor now since 1981 and has created several more well-received books, three prize winners among them. In addition to *No Scarlet Ribbons,* which was a Library of Congress Children's Book of the Year, *Wings and Roots* was a Junior Literary Guild selection, recounting how the polio epidemic of the 1950s affected the lives of two young people: a teenage boy who is a victim of the disease, and a girl of the same age who becomes emotionally attached to him. *Nell's Quilt* was an ALA Best Book for Young Adults in 1987, as well as a Silver Medalist in the Commonwealth Club of California Book Awards and a recipient of the Feminist Fortnight award in England. It tells the story of an 18-year-old girl whose life is threatened by what we would now call anorexia. Nell lives in Amherst, Massachusetts and the year is 1899. Her needy parents want her to marry a well-off widowed cousin, and Nell, who has dreams of college and living in Boston, not of being a drudge on the farm, retreats inside herself. As Nell daily portions out smaller and smaller amounts of food to herself, she also stitches together a quilt with scraps which she belives to have come from her suffragette grandmother. Terris stretches the drama to the final page, for it is only there the reader learns whether Nell's innate joy and love of life will save her or not.

Terris is not afraid to take chances in technique or subject matter: as Nell goes ever deeper into her pursuit of insignificance, the narrative voice shifts from first to third person. With *Octopus Pie* Terris verges into the mystery genre and tells the story partly in journal format. Two sisters keep an octopus in their room and when the older sister takes it to her Gifted and Talented class at school, the octopus is stolen. The journal is the younger sister's, who is suspected of the theft. *Baby-Snatcher,* from 1984, explores adolescent romance and the dangers of the adult world when Laurel, a 13-year-old girl, falls in love with an anachronistic hippy sculptor who, along with his little daughter, seem to be hiding away near a Minnesota lake. "Terris builds to the suspenseful conclusion of *Baby-Snatcher* quickly and relentlessly," wrote *Los Angeles Times Book Review* contributor Dale Pollock. "In the process, Laurel matures, learning more about love and responsibility." Again, Terris's characters experience an epiphany or turning point in their lives.

"I'm not sure where I get my ideas," Terris said in her interview. "But once they come, I don't touch them. I just let them accumulate without me interfering. They're like a snowball at this stage, and when the snowball gets so big that I can no longer get around it, then I know it's time." Time in this case means the second and third steps in Terris's creative process. "Next I do character sketches and a chapter-by-chapter outline. But I don't look at any of this once I start writing. Only a glance at the chapter outline, but it's not so thorough that I can't still be surprised." The last step before beginning the writing is research. "Having been trained in research, I'm a big advocate of it. But I use it on the iceberg theory: only one tenth of the research shows, but the rest adds incredible depth and richness to a book." For *Octopus Pie* Terris interviewed a score of sisters, both separate and together; for *Whirling Rainbows* she spoke with parents of adopted children as well as adoptees themselves; for *The Drowning Boy* she went to a gun shop to learn how to clean a rifle; for *Wings and Roots* she interviewed polio victims, therapists, parents and doctors; and for *The Latchkey Kids* she talked with social workers, counselors and actual latchkey kids.

"I work in a tiny office on the bottom floor of my San Francisco home," Terris told *SATA*. "It looks out onto a small city backyard, all green and bright with a tree in the middle. My one requirement for work is absolute quiet. When my own kids were at home, I was usually two floors away and they had a separate phone line to call me." Terris generally works in the morning from 8:30 to about 1 or 2 p.m., and works in intense three-month blocks when she is creating a first draft. Her 1990 novel, *Author! Author!,* followed this pattern and held more than the usual element of autobiography: Valerie Myerson is 12 when she has her first children's book published—not unlike Terris herself, who first broke into print at age 12. But as with all her books, Terris blends this autobiographical element into a richer compound: Val's initial success turns sour as a second book is expected, and adolescent growing pains alienate her from her family and herself. In the process, the reader is treated to a "fine fictional look at one teenager's coming of age," according to Bob Thompson in the *San Francisco Chronicle*. A *New York Times Book Review* critic considered *Author! Author!* to be an "intelligent" novel that "addresses familiar confusions and fantasies with sophisticated discretion."

For Terris, her favorite book "is always the one I'm working on." But she does more than write children's books; she also plays mentor to other authors, both in the writing classes she instructs, as well as on a one-to-one basis with promising writers who seek her out. "Children's book writers in general are very generous people," Terris said. "We are giving of time and considerate of other people's work as well as our own. I was helped when I began and I'm repaying the favor." But Terris feels you are doing no one a favor by not being honest with them, by providing real criticism. "Everyone can and should be a writer," she said, "but not everyone can be an author." She tells an anecdote about seeing a young couple on the street outside her home with a toddler just learning to walk. When the child would fall down, the parents yelled "Good falling!" "That's what I tell my proteges sometimes: Good falling." Writing would seem to be in the Terris blood: her oldest son, Dan, is, in addition to being a provost at Brandeis University, a writer of children's biographies, and Michael works as a political consultant, writing speeches and press releases. Terris is also involved in politics, especially women's issues. "If politicians more nearly reflected our population," she told *SATA,* "we would be in better shape."

But at the end of the day, it is writing where Terris makes her stand, where she hopes she is able to reach people. "In a world filled with doubt and pessimism, I'm still an optimist," she said. "And because I believe that sooner or later—preferably between ten and fourteen—everyone has to turn around, take a stand, and say, 'This is me. I'm going to struggle. I'm going to take risks. What I *do* can make a difference.' And I hope my books will also make a difference."

■ Works Cited

Review of *Author! Author!, New York Times Book Review,* March 10, 1991, p. 29.

Review of *On Fire, Publishers Weekly,* January 17, 1972, p. 59.

Pollock, Dale, review of *Baby-Snatcher, Los Angeles Times Book Review,* February 10, 1985, p. 3.

Terris, Susan, interview with J. Sydney Jones for *Something about the Author,* August, 1993.

Thompson, Bob, review of *Author! Author!, San Francisco Chronicle,* January 27, 1991, p. 37.

Review of *Whirling Rainbows, Library Journal,* October 15, 1974, pp. 2742-43.

■ For More Information See

PERIODICALS

English Journal, Volume 78, number 7, 1989, p. 82; Volume 80, number 5, 1991, p. 84.

Horn Book, December, 1975, p. 596; August, 1981, p. 438.

Library Journal, December 15, 1971, p. 4181; October 15, 1973, p. 3160; March 15, 1974, p. 896.

Publishers Weekly, March 24, 1974, p. 60; June 2, 1975, p.53; August 10, 1990, p. 446.

Times Educational Supplement, March 10, 1989, p. B14.

Washington Post Book World, November 6, 1983, p. 16.

—*Sketch by J. Sydney Jones*

THOMSON, Pat 1939-

■ Personal

Born April 28, 1939, in Norwich, England; married Roy Thomson (a leather chemist), June 6, 1961; children: Susanna, Alexander. *Education:* University of Leeds, B.A. (honors), 1960, post-graduate certificate in education, 1961; University of Loughborough, M.L.S., 1982, Diploma in Librarianship, 1982. *Hobbies and other interests:* Opera and collecting baby rattles ("I make sure that the baby has finished with them, of course.")

■ Addresses

Home—The Long House, Behind 43 West St., Oundle PE8 4EJ, England. *Office*—Nene College, Boughton Green Rd., Northampton NN2 7AL, England. *Agent*—Laura Cecil, 17 Alwyne Villas, London N1 2HG, England.

■ Career

Nene College, Northampton, England, education librarian, 1975—. Has also taught French. *Member:* Federation of Children's Book Groups (honorary vice president), Society of Authors, Children's Book History Society.

■ Writings

(Compiler) *Rhymes around the Day,* illustrated by Jan Ormerod, Lothrop, 1983.

Trouble in the Cupboard, Yearling, 1987.

Family Gathering: A Collection of Family Stories, illustrated by Toni Goffe, Dent, 1988.

Strange Exchange, Gollancz, 1991.

Beware of the Aunts!, illustrated by Emma Chichester Clark, McElderry Books, 1992.

Tales Told after Lights Out (short stories), HarperCollins, 1993.

"SHARE-A-STORY" SERIES

The Treasure Sock, illustrated by Tony Ross, Gollancz, 1986, Delacorte, 1987.

One of Those Days, illustrated by Bob Wilson, Delacorte, 1986.

Can You Hear Me, Grandad?, illustrated by Jez Alborough, Delacorte, 1986.

My Friend Mr. Morris, illustrated by Satoshi Kitamura, Delacorte, 1987.

Thank You for the Tadpole, illustrated by Mary Rayner, Delacorte, 1987.

Good Girl Granny, illustrated by Faith Jaques, Delacorte, 1987.

Dial D for Disaster, illustrated by Paul Demeyer, Trafalgar Square, 1990.

No Trouble at All, illustrated by Jocelyn Wild, Trafalgar Square, 1990.

Best Pest, illustrated by Peter Firmin, Trafalgar Square, 1990.

The Best Thing of All, illustrated by Margaret Chamberlain, Trafalgar Square, 1990.

"JETS" SERIES

Jacko, illustrated by Caroline Crossland, Black, 1989.
Rhyming Russell, illustrated by Crossland, Black, 1991.
Messages, illustrated by Crossland, Black, 1992.

EDITOR OF ANTHOLOGIES

A Basket of Stories for Seven Year Olds, illustrated by
   Rachel Birkett, Doubleday, 1990.
A Sackful of Stories for Eight Year Olds, illustrated by
   Paddy Mounter, Doubleday, 1990.
A Bucketful of Stories for Six Year Olds, illustrated by
   Mark Southgate, Doubleday, 1991.
A Chest of Stories for Nine Year Olds, illustrated by
   Peter Bailey, Doubleday, 1991.
A Pocketful of Stories for Five Year Olds, illustrated by P.
   Dann, Doubleday, 1992.
A Satchel of Stories, illustrated by Doffy Weir, Double-
   day, 1992.
A Stocking Full of Christmas Stories, illustrated by
   Bailey, Doubleday, 1992.

OTHER

Nonfiction editor of *Books for Your Children.* Contributor to *Books for Keeps, School Librarian, Bookmark,* and
*International Review of Children's Literature and Libra-
rianship.*

Jacko has been published in Welsh, Finnish, and
Catalan.

■ Sidelights

"I began writing rather late," Pat Thomson told *SATA.*
"I was the typical, avid child reader; but it was not until
I returned to work when my children were growing up
that I decided to work with books in a teacher training
college. I became particularly concerned with the quality
and nature of early reading material, wondering if
boring, banal 'readers' actually made children not want
to read. Consequently, my first books had in mind
children who were only just getting to grips with print,
but who surely needed the pleasures of lively language
and challenging imaginings."

Thomson created the unique "Share-a-Story" series so
that young children and their parents could enjoy
reading together. In the "Share-a-Story" books, the text
on the right is written in a simpler style than the text on
the left. The parent reads on the left side, while the child
reads on the right; the goal is for the parent to teach the
child to read the text on the left, and hence to be able to
read the book on his or her own.

Thomson's books feature an assortment of lovably
eccentric characters. In *Beware of the Aunts,* a young girl
describes her nine aunts' unusual habits: one wears
strange clothes, one overeats, and one might be a witch.
All, however, are very generous, as a Christmas get-
together proves. The title character of *My Friend Mr.
Morris* interprets everything he hears literally; for example, he believes that a hat band is a band which performs
on a hat.

"I draw a great deal on family life for my stories,"
Thomson explained. "*Beware of the Aunts!* celebrates
the funny, strong-minded, and highly individual women
in my extended family. *Good Girl Granny* is based on
episodes in my grandmother's childhood. School life is
also a rich source of amusement and inspiration."

In addition to writing books, Thomson has compiled
several anthologies of stories for children, including the
Doubleday anthologies, a collection of books antholo-
gized by age that includes *A Pocketful of Stories for Five
Year Olds* and *A Bucketful of Stories for Six Year Olds.*
She has also written articles about children's books and
library studies for several magazines, including *Books
for Keeps, School Librarian,* and *Bookmark.*

Thomson told *SATA:* "I believe I have a strong sense of
the audience I am writing for, but I suppose one always
ends up 'writing for oneself' to some degree, especially
when the characters seize the imagination. That is the
greatest pleasure—to live richly in one's head and to
share that with young readers."

**Pat Thomson uses some of her family members as
models for the nine quirky aunts featured in this
humorous romp.** (Cover illustration by Emma
Chichester Clark.)

■ For More Information See

PERIODICALS

Publishers Weekly, December 25, 1987, p. 73; March 9, 1992, p. 57.
School Library Journal, February, 1987, p. 35; September, 1988, p. 66; January, 1989, p. 67; February, 1991, p. 21; July, 1992, p. 65.
Times Educational Supplement, November 14, 1986, p. 40; July 11, 1988, p. 30; March 24, 1989, p. 25; September 21, 1990, p. R4.

* * *

THORNHILL, Jan 1955-

■ Personal

Born June 3, 1955, in Sudbury, Ontario, Canada; daughter of Philip (a metallurgical engineer) and Mia (an artist) Thornhill; married Fred Gottschalk (an artist), August 10, 1985. *Education:* Graduated from Ontario College of Art, 1977. *Hobbies and other interests:* Organic gardening, travelling, wild-mushrooming, camping, canoeing, birding, herbalism.

■ Addresses

Home—RR #1, Havelock, Ontario K0L 1Z0, Canada.

JAN THORNHILL

■ Career

Freelance editorial illustrator, 1978—; author and illustrator of children's books, and short stories for adults. *Member:* Canadian Society of Children's Authors, Illustrators, and Performers, Canadian Children's Book Centre.

■ Awards, Honors

Award of Merit, Art Directors Club of Toronto, 1988, for *The Wildlife A-B-C: A Nature Alphabet;* finalist for Governor General's Award (illustration), Canada Council, 1989, for *The Wildlife A-B-C,* and 1990, for *The Wildlife 1 2 3: A Nature Counting Book;* UNICEF-Ezra Jack Keats International Award for Excellence in Children's Book Illustration, 1990, for *The Wildlife 1 2 3;* Information Book Award, Children's Literature Roundtables of Canada, 1992, for *A Tree in a Forest.*

■ Writings

SELF-ILLUSTRATED

The Wildlife A-B-C: A Nature Alphabet, Greey de Pencier, 1988, Simon and Schuster, 1990.
The Wildlife 1 2 3: A Nature Counting Book, Greey de Pencier, 1989, Simon and Schuster, 1989.
A Tree in a Forest, Greey de Pencier, 1991, Simon and Schuster, 1992.
Crow and Fox and Other Animal Legends, Greey de Pencier, 1993, Simon and Schuster, 1993.

■ Sidelights

Jan Thornhill is an award-winning author and illustrator whose detailed paintings complement prose which teaches young children about the value and fascination of nature. Thornhill captured critical attention with her first work for children, *The Wildlife A-B-C: A Nature Alphabet.* Reviewers found charm in the book's rhyming prose and colorful illustrations framed by borders incorporating each highlighted animal. *The Wildlife A-B-C* also features a section that offers additional information about each animal as well as other species and plants featured in Thornhill's paintings. Mary Ellen Binder, a reviewer for *Canadian Children's Literature,* remarked: "While this book is aimed at 2-6 year-olds, the wealth of informative detail in its illustrations and the additional notes at the end make it enjoyable and educational for older children as well."

Thornhill utilized the same format for her next effort, *The Wildlife 1 2 3: A Nature Counting Book,* in which detailed pictures of animals in their natural habitats are represented within ornamental frames. It also includes notes instructing children about the wildlife featured in the book. While some reviewers felt that Thornhill's presentation was too complex for children just learning how to count, her artwork was largely praised. Patricia Feltham, reviewing *The Wildlife 1 2 3* in *Canadian Children's Literature,* stated: "This enchanting book is a must for the budding biologist or for that special pre-schooler with small hands." In a review for *Junior*

By focusing on the two-hundred-year life of a sugar maple, Thornhill depicts the interdependent lives of plants and animals in his self-illustrated work.

Bookshelf Marcus Crouch commented that Thornhill's "book is as beautiful as it will be useful in teaching children."

A Tree in a Forest spans two hundred years in the life of a sugar maple as it grows from a seed and eventually weathers a fire, an icestorm, drought, and being struck by lightning. When the tree finally dies, it becomes the host for a new seedling. Through detailed illustrations Thornhill also offers a view of the changing lives of humans in North America, for the background of each picture contains Native Americans, then pioneer settlers, farmers, and finally suburban commuters. A reviewer for *Publishers Weekly* remarked: "This compelling presentation of the interdependency and rhythmic round of life will surely nourish readers." And in the *School Library Journal* Sharon Levin concluded that *A Tree in a Forest* is "a good read-aloud for ecology units, while individual readers will enjoy poring over it."

Thornhill told *SATA:* "By 1987 I'd been doing magazine and newspaper illustration for almost ten years and was getting pretty darn tired of drawing computers and money. At the same time, I was living deep in the heart of Toronto and got swept into the environmental movement because of a severe lead pollution problem in my neighbourhood. So out of the blue I decided to kill a few birds with one stone—I'd do a kids' book. The concept was an alphabet book about North American wildlife so that a) I could draw animals again like I used to when I was a happy, young, naturalist kid, b) I could do my part for the environment by educating kids, and c) I could get rich. Ha ha.

"I haven't become rich, but my husband and I *did* manage to escape the city—a long-time goal—first to a rented farm with friends, and then to a little piece of wooded land in central Ontario where we have since built a house.

"It was a spring of making maple syrup that inspired *A Tree in a Forest.* We were out in the sugar bush every day for a couple of weeks, collecting sap, boiling sap, skimming scum off boiling sap, and staring at naked maple trees. I couldn't help but ponder their lives as I watched huge pileated woodpeckers flying from trunk to trunk looking for the perfect nesting hole. It just seemed natural after that to write the biography of a tree."

■ Works Cited

Binder, Mary Ellen, review of *The Wildlife A-B-C: A Nature Alphabet, Canadian Children's Literature* 60, 1990, pp. 116-17.
Crouch, Marcus, review of *The Wildlife 1 2 3: A Nature Counting Book, Junior Bookshelf,* February, 1990, p. 19.
Feltham, Patricia, review of *The Wildlife 1 2 3, Canadian Children's Literature* 59, 1990, p. 107.
Levin, Sharon, review of *A Tree in a Forest, School Library Journal,* July, 1992, p. 71.
Review of *A Tree in a Forest, Publishers Weekly,* April 13, 1992, p. 57.

■ For More Information See

PERIODICALS

Publishers Weekly, October 27, 1989, p. 63.

* * *

THREADGALL, Colin 1941-

■ Personal

Born April 28, 1941; son of Hilda Brown Mapstone; married, December 2, 1986; wife's name, Liz (a secretary). *Education:* Secondary School for Boys, Eight Certificates, 1959; Colchester School of Art, National Diploma of Design, 1963. *Politics:* Liberal Democrat. *Religion:* Church of England.

■ Addresses

Office—c/o Julia MacRae Books, Random House, 20 Vauxhall Bridge Road, London SW1V 2SA, England.

COLIN THREADGALL

■ Career

Writer and illustrator. Worked in public exhibition and design department at Natural History Museum, South Kensington, England, 1963-90. Part time lecturer in art schools. *Member:* British Entomological and Natural History Society.

■ Writings

A Visit from Bear, Julia MacRae Books, 1990.
(Illustrator) Graham Peacock, *Science Learning Book,* Walker Books, 1990.
Proud Rooster and the Fox, Julia MacRae Books, 1991.
Dinosaur Fright, Julia MacRae Books, 1992.
The World of Dinosaurs, Julia MacRae Books, 1992.
Find My Mother, Julia MacRae Books, 1993.
Find My Wheels, Julia MacRae Books, 1993

■ Work in Progress

Find My Dinosaur, and *Find My Legs,* novelty books, as well as "ideas for several new novelty books"; a new story picturebook.

■ Sidelights

Colin Threadgall told *SATA,* "I began trying to write and illustrate story picturebooks for young children a few years ago. Until then, most of my working life had been in the Natural History Museum, South Kensington, London, England, working in the public exhibition and design department.

"The department was much smaller than it is now when I first began to work there, only a handful of people, in fact. We all had to 'muck in' and do all sorts of things—like carefully brushing off the dust from the mounted birds in the bird exhibits using the wing-feather of a bird! Once I brushed an owl too hard. It had either a bad skin, or had been got at by 'something.' Suddenly, the air was full of downy feathers!

"While at the museum, I illustrated a number of nonfiction books on natural history for young readers. I also taught drawing and held various drawing workshops in art schools. Writing and illustrating story picturebooks for young children, however, is definitely a new departure. I'm still a newcomer, and have so far completed just three story picturebooks and two mix-and-match novelty books.

"Perhaps it's no great surprise, because of my background, that most of my story picturebook ideas—so far at least—are tales or fables about animals. At the moment I prefer to keep my animal characters as animals in natural surroundings rather than dress them up in clothes or put them in houses and make them behave like people. Having said that, of course, along could come some idea that could soundly break those particular 'rules.'

"I keep a great number of jottings in the form of ideas for stories. I rarely seem able to write the simplest story by starting at the beginning and working through to the end with everything nicely sorted out and in place. Things get chopped and changed around constantly. In

"Go away!" cried the other dinosaurs.

Colin Threadgall initially planned this playful tale to be about elephants, but when dinosaurs invaded his first illustrations for the story he decided to switch subjects.

fact, I often seem to start with the ending of the story first. I knew the ending for Proud Rooster, for example, long before I finally decided upon the actual beginning and middle of the story. Story picturebook ideas can actually start anywhere. I even seem to have begun this piece of writing in the middle somewhere, and am sort of working backwards and forwards.

"I find that knowing an ending first creates a lot of freedom and flexibility. You can travel anywhere on the way. It's a little like setting out on a journey with no fixed itinerary, apart from knowing your final destination. You can go wherever the whim takes you, stop over longer at one particular place if it takes your fancy, or press on with more speed if you have the urge to. You can change pace whenever you want. Knowing you have a particular place to arrive at provides the impetus.

"I like to keep ideas as loose as possible. I start each story picturebook with a rough dummy. I like to plan both the writing and the illustrations together rather than to write the story first and then produce the illustrations. There may be three or four rough dummy stages—even more sometimes—before I feel that both the text and illustrations work well together. I may also spend some time working on the characters to get a better feel for them before I start a final dummy.

"The story idea generally determines the kind of illustrations, of course, but an idea for an illustration may also determine the form the story takes, too.

"My last story picturebook for young children, called *Dinosaur Fright*, actually started off as a story about elephants! I did an illustration of some elephants jumping into a lake creating enormous splashes but couldn't somehow shake the idea of dinosaurs jumping into a lake instead, creating even bigger splashes—and gradually the idea about dinosaurs took over. I find it is important to know when to 'switch off' too. I often leave an illustration not quite finished at the end of a day or evenings work, which makes it easier to resume again the following morning. Once started, it's a lot easier to carry on into other things.

"My wife and I enjoy exploring new places, and taking our time doing so. Earlier this year we visited Wales. An artist friend took us to see a particularly precipitous stretch of coast. It was very dramatic, with great chunks and slabs of rock punching up almost vertically out of dark, slapping waves. Huge tumbles of rock had also collapsed into the sea. They dotted the coast line, into the distance, looking, somehow ... like ... like an army of monstrous stone giants, sprawling there, half submerged. Had they been, like the trolls in the *Hobbit*, beguiled by a clever wizard, and turned to stone by the first bright rays of morning? Or had they been enchanted in some way, and were now waiting for some unbinding spell ...?

"I always take a pad with me wherever I go to write and scribble in. Odd thoughts can drop into your head from nowhere at any moment, often quite unconnected with what you might be working on at that particular time. It's important to note things down. Who knows where your inclinations will lead to in the future? And ideas are like seeds really, except you never quite know when they are going to sprout—or what form they'll actually take when they do!"

■ For More Information See

PERIODICALS

Junior Bookshelf, December, 1991, p. 246; February, 1993.
Nursery World, October, 1991.
Parent Magazine, August, 1993.
Times Educational Supplement, May, 1993.

* * *

TIFFAULT, Benette W. 1955-

■ Personal

Name is pronounced "ben-*net tee*-foe"; born December 17, 1955, in Syracuse, NY; daughter of Benjamin Newton (a purchasing agent) and Jeanette (a homemaker; maiden name, Forger) Whitmore; married Lee James Tiffault (a musician), August 4, 1984; children: Eli Benjamin, Kallie Elizabeth. *Education:* Queen's University, B.A., 1977; Syracuse University, M.A., 1980. *Politics:* Independent.

■ Addresses

Home—923 Cumberland Ave., Syracuse, NY 13210. *Office*—Community-General Hospital, Broad Rd., Syracuse, NY 13215.

BENETTE W. TIFFAULT

■ Career

Cazenovia College, Cazenovia, NY, director of public relations and journalism instructor, 1980-82; Sargent-Webster-Crenshaw & Folley (architectural firm), Syracuse, NY, publications director, 1982-90; Community-General Hospital, Syracuse, media specialist, 1990—; Onondaga Community College, Syracuse, adjunct faculty member, 1992—; Le Moyne College, Syracuse, adjunct professor of English, 1993—; SUNY College of Environmental Science and Forestry, Syracuse, adjunct professor of technical writing, 1993—; author. *Member:* Society of Children's Book Writers and Illustrators.

■ Awards, Honors

First place award for most effective newsletter, 1983, for Westcott Recycles, Inc. newsletter; Award of Merit for Outstanding Achievement in External Publications, International Association of Business Communicators/Business and Industry Communicators Council, 1986; Silver Award for Outstanding Achievement in Writing, MerCom Inc., 1989; award for artistic excellence, Cultural Resources Council of Onondaga County, 1991, for a graphic design poster.

■ Writings

A Quilt for Elizabeth, illustrated by Mary McConnell, Centering Corp., 1992.
The Little Shoe Book, Random House, 1993.

Also author of seventeen episodes for *Pappyland* (children's television series), to be broadcast by PBS in 1994. Contributor to periodicals, including *House Beautiful, School and College, Architecture, Consulting-Specifying Engineer, Corporate Design, Building Design and Construction,* and *School Product News.*

■ Work in Progress

Great Gobs of Gooey Gum, to be published by Random House. *I'll Give You the Ocean, Jimmy Lee; Dragon Eyes and the Kite Flyer; Forever Aunt Christina; The Little Hat Book;* and *The Little Midnight Book.*

■ Adaptations

The film rights to *A Quilt for Elizabeth* have been acquired by FilmFair Communications, for adaptation into a short animated film.

■ Sidelights

Benette W. Tiffault told *SATA:* "I am particularly interested in writing concept picture books about children coping with problems in their worlds. These kinds of books are important, not only for children who have certain problems, but also for other children, to help create a greater awareness of and sensitivity to various life circumstances. My greatest challenge in writing this type of book is to develop and maintain a strong story line and in the process to avoid being didactic in my presentation."

*   *   *

TOMEY, Ingrid 1943-

■ Personal

Name is pronounced "tow-me"; born May 25, 1943, in Port Huron, MI; daughter of Frank (a lab technician) and Georgena (a writer; maiden name, Carter) Goff; married Paul Tomey (a furniture company representative), August 28, 1965; children: Paul Matthew, Kristin. *Education:* Michigan State University, B.A., 1965; Oakland University, M.A., 1977; University of Michigan, M.F.A., 1985. *Hobbies and other interests:* Gardening, tennis, jogging, recycling, listening to silence.

■ Addresses

Home and office—7565 Lilac Ct., West Bloomfield, MI 48324.

■ Career

Writer. Michigan Literacy Program, instructor, 1986-89. *Member:* Society of Children's Book Writers and Illustrators, Detroit Women Writers (vice-president),

INGRID TOMEY

Westacres Women's Club (president, 1976-77), Westacres Garden Club.

■ Awards, Honors

American Poets Prize, University of Michigan, 1985, for "Baby in a Tree" and "Where Skies Are Not Cloudy"; Tyson Award, Most Promising Novel, University of Michigan, 1985, for *Loss Events.*

■ Writings

Neptune Princess, Bradbury, 1992.
Grandfather's Day, Boyds Mills, 1992.
Savage Carrot, Scribners, 1993.
The Queen of Dreamland, Scribners, 1993.

Author of the poems "Baby in a Tree" and "Where the Skies Are Not Cloudy." Also author of a novel for adults, *Loss Events,* as well as articles for *Woman's Day, Detroit Monthly, Michigan, Cricket, Los Angeles Times, Sailing,* and *Islands.*

■ Sidelights

Ingrid Tomey's first novel for children, *Neptune Princess,* won praise from reviewers. In the story, Poppy Field is eager to win a swimming contest and become the Neptune Princess, but she breaks her leg before the competition and blames it on the old woman next door, who Poppy thinks may really be a witch. A *Kirkus Reviews* critic remarked that "characters are nicely individualized, sharply drawn, and engaging; their lively dialogue keeps the story moving.... An unusually promising debut." And Deborah Abbott in *Booklist* stated, "this refreshing novel is like a cool dip on a hot day." Tomey's second children's novel, *Grandfather's Day,* was also well received. When Raydeen's grandpa comes to live with her family, Raydeen gives him her bedroom and, eventually, her heart. "Children will enjoy [Raydeen's] success in breaking down the barriers with her grandfather," wrote Anne Connor in the *School Library Journal.* A *Publishers Weekly* reviewer suggested "this poignant novel about life, love and the grieving process" is inspiringly portrayed.

Tomey shared the secret of her success with *SATA:* "The most nourishing thing I do for myself as a writer and as a person is spend one week out of every month alone, in silence. I drive four and a half hours from my home to a small town in northern Michigan where I have a bed, a typewriter, and silence. I don't watch TV or listen to the radio. I listen to the inside of my head. And I go slow. Sometimes I sit at the window for an hour, sipping tea and watching the snow fall. Some days I can write for eight hours. Other days I merely ruminate. And, of course, I read. A week of silence is better than a vacation, better than a spa. It renews me mentally and spiritually."

■ Works Cited

Abbott, Deborah, review of *Neptune Princess, Booklist,* July, 1992, p. 1940.
Connor, Anne, review of *Grandfather's Day, School Library Journal,* October, 1992.
Review of *Grandfather's Day, Publisher's Weekly,* August 31, 1992, p. 80.
Review of *Neptune Princess, Kirkus Reviews,* May 1, 1992.

■ For More Information See

PERIODICALS

Detroit Free Press, November 18, 1992.

* * *

TURNER, Ann (Warren) 1945-

■ Personal

Born December 10, 1945, in Northampton, MA; son of Richard Warren (a printer) and Marion Warren (an artist); married Richard E. Turner, June 3, 1967; children: Benjamin, Charlotte. *Education:* Bates College, B.A., 1967; attended Oxford University, received certificate of study; University of Massachusetts, M.A.T., 1968. *Politics:* Liberal Democrat. *Religion:* Protestant. *Hobbies and other interests:* Gardening, tennis, cooking, sailing.

■ Addresses

Home and office—60 Briar Hill Rd., Williamsburg, MA 01096. *Agent*—Marilyn E. Marlow, Curtis Brown Ltd., 10 Astor Place, New York, NY 10003.

■ Career

High school English teacher in Great Barrington, MA, 1968-69; writer, 1970—; Antioch University, Northampton, MA, assistant director, 1978-80. Affiliated with Friends of Meekins Library, 1986-87; instructor of writing at University of Massachusetts. *Member:* Society of Children's Book Writers and Illustrators.

■ Awards, Honors

First prize, *Atlantic Monthly* college creative writing contest, 1967; New York Academy of Sciences honor book citation, 1976, for *Vultures;* American Library Association notable children's book citations, 1980, for *A Hunter Comes Home,* and 1985, for *Dakota Dugout;* IRA/CBC children's choice, 1988, for *Nettie's Trip South;* NCSS Notable Book citations in the field of social studies, 1989, for *Heron Street* and *Grasshopper Summer,* 1990, for *Through Moon and Stars and Night Skies,* and 1991, for *Stars for Sarah; Rosemary's Witch* was a *School Library Journal* Best Books selection, 1991.

■ Writings

Vultures (nonfiction), illustrated by Marian Gray Warren, McKay, Harper, 1976.

Houses for the Dead (nonfiction), McKay, Harper, 1976.

A Hunter Comes Home (novel), Crown, 1980.

The Way Home (historical fiction), Crown, 1982.

Dakota Dugout (historical poem), illustrated by Ronald Himler, Macmillan, 1985.

Tickle a Pickle (poems), illustrated by Karen Ann Weinhaus, Macmillan, 1986.

Street Talk (poems), illustrated by Catherine Stock, Houghton, 1986.

Third Girl from the Left (novel), Macmillan, 1986.

Nettie's Trip South (historical poem), illustrated by Ronald Himler, Macmillan, 1987.

Time of the Bison (fiction), illustrated by Beth Peck, Macmillan, 1987.

Grasshopper Summer (novel), Macmillan, 1989.

Hedgehog for Breakfast (picture book), illustrated by Lisa McCue, Macmillan, 1989.

Heron Street (picture book), illustrated by Lisa Desimini, Harper, 1989.

Through Moon and Stars and Night Skies (picture book), illustrated by James Graham Hale, Harper, 1990.

Mathilda's Revenge (novel), Harper, 1991.

Stars for Sarah (picture book), illustrated by Mary Teichman, Harper, 1991.

Rosemary's Witch (fiction), Harper, 1991.

(With Robert J. Blake) *Rainflowers*, Harper, 1992.

Katie's Trunk, illustrated by Ron Himler, Macmillan, 1992.

Grass Songs: Poems, illustrated by Barry Moser, Harcourt, 1993.

Apple Valley Year, illustrated by Sandi Wickersham Resnick, Macmillan, 1993.

Also author of *Rituals of Birth* (nonfiction).

■ Work in Progress

Riversong, the second volume of *Elfsong* trilogy; *No Maybes*, a novel about two young girls, for Harper; *The Burnt Stick*, "poems of Native Americans at the moment of contact with Anglo culture"; two picture books for Macmillan, due 1994.

■ Sidelights

Ann Turner is a writer of wide interests and talents whose treatment of historical material in fiction, nonfiction, and poetry for children and young adults has earned her a special reputation and many awards. "My upbringing influenced my writing," Ann Turner once commented in *Contemporary Authors, New Revision Series* (*CANR*). "Possibly because my liberal family was somewhat 'different' from the New Englanders of our town, I grew up being interested in different people and cultures. Living in the country and having an artist for a mother gave me a certain way of seeing, an eye for beauty and interest in what others might think ugly or dull: dead weeds, old men and women, fat ladies at the beach, ancient and venerable crows, and vultures."

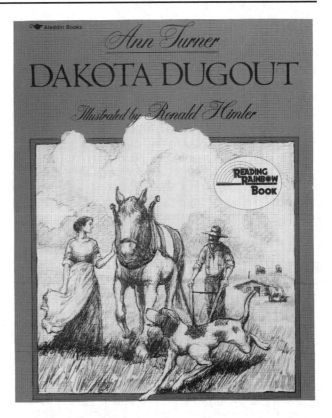

In one of her more serious works, Turner's verses recall the hard, lonely life that early settlers had on the American prairie during the nineteenth century. (Cover illustration by Ronald Himler.)

Turner's first book is in part the offspring of this interest. *Vultures*, illustrated by her mother, Marion Warren, is a scientific but accessible study of a type of bird that many might find repulsive. Yet as Warren points out in the introduction, vultures are "clean birds and bathe often in streams and rivers. After eating, they carefully wipe their heads clean on grass or sand. And though not Birds of Paradise, vultures can be handsome, for they are magnificent and graceful in flight."

Explores Life in Different Lands and Times

Turner's interest in other cultures was evident almost from the start of her career. In *A Hunter Comes Home* a fifteen-year-old Eskimo boy named Jonas returns to his village after a year away at a boarding school, where he was exposed to white culture. Now, he wants to go hunting with his grandfather to learn the ways of the Eskimo tradition. Making the transition from modern to traditional, however, does not come easily to Jonas. "The author shows extraordinary sensitivity in revealing the feelings of schoolboys surrounded by a totally unfamiliar atmosphere," wrote reviewer Virginia Haviland in *Horn Book*. By the end of the story, as described in *Kirkus Reviews*, "Jonas has come to terms with himself by coming to terms with his imposing, demanding grandfather, not by flatly rejecting the new for the old—which saves this from being still another polemical exercise."

"Perhaps because I was small and skinny with frizzy hair and an unusual family, I grew up thinking a lot about survival," Turner recalls. The theme emerges in *The Way Home,* in which she widens her cultural and historical range, telling of Anne, a teenage girl living in fourteenth-century England. Anne is forced to flee her village upon cursing a local tyrant. After hiding in a marsh and surviving by living off the land for a summer, she returns to her village to find everyone has died from the Black Plague. According to a reviewer in the *Bulletin of the Center for Children's Books,* "the book holds up nicely: vivid details in the setting, good dialogue and adequate characterization, a focused development, and a strong sense of narrative."

History and Nonsense Fill Poems

"My first love will always be poetry," says Turner. "I like writing silly poems, such as the ones in *Tickle a Pickle,* about things we did as children—throwing Daddy's shoes into the toilet and sprinkling them with perfume. We called it 'making soup.' But I also like to write serious poems, often about true events or history." *Dakota Dugout,* written for preschool through third grade readers, falls into this latter category. A grandmother recalls for her granddaughter life with her husband in a sod house on the Dakota prairie in the late nineteenth century—the loneliness, the slow spring, a summer drought, and finally a successful crop and the building of a clapboard house. "The spare text, like poetry pruned of any excess words but rich in emotional

With the help of glowing stars on her bedroom ceiling to keep the darkness away, a young girl faces her fears of moving into a new house. (Cover illustration by Mary Teichman.)

impact, is perfectly attuned to the splendid black-and-white drawings," wrote Mary M. Burns in *Horn Book,* while *New York Times Book Review* contributor Mark Jonathan Harris found that "the impressionistic pictures combine with the vivid prose to create a moving memoir."

Tickle a Pickle is a collection of mostly nonsense poems: "Tickle a pickle / greet a beet / say 'eek!' to a leek . . . . " A reviewer in *Kirkus Reviews* commented that "the images and rhythms are energetic and unusual, and the sheer nonsensical and offbeat aspects will delight some readers." Among Turner's other poems is *Street Talk,* a collection of free verse, such as "Pizza-pepper plucking / at my throat / (Hey-hot! hey-hot!) / fizzy Coke tickly / my nose (sssz-bam! ssssz-bam!)." A reviewer for the *Bulletin of the Center for Children's Books* writes that "what [Turner] sees, the way she sees it, and the way she makes readers see it are full of fresh flashes."

Family History Inspires Picture Books

In the two picture books *Katie's Trunk* and *Nettie's Trip South,* Turner draws upon personal anecdotes from her family history. Young Katie, member of a Tory family during the Revolutionary War, is confused by the enmity of her former friends and neighbors. In *Bulletin of the Center for Children's Books,* reviewer Deborah Stevenson finds that *Katie's Trunk* "hints at the complexities of rebellion and dissent in a way that should provoke thought and discussion." In *Nettie's Trip South,* inspired by the author's great-grandmother's diary of a journey made in 1859, Turner describes a ten-year-old northern girl's encounter with slavery. *School Library Journal* contributor Elizabeth M. Reardon calls the book "compelling and thought-provoking ... sure to arouse readers' sympathies." Another picture book for young readers is *Heron Street,* which charts the changes in a marsh from before the American Revolution to the present. "Unlike other books on the topic, this implies an appreciation of progress—a refreshing change—as well as dismay over the loss of nature," comments Ilene Cooper in *Booklist.*

The events in *Hedgehog for Breakfast* are triggered by the misinterpretation of the statement made by Papa Fox that "I'd like to have Mrs. Hedgehog for breakfast." *Through Moon and Stars and Night Skies* is about the cross-cultural adoption by an American family of a young Asian boy. The boy retells the story of his adoption and his fear at first of what he encounters before the love of his new family gradually draws him in. *Horn Book* contributor Ellen Fader found that the story "illuminates in a lyrical and compassionate way" the process of adapting faced by a child from a faraway country. *Stars for Sarah* concerns a young child's fears of moving to a new house. "The people and objects are pictured from close and realistic perspectives, giving them an immediacy that reinforces the intimate feeling," comments Jane Marino in *School Library Journal.*

Pioneer Life and Lonely Witches

Turning to write fiction for a somewhat older audience, Turner produced *Grasshopper Summer*, which revisits the period and setting of *Dakota Dugout*. Twelve-year-old Sam must, with his younger brother and parents, make the transition from his grandfather's orderly Kentucky farm to the undeveloped Dakota prairie. "Both a family story and an account of pioneer living, the book is accessible as well as informative," writes Mary M. Burns in *Horn Book*. In *Rosemary's Witch*, young Rosemary finds a 150-year-old witch hiding in the woods near the old New England house to which her family has recently moved. Mathilda, the witch, was an unloved child driven out of the house by villagers. Mathilda, who still longs for affection, plays pranks on the nine-year-old Rosemary, such as stealing her bike, to gain attention. Eventually Rosemary comes to empathize with the childish and lonely witch. In the *Bulletin of the Center for Children's Books*, reviewer Roger Sutton found "the alternation of Rosemary's and Mathilda's point of view ... intensely effective." A *Kirkus Reviews* contributor revealed that "Turner thoughtfully explores the idea of home and how it can be shared," calling the work "skillfully written" and "entertaining."

Grass Songs is a collection of seventeen poems inspired by the correspondence and diaries of pioneer women. The poems treat subjects such as marriage, childbirth, Indian raids, and death. A *Kirkus Reviews* contributor found the work "even more vivid and personalized" than Turner's other historical work. *Bulletin of the Center for Children's Books* reviewer Betsy Hearne states that regarding these pioneer women "Turner has matched the intensity of their struggle with a poetic intensity of her own, spare and plainspoken."

"Don't ever think that you *can't* be a writer," advises Turner. "No one knows what they will be. No one knows what creations and lovely life will come out of them. If you think you want to write, then do it. And keep going. Start with a journal. Carry a notebook with you and jot down things when you're at the movies, the mall, the beach. How do people walk? What do their voices sound like? Why is that person angry? How does a sad person walk? Then, who knows, you may arrive at adulthood—as I did—with all your journals intact with a wonderful knowledge of people, ready to write and imagine your own books."

■ Works Cited

Burns, Mary M., review of *Dakota Dugout*, *Horn Book*, January, 1986, p. 52.

Burns, Mary M., review of *Grasshopper Summer*, *Horn Book*, September, 1989, p. 624.

Contemporary Authors, New Revision Series, Volume 31, Gale, 1990, pp. 437-38.

Cooper, Ilene, review of *Heron Street*, *Booklist*, May 15, 1989, p. 1657.

Fader, Ellen, review of *Through Moon and Stars and Night Skies*, *Horn Book*, May 6, 1990, p. 330.

Review of *Grass Songs*, *Kirkus Reviews*, February 15, 1993, p. 235.

Harris, Mark Jonathan, review of *Dakota Dugout*, *New York Times Book Review*, January 12, 1986, p. 25.

Haviland, Virginia, review of *A Hunter Comes Home*, *Horn Book*, October, 1980, p. 529.

Hearne, Betsy, review of *Grass Songs*, *Bulletin of the Center for Children's Books*, June, 1993, p. 331.

Review of *A Hunter Comes Home*, *Kirkus Reviews*, September 15, 1980. p. 1237.

Marino, Jane, review of *Stars for Sarah*, *School Library Journal*, February, 1992, p. 79.

Reardon, Elizabeth M., review of *Nettie's Trip South*, *School Library Journal*, July/August, 1987, p. 88.

Review of *Rosemary's Witch*, *Kirkus Reviews*, March 15, 1991, p. 400.

Stevenson, Deborah, review of *Katie's Trunk*, *Bulletin of the Center for Children's Books*, December, 1992, p. 123.

Review of *Street Talk*, *Bulletin of the Center for Children's Books*, June, 1986, p. 197.

Sutton, Roger, review of *Rosemary's Witch*, *Bulletin of the Center for Children's Books*, May, 1991, p. 230.

Review of *Tickle a Pickle*, *Kirkus Reviews*, March 15, 1986.

Turner, Ann, Macmillan publicity flyer, 1989.

Review of *The Way Home*, *Bulletin of the Center for Children's Books*, February, 1983, p. 118.

■ For More Information See

PERIODICALS

Booklist, April 1, 1991.

Bulletin of the Center for Children's Books, September, 1991, p. 24.

Horn Book, September, 1989, p. 616.

Kirkus Reviews, March 15, 1986; September 1, 1992, p. 1136.

School Library Journal, February, 1983, p. 84.

—Sketch by Scott Gillam

*   *   *

TURNER, Robyn 1947-

■ Personal

Born March 20, 1947, in Amarillo, TX; daughter of R. L. Robertson and Pauline Robertson; married; children: Trent, Tara. *Education:* University of Texas at Austin, B.S., 1968, M.A., 1982, Ph.D., 1989. *Politics:* "Yellow-Dog Democrat." *Religion:* Society of Friends (Quaker). *Hobbies and other interests:* Music, art, dance, playwriting.

■ Addresses

Office—3408 Werner Avenue, Austin, TX 78722.

ROBYN TURNER

■ Career

Amarillo Community Center, Amarillo, TX, visual arts coordinator and teacher, 1974-78; Campbell Elementary, Austin Independent School District, Austin, TX, teacher, 1979-85; Holt, Rinehart and Winston, senior editor, 1985-89, script writer and editor of video programs, 1987-88, national marketing manager for the school division, 1989-1990; St. Edward's University, Austin, adjunct professor, 1991—; Robyn Turner and Associates, owner and manager, 1991—. Consultant for various institutions, including Harcourt Brace Jovanovich, 1988-89, 1990; Women and Their Work, 1989-90; Davis Publishing Company, 1991; Houston Museum of Fine Arts, 1992; and McGraw-Hill Publishing Company, 1992. Austin Independent School District, Austin, TX, conducted writing workshops, 1982-84. Member of Texas Hill Country Writers' Project, 1983—, and advisory board member of Leadership Enrichment in the Arts Program (chair of evaluation committee, 1990-92), and Austin Performing Arts League, 1992. Guest lecturer at various institutions. *Member:* National Art Education Association, Texas Art Education Association, Texas Women's History Network, Kappa Delta Pi.

■ Writings

"PORTRAITS OF WOMEN ARTISTS FOR CHILDREN"
SERIES

Rosa Bonheur, Little, Brown, 1991.
Georgia O'Keeffe, Little, Brown, 1991.
Mary Cassatt, Little, Brown, 1992.
Frida Kahlo, Little, Brown, 1993.
Faith Ringgold, Little, Brown, 1993.
Dorothea Lange, Little, Brown, 1994.

OTHER

(Author and photographer) *Austin Originals: Chats with Colorful Characters,* foreword by Cactus Pryor, Paramount Publishing Company, 1982.

Contributor to *The Textbook Controversy,* edited by J. G. Herligy, Ablex, 1990. Contributor or articles to periodicals, including *National Art Association Journal, Third Coast,* and Texas *Observer.* Columnist, *Austin American Statesman,* 1983-91.

■ Work in Progress

High school art text book with a teacher's edition, for Davis Publications; play about Georgia O'Keeffe and Frida Kahlo.

*   *   *

USHER, Margo Scegge
  See McHARGUE, Georgess

W

WALLIS, Diz 1949-

■ Personal

Born January 15, 1949, in Brighton, England; daughter of Kenneth Horatio (a Royal Air Force officer and autogyro designer and builder) and Peggy Mary (a homemaker; maiden name, Stapley) Wallis; married Barry Macmahon; children: Chloe Elizabeth. *Education:* Attended Hammersmith College of Art, London. *Hobbies and other interests:* Natural history.

■ Career

Freelance commercial illustrator for numerous clients, including Shell, Canon, Guiness, Boots, and Omni, 1977—; author and illustrator of Children's Books, 1990—.

■ Writings

SELF-ILLUSTRATED

Something Nasty in the Cabbages, Caroline House, 1991.
A Jar Full of Mice, Caroline House, 1991.
Prune's Adventure, Ragged Bears, 1991, published in the United States as *Pip's Adventure,* Caroline House, 1991.
Battle of the Beasts, Ragged Bears, 1993.
Mandarins and Marigolds: A Journey through Color, Ragged Bears, 1994.

ILLUSTRATOR

(With Brian McIntyre, John Butler, Philip Hood, Roy Woodard, and Gary Marsh) Dougal Dixon, *Afterman,* Granada, 1982.
(With William Rushton and Hood) Robert Mash, *How to Look after Your Dinosaur,* Andre Deutsch, 1984, published in the United States as *How to Keep Dinosaurs,* Penguin Books.
Marie Farre, *Qui a peur des crocodiles?,* Gallimard, 1985.
(With Sylvaine Perols) Christine Lazier, *Malins commes les singes,* Gallimard, 1986.

DIZ WALLIS

Andre Lucas, *Les Architects de la nature,* Gallimard, 1987.
Lazier, *Des animaux de bonne companie,* Gallimard, 1988.

■ Work in Progress

Illustration work for two stationary projects, including diaries and cards.

■ Sidelights

The first books Diz Wallis wrote as well as illustrated received critical acclaim. *Something Nasty in the Cab-*

223

bages, a retelling of Pierre de Saint-Cloud's story "Chantecler and the Fox," is about a cock which uses its wits to escape a fox that has captured him through trickery. A *Bulletin of the Center for Children's Books* reviewer stated that Wallis's approach to the story "is modern, with an immediacy of narrative and artistic tone." A critic for *Kirkus Reviews* noted that the illustrations in *Something Nasty in the Cabbages* are "lovingly rendered in exquisite, precisely observed detail." Betty Root, reviewing the book for *Growing Point,* commented that "the words are little more than indicators to the glowing pictures ... in a romping version tailored expertly for young listeners/viewers."

The relationship between the several cats and plentiful mice of a household forms the plot of *A Jar Full of Mice.* A critic in *Kirkus Reviews* wrote that Wallis's "diminutive illustrations are precisely executed and charmingly detailed."

Wallis told *SATA:* "I was always a very nosy child. Forbidden cupboards and drawers held the most fascination, filled as they were in our home with unlikely and highly desirable clutter. Bottled fruit shared the same space as nests of kittens and jewelled lipstick cases. The house was full of promise for the curious, especially the larder with its jars and packets and great, glass demijohn which held an evil, gurgling ginger beer plant, behind which many a mouse sought refuge. The garden too was a treasure trove of secret worlds where ants scurried over fallen bird eggs and woodlice and burnished beetles went about their business.

"My childhood is relived in all the work I do, almost every illustration contains details from it. And when I write I am aware that the rhythms I use were laid down long ago, by my mother as she read to me."

◼ Works Cited

Review of *A Jar Full of Mice, Kirkus Reviews,* October 15, 1991.
Root, Betty, review of *Something Nasty in the Cabbages, Growing Point,* May, 1991, p. 5538.
Review of *Something Nasty in the Cabbages, Bulletin of the Center for Children's Books,* February, 1992, p. 171.
Review of *Something Nasty in the Cabbages, Kirkus Reviews,* August 1, 1991.

◼ For More Information See

PERIODICALS

Bookseller, September 3, 1993, pp. 28, 30.
New York Times Book Review, November 13, 1983.

HELEN WILLIAMS

WILLIAMS, Helen 1948-

◼ Personal

Born March 1, 1948, in Gloucester, England; daughter of Lionel Marks (a hairdresser) and Esther Marks (a hairdresser; maiden name, Lisgarten); married Kir Williams (divorced, 1979); married Chris Robertson (divorced, 1988); children: Abigail, Isabella, Stephanie, Tessa. *Education:* Attended Gloucestershire College of Art and Design, 1966-67; Canterbury College of Art, B.A. (with honors), 1970; University of Bristol School of Education, art teacher's diploma and post graduate certificate in education, 1971. *Politics:* British Green Party. *Religion:* Roman Catholic. *Hobbies and other interests:* Swimming, theatre, music, diary writing, nature, hosting poetry readings.

◼ Addresses

Home and office—The Doll's House, 76 Middle St., Stroud, Gloucestershire GL5 IEA, England. *Agent*—Jess Wilder, Portal Gallery, 16a Grafton St., Bond Street, London WIX 3LF, England.

■ Career

Redbourne Upper School, Ampthill, Bedfordshire, England, teacher of general art, graphics, and textiles, 1971-73; Stamford High School for Girls, Stamford, Lincolnshire, England, instructor in art and calligraphy, 1973-74; self-employed artist, designer, and illustrator, 1974—; Stroud High School, Stroud, Gloucestershire, England, instructor in art, textiles fashion, and design, 1989—; exhibitor at museums, galleries, and art fairs throughout England, and in Los Angeles, CA, Atlanta, GA, and Nashville, TN. Instructor of English using the "Parosi" scheme, 1977-79; artist in residence at Churchdown School, Gloucestershire, 1989. *Member:* British Mensa, Institute of Advanced Motorists, Society for the Protection of the Unborn Child.

■ Writings

Stories in Art, Millbrook Press, 1992.
People in Art, Merlion Publishing, 1992.

ILLUSTRATOR AND COMPILER

The Miracles of Thomas Beckett (history), Canterbury College of Art, 1970.
In Abigail's Garden (poetry), Dutton, 1986.
A Garden for Isabella, Dutton, 1987, also published as *A Language of Flower.*

ILLUSTRATOR

Christopher Tower, *Song of Raymond* (history, philosophy, religion), Weidenfeld & Nicholson, 1987.
Roger Davidson, *Five Particular Places* (poetry), Pear-Tree Press, 1987.

■ Work in Progress

Jam Tomorrow, a book of poems with Bryan Langley; artwork involving pastels, embroidery, graphics, and ceramics.

■ Sidelights

Helen Williams told *SATA:* "Since my earliest memories, I've been fascinated with stories. My grandfather and my mother were great storytellers and readers. The illustrating came about because I found that I enjoyed drawing and painting more than anything else in the world and was given early credit for these skills from teachers and professional artists. I hope to achieve a joy and expression of hope, a love for the beauties of the world through my illustrations and paintings. Through my writing of poetry I hope to turn people's attention to a moment caught in time—fleeting, floating—like the Japanese *Ukiyo-e* prints and poems. I love Japanese haiku poetry, the early medieval illuminated manuscripts, Indian and middle eastern decorative art, the works of Claude Monet and Henri Matisse. With my art-history writing, I hope to share a deep love of the art of the past and across many cultures. I like to make art and craft of the past live now. Art and art history, craft and design are my passions; I cannot separate work from leisure as they are both my constant indulgence."

WILLIAMS, Sheron 1955-

■ Personal

Born September 13, 1955, in Hampton, VA; daughter of Ruel L. (a serviceman) and Clara (Simpson) Williams; married Cecil Brooks (a director of social work); children: Tiffany, Ebony, Richard. *Education:* Indiana University, B.A., 1983; Governors State University, M.A., 1985. *Politics:* Liberal. *Hobbies and other interests:* Cooking, crabbing (fishing for crabs).

■ Addresses

Office—Arts Management Department, Columbia College, 600 South Michigan Ave., Chicago, IL 60603.

■ Career

Columbia College, Chicago, IL, part-time faculty, 1990—. *Member:* African Arts Alliance (board member), National Association of Black Journalists, National League of Black Women, Chicago Association of Black Journalists.

■ Writings

And in the Beginning, Macmillan, 1992.
Hip Hop City Saturday, Hip Hop Publishers, 1992.

■ Work in Progress

Fairy Tale Land Lies Just beyond the "L" Tracks.

■ Sidelights

Sheron Williams told *SATA:* "When I was a little girl on the south side of Chicago I never imagined that anyone would take in what I wrote, and think the same thoughts. I knew they were great thoughts, though. It always impressed me that ancient people could leave behind their thoughts, preserved as though they'd been pondered only yesterday. That fascination with the preservation of the who/what/why that I am is what pushes me to write. I long to preserve the thought that is me. My secret fantasy is to have a book of my thoughts cracked open to a particularly salient passage hundreds of years from now, where it will again be examined, taken in and thought through all over again."

*   *   *

WINFIELD, Julia
See ARMSTRONG, Jennifer

*   *   *

WRIGHT, J. B.
See BARKAN, Joanne

Y

YATES, Janelle K(aye) 1957-

■ Personal

Born December 10, 1957, in Big Springs, TX; daughter of Wayland Davis Yates (a journalist) and Dorothy Ellen Kincaid (a teacher and artist; maiden name, Book); married Luciano David Cano (divorced, 1981); children: Alexander Cano, Adrienne Cano. *Education:* Angelo State University, B.A. (magna cum laude), 1983; New York University, M.A., 1988. *Hobbies and other interests:* Piano, flute and Irish tin whistle, American and Irish folklore and music, Irish folk dancing, books, travel.

■ Addresses

Home—49 Curtis Place, Staten Island, NY' 10301.

■ Career

Freelance writer and editor, New York City, 1986—. Has conducted writing workshops for homeless men, women, and young adults, 1990—.

■ Awards, Honors

Benjamin Franklin Award, 1992, for *Zora Neale Hurston: A Storyteller's Life.*

■ Writings

JUVENILE

Zora Neale Hurston: A Storyteller's Life, Ward Hill Press, 1991.

* * *

YORK, Carol Beach 1928-

■ Personal

Born January 21, 1928, in Chicago, IL; daughter of Harold and Mary (Cantwell) Beach; married Richard

CAROL BEACH YORK

Marten York, 1947 (divorced, 1969); children: Diana Carol. *Education:* Attended Thornton Junior College.

■ Addresses

Home—860 North DeWitt Pl., Chicago, IL 60611. *Agent*—Gloria R. Mosesson, GRM Associates, 240 West End Ave., New York, NY 10023.

■ Career

Author of books for children and young adults. Worked as a page girl, receptionist, and title examiner for Chicago Title & Title Co., beginning in 1944. *Member:*

Society of Children's Book Writers and Illustrators, Children's Reading Roundtable.

■ Writings

Sparrow Lake, Coward-McCann, 1962.
(With Mary Cantwell Beach) *One Summer,* Coward-McCann, 1963.
Where Love Begins, Coward-McCann, 1963.
The Doll in the Bakeshop, F. Watts, 1965.
The Ghost of the Isherwoods, F. Watts, 1966.
Until We Fall in Love Again, F. Watts, 1967.
The Blue Umbrella, F. Watts, 1968.
The Mystery of the Diamond Cat, F. Watts, 1969.
Nothing Ever Happens Here, Hawthorn Books, 1970.
Mystery at Dark Wood, F. Watts, 1972.
Dead Man's Cat: A Mystery, F. Watts, 1972.
The Tree House Mystery, Coward-McCann, 1973.
The Midnight Ghost, Coward-McCann, 1973.
The Mystery of the Spider Doll, F. Watts, 1973.
Takers and Returners: A Novel of Suspense, Hawthorn Books, 1973.
I Will Make You Disappear, Thomas Nelson, 1974.
The Witch Lady Mystery, Thomas Nelson, 1976.
Beware of This Shop, Thomas Nelson, 1977.
Revenge of the Dolls, Elsevier/Nelson Books, 1979.
When Midnight Comes, Elsevier/Nelson Books, 1979.
The Look-Alike Girl, Beaufort Books, 1980.
Remember Me When I Am Dead, Elsevier/Nelson Books, 1980.
Stray Dog, Beaufort Books, 1981.
Ghost Story Mysteries, Watermill Press, 1982.
Magic Word Mysteries, Watermill Press, 1982.
Mysteries for Midnight, Watermill Press, 1982.
The Secret, Scholastic, 1984.
Not Your Type, Tempo Books, 1984.
Make a Wish, Ballantine, 1985.
A Likely Story, Ballantine, 1985.
On That Dark Night, Bantam, 1985.
Secrets in the Attic, Scholastic, 1986.
Where Evil Is, Pocket Books, 1987.
Nights in Ghostland, Pocket Books, 1987.
Once upon a Dark November, Holiday House, 1989.
Pudmuddles, HarperCollins, 1993.
Please Write ... I Need Your Help, Scholastic, 1993.
Key to the Playhouse, Scholastic, 1994.

Also author of short stories and nonfiction for women's and children's magazines.

"MISS KNOW IT ALL" SERIES

Miss Know It All, F. Watts, 1966.
The Christmas Dolls, F. Watts, 1967.
The Good Day Mice, F. Watts, 1968.
Good Charlotte, F. Watts, 1969.
The Ten O'Clock Club, F. Watts, 1970.
Miss Know It All Returns, F. Watts, 1972.
Kate Be Late, Scholastic, 1987.
Miss Know It All and the Wishing Lamp, Bantam, 1987.
Miss Know It All and the Three-Ring Circus, Bantam, 1988.
Miss Know It All and the Magic House, Bantam, 1989.
Rabbit Magic, Scholastic, 1991.

The little things that start to go wrong in the Bridgeport home after Cousin Wilma comes to visit grow more and more disturbing with each passing day in this suspenseful story. (Cover illustration by Lydia Rosier.)

The Secret House, Scholastic, 1992.

FOLK STORIES FOR CHILDREN

Casey Jones, Troll Associates, 1980.
Febold Feboldson, the Fix-it Farmer, Troll Associates, 1980.
Johnny Appleseed, Troll Associates, 1980.
Mike Fink, Troll Associates, 1980.
Old Stormalong: The Seafaring Sailor, Troll Associates, 1980.
Sam Patch: The Big Time Jumper, Troll Associates, 1980.
Washington Irving's Ichabod Crane and the Headless Horseman, Troll Associates, 1980.
Washington Irving's Rip Van Winkle, Troll Associates, 1980.

■ Sidelights

"I loved reading as a child, and I started writing as soon as I learned to write ... and long before I could spell," Carol Beach York laughed in an interview with *SATA.* York, who has written more than 60 books for children and young adults, recalled one of her earliest memories of writing. "I was about seven years old, in the second grade," she told *SATA.* "I remember my school was having a hobby show, where all the children were supposed to bring their hobbies in to share. Lots of the children had collections—stamps, dolls, coins and things like that. I told my teacher that I didn't have a hobby. When she asked me what I did when I had leisure time, I told her I liked to write little stories. She said, 'That's your hobby,' and told me to bring in one of my books. My mother got me a big scrapbook, and I cut out pictures from magazines and newspapers and pasted them in the book. Then I wrote little stories about each one. My teacher was very impressed, and she wrote me a nice little note saying she knew I'd be a writer one day."

Reading—and later, writing her own stories—was an important part of York's life from a young age. Growing up in a north Chicago apartment during the Great Depression, York and her mother, younger sister and grandmother lived a modest life. A trained musician, York's mother earned a living for her family giving piano and violin lessons. When York was about eight, Mrs. Beach went back to school and earned her teaching degree from Chicago Teacher's College. "She was a very plucky woman to go back to college when she had two small children. That type of thing wasn't done a lot in those days," said York. "I admired her a lot."

At about the age of seven, York began writing poems and short stories. "I couldn't spell very well yet, and some of the words looked really funny," she recalled in her *SATA* interview. By the time she was ten, she'd written her first book, which she titled *Mr. Dilly's Toy Shop.* "It wasn't a very original idea—a typical story about the toys in a toy shop coming alive at night," she remarked. "Back then my mother was my only reader, and she was very supportive."

When she was twelve, York belonged to a small girl's club whose members would, among other activities, exchange gifts at Christmas. "We'd each draw one name from a grab bag, and we were supposed to spend ten cents on the gift," she said. "I remember I spent my dime for a little spiral notebook, and wrote stories to fill it up. The little girl I gave it to was also a great reader, so she loved it. Even now, after all these years, I still keep in touch with her. She doesn't have that book any more, but she still remembers it."

While she continued to read avidly—she particularly enjoyed the Laura Ingalls Wilder books, as well as Arthur Payson Terhune, Jack London and other authors of adventure-type books—York didn't write as frequently during her teen years. "At the time I was in high school and college, there were no creative writing courses in the school I attended," she explained. "To me, the idea of actually being a writer didn't seem real. I thought getting books published would be like getting into the movies—it just didn't happen to real people."

York received a scholarship to Thornton Junior College, which she attended in 1946 and 1947. In her second year there, she met Richard York, an Air Force veteran and photographer, and the two were married in 1947. After college, York worked at the Chicago Title & Title

A year after their mother's death, Jenny and Sara are haunted by mysterious messages that seem to be coming from beyond the grave. (Cover illustration by Lydia Rosier.)

Co., where she had been employed part-time since she was 16. She served in various positions there, starting out as a page girl, then becoming a receptionist and later a title examiner for the company.

Discovers Love of Writing for Children

Living with her husband in Harvey, a Chicago suburb, York continued to read a lot and soon developed the urge to go back to writing more actively. "I remember my husband bought me a typewriter for a Christmas present, and that was a great occasion." York began to study women's magazines that were available at the time and started sending short stories and articles to them. That was when she learned one of her most valuable lessons about writing: "You really can't write something well if you don't enjoy reading it," she told *SATA.* While she had some success with the women's magazines—her first published short story appeared in *Seventeen* magazine in 1953 and she sold two short stories to *Family Circle*—she realized this was not the kind of writing she really wanted to do. So, she began writing short stories for children.

"I think doing short stories is a good way to begin in writing," York said in her interview, "because you can usually finish them before you get too discouraged!" Using *The Writer* magazine as her main source for listings of opportunities in various categories of writing, York began submitting her stories to children's magazines. She had immediate success, selling stories to *Highlights for Children,* a teacher's guide called *Grade School Teacher,* and other children's publications. Her quick success inspired her to elaborate on her stories until they became books. "Once I starting writing books, I never went back to short stories. I still love typing 'Chapter One' on the top of a fresh page. The possibilities seem so exciting."

York's first full-length book was *The Doll in the Bakeshop,* which she wrote in 1960 about a doll that gets lost in a bakery. It wasn't published until 1965, but one editor who read the manuscript, which York had written for children ages eight to ten, told York she should try writing books for teenage girls. So she did just that, writing *Sparrow Lake,* a book about a teenage girl who moves from New York City to a small town with her wealthy aunt, then meets and falls in love with a town boy whom her family doesn't think is suitable for her. *Sparrow Lake* was York's first published book.

Katie's crush on her freshman English teacher Mr. Herron leads to danger when his sinister cousin Martin comes to town. (Cover illustration by Alan Olson.)

York gets ideas for her books from her own life and from the lives of people she knows. *Sparrow Lake* was inspired when York and her husband visited a friend at her summer home on a New Jersey lake. "This woman was an artist, and very wealthy. She'd spend her winters in New York City and her summers on the lake, arriving there in a chauffeur-driven limousine. The area was so beautiful and her lifestyle was so far removed from anything I had known that I was fascinated." York wrote many other romances for teenagers, basing many of her stories on experiences from her own high school days. *Where Love Begins* is about teenage girls, who like York and a high school friend, fall in love with two trapeze performers at a circus. *Until We Fall in Love Again* is also based on York's experiences as a teenager.

After her daughter was born in 1956, York had a new source of inspiration. *Blue Umbrella* is the story of an imaginative young girl caught up in her own world of reading, writing stories and playing make-believe. "*Blue Umbrella* was one of my favorite books to write because the girl in the story was just like Diana," said York. In 1966, York began writing a series of books inspired by a girl York had seen at one of her daughter's school functions. "When my daughter was about eight, I remember going to her fair at school," she told *SATA.* "Most of the children were very neatly dressed and looked well-cared for, but there was one little girl who struck me as looking like an orphan—she was small, and not very well dressed, a little untidy. I remember her as appealing, even though she looked this way." That girl became one of the characters in York's book *Miss Know It All,* which introduced a group of girls who lived in a "happy orphanage run by two dear old ladies.... Wonderful adventures were always happening there," York explained. After *Miss Know It All,* York wrote five more books in the series, which was intended for ages seven through ten. In the late 1980s, an editor at Scholastic asked York to write more of the stories. *Kate Be Late* was published in 1987, followed by five more tales, including *Miss Know It All and the Magic House* and *The Secret House.* Four of the original stories were reprinted by Scholastic beginning in 1993 under the series title "Girls of the Good Day Orphanage."

Mysteries Inspired by Favorite Authors

One area of writing that York has particularly enjoyed is mysteries. Her own love for mysteries—she reads Agatha Christie, Colin Dexter and Ruth Rendell, among other adult mystery writers—inspired her to write them for young readers. "I've always loved to read mysteries, both for children and adults, and I knew they were always popular with young readers," York explained in her interview. "It's always been a lot of fun to decide clues I can give my readers without giving the mystery away." *The Mystery of the Diamond Cat,* one of her earlier mysteries, is about a young boy and girl who, during a visit to their aunt, help solve the mystery of a stolen diamond cat pin. York has also written many suspense stories and books focusing on the supernatural. "People ask me how I get ideas for those books, and it certainly isn't from my experience," the author remarked. "I just have to make those stories up!"

For instance, *Beware of This Shop* is the tale of two girls who, after visiting a mysterious old shop, become terrorized by bad dreams and mysterious illnesses. A *Publishers Weekly* reviewer notes that the author immediately creates "the ominous atmosphere necessary to her eerie entertainment ... and sustains it expertly." A *Booklist* writer likewise called the witchcraft story *I Will Make You Disappear* "fast, good reading," adding that York's conventional plot is treated with "surprising originality, adding plenty of action and some chilling descriptive passages."

While many of her books have been intended for late grade school-age children and teens, York has written a few beginning reader books such as *The Midnight Ghost* and *Pudmuddles,* the whimsical story of a man who does everything backward. She has also written books for young adults, including *Nothing Ever Happens Here,* the story of a teenage girl frustrated with the "boring" life in her small town and *Takers and Returners: A Novel of Suspense.* "I've explored just about all age levels in my writing," said York. In *Nothing Ever Happens Here,* the main character is a teenage girl who longs for glamour and sophistication, but learns there are more important things in life. She meets a young couple, deeply in love and living a quiet, decidedly unglamorous life. "From them, she learned you don't have to be rich or beautiful or glamorous to have a happy life," recounted York. *Publishers Weekly* describes *Takers and Returners,* a book about a group of teens who embark on a stealing game to break the monotony of their vacation, as one of York's best books: "York's adroit telling results in one of the best suspense novels of her career."

In 1980, York branched out into yet another genre of writing, completing eight books about folk heroes. "I enjoyed doing them, because the subjects were interesting," York said during her *SATA* interview. These books, all published by Troll Associates in 1980, included tales about Casey Jones, Johnny Appleseed, Mike Fink and others. Besides writing, York's interests include reading, art, history and philosophy. In addition to mysteries, York enjoys authors such as Willa Cather and Annie Dillard, as well as poetry by Robert Frost and others. She also enjoys attending the ballet and opera and visiting Chicago's Art Institute.

York noted that in her early years as a writer, "I would always finish a book and hope that soon I'd think of another idea." She soon learned to carry a small spiral notebook so she could jot down ideas as they came to her, wherever she was. She looks through her "idea notebook" when looking for ideas for a book. "Sometimes I jot down ideas that may be only a sentence or two, but they could lead to a good story," she concluded. "Now I never feel like I will run out of ideas."

■ Works Cited

Review of *Beware of This Shop, Publishers Weekly,* October 10, 1977, p. 70.
Review of *I Will Make You Disappear, Booklist,* February 15, 1975, p. 622.
Review of *Takers and Returners, Publishers Weekly,* November 26, 1979, p. 53.
York, Carol Beach, interview with Pat Matson Knapp for *Something about the Author,* August 11, 1993.

■ For More Information See

PERIODICALS

Bulletin of the Center for Children's Books, April, 1968, p. 136; February, 1975, p. 102; October, 1980, p. 43.
New York Times Book Review, December 3, 1967, p. 68.
School Library Journal, December, 1977, p. 62; October, 1980, p. 165; February, 1981, p. 72.
Times Literary Supplement, November 30, 1967, p. 1153.
Voice of Youth Advocates, October, 1984, p. 203.

—*Sketch by Pat Matson Knapp*

*   *   *

YOSHIDA, Toshi 1911-

■ Personal

Born in Tokyo, Japan; son of Hiroshi Yoshida (a painter and printmaker); married; wife's name, Kiso; children: Akihiro, Takashi, Koubun, Hitoshi, and Tsukasa (all sons). *Education:* Attended School of the Pacific Arts Association.

TOSHI YOSHIDA

■ Addresses

Agent—Japan Foreign-Rights Centre, 27-18-804 Naka Ochiai 2-chome, Shinjuku, Tokyo 161, Japan.

■ Career

Hanga (traditional wood-block print) artist, author and illustrator of children's books. *Exhibitions:* Works held in permanent collections of New York Museum of Modern Art, Boston Museum of Fine Arts, and Yoshida Hanga Collection, Tokyo, Japan.

■ Writings

SELF-ILLUSTRATED

Maigo, Fukutake-shoten, 1983.
Young Lions (translation of *Hajimete no kari*), Philomel, 1989.
Elephant Crossing, Philomel, 1989.
Kanchigai, translation by Susan Matsui published as *Rhinoceros Mother,* Philomel, 1991.

OTHER

Also author of *Japanese Print-Making,* 1967.

■ Sidelights

Artist and author Toshi Yoshida, born into a family of renowned artists, showed exceptional talent at an early age for the traditional Japanese wood-block art practiced by his father. His picture books are praised for their realistic portrayal of animals in the wild and for their rich colored-pencil illustrations.

After attending the School of the Pacific Arts Association, Yoshida began traveling throughout the world, giving lectures and exhibiting his works. His first picture book in English translation, published in 1989, was *Young Lions,* the story of three lion cubs who venture out on their first hunt. Through their encounters with other predators and possible prey, the young reader learns about the animals of the East African plain and their habits. Frances E. Millhouser, reviewing *Young Lions* for *School Library Journal,* noted that the author "captures the essence of each creature" the cubs encounter, and declared *Young Lions* "a beautiful, powerful introduction to animal life on the African plain." Roger Sutton, writing in the *Bulletin of the Center for Children's Books,* concluded, "Honest but never brutal, [*Young Lions*] informs natural selection with natural suspense." Diane Roback, reviewing the work for *Publishers Weekly,* described the translated text as "a bit

In this self-illustrated story, Yoshida follows three lion cubs on a journey of discovery on the African plains.

stilted and simplistic sounding," but identified the story's "magnificent, realistic" drawings as the highlight of the book.

Yoshida's next work to appear in English translation, *Elephant Crossing,* is set in East Africa as well and follows a small herd of elephants crossing the desert plain in search of a green forest. After fending off some prowling lions, the leader, an old great-grandmother elephant, remembers the destruction caused long ago by a swarm of grasshoppers that devoured all the plant life and caused the herds of animals to stampede. In a *Publishers Weekly* review, Roback noted that "Yoshida's illustrations are stunning and varied," employing tools and techniques that imitate the elephant's skin texture, the grasshoppers' movements, and the visible heat waves of the African plain. Millhouser, in a *School Library Journal* review, found that Yoshida's drawings "evoke the grandeur of the African landscape" with colors that "delight the senses at every turn of the page." *Quill and Quire* reviewer Susan Perren concluded, "The reader is awed by the talent exhibited here and will look forward to future books."

Yoshida's third book is, like *Young Lions* and *Elephant Crossing,* notable for its stark portrayal of animal survival in Africa. *Rhinoceros Mother* opens with a drawing of a baby rhino standing next to its wounded mother, then considers a number of possibilities, depicted in black-and-white, for what might have caused the wound. The book returns to full-color drawings as Yoshida describes what actually happened: the baby rhinoceros approached a baby elephant out of curiosity, and its mother attacked in order to protect its young. The mother rhinoceros would die if its wound became infected, but the tickbirds which feed on the types of insects that would infect the rhino's wound prevent this from happening. Sutton remarked in the *Bulletin of the Center for Children's Books,* "This is a fierce tale that will engage readers' sympathies more deeply than tamer offerings, an effect all the more remarkable for its resistance to anthropomorphism." *Kirkus Reviews* contributor Joanna Rudge Long noted that Yoshida's depiction of the animals' struggle to survive fails to mention the role of human beings, who often hunt the endangered species Yoshida takes as his subject. Long noted that although *Rhinoceros Mother* does not mention the animal's endangered status, "still, the lovely, panoramic spreads make a potent implicit plea for its vanishing world." *School Library Journal* contributor Diane Nunn advised, "Place [*Rhinoceros Mother*] alongside *Young Lions* and *Elephant Crossing* for a picturesque and informative collection on African animal life."

■ Works Cited

Long, Joanna Rudge, review of *Rhinoceros Mother,* *Kirkus Reviews,* June 1, 1991, p. 734.
Millhouser, Frances E., review of *Young Lions,* *School Library Journal,* April, 1989, p. 100.
Millhouser, Frances E., review of *Elephant Crossing,* *School Library Journal,* December, 1989, p. 97.
Nunn, Diane, review of *Rhinoceros Mother,* *School Library Journal,* July, 1991, p. 71.
Perren, Susan, review of *Elephant Crossing, Quill and Quire,* February, 1990, p. 16.
Roback, Diane, review of *Young Lions, Publishers Weekly,* April 28, 1989, p. 76.
Roback, Diane, review of *Elephant Crossing, Publishers Weekly,* October 13, 1989, p. 52.
Sutton, Roger, review of *Rhinoceros Mother, Bulletin of the Center for Children's Books,* June, 1991, p. 255.
Sutton, Roger, review of *Young Lions, Bulletin of the Center for Children's Books,* March, 1989, p. 185.

■ For More Information See

PERIODICALS

Booklist, April 1, 1985, p. 1127; June 15, 1991, p. 1970.
Bulletin of the Center for Children's Books, January, 1990, p. 126.
Choice, July, 1967, p. 527.
Kirkus Reviews, September 1, 1989, p. 1335.
Library Journal, January 15, 1967, p. 228.

*   *   *

YOUNKIN, Paula 1942-

■ Personal

Born October 15, 1942, in Pomona, CA; daughter of Harold (a dairy man) and Ruth (a homemaker; maiden name, Brown) Younkin; married Nikolai Gregoric (an artist), November 20, 1981. *Education:* University of California at Riverside, B.A., 1964, California teaching credential, 1966.

■ Addresses

Home—Seattle, WA.

■ Career

Freelance writer, 1987—. Works at various editorial jobs and writes teacher guides. Taught English to grades five through twelve in California and Washington, 1966-86; spent one year as a flight attendant.

■ Writings

Indians of the Arctic and Subarctic (young adult nonfiction), Facts on File, 1991.
The Spirit of St. Louis, Macmillan (Toronto), 1993.
The V-2 Rocket, Macmillan (Toronto), in press.

■ Sidelights

Paula Younkin wrote *SATA:* "Whenever I see the various forms of writing categorized into *creative* versus *factual,* I worry. I envision innocent children slumped over factual texts, mining for truth. The truth is that no text happens without a writer who chooses which facts to put in or to leave out. The writer also chooses the words and ways to tell a story, whether fact or fiction.

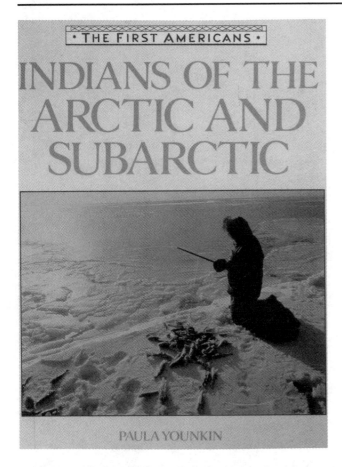

Paula Younkin explores the diverse cultures of northern Indian tribes from their prehistoric roots to the present day in this debut book.

Therein lies creativity. It's also power. And it's the reason books get banned. Fortunately, reading is interactive. A writer can only get through to a mind while it is working. Thus any book is far less dangerous than TV.

"For me, writing is all about making discoveries and connections. To stir interest, provoke thought, evoke a laugh, or get a nod is like joining two hot wires. Sparks fly. With each new reader is the potential for the fun to start all over again.

"My off-duty pleasures include puttering with plants, hobnobbing with neighborhood cats, stumping for animals' rights, and working with people in prison. I run with the thought that the day will come when we look back in disbelief that human beings ever chose to live any other way than in harmony and freedom. I keep hoping that something I write can help hasten the day."

Cumulative Indexes

Illustrations Index

(In the following index, the number of the volume in which an illustrator's work appears is given *before* the colon, and the page number on which it appears is given *after* the colon. For example, a drawing by Adams, Adrienne appears in Volume 2 on page 6, another drawing by her appears in Volume 3 on page 80, another drawing in Volume 8 on page 1, another drawing in Volume 15 on page 107, and so on and so on....)

YABC

Index citations including this abbreviation refer to listings appearing in *Yesterday's Authors of Books for Children,* also published by Gale Research Inc., which covers authors who died prior to 1960.

Author Index

The following index gives the number of the volume in which an author's biographical sketch, Brief Entry, or Obituary appears.

This index includes references to all entries in the following series, which are also published by Gale Research Inc.

YABC—*Yesterday's Authors of Books for Children: Facts and Pictures about Authors and Illustrators of Books for Young People from Early Times to 1960*
CLR—*Children's Literature Review: Excerpts from Reviews, Criticism, and Commentary on Books for Children*
SAAS—*Something about the Author Autobiography Series*